Virginia Woolf is now hailed as one of the greatest, most innovative writers of our age. This landmark collection of essays by leading scholars in the field addresses the full range of her intellectual perspectives – literary, artistic, philosophical and political. *The Cambridge Companion to Virginia Woolf* provides original, new readings of all nine novels and fresh insight into Woolf's letters, diaries and essays allowing easy reference to individual themes and texts. The progress of Woolf's thinking is revealed from Blooms-bury aestheticism through her hatred of censorship, corruption and hierarchy to her concern with all aspects of modernism. The volume reflects the changing face of Woolf scholarship especially in the light of new feminist approaches, and explores the immense range of social and political issues behind her ongoing search for new narrative forms.

Sue Roe's books include *Estella, Her Expectations*, *The Spitfire Factory* and *Writing and Gender: Virginia Woolf's Writing Practice*. She also edited the Penguin Modern Classics edition of Virginia Woolf's *Jacob's Room*. She is currently writing a biography.

Susan Sellers is Professor of English and Related Literature at The University of St Andrews. Her books include *Language and Sexual Difference* (1991, 1995) and *Hélène Cixous: Authorship, Autobiography and Love* (1996). She is co-author with Sue Roe and Nicole Ward Jouve of *The Semi-Transparent Envelope: Women Writing* (1994) and editor of *The Hélène Cixous Reader* (1994, 1995).

THE CAMBRIDGE
COMPANION TO

VIRGINIA WOOLF

CAMBRIDGE COMPANIONS TO LITERATURE

THE CAMBRIDGE
COMPANION TO
VIRGINIA WOOLF

EDITED BY

SUE ROE

AND

SUSAN SELLERS

PUBLISHED BY THE PRESS SYNDICATE OF THE UNIVERSITY OF CAMBRIDGE
The Pitt Building, Trumpington Street, Cambridge, United Kingdom

CAMBRIDGE UNIVERSITY PRESS
The Edinburgh Building, Cambridge CB2 2RU, United Kingdom
40 West 20th Street, New York, NY 10011–4211, USA
477 Williamstown Road, Port Melbourne, VIC 3207, Australia
Ruiz de Alarcón 13, 28014 Madrid, Spain
Dock House, The Waterfront, Cape Town 8001, South Africa

http://www.cambridge.org

© Cambridge University Press, 2000

First published 2000
Third printing 2003

Printed in the United Kingdom at the University Press, Cambridge

Typeset in Sabon 10/13 pt. [CE]

A catalogue record for this book is available from the British Library

Library of Congress cataloging in publication data
The Cambridge companion to Virginia Woolf / edited by Sue Roe and Susan Sellers.
p.   cm. – (Cambridge companions to literature)
Includes bibliographical references and index.
ISBN 0 521 62393 6 (hardback). – ISBN 0 521 62548 3 (paperback)
1. Woolf, Virginia, 1882–1941 – Criticism and interpretation.
2. Women and literature – England – History – 20th century.
I. Roe, Sue. II. Sellers, Susan. III. Series.
PR6045.072Z5655   2000
823'.912–dc21   99–38435   CIP

ISBN 0 521 62393 6 hardback
ISBN 0 521 62548 3 paperback

CONTENTS

ix

CONTENTS

CONTRIBUTORS

DAVID BRADSHAW, Worcester College, Oxford

JULIA BRIGGS, De Montfort University, Leicester

MARIA DiBATTISTA, Princeton University

SUSAN DICK, Queen's University, Kingston, Ontario

HERMIONE LEE, New College, Oxford

LAURA MARCUS, University of Sussex

ANDREW MCNEILLIE is the editor, with Anne Olivier Bell, of *The Diary of Virginia Woolf*

NICOLE WARD JOUVE, University of York

SUZANNE RAITT, University of Michigan

SUE ROE is a freelance writer and editor of the Penguin Modern Classics edition of *Jacob's Room*

SUSAN SELLERS, University of St Andrews

MICHAEL WHITWORTH, University of Wales, Bangor

PREFACE

She had 'the worn beauty of a hare's paw'.[1] She pinned up her clothes with brooches because she hated mending. She adored and was a regular source of amusement to her small nephews, Quentin and Julian Bell. She was deeply committed to and fond of her sister Vanessa Bell; devotedly married to the writer and political activist, Leonard Woolf. Her most inspiring friend seems to have been the painter and art theorist, Roger Fry. There she is: striding across the Downs, all thighs and shins; or smoking a cheroot with Lytton Strachey, laughing; or writing – recklessly, rapidly, brilliantly – in her room in the garden of her home in Sussex, Monks House. Here in this volume of new, especially commissioned chapters, written specifically for our students, we are concerned with her mind: the breadth of her intellectual range; her impulsive flights of creative brilliance, the long labours of composition; her conversations with the present; her arguments with history. She seems to have a range of personae, a myriad selves. As soon as we begin to read her writing and enter her thoughts, it is like being given access to a range of great minds, all conversing with one another.

All the chapters in this book have been commissioned with the intention of reflecting the broad range of Virginia Woolf's concerns as a writer and thinker. It includes a chapter on each of the main foci of her intellectual thought: intellectual ideas which underpin, inform and effect transformations and transpositions within her fiction. The ideas of the Bloomsbury Group formed the basis of her thinking, from which emerge her political ideas and social convictions. Her feminist perspectives, at a deep level and in radical, subtle ways, emerged as she wrote, and have over the years been subject to a range of styles of evaluation. As an artist, she was influenced as deeply by contemporary painting as by politics or philosophy, and the unique languages of her essays have a visual application and register. She was profoundly aware of herself as a 'modern' addressing her contemporaries, but her conversations with the past consistently inform all her writing, both fiction and non-fiction. Her nine novels form the backbone of all she produced, and the languages of them are addressed throughout this book, and specifically in the chapters on her early, middle and later fiction.

The daughter of Sir Leslie Stephen, eminent Editor of the *Cornhill Magazine* and of the *Dictionary of National Biography*, and of Julia Duckworth Stephen, niece of Julia Margaret Cameron, the Victorian photographer, Virginia Stephen married the writer Leonard Woolf, in the process exchanging one era and style of thought for another. On the border of two worlds in time was 'Bloomsbury', the name given to the group of intellectuals emerging from Cambridge at the turn of the century. Andrew McNeillie's masterly analysis of the Bloomsbury Group's intellectual background shows us that English aestheticism at the turn of the century was underpinned by Plato, influenced by Kant and re-awakened by G. E. Moore, who reconciled moral philosophy with aesthetics. For the young Virginia Stephen, the search for truth therefore had a classical history and a modern application. Amorality and the search for significant form arose out of Bloomsbury's aesthetic; in her fiction, Virginia Woolf developed these ideas into new formal ideas of her own. In her early novels she is concerned with the problems of post-Industrial modernism which have arisen out of British nineteenth-century thought, as David Bradshaw's chapter shows; the question of how to define 'civilisation' emerges, and remains central to her thinking. The other strand of Bloomsbury's influence was the visual arts. Through her sister, Vanessa Bell, her husband Clive Bell and her friend Roger Fry, Virginia Woolf became familiar with the developments of post-impressionism and with the ideas and techniques of painting. These ideas, and the liberating effect of drawing visual ideas into her writing, underpinned her experimentation in fiction, enabling her to pursue ideas in her short stories which led to the breakthrough of experimentalism which characterises her work. She learned, in her writing, to train the reader's eye as she described inner and outer forms, radically questioning relationships between surface and depth and finding new frameworks and forms for narrative. Sue Roe's chapter on the impact of post-impressionism shows up the extent to which Virginia Woolf visualised and designed her fiction and, like the post-impressionist painters, experimented with her own classical past while at the same time ceaselessly trying for a new quality of immediacy.

For the first three decades following her death, Virginia Woolf was largely regarded as an aesthete; arguably, it was Feminism which re-discovered her, reviving her as a major figure in the 1970s and subjecting her work to new scrutiny. Laura Marcus's chapter draws attention to the complexity of Virginia Woolf's feminist positions, and to the flexibility with which she may be read as a feminist. The conversations she has with herself as a feminist – in her letters and diaries, as well as in her fiction and non-fiction – are ongoing, as Susan Sellers's chapter shows. New feminist perspectives may bring her own feminist ideas and intuitions into connection with radical feminism; since the 1970s, feminist theorists and writers such as Nicole Ward Jouve have brought psychoanalytic theory to bear on her thinking; and new feminist readings bring out the extent to which her unique style of feminism informs her politics and her view of what she called the 'social system'. As Hermione Lee points out in her chapter on Virginia Woolf's essays, our readings of her seem to have transformed her writings, over the years. Since the 1970s an increasingly charismatic Virginia Woolf has emerged; the deceptive lightness of touch in her essays is consistent with a multi-faceted intellectual engagement, an inimitable talent for portraiture in writing and a formidable knowledge of literature. The interconnection between essays and fiction was lifelong, and her preoccupation with audience, access and market-place is reflected in her strategies for publishing her non-fiction. In that work, we may see the extent of her hatred of censorship, corruption and hierarchy; with her desire to explore the inner life in her fiction she reconciled an ongoing desire to earn her own living and to communicate with her audience, whom she thought of as 'the common reader'. In all her novels, as well as in her non-fiction, she is deeply concerned with the definitions and value of community.

As Michael Whitworth's chapter demonstrates, all these issues converge in the multi-perspectival issue of what, for Virginia Woolf, constituted modernism, which was 'intellectual, technological, social, and literary'. The political issues of modernism are deeply concerned with the issue of styles of disseminating knowledge. The whole notion of what constitutes consciousness is called into question, and Virginia Woolf's formal discoveries are brought into play to draw the complex perspectives of modernism into juxtaposition. Time and place are of the essence; there is no consensus about what constitutes subjectivity; primitivism underpins radicalism and the question of character needs to be revised. The languages of fiction become endlessly flexible, elastic; now solid, now 'thinned to transparency' (Virginia Woolf's own phrase, from *Between the Acts*). Maria DiBattista's inspiring exploration of the language of the fiction shows us how language, for Virginia Woolf, 'might be used *before* the seeking and questing and knocking of words together'. Words are now solid, now shifting; endlessly nuanced and refined. Late in her life, Virginia Woolf thought that authors might be divided into two kinds: soliloquists and ventriloquists. Maria DiBattista shows her progress as an author as a series of intricate, ongoing attempts to orchestrate these two styles of literary performance.

The nine novels form the basis and backbone of her endeavour: Suzanne Raitt, Susan Dick and Julia Briggs offer detailed readings of the individual early, middle and late fiction. Virginia Woolf's technical explorations and the rhythms of the artist's imagination at work find their way into the finished works. Her early novels are *about* finding a creative voice. As Suzanne Raitt shows, the starting-point for a novel had to be arrived at many times, and the voice which emerges in the early fiction has to address history as well as the present; the hallucinatory imagination as well as the refined intellect. She tells us that Woolf 'struggled horribly' with the style of the novel, gradually moving from the shifting frameworks of *The Voyage Out*, which harks back to the intellectualism of 'Bloomsbury', through the overtly feminist *Night and Day* into the complex disruptions and seductions of *Jacob's Room*. That novel throws up all sorts of questions for her subsequent works, here considered by Susan Dick, about how character in the modern novel might be created and about how narrative might now be formed. *Mrs Dalloway*, with its ingenious juxtaposition of two apparently dissimilar principal characters, constitutes a definitive formal challenge to the idea of representational realism which is fully realised in *To the Lighthouse*, with its three-tiered structure which explores the character of time itself. The satire, fantasy or mock-biography, *Orlando*, finds new, superficially amusing ways of addressing the issues of history and community; in *The Waves* Woolf delves deeply into the inner lives of each of her individual characters, finding in the relationship between the individual and the idea of community further depths of complexity.

'Virginia Woolf's fiction explores the nature of the human condition': Julia Briggs explores Woolf's fundamental concern, in her three final novels, *The Waves*, *The Years* and *Between the Acts*, with human consciousness in time and place. In her final novels, Virginia Woolf calls into question the whole notion of story, reveals her impatience with history and brings into play a concern with regeneration. *The Years* reveals the ways in which language has been used, throughout history, for concealment as well as revelation; *Between the Acts* hints at unperformed dramas, as well as playing on the whole notion of performance. In her final novel, Virginia Woolf brings together the rhythms and passions of language and the body with the historical specificity of a moment of national crisis, whilst still retaining 'a Yeatsian "Gaiety transfiguring all that dread"'. Its concern is all-encompassing: with design and chaos, with cultural assumptions and with the relation of the artist to her materials.

This book would not have come to fruition at all without the inspiration, support and infinite patience of Andrew Brown, Josie Dixon and Kevin

Taylor: heartfelt thanks to them for their exceptional contributions to this book. Grateful thanks also to all the friends and fellow Virginia Woolf scholars whose work here comprises *The Cambridge Companion to Virginia Woolf.*

Sue Roe

NOTE

1 Angelica Garnett's memoir of her aunt, 'Virginia and Vanessa', is published in Angelica Garnett, *The Eternal Moment* (Maine: Puckerbrush Press, 1998), p. 50.

ACKNOWLEDGEMENTS

The editors gratefully acknowledge the assistance of the School of English at the University of St Andrews and in particular the work of Jill Gamble in preparing the typescript for publication. Thanks are also due to Ian Blyth.

Excerpts from *The Diary of Virginia Woolf*, volumes 1–5, edited by Anne Olivier Bell (Penguin: London, 1977–84), copyright © 1984 by Quentin Bell and Angelica Garnett, reprinted by permission of the Executors of the Virginia Woolf Estate, The Hogarth Press and Harcourt Brace & Company. Excerpts from *The Letters of Virginia Woolf*, edited by Nigel Nicolson (The Hogarth Press: London, 1975–80), reprinted by permission of The Hogarth Press. Extract from Leonard Woolf's paper to the Apostles (SxMs13IIO) printed with permission of the Librarian and the University of Sussex. Vanessa Bell's 'Three Women' reproduced with permission of the Estate of Vanessa Bell c. 1961. Excerpts from *The Voyage Out*, copyright 1920 by Harcourt Inc. and renewed 1948 by Leonard Woolf, reprinted by permission of the publisher and The Society of Authors as the Literary Representative of The Estate of Virginia Woolf. Excerpts from *Jacob's Room*, copyright 1922 by Harcourt Inc. and renewed 1950 by Leonard Woolf, reprinted by permission of the publisher and The Society of Authors as the Literary Representative of the Estate of Virginia Woolf. Excerpts from *To the Lighthouse*, copyright 1927 by Harcourt Inc. and renewed 1955 by Leonard Woolf, reprinted by permission of the publisher and The Society of Authors as the Literary Representative of the Estate of Virginia Woolf. Excerpts from *The Years*, copyright 1937 by Harcourt Inc. and renewed 1965 by Leonard Woolf, reprinted by permission of the publisher and The Society of Authors as the Literary Representative of the Estate of Virginia Woolf.

ABBREVIATIONS

BA	Between the Acts
CE	Virginia Woolf: The Collected Essays
CSF	The Complete Shorter Fiction
D	The Diary of Virginia Woolf (5 vols.), ed. Anne Olivier Bell (London: Penguin, 1977–84)
Draft TL	To the Lighthouse: The Original Holograph Draft
Draft W	The Waves: The Two Holograph Drafts
E	The Essays of Virginia Woolf
EJ	A Passionate Apprentice: The Early Journals: 1897–1909
Hours	'The Hours': The British Museum Manuscript of Mrs Dalloway
JR	Jacob's Room
L	The Letters of Virginia Woolf (6 vols.), ed. Nigel Nicholson (London: Hogarth, 1975–80): The Flight of the Mind: The Letters of Virginia Woolf Volume 1 1888–1912, The Question of Things Happening Volume 2 1912–22, A Change of Perspective Volume 3 1923–28, A Reflection of the Other Person Volume 4 1929–31, The Sickle Side of the Moon Volume 5 1932–35 and Leave the Letters Till We're Dead Volume 6 1936–41
MB	Moments of Being
Mrs D	Mrs Dalloway
ND	Night and Day
O	Orlando
RF	Roger Fry: A Biography
ROO	A Room of One's Own
SSS	Selected Short Stories
TG	Three Guineas
TL	To the Lighthouse
VO	The Voyage Out
W	The Waves
Y	The Years

CHRONOLOGY

1882   Adeline Virginia Stephen born 25 January at 22 Hyde Park Gate, London.

1895   Her mother Julia Stephen dies. First mental breakdown.

1897   Begins her first diary.

1902   Begins her correspondence with Violet Dickinson.

1904   Her father, Leslie Stephen dies. Second mental breakdown. Publishes her first review. Moves to 46 Gordon Square with Vanessa, Thoby and Adrian.

1905   Thoby Stephen's 'Thursday Evenings' herald the start of the 'Bloomsbury Group'. Starts teaching at Morley College. Publishes her first review for *The Times Literary Supplement*.

1906   Thoby dies from typhoid caught on holiday in Greece.

1907   Vanessa marries Clive Bell. Moves to 29 Fitzroy Square with Adrian. Starts work on *Melymbrosia* (later published as *The Voyage Out*).

1908   Julian Bell born.

1909   Engaged, fleetingly, to Lytton Strachey. Starts working for Women's Suffrage.

1910   Takes part in the 'Dreadnought' Hoax. Roger Fry organises the first Post-Impressionist exhibition. Quentin Bell born.

1911   Moves to 38 Brunswick Square with her brother Adrian, Maynard Keynes, Duncan Grant and Leonard Woolf.

1912   Marries Leonard Woolf.

1913   *The Voyage Out* accepted for publication by Duckworth. Third mental breakdown begins.

1914   Vanessa leaves Clive Bell for Duncan Grant.

1915   Tries writing a diary for the first time since her marriage, it lasts six weeks. *The Voyage Out* published. The Woolfs move to Hogarth House.

1916   (Approx.) Meets Katherine Mansfield.

1917   The Woolfs buy a printing press. The Hogarth Press publishes *Two Stories* (Virginia Woolf's 'The Mark on the Wall' and Leonard Woolf's 'Three Jews'). Begins to keep the diary she will continue with, almost uninterrupted, for the rest of her life.

1918   Angelica Bell born.

1919   Hogarth Press publishes *Kew Gardens*. Duckworth publish *Night and Day*. Publishes 'Modern Novels' in the *TLS* (revised and reprinted as 'Modern Fiction' in *The Common Reader* in 1925). The Woolfs buy Monks House, Rodmell.

1920   First meeting of the 'Memoir Club'.

1921   Hogarth Press publishes *Monday or Tuesday* (all subsequent publications are through the Hogarth Press).

1922   Publishes *Jacob's Room*. The Hogarth Press begins to publish the works of Freud. Meets Vita Sackville-West.

1923   Katherine Mansfield dies. Co-operates on a translation of Tolstoy's love letters.

1924   The Woolfs leave Hogarth House for 52 Tavistock Square. Publishes *Mr Bennett and Mrs Brown*.

1925   Publishes *The Common Reader* and *Mrs Dalloway*. Begins her love affair with Vita Sackville-West.

1927   Publishes *To the Lighthouse*.

1928   Publishes *Orlando*. Lectures on 'Women and Fiction' at Newnham and Girton Colleges, Cambridge. Awarded the 1927–28 *Prix Femina* for *To the Lighthouse*.

1929   Publishes *A Room of One's Own*.

1930   Meets Ethel Smyth.

1931   Publishes *The Waves*.

1932   Lytton Strachey dies. Publishes *A Letter to a Young Poet* and *The Common Reader: Second Series*. Begins work on *The Pargiters* (published as *The Years*). Turns down Cambridge University's invitation to give the Clark lectures.

1933   Publishes *Flush*. Refuses an honorary degree from Manchester University.

1934   Roger Fry dies.

1935   First performance of *Freshwater*. The Woolfs visit Nazi Germany, distracting the border guards with Leonard's marmoset.

1937   Publishes *The Years*. Julian Bell killed in the Spanish Civil War.

1938   Publishes *Three Guineas*.

1939   The Woolfs leave Tavistock Square for 37 Mecklenburgh Square, but spend most of their time at Rodmell as war approaches. Refuses an honorary degree from Liverpool University. Begins writing 'A Sketch of the Past'.

1940   Publishes *Roger Fry*. Mecklenburgh Square is bombed.

1941   In anticipation of her fourth mental breakdown, Virginia Woolf drowns herself in the River Ouse on 28 March. *Between the Acts* is published posthumously.

I

ANDREW McNEILLIE

Bloomsbury

The entry on Virginia Woolf in the old *Dictionary of National Biography*, a piece by David Cecil (who married a daughter of the Bloomsbury Group), speaks of 'the shimmering felicities of her style' and concludes that in her work 'the English aesthetic movement brought forth its most exquisite flower'.[1] In such light, where the language of biography trespasses upon eulogy and teeters floridly towards obituarese, we might recall how Woolf's father, Leslie Stephen, the *DNB*'s founding editor, pursued a policy of 'No flowers by request' when briefing his contributors.[2] Stephen died in 1904. The incumbents at the dictionary in Cecil's day were obviously more relaxed about floral arrangements. They let him get away with not just a flower (a Wildean lily?) but a whole bouquet. For what after all is or was the *English* aesthetic *movement*? To put the question is not to suggest that there are no lines of relation between the diverse stock of, say, John Ruskin, Walter Pater, and Oscar Wilde, and that of a no less diverse Bloomsbury Group. Rather it is to ask what is the nature of that relation? If it is at all important, how important is it in the cultural formation of Bloomsbury?

For present purposes let us take Bloomsbury to include, but not always or equally to involve: the novelists Virginia Woolf (1882–1941) and E. M. Forster (1879–1970); the literary journalist Desmond MacCarthy (1877–1952); the critics Roger Fry (1866–1934, also a painter) and Clive Bell (1881–1964); the biographer and essayist Lytton Strachey (1880–1932); the painters Duncan Grant (1885–1978) and Vanessa Bell (1879–1961, Virginia Woolf's sister); the political writer and worker, publisher and autobiographer Leonard Woolf (1880–1969); and the economist John Maynard Keynes (1883–1946). To give an example specifically concerned with aesthetics, Clive Bell's book *Art* (1914), a radical formalist polemic, owes more, and acknowledges its debt, to the writings of the Cambridge philosopher G. E. Moore and to Roger Fry than it can begin to be said to owe to Pater, or to Wilde (with whom its thought is considerably at odds), while its Ruskinian legacy is more pervasive than is perhaps generally appreciated. Yet Forster would declare that he believed in art for art's sake, alluding to Wilde in what English readers might regard as 'eighteen-eighties' language, rather than a more Bloomsburyean formulation.[3] The phrase 'art for art's sake' – as *l'art pour l'art* – derives from nineteenth-century France.[4] Whatever else informs it (including Pater's Hellenism and Roman religion) 'English aestheticism' of the 1880s is significantly French in derivation. This is not a tradition to which Bloomsbury belongs in any direct sense. Paterian theories certainly acted as a stimulant in the formation of Woolf's ideas of art and beauty. So later did aspects of Moore's distinctly Platonic philosophy. (His Socratic methodology too was mediated to her in imitations by her male friends, as we will see later.) But we look elsewhere, to Woolf's extensive, independent reading in Plato, her fascination with 'Greek', for another grounding to her aesthetic values (prior, as far as Bloomsbury is concerned, if consanguineous) and for the Socratic roots to many of her most deeply held humane beliefs, concerning sexuality, androgyny and personal relations.

Movements are active fictions, involving differences as well as difference, whether formed by minorities or majorities, and even when highly disciplined and organised into political parties. But it is more than doubtful that there was ever anything that might truly be described as an English aesthetic movement, extending from Pater to Woolf, still less, as we have seen, a specifically English aesthetic. Was Oscar Wilde ever an Englishman? Was Théophile Gautier? Was Immanuel Kant? Pater was of Dutch descent. And were even the members of Bloomsbury English? Desmond MacCarthy was descended from Ireland. Leonard Woolf was a Jew. Duncan Grant and the mother of the Stracheys were Scottish aristocrats ('Is Mary Garden in Chicago still / And Duncan Grant in Paris – and me fou'?' wrote Hugh MacDiarmid, making ironic waves for his Scottish renaissance, in 'A Drunk Man Looks at the Thistle', 1926).[5] And while Roger Fry certainly was English, his contempt for the philistinism of his compatriots was only equalled by the passion of his francophilia. Otherwise, we might just say, Bloomsbury was in origin Victorian and by acculturation securely British upper-middle class, if in more cases than Fry's alone conspicuously francophile, especially with regard to the visual arts. (Beyond the visual arts, Gautier and Baudelaire can scarcely be said to have concerned them; though Mallarmé and Proust, belatedly, did.)

Among the Bloomsbury group's forebears and relations were noted opponents of slavery, belonging to the Clapham Sect,[6] lawyers and civil servants, members of the judiciary, agents of Empire, Cambridge dons, Quakers, manufacturers of chocolate, coal-owning huntin'-shootin'-and-fishin' self-styled gentry,[7] at least one eminent Victorian agnostic, but not for generations a peasant, and never it seems a proletarian. Bloomsbury was neither an organisation nor self-consciously a movement (or part of a movement), still less a political party, which is not to say it had no politics. It did not organise itself, though for periods some of its members edited and or owned influential organs (e.g. *Nation & Athenaeum*, eventually absorbed into the *New Statesman*).[8] It had no manifesto, notwithstanding at least one attempt to claim *Art* as a platform for the group cause.[9] Whatever else it was, it was a group of friends, held together by ties of marriage and affection. It placed great emphasis on 'personal relations': 'personal relations are the important thing for ever and ever, and not this outer life of telegrams and anger', wrote Forster, and, more famously, 'if I had to choose between betraying my country and betraying my friend, I hope I should have the guts to betray my country'.[10] This is a position regarding patriotism that Woolf, in her feminist polemic *Three Guineas* (1938), radically took further, into the realms of telegrams and anger, in sisterly solidarity, with regard to women and war, much to the embarrassed disapproval of her Bloomsbury friends. She certainly thought women should either weep or unite[11] and withhold their co-operation from the male-run state intent on war – it was a perilous hour at which to go public with so radical a view. Nor for a moment was it appeasement she had in mind (it is important always to make this clear). In *Three Guineas* Woolf offended Bloomsbury's rationalism, by which they set such store. They had otherwise discovered their version of patriotism (a word so close to patriarchy), in the face of rising fascism (which in 1937 had killed Woolf's nephew in a tragic incident during the Civil War in Spain).[12]

The issues raised by *Three Guineas* were highly serious, on both sides, but Bloomsbury, however 'highbrow', was quite commonly conceived as wanting seriousness, as being frivolous. Privilege and frivolity in public life may always make a provoking sight. Bloomsbury enjoyed the potent privileges of their class, if not always as tangibly as they would have liked, however much they warred within and against that class. Raymond Williams has most accurately described them as a dissenting 'fraction' of the upper class, a civilising fraction.[13] Their heightened sense of 'difference' in this respect wasn't so readily visible to others, though their works betrayed it amply (consider for example Clive Bell's pamphlet *Peace at Once*, 1914, destroyed by the authorities, or the tenor of his book *On British Freedom*, 1923; or J. M. Keynes's *Economic Consequences of the Peace*, 1919; or Leonard Woolf's radical condemnation of imperialism in

Empire & Commerce in Africa, 1920). Bloomsbury were serious but not serious in the overwhelming style of such acquaintances as Sidney and Beatrice Webb (Fabian socialists prepared to have their heads turned by Stalin). They believed in laughter. (Laughter, in all its registers, from cruel to merry, resounds in Woolf's work, not least in her diary and letters.) Laughter, it should be said, satirical and otherwise, plays a key and provocative role in Bloomsbury aesthetics, as satire does more generally in modernism. In Bloomsbury's case it may be related in part to the ethos of the Cambridge Apostles and their concern, as described by Henry Sidgwick, 'to understand how much suggestion and instruction may be derived from what is in form a jest – even in dealing with the gravest matters'.[14] It would be a naive reader who believed that Strachey's purpose in *Eminent Victorians* (1918) isn't profoundly serious, for all the witty tricks he plays with the genres of history and biography. In a far more flamboyant and fanciful case, the same can be said of Woolf's *Orlando: A Biography* (1928). (The practice of the 'new' biography, of the biographical essay, and of the autobiographical memoir – life-writing as Woolf called it – were to one degree or another common across Bloomsbury. In many ways Bloomsbury ensured its continuity by recycling its life in common through the art of memoir.)[15]

When in the culture wars of the first half of the twentieth century Bloomsbury came under attack, as it commonly did, its enemy, whether (self-styled) Wyndham Lewis or F. R. Leavis in *Scrutiny*, or any number of others (including, famously, D. H. Lawrence), might at last be accused, in Quentin Bell's quaint rural expression, of 'firing into the brown'.[16] The challenge offered, as by Clive Bell, was for the enemy to target names, to relate charges to individuals. The same must apply to critics with regard to claims concerning the lives and works of the so-called Bloomsbury Group. Which is where the rub resides, the paradigmatic difficulty. How can we speak collectively of 'Bloomsbury' and make defensible sense? 'Only connect' was Forster's epigraph to *Howards End* (1910). Just as in the study of any other disparate cultural formation, or even a single author's *œuvre*, how to connect, and not compromise, is the commonsense task in hand here. (It is a minor irony that the most peripheral, yet still major, figure within Bloomsbury, E. M. Forster, is the one writer whose ideas critics are generally happiest to cite as representatively Bloomsburyean.)

The most comprehensive literary historical attempt to grapple with the difficulty of connecting Bloomsbury is currently in process of being made by S. P. Rosenbaum, across a number of surprisingly extensive volumes.[17] These cover their ground by monarchical epoch: Victorian, Edwardian, and (as yet still in the writing) Georgian, in a minutely graded chronological progression. Their scholarship is unequalled but their very methodology precludes the provision of a synoptic view, unless that is to be ventured in a final volume. This essay in their shadow offers the merest sketch of its subject, and from a very particular perspective. It hopes to provide, in an open and elastic, if brief, account, a helpful synopsis of the Bloomsbury mentalité, especially in so far as it concerns Virginia Woolf.

To do that, it is necessary to begin before Bloomsbury was anything but a name on the map of London. For present purposes perhaps the most convenient place and point in time at which to make such a start is in Kensington, London, in 1897, the year of Queen Victoria's Diamond Jubilee (an event viewed in procession, by Woolf and her siblings, from a vantage-point at St Thomas's Hospital).

Before Bloomsbury

The Stephen family, and Duckworth step-family, lived in Kensington, at 22 Hyde Park Gate. In 1897 their lives were still painfully shadowed by the death two years before of Stephen's second wife, Julia, née Jackson, *quondam* Duckworth, model-to-be for Mrs Ramsay in *To the Lighthouse* (1927). A woman of noted 'beauty', descended from the upper but also from the artistic echelons of Victorian society (the pioneering photographer Julia Margaret Cameron was her aunt), Julia Stephen was a devoted wife and mother. The tragedy of her death was to prompt her daughter Virginia's first mental breakdown. Julia seems to have worn herself out prematurely in devotion to her family and, through good works, to the service of others less favourably circumstanced (she was the author of *Notes from Sick Rooms*, 1883, as well as a number of stories for the diversion of her children). In her abnegating and caring way, she had been especially adept at the management of her husband's palpably thin-skinned ego, a role bequeathed to her Duckworth daughter, Stella, and to Virginia's older sister Vanessa. Stella was now, in 1897, herself shortly to die, of peritonitis, under the surgeon's knife. It was a most grievous death hard upon her marriage and it redoubled the misery at Hyde Park Gate, deepening the 'Oriental gloom' that had begun with Julia's death.[18]

The phrase 'Oriental gloom' might serve to prompt us, in the present shorthand, and with Bloomsbury's decorative aesthetics in mind, to consider the general gloom of Victorian domesticity: gaslit and darkly furnished with cumbersome pieces from William Morris's repertoire, and the staggeringly lifeless painting of G. F. Watts, as found at No. 22.[19] (The Pargiters' home in Abercorn Terrace, in the 1880 opening chapter of Woolf's novel *The Years*, 1937, evokes such a world, as more directly do

Woolf's memoirs '22 Hyde Park Gate' and 'A Sketch of the Past'. A similar scene is described in Lytton Strachey's 'Lancaster Gate', an essay which begins, with appropriate emphasis upon the gulf between generations: 'The influence of houses on their inhabitants might well be the subject of a scientific investigation . . . Our fathers, no doubt, would have laughed at such a speculation'.)[20] As to that despotic 'Oriental' itself, we might also pick up in passing an intriguing interest of Julia Stephen: Thomas de Quincey's *Confessions of an Opium-Eater* (1822).

This wonderful classic of Romanticism, a text claimed for modernism in French translations by Baudelaire,[21] is a drug addict's account of life both down and out and high, in London and elsewhere. According to Woolf it was also one of her mother's favourite bedside books. What in De Quincey's confessional might attract a respectable Victorian lady of Julia Stephen's probity? We might suppose (though the Stephen family were dyed-in-the-wool Thackerayeans), that it was the proto-Dickensian, transparently humane elegist to the street-life companionship of Ann that enthralled and compelled her interest, and not, surely, so much as the slightest tincture, even by proxy, of the drug itself? (For that you must turn to Mr Carmichael, the somewhat anachronistic emergent war poet in *To the Lighthouse*, with the tell-tale yellow stains in his beard; De Quinceyean aesthetics are in fact central to the 'Time Passes' section of that novel.) Indeed, De Quincey was a writer on whom Woolf wrote at some length (her essay 'Impassioned Prose' was composed as she simultaneously worked at *To the Lighthouse*).[22] One of her earliest published articles, and one of her longer pieces at this time, 'The English Mail Coach' (1906), is about him.[23] He is at least as important to her aesthetics as Walter Pater on whom she only ever comments briefly in passing. In fact the most extensive of her few published observations on Pater occurs in 'The English Mail Coach', which ends in praise of De Quincey's rapid and reverberating style, a style incapable of being groomed to suit a Paterian sentence, or tamed and housed in a Paterian architecture. Woolf's father also wrote a study of De Quincey, describing him as being 'like the bat, an ambiguous character, rising on the wings of prose to the borders of the true poetical region'.[24] But then Stephen, alpinist extraordinaire, conqueror of the Shreckhorn (and celebrated as such in a poem by Thomas Hardy), was a post-Romantic Victorian, a Wordsworthian, if of Whiggish cast, as well as, paradoxically, given Wordsworth's religious belief, the post-Darwinian author of *An Agnostic's Apology* (1893).[25]

Stephen was a prolific and formidably accomplished man, if not the genius he had wanted to be, and, for all the reductive rhetoric so often couched against him, an attractive figure, in his liberalism and hard-thinking scepticism, and the passion with which he held what were in those days controversial views, sufficient to cost a conscientious man his living as a Cambridge don. He resigned his fellowship for which he had been ordained on acknowledging that he did not believe, and never had believed, in the literal truth of the Bible. Anyone doubting Stephen's passion and its humanity should read his pamphlet *The Times on the American War* (1865), or, more accessible, consider the letter from America he wrote to Anne Thackeray in 1868.[26] As befitted a descendant of the abolitionist Clapham Sect, he held the Southern cause in sharp contempt. Stephen was admired by women, and played manipulatively to their admiration. He was revered and loved by male friends from, to focus upon the literary, George Meredith to Thomas Hardy and Henry James. He knew and was respected by all the great literati of his day: Matthew Arnold, Thomas Carlyle, George Eliot, Alfred Tennyson, Anthony Trollope. But he was not just a literary man, successor to his one-time father-in-law, the novelist Thackeray, as editor of the *Cornhill Magazine*; a biographer and a literary historian, he also had philosophical ambitions. He was an ardent disciple of J. S. Mill and an historian of the utilitarian philosophers, as well as the failed exponent of *The Science of Ethics* (1882, the year of Virginia Woolf's birth).

It is important to bear these matters in mind if we are to begin to understand the intellectual ambience at Hyde Park Gate, and to do any kind of justice to Stephen, or to the profoundly ambivalent love his daughter bore him, and the ineradicable esteem in which she held him, throughout her life, for all that in his last years he became an emotional bully and domestic tyrant, one whom she, in the last years of her life, would excoriate in her memoir, 'A Sketch of the Past'. The household Stephen presided over, we should note, was by now one in which his stepson George Duckworth, a somewhat dim-witted and sentimentally 'well-meaning' socialite, might impose upon Virginia, already traumatised by a multitude of griefs, late-night sexual fumblings as she lay in her bed, and other equally unwanted diversions as her social chaperone, criticising her manners and her choice of clothes, with who knows what consequences for her social self-assurance and sexuality? 'I shrink from the years 1897–1904,' wrote Woolf in 'A Sketch of the Past', 'the seven unhappy years.'[27]

In 1897 Adeline Virginia Stephen celebrated her fifteenth birthday (on 25 January) and had just begun (3 January) to keep a diary.[28] This almost daily shorthand record of the year reveals its author's great humour and resilience in the midst of the little comedy, and greater tragedy (as now

Stella dies), of life at Hyde Park Gate. But of more immediate interest here, in mapping the years before Bloomsbury, is the account the 1897 diary provides of her literary education or, more accurately, the extent of her uncommon common reading. Her booklist is monumental: Thackeray, Dickens, George Eliot, Trollope, Hawthorne, Washington Irving, Henry James, W. E. Norris form the lighter part of it (and mark the beginnings of the uncanonical catholicity of her subsequent critical career, something characteristic also of her father's critical output). The more forbidding works and authors consumed, eminent Victorians furnished by her father, include: Mandel Creighton's *Queen Elizabeth*, Froude's life of Carlyle, Carlyle's *French Revolution, Life of Sterling*, and *Reminiscences* (for the second time), Sir James Stephen's *Essays in Ecclesiastical Biography*, Lockhart's life of Scott ('my beautiful Lockhart') in ten volumes, Macaulay's history of England. Stephen escorts her to Cheyne Row to visit Carlyle's house. They walk together in Kensington Gardens almost daily. He tells her stories about Macaulay 'and various old gentlemen'. At night he reads to the family, from Thackeray's *Esmond*, Scott's *Antiquary*, Godwin's *Caleb Williams*, or recites Wordsworth, Tennyson, Arnold, Meredith. Only once or twice do we glimpse the parent prone to tantrums, with whom we may already be familiar in the guise of Mr Ramsay, as when a reading of Coleridge's *Ancient Mariner* goes wrong and almost ends in the middle 'furiously'. In October she attends classes in Greek and History at King's College, London. The history lessons, for which she had to write essays, seem to give way by early 1898 to a diet of Greek from Dr George Warr (a founder in 1877, note the terminology, of the 'Ladies Department' at King's) and later that year of Intermediate Latin, consisting, if we can trust to her account, of reading Virgil under the guidance of Clara Pater, Walter Pater's sister. (She was acquainted with both Paters socially.)

In the next year her older brother Thoby left his public school, Clifton College in Bristol, and entered Trinity College, Cambridge, and so began to filter into Hyde Park Gate news of embryonic Bloomsbury and its undergraduate life. In 1902 we find Woolf beginning private lessons in Greek with Janet Case, lessons resumed in 1903, but not in 1904, the year of Leslie Stephen's death, a momentous year in which the Stephen children moved, from the London borough of Kensington to set up home in the then markedly shabbier district of Bloomsbury. Greek had become Woolf's 'daily bread, and a keen delight' (*L1*, p. 35). It was a subject she could share with her brother Thoby. Her studies in it were to continue throughout her life, often with great practical intensity, as she made translations and notes, reading and re-reading the poets, philosophers and dramatists in the production of such essays as 'The Perfect Language' and, more important,

'On Not Knowing Greek',[29] as well as otherwise, in service of her thought and writing. Greek became a marker for her, a gendered trope (just as for another student of Greek, the autodidact Thomas Hardy, it may be seen as a class trope). It is a figure, for example, resurgent in *Three Guineas*, pointing up the educational privileges afforded her brothers and male peers, especially those now embarked on life at Cambridge – Cambridge being, as we should know, the university to which Virginia Woolf did not go, an ambivalent matter for her, of both pride and grievance.

'Embryo' Bloomsbury and after

In the jargon of the elite Cambridge Conversazione Society or Apostles, an 'embryo' was a candidate for election; an 'abortion' a failed candidate. Candidates were observed by active Society members and were either oblivious or only solipsistically hopeful of their candidature. Leonard Woolf once read a paper to the Apostles entitled 'Embryos or Abortions?'[30] The gynaecological terminology is revealing. We are in the domain here of the English public school male, if at the priggish and intellectual rather than the hearty end of the spectrum. There were usually no more than six or seven active Apostles at any one time. Departed brethren or 'angels' maintained links with the Society, often quite closely. The Apostles played an important part in the formation of Bloomsbury: Fry, MacCarthy and Forster, of the older generation, Woolf, Strachey and Keynes, of the younger, were all members. There were no women Apostles. Nor was the Society an avowedly political one (something Leonard Woolf was deeply inclined to question),[31] though there certainly came to be more than one or two notoriously politically active members in the 1930s. In tenor like Cambridge itself, as distinct from Oxford, the Apostles were unworldly. (They wrote the name of the other place with a disdainful lower case 'o'.) Even Leslie Stephen in his time was deemed to be too much the muscular Christian to pass through the eye of the Apostolic needle. His son Thoby (Woolf's adored brother, nicknamed the 'Goth') was also debarred, as was the *parvenu* Clive Bell, a figure in many ways far more adventurous intellectually than some of his closer Cambridge friends, at least in his earlier years, above all in his interest in modern painting.[32] The visual arts were largely a blind spot in Apostolic discourse. Nor did music feature much, except in a cult for German *lieder*, as rendered occasionally by G. E. Moore, and a certain fashionable interest in Wagner.

All non-Apostles (the rest of us) were referred to by the elect as 'phenomena' (echoing Kant), benighted persons living in unenlightened unreality, like denizens of Plato's cave. The Society itself dates back to 1820, when it was founded as an undergraduate discussion club. Little by little it evolved into a semi-secret kind of 'freemasonry of the intellect', as Quentin Bell has called it.[33] The poet Tennyson and his friend Hallam were Apostles. There are arcane allusions to the Society in *In Memoriam* (1850 – begun in 1833), Tennyson's elegy to Hallam. Homoerotic (and, certainly under Lytton Strachey's influence, actively homosexual) friendship was an inevitable if unproclaimed feature of Apostolic life. (The fateful shadow of the law and of Oscar Wilde certainly falls upon Bloomsbury here.)

Celebrated historic figures like Plato, Aristotle, and Bishop Berkeley, unfortunate enough never to attend Cambridge, whether before or after 1820, were granted honorary Apostolic status. So Leonard Woolf could begin another of his Saturday night papers to the Society:

> Our brother Plato tells us that this world with its changing and fickle forms of things, with its false justice, false morality, false Education and false govern-ment is a gloomy fire-lit cave, wherein men sit bound prisoners guessing at these shadows of reality and boasting that they have found the Truth. Outside blaze the clear sun and the wide world of Reality and only the man who has struggled up the narrow path and looked upon the sun can hope to set in order the chaos of the cave.[34]

If Plato was a haunting presence for the Apostles, so too was the German philosopher Immanuel Kant. Apostolic jargon has been described as 'a neo-Kantian argot'.[35] G. E. Moore, by the turn of the century about to become the most powerfully influential figure in the Society, had written a fellow-ship thesis on Kant – a philosopher important to Romanticism and the formulation of subsequent aesthetic theory, whether as appropriated by Coleridge, or as misrepresented by Henry Crabb Robinson, De Quincey, and others[36] – and Kantian loyalties figure in Moore's 1899 contribution to *Mind*, 'The Nature of Judgement'. Roger Fry's preface in 1912 to the Second Post-Impressionist Exhibition would allude to Kant's definition of the proper object of aesthetic emotion, and Desmond MacCarthy in the same year would publish an essay on 'Kant and Post-Impressionism',[37] thus perhaps reminding us of at least some of the connections between moder-nist and Romanticist aesthetics and subjectivities.

It was as a commonsense philosopher that Moore left his mark within the analytical tradition. But he was earlier to be celebrated for his philosophical realism, for liberating not just Bertrand Russell (another Apostle) but Cambridge philosophy itself from the trammels of neo-Hegelian thought, and, particularly, of Berkeleyan idealism. It was Russell who persuaded Moore, a classicist, to take up the study of philosophy (perhaps this background explains Moore's penchant for Plato). In 1897 Moore subscribed to such neo-Hegelian ideas as the unreality of time. But, as we have seen, by 1899 he had exchanged such idealism for realism and, with Russell for a convert to his cause, he had begun his onslaught on the Hegelian tradition. Most immediately at stake at Cambridge was the neo-Hegelianism pursued by J. E. McTaggart (another Apostle and a former schoolfellow of Roger Fry; and one whom, Moore notwithstanding, Virginia Woolf would read in 1936, remarking as she did so her surprise at discovering 'how interesting mystic Hegelianism is to me') (L6, p. 6). Moore knocked McTaggart from his predominant position in Cambridge philosophy. According to Russell, Moore found the Hegelian philosophy inapplicable to chairs and tables, while Russell found it inapplicable to mathematics: 'with a sense of escaping from prison,' wrote Russell, employing all but a Platonic trope, 'we allowed ourselves to think that the grass is green, that the sun and stars would exist if no one was aware of them'.[38]

But when Moore wrote his paper 'A Refutation of Idealism', published in 1903, it was Bishop Berkeley he sought to contradict. Berkeleyan ideas about being and perception open Forster's *The Longest Journey* (1907), a novel, we should note, that bears an Apostolic dedication: '*Fratribus*'. (Forster never fell under Moore's Socratic spell as others did; he was of an earlier Apostolic generation and remained, as ever, elusively his own man, although we know he read Moore's paper on Idealism, and he would later attest to losing his Christianity in part through Moore's influence.) There are local effects in *The Longest Journey*, for example, in the opening pages where the Cambridge undergraduates discuss whether objects (in this case a cow) exist 'only when there is someone to look at them'; and profounder philosophical bases, linking the novel to Moore's paper.[39] In *To the Lighthouse*, Andrew's reported excursion on 'Subject and object and the nature of reality' with its injunction to 'Think of a kitchen table . . . when you're not there' is Berkeleyan too.[40] The example of a table is used in the account of Berkeley's philosophy by Leslie Stephen in his *History of English Thought in the Eighteenth Century* (1876), and Moore brings it into his 'Refutation', a paper which argues for the necessary co-existence of both objects and perceiving states of mind.

But the work that really impacted on the Apostolic undergraduates of 1903 was Moore's *Principia Ethica* (1903). This is the 'black volume of philosophy' read by Helen Ambrose in Woolf's first novel *The Voyage Out* (1915), from which the politician Richard Dalloway (slightly mis)quotes. '"Good, then, is indefinable"' he reads, and continues 'How jolly to think that's going on still! "So far as I know there is only one ethical writer,

Professor Henry Sidgwick, who has clearly recognised and stated this fact."
That's just the kind of thing we used to talk about when we were boys.
Whether we came to any conclusion – that's another matter. Still, it's the
arguing that counts.'[41] His reflection that it is 'the arguing that counts' is
truly, and ironically in the light of 'when we were boys', Moorean in spirit
(though in any other context it could as reasonably be described as
sounding like Kant). It is a like case with the sentence 'the journey not the
arrival matters', as Leonard Woolf would later name a volume of his
autobiography (1969); or with Virginia Woolf's conclusion to her essay
'How Should One Read a Book?': 'Yet who reads to bring about an end,
however desirable? Are there not some pursuits that we practise because
they are good in themselves, and some pleasures that are final?'[42] It is not
hard to see how thinking of this kind expresses ideas of autonomy, of the
work of art as autonomous, or of 'significant form', in Clive Bell's
(admittedly circular and self-justifying) version:

> For either all works of visual art have some common quality, or when we
> speak of 'works of art' we gibber. . . There must be some one quality without
> which a work of art cannot exist; possessing which, in the least degree, no
> work is altogether worthless. What is this quality? What quality is shared by
> all objects that provoke our aesthetic emotions? What quality is common to
> Sta. Sophia and the windows at Chartres, Mexican sculpture, a Persian bowl,
> Chinese carpets, Giotto's frescoes at Padua, and the masterpieces of Poussin,
> Piero della Francesca, and Cézanne? Only one answer seems possible –
> significant form. In each, lines and colours combined in a particular way,
> certain forms and relations of forms, stir our aesthetic emotions. These
> relations and combinations of lines and colours, these aesthetically moving
> forms, I call 'Significant Form'; and 'Significant Form' is the one quality
> common to all works of visual art.[43]

The four key strands of argument in Moore's *Principia* are: (i) that intrinsic
goodness is an unanalysable concept and the word 'good', when used in
this way, to mean a thing 'good in itself', is indefinable, like the colour
yellow; (ii) that instead of one thing, the Utilitarians' concept of 'pleasure'
being good in itself, there is a plurality of things that are, and the most
valuable of these are states of mind involving either the pleasures of human
intercourse (Forster's 'personal relations') or the enjoyment of beautiful
objects; (iii) that the rightness of an action derives from the character of its
consequences, which is a classic utilitarian idea, and one fundamental to
the economic thought of J. M. Keynes, for example, especially in its
emphasis upon the near future (regarding quantity theory in economics,
Keynes would observe famously that '*In the long run* we are all dead');[44]

(iv) Moore's version of idealism – that when we call a state of things 'ideal' we always mean to assert not only that it is good in itself, but that it is good in itself in a much higher degree than many other things.

It is clear, even put so summarily, that Moore and the Apostles were highly important for Bloomsbury's thought. But how precisely important were they for Virginia Woolf? Turning from Moore's pages to hers, it seems very hard to believe that so prosaic a philosopher (and Moore could be numbingly prosaic) can have been any kind of inspiration to Woolf. Her few comments on the experience of reading *Principia* may be summoned to support this view. But Woolf's voice in her letters, not least in her earlier correspondence where these comments are found, is intensely performative and recipient-specific in tone, and should not be lightly granted authority. We can't always take it that she 'means' what she says (and I mean that in a commonsense fashion). On the other hand, our wish to establish Woolf's intellectual seriousness, to retrieve her from the categories of mere 'impressionist' or of 'English aesthete', shouldn't throw us back upon a procrustean bed, there to lie forever locked in the wooden embrace of G. E. Moore, whatever his reputed charisma. There are far too many other factors in the case.

We should not pursue *Principia Ethica* to the exclusion, for example, of another 1903 publication associated with Cambridge, Jane Ellen Harrison's *Prolegomena to the Study of Greek Religion*. This classic work in anthropology was consumed widely in Bloomsbury (by Virginia Woolf and also, with especial interest, by Roger Fry who once, without evident irony, attributed to Harrison a 'really Apostolic mind').[45] When considering Woolf's development it would certainly be as much if not more to the point to consider the effect on her writing of her hellenic interests and, for that matter, her reading in Renaissance literature; or of the impact made by Eliot, or by Joyce and *Ulysses* (1922, read by Woolf in serial form from 1919), not to mention the examples of Dostoevsky, Chekhov, and Turgenev. These last were writers on whom Woolf wrote, as she never wrote on Moore, and who were evidently of great importance to her on into the 1920s in the development of her psychological method (a method that also owed much historically to the late fictions of Henry James; and one which, in her view, distinguished her dramatically from Joyce). Woolf's 'realism' was also of a psychological kind.

Of course, if we are to read her fully, we need to loosen up and take an inclusive view in accounting for her poetics, so as to recognise, for example, the neo-Hegelian features in *The Voyage Out*,[46] and the intensely Paterian nature of the epiphany centred on Rachel's vision of the tree, towards the end of chapter 13, in the same novel. We need to acknowledge firmly the presence of both Plato and Kant (however distorted in the latter case), imbricated in Woolf's post-Romantic thought, mediated by Coleridgean aesthetics, by Wordsworthian 'spots of time', by De Quinceyean 'involutes', also by Shelley's poetry (his version of Platonism). We must see these strands as intermeshed, unevenly and variously at different stages in her life, looping back now and again to be recycled through versions of Plato, incorporating post-impressionist theory amid echoes of Kant (to say nothing of the reverberations of Beethoven's late quartets).

Plato, it has to be said, was the philosopher Woolf read far more enthusiastically and extensively than ever she read Moore or any other philosopher. This should not surprise us: Plato was an especially literary writer (as far as the aesthetic goes, his republican's distrust of 'poetry' and the literary arts was long ago negotiated away); Moore, for all his Socratic presence, was an especially dry, analytic thinker, a philosopher's philosopher. We need to recognise Woolf's resistance, her difference, and admit her own trajectory, beyond Bloomsbury. We need to acknowledge in detail her own project, aesthetic, feminist and otherwise (her historicism and its twin commitment to contemporaneity, as notably in *The Years*, 1937), whether distinct in its particulars from 'Bloomsbury' or allied to something we can securely diagnose as Bloomsburyean. We ought to observe, to offer just one out of a myriad possible examples, how as she read and made notes for her essay 'On Not Knowing Greek' she ran up an agenda that replenished and renewed her earlier studies, in ways that sought to link Greek and Elizabethan culture: 'Some Homer: one Greek play; some Plato; Zimmern; Sheppard, as text book; Bentley's Life. If done thoroughly, this will be enough . . . Then there's the Anthology. All to end upon the Odyssey because of the Elizabethans. And I must read a little Ibsen to compare with Euripides – Racine with Sophocles – perhaps Marlowe with Aeschylus' (D2, p. 196). We need also to admit how in creating Judith Shakespeare in *A Room of One's Own* (1929) and retrieving in her essays the lives of obscure (male and female) writers, she pursued a philosophy about literary history and canonicity far from alien to her father's thinking, arch-patriarch and demon that he may be in some critical agendas, and alien as he might be to Bloomsbury's brand of modernist thought. Woolf, as the revisionist moves in her essays and *A Room* show, believed in community; but she was an outsider, stranded: from democracy by history, class, and gender (all governing tensions at the heart of her work) and, in an existentialist sense, from community itself by the ultimately tragic intensity of her vision, her driven need.

Bloomsbury

Bloomsbury began to come into being in 1904 following the death of Leslie Stephen, when the Stephen siblings moved to 46 Gordon Square. There, on Thursday nights, the younger generation of recent Cambridge graduates began to foregather. Unimpressed by their joint collection of poetry *Euphrosyne* (1905), and inclined to ridicule their overweening seriousness, Woolf at first tended to be sceptical about them. But they won her round and became, as it were, the student contemporaries she had otherwise been denied. The bond between them all grew closer in 1906 with the death, another tragic death, of Woolf's brother Thoby, for whom *Jacob's Room* (1922) is an ironic elegy. She described their encounters in her memoir 'Old Bloomsbury', recapturing the earnestnesses and awkwardnesses of the young men in pursuit of their favourite topics: 'beauty', 'good', 'reality':

> It filled me with wonder to watch those who were finally left in the argument piling stone upon stone, cautiously, accurately long after it had completely soared above my sight. But if one could not say anything, one could listen. One had glimpses of something miraculous happening high up in the air. Often we would still be sitting in a circle at two or three in the morning. Still Saxon would be taking his pipe from his mouth as if to speak, and putting it back again without having spoken. At last, rumpling his hair back, he would pronounce very shortly some absolutely final summing up. The marvellous edifice was complete, one could stumble off to bed feeling that something very important had happened. It had been proved that beauty was – or beauty was not – for I have never been quite sure which – part of a picture.[47]

According to Quentin Bell, Woolf's essay was read to the Memoir Club in about 1922, the year in which the highly hellenic *Jacob's Room* appeared. The memoir's language of 'piling stone upon stone', of soaring out of sight, has strong echoes in 'On Not Knowing Greek', for which she began reading later that same year (and on which she was still working in 1924):

> It is Plato, of course, who reveals the life indoors, and describes how, when a party of friends met and had eaten not at all luxuriously and drunk a little wine, some handsome boy ventured a question, or quoted an opinion, and Socrates took it up, fingered it, turned it round, looked at it this way and that, swiftly stripped it of its inconsistencies and falsities and brought the whole company . . . to gaze with him at the truth. It is an exhausting process . . . Are pleasure and good the same? Can virtue be taught? Is virtue knowledge? The tired or feeble mind may easily lapse as the remorseless questioning proceeds; but no one, however weak, can fail, even if he does not learn more from Plato, to love knowledge better. For as the argument mounts from step to step, Protagoras yielding, Socrates pushing on, what matters is not so much

the end we reach as our manner of reaching it. That all can feel – the indomitable honesty, the courage, the love of truth which draw Socrates and us in his wake to the summit where, if we too may stand for a moment, it is to enjoy the greatest felicity of which we are capable.[48]

It is interesting in these pieces not just to see the same transcendental figures in play, but also to recall the distorted echo of 'what matters is not so much the end we reach as our manner of reaching it' in Richard Dalloway's 'that's another matter. . . it's the arguing that counts'.

As to whether beauty is or is not part of a picture, Bloomsbury, though well served by Clive Bell on this score, had to await the arrival in their midst of Roger Fry and his first Post-Impressionist Exhibition of 1910 ('Manet and the Post-Impressionists') to begin to pronounce in public polemical positions of their own (post-impressionism is a term coined by Fry for the occasion of the exhibition). The same year saw publication of Forster's *Howards End*. His Schlegel sisters in that novel are based to some degree on Vanessa and Virginia Stephen. Their culture, literally, in the form of a falling bookcase, kills the working-class Leonard Bast – a type reconstituted, we might say, in an evolved form as Charles Tansley, and crushed if not killed in *To the Lighthouse*. Woolf's provocative assertion that 'on or about December 1910 human character changed'[49] comes from her later essay 'Character in Fiction' (1924), also reprinted as 'Mr Bennett and Mrs Brown', a watershed for Woolf in her war with those she called 'materialists': Arnold Bennett, H. G. Wells and John Galsworthy who, like Gissing and also Meredith, were exponents for Woolf of impure fiction (the equivalent in literature of 'descriptive painting').[50] 1910 was also the year in which Edward VII died and George V came to the throne, and it signalled for Woolf the dawning of a new 'Post-Impressionist age'[51] (Clive Bell referred to post-impressionism as 'the contemporary movement').[52] Up until 1910, 'Bloomsbury' can scarcely be said to have enjoyed or suffered a public profile, but now there began open conflict with the 'philistine' denizens of what Roger Fry liked to dismiss as 'Bird's Custard Island'.[53] Fry's exhibition was a high modernist event, and together with its sequel in 1912 it has spawned an extensive literature. The 'public' were shocked, as they were earlier, in 1910, by the 'Dreadnought' Hoax.[54]

We might say that Bloomsbury first entered the public sphere on a battleship, then on a rocking horse, tilting at naturalism (for which also read Woolf's 'materialism'): 'A good rocking-horse is more like a horse than the snapshot of a Derby winner' wrote Desmond MacCarthy in his (anonymous) preface to the first Post-Impressionist Exhibition.[55] MacCarthy's 1912 article in the *Eye-Witness*, 'Kant and Post Impressionism', offers itself not as a review of the (second) exhibition but a review of the 'prefaces' to that exhibition. For our purposes, it provides a highly pertinent, and very convenient, synopsis of Kant's theory of aesthetics as interpreted by MacCarthy:

> Kant laid great stress on the immediacy of the aesthetic judgment and its disinterestedness. By immediacy he meant that beauty was a quality perceived as directly as a colour itself; and that no analysis could reconstruct or explain that impression. Aesthetic judgments were therefore not susceptible of proof, they could only be evoked; and therefore there could be no such thing as scientific criticism. Art criticism in the last resort could only point . . . By disinterestedness he meant that the aesthetic emotion is one entirely detached from a sense of the qualities of things as they appeal to the imagination, or to the moral or practical judgment. He distinguished between 'free or disinterested beauty' and 'secondary beauty', which is felt through the medium of associated ideas. He refused to call 'secondary' beauty, beauty – why I cannot think . . . he denied that the human face (he had not, of course, seen Picasso's portrait of Buffalo Bill) could be beautiful in art, because the beauty of the human face must depend upon ideas, the idea of human qualities.[56]

MacCarthy saw that what Bell meant in his preface (on 'The English Group') by the term 'significant form' (a term so vital to the theories expounded in *Art*, a term too with marked Platonic associations) is what Kant meant by 'free beauty'.[57] Bell asks, 'How, then, does the Post-Impressionist regard a coal scuttle?' and answers: 'He regards it as an end in itself, as significant form related on terms of equality with other significant forms.' For Bell the work of the post-impressionists is 'plastic not descriptive'; it does not traffic in 'secondary' beauty or associated ideas.[58] MacCarthy also notes that (unlike Bell) Fry does not 'deny that "secondary" or "romantic" beauty is a proper object for aesthetic emotion; but he gives it much less importance'.[59] MacCarthy himself argued for the presence of both kinds of beauty, if a painting is 'to rank as magnificent work of art'.[60] Taken together, these different positions demonstrate how much we must discriminate and hesitate, at any given point of the group's history, before referring to a 'Bloomsbury' aesthetic. How can we make any such reference on behalf of Woolf? In 1912 she was yet to publish her first novel (in 1915). Whatever its (great) strengths, they are not strictly formal, still less post-impressionist; and if her second novel *Night and Day* (1919) is intensely formal, its formality is more that of an English tea-table than of a still-life by Cézanne.

Woolf's version of transcendental reality was hybrid, emphatically secular, yet also mystical. It is given perhaps its clearest critical expression in 'A Sketch of the Past', where she digresses 'to explain a little of my own psychology'.[61] Here she describes her experience in terms of 'being' and 'non-being' and of violent 'shocks' of recognition, one of which, concerning an intense epiphanic revelation (without revelation) centred upon a flower: '"That is the whole", I said. I was looking at a plant with a spread of leaves; and it seemed suddenly plain that the flower itself was a part of the earth; that a ring enclosed what was the flower; and that was the real flower; part earth; part flower.'[62] At first when she was young such shocks carried, she said, a painful burden. Later she recognised their usefulness and stored them as a resource for her writing. We might be content to class the example just given as Paterian, but it is the common stock of post-Romantic modernism with a far more extensive root system (as Frank Kermode has shown).[63] Woolf expands on the rapturous experience and supposes that 'the shock-receiving capacity'[64] is what makes her a writer. She has to explain the experience in writing. The shock or blow is 'a token of some real thing behind appearances', and here we discover a 'system' of thought that has nothing whatsoever to do with Pater:

> at any rate it is a constant idea of mine; that behind the cotton wool is hidden a pattern; that we – I mean all human beings – are connected with this; that the whole world is a work of art; that we are parts of the work of art. *Hamlet* or a Beethoven quartet is the truth about this vast mass that we call the world. But there is no Shakespeare, there is no Beethoven; certainly and emphatically there is no God; we are the words; we are the music; we are the thing itself. And I see this when I have a shock.[65]

That 'thing itself' clearly echoes the Kantian *Ding-an-sich*, or thing-in-itself; although for Kant, emphatically, God was something more of a problem. But there's also a register here just a little reminiscent of McTaggart.[66] If Woolf recognised 1910 as the beginning of a new 'Post-Impressionist age', it would take a long period of gestation, as we have seen, before she could fully realise that age's aesthetic theories as a novelist. *To the Lighthouse* is *the* post-impressionist novel. In it Lily Briscoe stands at her easel as surrogate author, the question for her, as by peculiar analogy for Woolf, being 'one of the relations of masses, of lights and shadows . . . how to connect this mass on the right hand with that on the left',[67] a world away from the kind of 'descriptive painting' loved by Mr Bankes. I say 'peculiar' because fiction is a linear verbal art, with a relatively direct (however ambiguous, however symbolic) semantic burden. The formalism of *To the Lighthouse* is at one level obvious, as is its epiphanic transcendentalism, as instanced in Lily's (Christian) 'It is finished'[68] near the novel's close. (On the eventual voyage to the lighthouse it is no coincidence either that the 'little shiny book'[69] Mr Ramsay reads can be identified, though not within the pages of the novel itself, as being by Plato.)

But these elements are either obvious or can only be tied fairly superficially to post-impressionist theory and related ideas. Where a closer relation to post-impressionism may be discovered is, perhaps, in Woolf's psychological realism (as opposed to what she saw to be the impressionism of Joyce), in the perfection in this novel of her technique (worked at progressively through *Jacob's Room* and *Mrs Dalloway* and which owes much indirectly to Henry James) of multiple points of view, where we come very close to Cézanne and his use, in still life, of multiple perspectives, and perhaps also to a species of cubism. We maybe find it too in Woolf's synthesis of forms and genres.[70] Woolf was to regret her decision, in the end, not to dedicate her book to Roger Fry. We may similarly regret that she did not expand more directly, and in greater detail, upon what she saw to be the nature of her debt to him (even in her biography of Fry, she is evasive).

But Woolf always tended to prefer obliquity: it was part and parcel of her aesthetic to do so, and in the case of her novel obliquity is key ('I meant *nothing* by The Lighthouse. One has to have a central line down the middle of the book to hold the design together' she would spell out, with no little irony, to the formalist Fry) (*L3*, p. 385). The three panels of her triptych 'The Window', 'Time Passes', 'The Lighthouse' hang so, sideways-on to each other, their narrative lines suspended, bracketed, in parenthesis. In considering other modes and works – her essays; *The Pargiters* – Woolf had occasion to question what she called her 'sidelong' approach.[71] She put it down to her Victorian tea-table training (the angel of the house haunting her practice), thus showing her aesthetic to be, in some senses, the product of Victorian social conditioning: a kind of conforming good manners, expressing also, we should note, a hierarchy in which women fussed around men. None the less, she continued to believe more could be achieved by obliquity than by directly speaking out.

After Bloomsbury?

By the 'dirty decade' of the 1930s 'Bloomsbury' began to seem redundant. Urgent political events in Europe, the march of fascism (against which Woolf – the wife of a Jew – campaigned, actively and in print), all conspired to make the Moorean contemplation of 'beautiful objects', and so on, a luxury no one could justify. (Woolf's work had already begun, from quite early in the decade, to show signs of fracturing, in a deep-structured response to these developments.) Keynes would tease the younger generation regarding the aesthetic in a famous memoir, 'My Early Beliefs', read to his Bloomsbury friends in 1938 (published in 1949, and too often, as by A. J. Ayer, taken for fact). He maintained that the undergraduates of 1903 'accepted Moore's religion . . . and discarded his morals'.[72] In short, they were hedonists, heedless of consequences, uninterested in the fifth chapter of *Principia*, 'On Ethics in relation to Conduct'.[73] This was an argument Leonard Woolf would resolutely contest in his autobiography. Even the hedonistic Clive Bell had, in *Art*, used Moore to frame a moral justification for the aesthetic. The irony of all this is that there was no greater 'consequentialist' than Keynes, as his response to the Treaty of Versailles, to Churchill's disastrous return to the gold standard, and, indeed, his own work at the Bretton Woods Conference in 1944, all show.

But for Quentin Bell as he sat listening to Keynes in the summer of 1938 it seemed Bloomsbury now had no future as anything but history.[74] As suggested earlier, the historical interpretation of Bloomsbury originally began from within. The first extended public manifestation of this was Virginia Woolf's life of Roger Fry, published in 1940, and the last of her books she would see to the press. Fry had died in 1934. But her biography of him could hardly embody the 'truth-telling' ideals that Bloomsbury sought to live by.[75] Too many of her *dramatis personae* were still alive. Those ideals would have to wait in the wings to be revived by future biographers, led by Michael Holroyd in his 1967–8 two-volume, distinctly not 'new-biographical' account of Lytton Strachey (who had died in 1932). Virginia Woolf committed suicide in 1941. She is now a cultural icon, a figure as immediately recognisable in western intellectual culture as Van Gogh. As far as her posthumous reception goes, she would largely wait until the 1970s to begin to find such strange celebrity. Quentin Bell's biography, the publication of her diaries and letters, and, not least, the challenge of deconstructive feminism, all coincided to enable her escape to a new eminence in the canon, from beneath the weight of (largely) male 'new criticism' and such views as we began with, in that Victorian monster of Stephen parentage the *Dictionary of National Biography*, where David Cecil so effusively pressed her, like a flower.

NOTES

1 See the entry on Woolf, Virginia, in the *Dictionary of National Biography 1941–1950* (Oxford University Press, 1959), pp. 975–6.

2 Leslie Stephen founded the *DNB* at the invitation of the publisher George Smith (owner of the *Cornhill Magazine* of which Stephen was then editor) in 1882, the year of his daughter Virginia's birth. 'No flowers by request' was Alfred Ainger's

encapsulation of Stephen's policy on eulogy. See Noel Annan, *Leslie Stephen. The Godless Victorian* (London: Weidenfeld & Nicolson, 1984), p. 84.

3 See E. M. Forster, *Two Cheers for Democracy* (London: Edward Arnold, 1972), 'Art for Art's Sake', p. 87:

> I believe in art for art's sake. It is an unfashionable belief, and some of my statements must be of the nature of an apology. Sixty years ago I should have faced you with more confidence. A writer or a speaker who chose 'Art for Art's Sake' for his theme sixty years ago could be sure of being in the swim, and could feel so confident of success that he sometimes dressed himself in aesthetic costumes suitable to the occasion – in an embroidered dressing-gown, perhaps, or a blue velvet suit with a Lord Fauntleroy collar; or a toga, or a kimono, and carried a poppy or a lily or a long peacock's feather in his medieval hand.

There were never any velvet suits or Fauntleroy collars, no lilies or peacock feathers in Bloomsbury (although the Omega Workshops – established by Fry in 1913 – seem to have inspired a distinctive form of female attire); and there was no medievalism either.

4 Generally associated with Gautier, Baudelaire, de Banville, and Flaubert, the term *l'art pour l'art* in fact has an earlier and, from the point of view of this essay, a more intriguing provenance. For it occurs, perhaps for the first time in print, in connection with Schelling and Kant, in an 1804 entry in Benjamin Constant's *Journal intime*, noting a conversation with Henry Crabb Robinson. Neither of Théophile Gautier's seminal manifestos on the idea of *l'art pour l'art*, the prefaces to his poem *Albertus* (1832) and to his novel *Mademoiselle de Maupin* (1835), use the phrase with which his name is associated. For Benjamin Constant's usage see *Journal intime de Benjamin Constant* (Paris: 1895, introduced by D. Melegari), Le 20. *pluviôse* [fifth month of the calendar of the First French Republic (20 January – 18 or 19 February)] 1804, p. 7:

> Il est vrai que les poésies fugitives des Allemands sont d'un tout autre genre et d'une tout autre profondeur que les nôtres. J'ai une conversation avec Robinson, élève de Schelling. Son travail sur l'*Esthétique* de Kant a des idées très énergiques. L'art pour l'art, sans but, car tout but dénature l'art. Mais l'art atteint au but qu'il n'a pas.

> It's true that the fugitive poems [i.e. individual lyric poems] of the Germans are of a totally different kind from ours and of quite another profundity. I spoke with Robinson, pupil of Schelling. His work on Kant's *Aesthetic* contains some very powerful ideas. Art for art's sake, without purpose; any purpose adulterates art. But art achieves a purpose which is not its own.

Henry Crabb Robinson (1775–1867), friend of Wordsworth, Coleridge and other Romantics (a term as fraught as 'Bloomsbury'), as well as of Thomas Carlyle, played a key part in disseminating (as well as distorting) Kantian thought in England (see also note 37 below). For Walter Pater's version of the phrase see the conclusion to his *The Renaissance* (1873):

> Great passions may give us this quickened sense of life, ecstasy and sorrow of love, the various forms of enthusiastic activity, disinterested or otherwise, which come naturally to many of us . . . Of such wisdom, the poetic passion, the desire of beauty, the love of art for its own sake, has most. For art comes to you proposing frankly to give nothing but the highest quality to your moments as they pass, and simply for those moments' sake.

5 Hugh MacDiarmid, *Complete Poems*, vol. 1, ed. Michael Grieve and W. R. Aiken (Manchester: Carcanet, 1993), 'A Drunk Man Looks at the Thistle', p. 84.

6 The Clapham Sect was a group of Evangelical anti-slavery campaigners that included William Wilberforce and, among others, Thornton and Stephen, ancestors of E. M. Forster and Virginia Woolf respectively. In a chapter on 'The Clapham Sect' in vol. 2 of his *Essays in Ecclesiastical Biography* (London: Longman, Brown, Green and Longmans, 1849), Sir James Stephen, Virginia Woolf's grandfather, wrote regarding the Sect in terms that have some resonance for (godless) Bloomsbury (pp. 307–8):

> It is not permitted to any coterie altogether to escape the spirit of coterie . . . The [Clapham] commoners admired in each other the reflection of their own looks, and the echo of their own voices. A critical race, they drew many of their canons of criticism from books and talk of their own parentage; and for those on the outside of the pale, there might be, now and then, some failure of charity . . . They mourned over the ills inseparable from the progress of society, without shrieks or hysterics. They were not epicures for whose languid palates the sweets of the rich man's banquet must be seasoned with the acid of the poor man's discontent. Their philanthropy did not languish without the stimulant of satire; nor did it degenerate into a mere ballet of tender attitudes and sentimental pirouettes. Their philosophy was something better than an array of hard words. Their religion was something more than a collection of impalpable essences; too fine for analysis, and too delicate for use. It was a hardy, serviceable, fruitbearing, and patrimonial religion.

7 Clive Bell's family lived in a pseudo-gothic pile 'Cleeve House', at Seend in Wiltshire, a monstrosity built largely on profits from coal and transport. Bell's father William Heward Bell (1849–1927) was a Justice of the Peace, a director of the Great Western Railway, High Sheriff of Wiltshire (1912), and member of the Avon Vale Hunt. Together with Clive Bell's older brother, Lieutenant-Colonel W. C. Heward Bell (1875–1961), sometime Unionist MP for Devizes and High Sheriff of Wiltshire, he was also a director of Nixon's Navigation Co. Ltd, a company founded in the nineteenth century and one hugely instrumental in the development of the Welsh coal industry.

8 Maynard Keynes and a consortium of other Liberals acquired control of the *Nation & Athenaeum* in 1923; Leonard Woolf became the paper's literary editor that year, and remained so down to 1930, when the *N&A* merged with the *New Statesman*, of which Desmond MacCarthy was literary editor from 1921 to 1927.

9 See the introduction to J. B. Bullen's edition of *Art* (Oxford University Press, 1987), p. xxii: 'First and foremost *Art* was a manifesto of Bloomsbury aesthetics . . .' Strictly, it was a manifesto of Clive Bell's aesthetics, whatever its debt to Roger Fry (note Fry's seminal 'An Essay in Aesthetics', 1909, reprinted in *Vision and Design*, London: Chatto & Windus, 1920).

10 For the first quotation see Forster, *Howards End* (1910; Harmondsworth: Penguin, 1969), ch. 19, p. 163; and for the second, *Two Cheers for Democracy* (London: Edward Arnold, 1951; Abinger Edition, London: 1972), 'What I Believe', p. 66: 'I hate the idea of causes, and if I had to choose . . .'

11 Virginia Woolf published a condensed version of *Three Guineas* under the title 'Women Must Weep – Or Unite Against War' in *Atlantic Monthly*, May and June 1938. She later retrenched her position.

12 Pacifist associates of Bloomsbury (like Frances Partridge) apart, there developed a broad consensus within Bloomsbury that the war against Hitler was the just war that must be fought. Even Clive Bell would retreat from the myopic recklessness of his pamphlet *War Mongers*, published by the Peace Pledge Union in 1938, in which he had asserted that 'the authentic people, the peasants and labourers, know well enough, when their minds have not been inflamed and distorted by propaganda, that *the worst tyranny is better than the best war*' (p. 5). It was in the pacific role of ambulance driver with the British Medical Unit that Julian Heward Bell (*b.* 1908), son of Clive and Vanessa Bell, was fatally wounded on 18 July 1937 by a shell fragment, while serving on the Brunete Front in the war against fascism in Spain.

13 Raymond Williams, *Problems in Materialism and Culture* (London: Verso, 1980), 'The Bloomsbury Faction', pp. 148–69. See especially Williams on Bloomsbury's 'social conscience', *ibid.*, pp. 155ff. In connection with Williams' comparative discussion of 'Godwin and his Circle' and of 'The Pre-Raphaelite Brotherhood', consider also 'The Clapham Sect', as described in note 6 above.

14 Quoted by Leonard Woolf in the first volume of his autobiography (*Sowing*, London: 1960; see *An Autobiography*, 2 vols., Oxford University Press, 1980; vol. 1: *1880–1911*, 'Cambridge', p. 82). Henry Sidgwick (1838–1900), Professor of Moral Philosophy at Cambridge, author of *The Methods of Ethics* (1874).

15 For Virginia Woolf's essay on 'The New Biography' see *E*4, p. 473. Bloomsbury's Memoir Club first met in March 1920, at the instigation of Molly MacCarthy, and met fairly often but irregularly thereafter.

16 See Quentin Bell, *Bloomsbury* (London: Weidenfeld & Nicolson, 1968), p. 13: 'Thus Bloomsbury is always fair game because it can stand for whatever prey the sportsman wishes to kill and easy game because he can "fire into the brown".' For Wyndham Lewis (1882–1957), F. R. Leavis (1895–1978) and D. H. Lawrence (1885–1930) and Bloomsbury, see the section on 'Criticisms and Controversies' in *The Bloomsbury Group*, ed. S. P. Rosenbaum (University of Toronto Press: 1975). For Clive Bell's challenge, see 'Bloomsbury' in *Old Friends* (London: Chatto & Windus, 1956).

17 S. P. Rosenbaum, *Victorian Bloomsbury: The Early Literary History of the Bloomsbury Group. Volume One* and *Edwardian Bloomsbury ... Volume Two* (Basingstoke and London: Macmillan, 1987, 1994).

18 Virginia Woolf, *Moments of Being. Revised and Enlarged Edition*, edited by Jeanne Schulkind (London: Hogarth, 1985), 'Reminiscences', p. 40: 'Her death, on the 5th of May, 1895, began a period of Oriental gloom, for surely there was something in the darkened rooms, the groans, the passionate lamentations that passed the normal limits of sorrow, and hung about the genuine tragedy with folds of Eastern drapery.'

19 See Vanessa Bell, 'Notes on Bloomsbury' in *The Bloomsbury Group*, ed. S. P. Rosenbaum, p. 75: 'Yet many of the rooms were pitch dark, Virginia Creeper hung down in a thick curtain over the back drawing room window, the kitchen and other basement rooms could only be seen by candle or lamp light and most of the paint was black. Not until quite a short time before my father's death did we have electric light and even then not everywhere.'

20 See Lytton Strachey's 'Lancaster Gate' in *The Shorter Strachey*, ed. Michael

Holroyd and Paul Levy (Oxford University Press, 1980), p. 1. For Woolf's memoirs see *MB*.

21 Charles Baudelaire, *Les paradis artificiels. Précédé de La Pipe d'opium, Le Hachich, Le Club des Hachichins par Théophile Gautier* (1860). An enlarged version of De Quincey's book was published in 1856.

22 For 'Impassioned Prose' see *E4*, p. 361.

23 For 'The English Mail Coach' see *E1*, Appendix 1, p. 365.

24 Leslie Stephen, *Hours in a Library* (4 vols., London: Smith, Elder & Co, 1874–1907), vol. 1, *De Quincey*, pp. 326–7.

25 For 'The Schreckhorn (*With thoughts of Leslie Stephen*) (June 1897)', see Thomas Hardy, *The Collected Poems* (London: Macmillan, 1962), 'Satires of Circumstance', p. 303:

> Aloof, as if a thing of mood and whim;
> Now that its spare and desolate figure gleams
> Upon my nearing vision, less it seems
> A looming Alp-height than a guise of him
> Who scaled its horn with ventured life and limb,
> Drawn on by vague imaginings, maybe,
> Of semblance to his personality
> In its quaint glooms, keen lights, and rugged trim . . .

For Stephen on Wordsworth, see 'Wordsworth's Youth' in *Studies of a Biographer*, 4 vols. (London: Duckworth & Co, 1898–1902), vol. 1, pp. 227–67.

26 *Selected Letters of Leslie Stephen*, ed. John W. Bicknell, 2 vols. (London: Macmillan, 1996), vol. 1, for 11 November 1868, pp. 63–4:

> I don't care much for Peere Freeman. He is of the haw-haw school in mind though not in manners & sometimes makes me savage about slavery. You may talk slightingly about such things but when one sees a real living & moving human being & thinks of another having a right to flog him or sell him or do with him, what he chooses – it makes me feel wicked. I could have joined John Brown with satisfaction. However, I hold my tongue – rather too much for an intelligent traveller.

Stephen had visited the United States in 1863

> to go to the North and see for himself at first hand American democracy at work. Leslie Stephen was one of the very few intelligent Englishmen who found the United States sympathetic. Still riled by the independence of the colonies, despising Americans as low-bred boors, a generation of English travellers from Harriet Martineau to Dickens confirmed their countrymen in their attitude of superiority. Stephen realised only too well that this upper-class dislike of the North sprang from dread of democracy.
> (Noel Annan, *Leslie Stephen: The Godless Victorian*, London: Weidenfeld & Nicolson, 1984, p. 52)

27 *MB*, 'A Sketch of the Past', p. 136.

28 See Virginia Woolf, *A Passionate Apprentice: The Early Journals 1897–1909*, edited by Mitchell A. Leaska (London: Hogarth, 1990), details from which are not noted here.

29 For 'The Perfect Language', see *E2* and for 'On Not Knowing Greek' see *E4*.

30 A copy of this paper, dated 14 May 1904, is in the Leonard Woolf Papers (see LWP, II, O), University of Sussex Library, Manuscripts Section.

31 See his paper of 9 May 1903, 'George or George or both?' (LWP, II, O), in which he concludes that he does want G. E. Moore to draft an Education Act.

32 As an undergraduate Bell showed a precocious if restricted interest in modern art: he admired the Impressionists; a Degas print hung in his rooms; and he possessed lithographs by Lautrec. A Byronic liaison begun in 1899 with Annie Raven-Hill (d. 1922), wife of the *Punch* illustrator and cartoonist Leonard Raven-Hill, seems to have played a part here in also initiating Bell's interest in painting. Leonard Raven-Hill's work shows that he had looked at some quite good painting in Paris, particularly that of Jean-Louis Forain (1852–1931), caricaturist and Impressionist painter (influenced chiefly by Manet and Degas).

33 See Quentin Bell's introduction to *D1*.

34 'George or George or both?' – see note 31 above.

35 Paul Levy, *Moore: G. E. Moore and the Cambridge Apostles* (Oxford University Press, 1979), p. 66.

36 See Rosemary Ashton, *The German Idea: Four English Writers and the Reception of German Thought, 1800–1860* (London: Libris, 1994) for the background to Kant's reception among the Romantic writers.

37 Desmond MacCarthy, 'Kant and Post-Impressionism', *Eye-Witness*, 10 October 1912, pp. 533–4.

38 Bertrand Russell, 'My Mental Development', in *The Philosophy of Bertrand Russell*, ed. P. A. Schilpp (New York: Harper & Row, 1963), vol. 1, p. 12. For a detailed account of this background see Rosenbaum, *Victorian Bloomsbury*; and see also A. J. Ayer, *Russell and Moore: The Analytic Heritage* (London and Basingstoke: Macmillan, 1973), being wary in the latter case of the account given of Moore's meaning for Bloomsbury as represented by J. M. Keynes (see below).

39 E. M. Forster, *The Longest Journey* (1907; Harmondsworth: Penguin, 1960), p. 7. For the background to this novel and Moore's paper, see S. P. Rosenbaum, *Edwardian Bloomsbury* (Basingstoke and London: Macmillan, 1994), ch. 9, 'E. M. Forster's Refutation of Idealism'.

40 *TL*, ch. 4, p. 23.

41 *VO*, ch. 5, p. 67.

42 Virginia Woolf, *The Common Reader. Second Series* (1932; London: Hogarth, 1986), 'How Should One Read a Book?', p. 270.

43 Clive Bell, *Art* (London: Chatto & Windus, 1914), 'The Aesthetic Hypothesis', pp. 7–8.

44 J. M. Keynes, 'A Tract on Monetary Reform', *Collected Writings. Volume IV* (30 vols., Basingstoke and London: Macmillan, 1971–89), ch. 3: 'The Theory of Money and of the Foreign Exchanges', p. 65.

45 *RF*, ch. 4, 'Chelsea: Marriage', p. 73.

46 See, for example, David Bradshaw, 'Vicious Circles: Hegel, Bosanquet, and *The Voyage Out*', in Diane F. Gillespie and Leslie K. Hankins (eds.), *Virginia Woolf and the Arts: Selected Papers from the Sixth Annual Conference on Virginia Woolf* (New York: Pace University Press, 1997), pp. 183–91.

47 *MB*, 'Old Bloomsbury', p. 190. Saxon Sydney-Turner (1880–1962), an Apostle, took a double first in Classics, and went to work in the Treasury. He could read Greek as others read the newspaper, Virginia Woolf noted in her sketch 'One of Our Great Men' (Monks House Papers, A 13c). Otherwise Sydney-Turner

remains the obscurest figure in Old Bloomsbury, a noted exegete of railway timetables, and a compulsive Wagnerian. 'Beauty' seems to have come round at regular intervals for the Apostles. Roger Fry read a paper to the Society in October 1889 with the title 'Are we compelled by the true and Apostolic Faith to regard the standard of beauty as relative?' (Fry Papers, King's College Library, Cambridge); in April 1904 Keynes addressed himself to the subject in connection with G. E. Moore (Keynes Papers, King's College Library, Cambridge).

48 Virginia Woolf, *The Common Reader. First Series* (1925), 'On Not Knowing Greek' – see *E*4, pp. 45–6. For the most detailed record of Woolf's classical studies to date, see Brenda Lyons, 'Textual Voyages. Platonic Allusions in Virginia Woolf's Fiction' (Oxford University, D.Phil., 1995).

49 Virginia Woolf, *E*3, 'Character in Fiction', p. 421.

50 Clive Bell, *Art*, 'The Aesthetic Hypothesis', pp. 16–17:

> The hypothesis that significant form is the essential quality in a work of art has at least one merit denied to many more famous and more striking – it does help to explain things. We are all familiar with pictures that interest us and excite our admiration, but do not move us as works of art. To this class belongs what I call 'Descriptive Painting' – that is, painting in which forms are used not as objects of emotion, but as means of suggesting emotion or conveying information.

51 Virginia Woolf, *The Flight of the Mind*, no. 574, to Vanessa Bell, 21 July 1911, p. 470: 'Oh how I'm damned by Roger! Refinement! and we in a Post Impressionist age.'

52 Clive Bell, *Art*, 'Aesthetics and Post-Impressionism', p. 47: 'Post-Impressionism, or, let us say the Contemporary Movement, has a future; but when that future is present Cézanne and Matisse will no longer be called Post-Impressionists. They will certainly be called great artists . . .'

53 Noted in conversation with Quentin Bell. The reference is to custard powder, implying stodginess and dullness and by extension complacency and lack of imagination.

54 HMS *Dreadnought*, flagship of the Commander-in-Chief of the Home Fleet, was the scene of a magnificent hoax staged on 10 February 1910 by Horace de Vere Cole, with Virginia Stephen, Adrian Stephen, Duncan Grant and others, in which the 'Emperor of Abyssinia' and his entourage visited Weymouth and were formally received by the British Navy aboard what was its most up-to-the-minute warship. There were shock and horror in the press when the story broke and questions in the House of Commons.

55 Desmond MacCarthy, 'The Post-Impressionists', from the catalogue to 'Manet and the Post-Impressionists', 1910–11 (London: 1910), p. 9. The essay is reprinted in S. P. Rosenbaum, *A Bloomsbury Group Reader* (Oxford: Blackwell, 1993).

56 Desmond MacCarthy, 'Kant and Post-Impressionism', *Eye-Witness*, 10 October 1912, pp. 533–4.

57 *Ibid.*, p. 534.

58 *Ibid.* This reference to plasticity and the absence of secondary beauty or associated ideas ought to remind us to acknowledge the (rarely acknowledged) seminal importance for Fry and for Bell of Bernard Berenson's *Florentine Painters of the Renaissance* (London and New York: G. P. Putnam's Sons,

1896), especially in his account of 'Giotto and Values of Touch', for example pp. 16–17: 'Now what is back of this power of raising us to a higher plane of reality but a genius for grasping and communicating real significance? What is it to render the tactile values of an object but to communicate its material significance?' Forster makes play with Berenson's ideas about Giotto and tactile values in *A Room With A View* (1908).

59 MacCarthy, 'Kant and Post-Impressionism', p. 534.

60 *Ibid.*

61 'A Sketch of the Past', p. 70.

62 *Ibid.*, p. 71.

63 Frank Kermode, *The Romantic Image* (London: Routledge, 1957).

64 'A Sketch of the Past', p. 72.

65 *Ibid.* For another seeming echo of Kant's '*Ding-an-sich*', see D3, p. 62, a passage written in a period when she was working on *To the Lighthouse* (1927) and also on her essay about De Quincey, 'Impassioned Prose': 'I have a great & astonishing sense of something there, which is "it"—It is not exactly beauty that I mean. It is that the thing is in itself enough: satisfactory; achieved.'

66 McTaggart argued for 'the principle that an all-inclusive harmony somehow underlies every bit of experience, and that a reference to it is somehow involved in every statement, however meagre, and could be made explicit if that statement was coherently thought out' – paraphrased by G. Lowes Dickinson in *J. McT. E. McTaggart* (Cambridge University Press, 1931), p. 55.

67 *TL*, p. 47.

68 *Ibid.*, p. 175 (given as Christ's last words in John 19: 30).

69 See *TL*, p. 188, note to p. 156: 'VW recalled her father's "little 'Plato"', which, being of a convenient size for his pocket, went with him on his journeys.'

70 The idea of 'synthesis' has a history in the formulation of post-impressionist theory. See MacCarthy, 'The Post-Impressionists', p. 12: 'He [the artist] aims at *synthesis* in design; that is to say, he is prepared to subordinate consciously his power of representing the parts of his picture as plausibly as possible, to the expressiveness of the whole design.'

71 'A Sketch of the Past', p. 150. *The Pargiters: A Novel Essay* (London: Hogarth, 1978).

72 J. M. Keynes, *Two Memoirs* (London: Rupert Hart-Davis, 1949), p. 82.

73 Yet Keynes, at that time working on the meaning of probability, gave a paper to the Apostles in c.1904, based on a text from Moore's fifth chapter (Apostles paper II, Keynes papers, King's College Library, Cambridge).

74 Quentin Bell, 'Reflections on Maynard Keynes' in Derek Crabtree and A. P. Thirlwall (eds.), *Keynes and the Bloomsbury Group* (London: Macmillan, 1980), p. 86 : 'It was the summer of 1938. Manchuria and Abyssinia had gone; Czechoslovakia was going and in Spain the battle was still raging. To us it seemed that if Lawrence talked dangerous nonsense, Moore talked trivial sense; if we had any ultimate faith it was not in the *Principia* . . . It was from that date, I think, that we really felt that Bloomsbury belonged to the past.' Yet this was surely premature. It was not until Margaret Thatcher's Friedmanic policies replaced Keynesian economics, and Keynesian ethics, with deregulated monetarism and moral bankruptcy (to say nothing of other forms of bankruptcy) that

Bloomsbury ceased to have relevance as anything more than history (a history too readily purveyed by the editors of broadsheet colour supplements as death-of-history heritage).

75 For a dissenting view of Bloomsbury in this connection, see Angelica Garnett, *Deceived with Kindness* (London: Chatto & Windus, 1984).

2

SUZANNE RAITT

Finding a voice: Virginia Woolf's early novels

On 26 July 1922, shortly after she finished writing her third novel, *Jacob's Room*, Virginia Woolf noted in her diary her feeling that in writing this novel, she had 'found out how to begin (at 40) to say something in [her] own voice' (*D2*, p. 186). Critics have often followed Woolf's lead in regarding *Jacob's Room* as a starting-point of some kind. Many monographs on Woolf discuss the novels that preceded *Jacob's Room* (*The Voyage Out* (1915) and *Night and Day* (1919)) only in passing, or not at all, and where they are given more sustained attention they are often dismissed as 'apprentice efforts'.[1] Woolf's comments appear to authorise developmental readings of her *œuvre*, readings which assume that her early novels were attempts to work out who she was as a novelist before, in early middle age, she found her characteristic fictional voice.

But Woolf made something of a habit of announcing new beginnings. About ten years after she made the diary entry on *Jacob's Room*, shortly after the publication of *The Waves*, she wrote excitedly in her diary:

> Oh yes, between 50 & 60 I think I shall write out some very singular books, if I live. I mean I think I am about to embody, at last, the exact shapes my brain holds. What a long toil to reach this beginning – if The Waves is my first work in my own style! (*D4*, p. 53)

Comments like these mean that we should treat her (and our) hailing of *Jacob's Room* as the definitive realisation of her fictional voice with a certain degree of reserve. Woolf's statement raises as many questions as it answers: did she, then, misrecognise the voice in *Jacob's Room*? Do we have different voices at different stages of our lives? Or is she writing about two separate phenomena in the two diary entries? Perhaps 'voice', the word she used in 1922, and 'style', the term she preferred in 1931, are not the same thing. In *A Room of One's Own* (1929), Woolf's most sustained meditation on women's relationship to their own writing, she uses neither term, insisting both that in the nineteenth century 'there was no common sentence ready for [women's] use' and that language must 'be adapted to the body'.[2] It seems, then, that in Woolf's aesthetics voice, style, sex and the body come together in crucially shifting ways to determine the different forms which a woman's writing might take.

In recent and contemporary criticism, Virginia Woolf has most often been associated with the articulation of the female *voice* in fiction. Virginia Blain in 1983, for example, remarked that Woolf's early novels are 'as experimental as any of the later fiction, in the sense that each is trying out means of breaking through the barriers of inherited male conventions towards the expression of an authentic woman's voice'.[3] 'Voice', for feminist criticism such as this, signifies the immediacy of a woman's experience and her authority. But in this chapter I shall be arguing that, far from endorsing the project of expressing 'an authentic woman's voice', Woolf's early work actually undermines the idea that voice, identity and body can be seen to express and coincide with one another in any straightforward or seamless way. It could even be said that her early work undermines many of the assumptions on which much feminist appreciation of her writing is based.

It seems at first obvious that the voice has an immediacy and an authenticity which writing lacks, especially in an era in which recorded sound threatens to take precedence over live performance, and the telephone is increasingly the medium for social as well as practical interactions. But even live voices do not uncomplicatedly locate a self. We see ourselves only intermittently, but most of us hear ourselves all the time, and although much psychoanalytic theory has been devoted to the necessary if traumatic effects of seeing our own image, in mirrors or in the desires of others, less work has been done on what it means endlessly to have to listen to our own voices.[4] Speech could be said to reveal the split in the subject: whenever I hear my voice, it is already outside myself, not subject but object of my consciousness. Is it 'me', or is it simply 'mine'? Freud noticed that our voices can seem to trick us: in *The Psychopathology of Everyday Life* he devotes pages to discussion of slips of the tongue, those moments when our voices seem to speak from somewhere outside of ourselves.[5] But even for Freud, master of the poetics of self-estrangement, slips of the tongue finally speak only a deeper truth, a more authentic and permanent identity. He stops short of arguing that our voices can undo us even as they express us.

Virginia Woolf was fascinated with what it meant to hear oneself say 'I am'. In a 1930 review of a biography of Christina Rossetti, Woolf quotes Rossetti's abrupt assertion of herself at a tea-party:

Suddenly there uprose from a chair and paced forward into the centre of the room a little woman dressed in black, who announced solemnly, 'I am Christina Rossetti!' and having so said, returned to her chair.[6]

Rossetti was a perfect example of a woman forced to perform her own self-enunciation. As Woolf well knew, and as Yopie Prins has beautifully demonstrated, Victorian women lyric poets were centrally concerned with the construction and de-construction of their own and their heroines' voices, and with the figure of voice itself.[7] Woolf's early novels show her wrestling with many of the same issues – the relations between voice and identity, between speech and silence – in some of the same terms. In a letter to her Greek teacher, Janet Case, shortly after the publication of Woolf's second novel, *Night and Day*, for example, Woolf wrote of her interest in 'the things one doesn't say; what effect does that have? and how far do our feelings take their colour from the dive underground?' (*L2*, p. 400). Terence Hewet in *The Voyage Out* wants to write 'a novel about . . . the things people don't say'; Rachel uses music to say 'all there is to say at once'; Terence's love for Rachel begins with 'the wish to go on talking'.[8] The difficulty for Terence and Rachel, as for Katharine and Ralph in *Night and Day*, is how to reconcile the world of silence with the world of conversation, in which even between lovers voices seem to distort and falsify the inner worlds they represent. For Rachel and Katharine there is the added difficulty of sex. As Woolf noted over and over again, for women, 'the accent never falls where it does with a man'.[9] *A Room of One's Own* is an extended meditation on the history of women's literary under-representation, and on the effort of establishing a feminine style when women constantly hear only the voices of men, telling women that they 'can't paint, can't write'.[10] Rachel must struggle to speak for herself when others endlessly seek to educate and speak for her; Katharine's life is 'so hemmed in with the progress of other lives that the sound of its own advance [is] inaudible'.[11] *Jacob's Room* abandons the project of developing its protagonist's voice altogether, and instead experiments with the voices of others speaking in his place, even down to the creaking of his empty chair. The early novels themselves all uneasily interrogate the concept of voice itself, suggesting that voices are duplicitous, that we cannot be sure when they are our own, that the assumption of both a personal and a literary 'voice' is precarious and dynamic rather than consoling.

Woolf herself was nearly destroyed by voices. She habitually talked to herself when she was out walking, or alone: the Woolfs' cook, Louie Mayer, remembers overhearing her through the ceiling in the bathroom: 'you would think there was somebody else in the bathroom'.[12] During the breakdowns with which Woolf battled, especially in the years just before and during her work on *The Voyage Out*, she was apparently subject to auditory hallucinations, as she describes in the 1921 memoir 'Old Blooms-bury': 'I had lain in bed at the Dickinsons' house at Welwyn thinking that the birds were singing Greek choruses and that King Edward was using the foulest possible language among Ozzie Dickinson's azaleas.'[13] Leonard Woolf expands on this scene in his autobiography:

> She spoke somewhere about 'the voices that fly ahead', and she followed them . . . when she was at her worst and her mind was completely breaking down again the voices flew ahead of her thoughts: and she actually heard voices which were not her voice; for instance, she thought she heard the sparrows outside the window talking Greek. When that happened to her, in one of her attacks, she became incoherent because what she was hearing and the thoughts flying ahead of her became completely disconnected.[14]

Hermione Lee points out that these accounts 'don't quite fit the usual pattern of auditory hallucinations in mania, which are usually either grandiose or paranoid'.[15] She prefers to read them as part of a strategic representation and interpretation on Woolf's part of her own mental illness, suggesting that 'she may have refashioned the frightening, unintelligible mental language of her hallucinations – a language which was, as it were, all Greek to her – into a more meaningful ensemble, either immediately afterwards or long afterwards'.[16] If this is the case, it urges us to acknowledge the privileged role that voice (and Greek) played in Woolf's epistemology. She chose to recall (or to imagine) aural hallucinations as the prime signifier of mental breakdown in *Mrs Dalloway*, for example (Septimus Smith hears the birds singing in Greek), even though she experienced visual hallucinations at least once, after her mother's death.[17] But it was displaced and invasive voices that most captured her imagination and aroused her fear.

This tragic history shadows the triumphant remark with which I opened about the emergence of her own voice in *Jacob's Room*. Her achievement there is tenuous: that voice bears the echoes (or, in Roland Barthes's word, the 'grain') of its earlier polyphony, its muffling, its appropriation.[18] In an early draft of *Mrs Dalloway* she describes this resonance in a woman's voice: there is

> a vibration in the core of the sound so that each word, or note, comes fluttering, alive, yet with some reluctance to inflict its vitality, some grief for the past which holds it back, some impulse nevertheless to glide into the recesses of the heart.[19]

The voice is insinuating, hopeful, marked by the emptiness of its own presence ('some grief *for* [not from] the past'), and ephemeral. To call on the figure of 'voice' to guarantee her early literary identity was, for Woolf, an extraordinarily risky thing to do. By 1931, in the diary entry on *The Waves*, 'voice' has been displaced by 'style'.

But it was, perhaps, exactly of the risk of voice that Woolf was thinking when she wrote those words in 1922. Both her imagination, and her aesthetic project, were unusually aural (unusual especially for Bloomsbury, none of whose avatars had much proficiency as musicians, although many – including the Woolfs – listened avidly to classical music).[20] Several times she describes moments of unusual inspiration as speaking in tongues, or hearing voices. Of the composition of *To the Lighthouse* and its exorcism of her obsession with her dead mother, she wrote:

> Then one day walking round Tavistock Square I made up, as I sometimes make up my books, *To the Lighthouse*; in a great, apparently involuntary, rush . . . Blowing bubbles out of a pipe gives the feeling of the rapid crowd of ideas and scenes which blew out of my mind, so that my lips seemed syllabling of their own accord as I walked. What blew the bubbles? Why then? I have no notion.[21]

Here writing is a form of ventriloquism: someone or something speaks through her. Once it has spoken, she 'ceased to be obsessed by my mother. I no longer hear her voice; I do not see her.'[22] This automatic speech is part of the work of successful mourning: voices from another place exorcise the dead.

This association appears again in her experience of writing *The Waves*. Leonard Woolf's vague memory in the passage quoted above – 'she spoke somewhere about "the voices that fly ahead"' – is of a sentence from Woolf's diary in which she describes writing the final pages of *The Waves*.

> I wrote the words O Death fifteen minutes ago, having reeled across the last ten pages with some moments of such intensity & intoxication that I seemed only to stumble after my own voice, or almost, after some sort of speaker (as when I was mad). I was almost afraid, remembering the voices that used to fly ahead. Anyhow it is done; & I have been sitting these 15 minutes in a state of glory, & calm, & some tears, thinking of Thoby & if I could write Julian Thoby Stephen 1881–1906 on the first page. (D4, p. 10).

Here the voice she hears speaks from a world beyond presence. It is not distinctly her own voice, or the voice of the dead, or a voice from the past, but neither does it encode fullness, embodiment, immediacy. Like the woman's voice in the *Mrs Dalloway* draft, it holds a history of grief and recovery: it urges her to write Thoby's epitaph. Voices finally drove her into her own grave. In a suicide note she wrote: 'I feel certain that I am going mad again: I feel we can't go through another of those terrible times. And I shan't recover this time. I begin to hear voices, and cant concentrate. So I am doing what seems the best thing to do.'[23]

Woolf associated the figure of voice, then, not only with the inception of a literary style (as in the quotation about *Jacob's Room*), but also with an inspirational – sometimes manic – sense of loss. It is entirely appropriate that she should have chosen as the plot of her first novel the story of a young woman whose struggle to develop an adult identity, and a voice, results in her death. For Rachel Vinrace, learning to be herself – or, as Rachel herself says it in her excitement, to 'be m-m-myself' (p. 90) – is synonymous with learning to die.[24] Rachel is accompanying her father Willoughby on a trading voyage to South America when her aunt, Helen Ambrose, also a passenger on the ship, invites Rachel to stay in Santa Marina with her and her husband Ridley for a few months while Rachel's father completes his journey. During her stay Rachel falls in love with a guest at the nearby hotel, Terence Hewet, but after a boat-trip into the jungle, during which the pair become engaged, Rachel falls ill and dies. The 'voyage out' is thus a voyage out of girlhood and out of life as well as out of England.

Woolf struggled horribly with the style of the novel, revising it over and over again. Leonard Woolf says she burned 'five or six' complete drafts; Quentin Bell thinks it was seven.[25] It certainly took her many years to complete it. Her nephew Quentin Bell suggests that she may already have been thinking about it during a trip to Manorbier in 1904 in the short period between her father's death and the breakdown in which she heard the birds talking in Greek.[26] The years during which she was working on it seriously (from 1907 to 1912) were marred by periods of mental instability: she was ill from March to August in 1910, ill again in June 1912 immediately before her marriage in August 1912, increasingly depressed and intermittently suicidal throughout 1913 and ill again from March 1915 until the end of the year (*The Voyage Out* was published on 26 March 1915). None of her other novels was composed and seen through publication in the midst of such pain. Louise DeSalvo argues that the writing of *The Voyage Out* was implicated in her uncontrollable distress, noting that each time Woolf wrote or tried to revise Rachel's death scene, 'she herself went mad and once tried to commit suicide'.[27] Even as Woolf worked to establish herself as a serious novelist, something in her was working to madden and silence her.

Throughout *The Voyage Out* Rachel fights, like Woolf, to develop a voice to which people will listen. Her preferred mode of self-expression is music: she is an exceptional pianist. The most assertive moment in an otherwise hesitant existence comes when she tells the pompous, arrogant St

John Hirst at a crowded dance: 'I . . . play the piano very well . . . better, I expect, than anyone in this room' (p. 171). But the three figures most explicitly concerned with her education, Helen Ambrose, Terence Hewet and her father, all seek to turn her towards books. Willoughby tells Helen that Rachel is 'a nice quiet girl, devoted to her music – a little less of *that* would do no harm' (p. 92); Helen 'desired that Rachel should think, and for this reason offered books and discouraged too entire a dependence upon Bach and Beethoven and Wagner' (p. 137). But Rachel defends her love of music in the teeth of Terence's adamant opposition.

> 'Novels,' she repeated. 'Why do you write novels? You ought to write music. Music, you see' – she shifted her eyes, and became less desirable as her brain began to work, inflicting a certain change upon her face – 'music goes straight for things. It says all there is to say at once. With writing it seems to me there's so much' – she paused for an expression, and rubbed her fingers in the earth – 'scratching on the match-box. Most of the time when I was reading Gibbon this afternoon I was horribly, oh infernally, damnably bored!'
>
> (p. 239)

Rachel's characterisation of music as 'going straight for things' anticipates Woolf's own aesthetic manifesto in *A Room of One's Own* where she advocates writing about 'things in themselves'; and her impatience with novels foreshadows Woolf's own rejection of the realist detail of writers such as John Galsworthy and Arnold Bennett.[28] Music allows Rachel to confront and articulate the world without mediation; it allows her to craft and to perform her own voice. As she practises, her face wears 'a queer remote impersonal expression of complete absorption and anxious satisfaction' (p. 58). She is freed both from her own personality and history – the little biography she gives to Terence of her life with her aunts – and from the personalities and wishes of others. Through music she can perform, rather than express, her self. In clinging on to music, she defends her own solitude and autonomy.[29]

The Voyage Out suggests that Rachel's relationship with Terence is somehow in conflict with the voice in which she speaks as she sits at the piano. When, after their engagement, Terence asks her opinion of some reflections he has written on the nature of women, Rachel refuses to answer and simply continues to play. She is irritated by Terence's constant interruptions, and he, for his part, dislikes it when she plays difficult music, like Beethoven, rather than 'nice simple tunes' (p. 340). Rachel's playing is like a form of physical exertion (at the beginning of the novel Rachel says her aunt is worried that practising will develop 'the muscles of the forearm – and then one won't marry' (p. 15)):

Rachel said nothing. Up and up the steep spiral of a very late Beethoven
sonata she climbed, like a person ascending a ruined staircase, energetically at
first, then more laboriously advancing her feet with effort until she could go
no higher and returned with a run to begin at the very bottom again.

(pp. 339–40)

With her voice as a musician comes a new, muscular body that strains to
master the difficulties of the music ('ruined' and tragic like the deaf
Beethoven). It is this body that Terence ridicules: 'I've no objection to nice
simple tunes – indeed, I find them very helpful to my literary composition,
but that kind of thing is merely like an unfortunate old dog going round on
its hind legs in the rain' (p. 340). Terence's remark of course recalls Samuel
Johnson's dictum about the woman preacher.[30] Rachel's heroic ascent and
descent are diminished into the meaningless and repetitive antics of a beast;
her muscular body becomes the mangy form of an old dog. The equation
that the narrator has already made between the self that Rachel builds as
she plays, and a body, is echoed in Terence's cruel teasing. At the piano
Rachel can develop a body Terence does not want her to have; thus he is
forced to caricature it.

It is in part this instinctive rhetorical association between body and voice
that Woolf is exploring in *The Voyage Out*. Its allure is apparent in
Barthes's work too, in his account of the voice's 'grain', 'the materiality of
the body speaking its mother tongue'.[31] In the singing of Russian basses, he
hears 'something which is directly the cantor's body, brought to your ears
in one and the same movement from deep down in the cavities, the
muscles, the membranes, the cartilages'.[32] But instrumental music too, he
says, has its own grain: 'the grain is the body in the voice as it sings, the
hand as it writes, the limb as it performs', and with pianists he can always
tell 'which part of the body is playing'.[33] Rachel can find no way to
introduce her body – the 'grain' of her voice – into her speech: even in
confessing her love she simply repeats Terence's 'we love each other'
(p. 316). But at the piano she can say things directly. The muscular grain of
her labouring self materialises there, as Terence is uneasily aware.

Barthes's analysis seems at first, then, to license a rhetorical association
between voice and body, such that the voice, at its best, fully expresses, for
the body that listens, the presence of the body that produces it. But Barthes
gestures towards the undoing of his own argument, and of the stability of
the voice–body association, by allowing the voice its own form of duplicity.
In words that are uncannily appropriate to Woolf's own experience, he
asks, of the mixture of abstraction and materiality in Panzera's rolled 'r':
'this phonetics – am I alone in perceiving it? am I hearing voices within the
voice? but isn't it the truth of the voice to be hallucinated? isn't the entire

space of the voice an infinite one?'[34] The voice now becomes a kind of necessary fiction, and the grain a ghostly body that has no context beyond the ear of the listener. If Barthes is right, the voice and the figurative body that Rachel engages at the piano are without foundation. Selves built on sound can never last.

Indeed, the hallucinatory world in which Rachel is immersed during the final scenes of the novel exposes the instability of her emerging 'self', the extent to which it relies on an audience (beyond her own ear) which it animates and inspires. As Christine Froula has observed, Rachel's battle with accepted paradigms reduces her to silence: 'in [the death scenes], Woolf advances the plot of the female artist-novel, representing not the death of the body but the symbolic death that her heroine undergoes when she finds no language in which to live'.[35] Froula's reading beautifully demonstrates the extent to which *The Voyage Out* reverses the usual trajectory of the *Bildungsroman* in tracing the increasing confusion and diminution of its heroine. But if we are to mistrust developmental readings of Woolf's own *œuvre*, perhaps we should also shift the frameworks in which we read the narratives of her novels themselves. Froula suggests that Rachel fights to realise a space for herself in the world, a 'language and culture with which to create and defend her destiny', and that she is overcome by forces beyond herself, 'the power of female initiation structures to overwhelm female desire'.[36] But in order to argue that Rachel's desire and selfhood are thwarted, Froula must assume that she is beginning to develop some form of autonomy, that she has some sense, at least in the first chapters of the novel, of a self that she is fighting for.

But Rachel's disintegration reveals the tenuousness of the autonomous voice she seemed to be developing through her music. Terence recognises it, but struggles to silence it. The images and figures which Rachel sees as she descends further and further into nightmare in the final scenes recapitulate images from the life she led before she became ill. For example, after Richard Dalloway kisses her on the boat on the way out, she dreams of a long damp tunnel with 'a little deformed man who squatted on the floor gibbering, with long nails' (p. 81). During her final illness the little man combines with the figure of her nurse to become 'little deformed women sitting in archways playing cards, while the bricks of which the wall was made oozed with damp, which collected into drops and slid down the wall' (p. 386). Later she sees 'an old woman slicing a man's head off with a knife' (p. 395), an image which recalls the women killing chickens that Rachel saw at the hotel (pp. 293–4). These hallucinatory reminiscences emphasise the incipient hysteria of Rachel's responses from the very beginning of the novel. As Freud noted, 'hysterics suffer mainly from reminiscences', and as

Rachel is increasingly taken over by memories of her own disintegration, the woman she previously appeared to be is gradually exposed as – or comes to seem – an empty illusion.[37] Rachel lives now in the delusional intensity with which she responded to every decisive moment in her life-story: Richard Dalloway's kiss, the talk with Evelyn just before she sees the women killing chickens, her engagement. Music has no meaning for her now, the self it seemed to give her unsustainable in the face of the imminence of sexual initiation.

Rachel's musical voice, then, cannot ground her in her self or in her body. Indeed it comes to signify the extent to which she will never be able to develop a mature sexual body or identity. Early in the novel she tells Terence that men and women are utterly incompatible: 'it's no good; we should live separate; we cannot understand each other; we only bring out what's worst' (p. 174). Her music, and Terence's dislike of it, emphasises both the fatal differences between them, and the extraordinary precarious-ness of the identity and the body she has even before their engagement. It is not just that, as Louise DeSalvo suggests, women cannot 'return from a journey of initiation unscathed': it is that even at their setting out, they are alienated, feeble, only dimly realised.[38] Pulling against the carefully deli-neated social context of the novel – the conversations in the hotel, the feeling of people coming and going – is a nihilistic sense of the inconsequen-tial nature of Rachel's life and being; of her, in Woolf's memorable phrase about herself, 'incomprehensible and quite negligible femininity' (L1, p. 329). Rachel's death barely makes any difference in her world. As Woolf wrote: 'what I wanted to do was to give the feeling of a vast tumult of life, as various and disorderly as possible, which should be cut short for a moment by the death, and go on again' (L2, p. 82). Rachel's identity, even her body, are scarcely formed; and the voice she seems to be developing at the piano remains suspended, provisional, misheard.

As the novel neared publication, Woolf seems to have had a similar sense of her own acute vulnerability and precariousness, of her 'incomprehen-sible' and 'quite negligible' fictional voice, with its unseen, threatening future audience. The day before *The Voyage Out* was published, in March 1915, Woolf entered a nursing-home, and for two months she was violent, refused to speak to Leonard and periodically refused to eat. As Lee remarks, *The Voyage Out* remained in Woolf's memory as one of the most difficult of her novels: reading the proofs of *The Years* more than twenty years later, she noted: 'I have never suffered, since The Voyage Out, such acute despair on re-reading, as this time.'[39] When she undertook her next novel, then, it was written almost as protection against a recurrence of this kind of desperation. This time the heroine manages to hold on to her wordless language, mathematics, through courtship and engagement. Woolf was determined that this time she and her heroine would not disintegrate as her first protagonist had done, and although Katharine Hilbery's voice is still muffled and uncertain throughout much of *Night and Day*, the novel's vision of women's possibilities is less uncompromisingly bleak than it was in *The Voyage Out*. *Night and Day* seeks to rescue some sense of the durability of women's voices but, in order to do so, Woolf made a number of formal choices which cost her dearly in terms of reviews and critical responses.

Woolf knew that *Night and Day* was a defensive (and defended) novel. She wrote to Ethel Smyth in 1930:

> When I came to, I was so tremblingly afraid of my own insanity that I wrote Night and Day mainly to prove to my own satisfaction that I could keep entirely off that dangerous ground. I wrote it, lying in bed, allowed to write only for one half hour a day. And I made myself copy from plaster casts, partly to tranquillise, partly to learn anatomy. Bad as the book is, it composed my mind, and I think taught me certain elements of composition which I should not have had the patience to learn had I been in full flush of health always.
>
> (*L*4, p. 231)

Woolf draws an analogy between the harmonious proportions of classical art (E. M. Forster called *Night and Day* 'a deliberate exercise in classicism') and the precarious harmony of her own mind.[40] The 'plaster casts' are the earlier forms on which *Night and Day* is so dependent: the comedies of Shakespeare, for example, or, as Jane Marcus has shown, the operas of Mozart.[41] The invalid voice that Woolf tried out in *Night and Day* was deliberately not quite her own, as if her own were too tenuous and too dangerous. The careful routines of her everyday life, orchestrated by Leonard, and the cautiously allusive structuring of her novel, were part of the same project to marginalise anarchic and disruptive voices: the voices of her madness, and, as she would later come to believe ('bad as the book is'), the voices of her creativity.

The plot concerns the courtships of Katharine Hilbery, Ralph Denham, William Rodney and Cassandra Otway. Katharine is the upper-middle-class grand-daughter of famous poet Richard Alardyce. She spends her days helping her absent-minded mother write a biography of her poet father: her time is given over to the past, to the dead, and to her family and domestic obligations. When the novel opens, Katharine is being courted by Government clerk William, and she soon agrees to marry him. Her misgivings about her lack of passionate feeling for him are confirmed by her developing friendship with Ralph Denham, who declares his love for her. William gradually comes to realise that he loves not Katharine, but her cousin Cassandra. Katharine is not sure how she feels about Ralph. This deadlock is broken by the arrival of Mrs Hilbery bearing branches from Shakespeare's tomb. She sorts out both couples and enables something of a happy ending.

Katharine differs from Rachel in a number of ways. She is older and more authoritative, and her fears of losing her solitude and her autonomy in love prove in the end to be unfounded. No one seeks to educate Katharine in quite the way that they do Rachel, although like Rachel she has no instinctive liking for text: '"yes, I do hate books," she continued. "Why do you want to be for ever talking about your feelings?"' (p. 149). Once again, Woolf creates a heroine who feels that books are just so much chat, a heroine who is suspicious of exactly the activities that Woolf loved – and feared – the most. Katharine's preferred language is the language of abstract symbol or of the stars – mathematics and astronomy:

> Perhaps the unwomanly nature of the science made her instinctively wish to conceal her love of it. But the more profound reason was that in her mind mathematics were directly opposed to literature. She would not have cared to confess how infinitely she preferred the exactitude, the star-like impersonality, of figures to the confusion, agitation, and vagueness of the finest prose. (p. 42)

Like Rachel, Katharine seeks a language that says things directly and without the impediment of personality or history. Writing is associated with domesticity and femininity: the words she (or the narrator on her behalf) uses to describe fiction could just as easily be associated with her mother, the writer, who can never stay with one train of thought long enough to finish it.[42] Furthermore, the task on which Katharine and her mother are engaged embeds Katharine firmly both in her filial identity, and in the past. Sometimes she feels that 'the past had completely displaced the present, which, when one resumed life after a morning among the dead, proved to be of an utterly thin and inferior composition' (p. 40). In writing Katharine is crowded out by other people, by the dead, by her mother's demands.

Part of Katharine's desire, indeed, is to escape from her own identity: her family name and, especially, her family house. Numbers and the stars inscribe formal relations which have nothing to do with human social interactions, with the annoyance and the distraction of voice: 'I want to work out something in figures – something that hasn't got to do with human beings', she tells her cousin Henry (p. 201). Katharine, unlike Rachel, is unusually taciturn and mistrustful of speech and, unlike Rachel's, her personal language is itself silent, demanding no listener. Katharine wants to marry in order to escape the restrictions of her home life, but marriage, she knows, is a compromise, 'no more than an archway through which it was necessary to pass in order to have her desire' (p. 224). There is an impossible contradiction, then, in Katharine's expectations of marriage. As Jane Marcus has commented, 'the ideal of the female utopia was to be in paradise alone, to work', but the only way that Katharine can imagine reaching that utopia is by entering into a relationship of exceptional intimacy.[43] Her challenge in the novel is to find a relationship in which, paradoxically, her solitude is guaranteed by the nearness of someone else. The cautious optimism of *Night and Day* is apparent in Woolf's decision to give Katharine such a marriage, a solution which Rachel, of course, is denied. In *The Voyage Out* Rachel's inner world is invaded by others, and the music of her own voice is drowned out; in *Night and Day* Katharine is amazed to find that it is possible to love without being silenced by it: 'she had now to get used to the fact that someone shared her loneliness. The bewilderment was half shame and half the prelude to profound rejoicing' (p. 518). Her 'loneliness' is not destroyed by being shared. Rather it is enriched and protected: Katharine dwells now in possibility.

It would be easy to assume that Woolf wrote *Night and Day* partly as a response to her own unease about the marriage to which she had committed herself a few years before she began working on the novel. *Night and Day* was the first novel written when she was a wife, the first novel whose writing had to contend with Leonard's anxious and affectionate control of her time and routine. At times she seems certainly to have resented his intrusions, as Lee notes: Woolf wrote to Violet Dickinson in 1912 that she must cancel her visit because 'Leonard made me into a comatose invalid'.[44] At other times, however, she described their marriage as a rich communion of solitudes, 'as if marriage were a completing of the instrument, & the sound of one alone penetrates as if it were a violin robbed of its orchestra or piano' (*D1*, p. 70). Her letter to Ethel Smyth implies that she was as frightened as Leonard was of damaging her fragile mental equilibrium in the first months of writing *Night and Day*, and eagerly co-operated with his attempts to control her activities. Her needs and expectations were, in fact, as contradictory as Katharine's: she wanted both to avoid illness – to silence the voices in her head – and to imagine an alternative world in which characters spoke and moved. In imagining the form and circumstances of Katharine's marriage she may also have been negotiating the conditions in which it would be safe to allow herself to speak again as a novelist. The story she told in *The Voyage Out*, of Rachel's failure to develop a voice that can resist the admonishments of others, was followed in *Night and Day* by the story of a woman who secures the right to express herself in the language she chooses. To put it crudely, Katharine finds a fiancé who wants her to study mathematics; whereas Rachel's insists that she stop playing the piano.

But *Night and Day* is hardly triumphant. For one thing, Katharine's silent work with numbers is much less disruptive of domestic peace than Rachel's noisy playing. In some ways, Katharine is *already* a more compliant heroine even at the beginning of the book. Secondly, *Night and Day* ends in tears. In the last pages Katharine and Ralph pause in the street to look at the light in the room of their friend Mary Datchet. Mary, having lost Ralph, whom she loves, to Katharine, has dedicated her life to social reform. She is an object of envy and awe for Katharine from the beginning of the novel: ' "I think you're very lucky," [Katharine] observed. "I envy you, living alone and having your own things" – and engaged in this exalted way, which had no recognition or engagement-ring, she added in her own mind' (p. 284). The presence of Mary in the novel dulls the triumph of Katharine's successful negotiation of transition. Marriage to Ralph may have been the best that Katharine could have hoped for, since, given her class position and her personality, she could never have left her family and struck out on her own except through marriage. But Mary's burning light at the end of the novel reminds Katharine of how few choices she has. Woolf herself acknowledged the sombre tone of the ending:

> L. finds the philosophy very melancholy . . . Yet, if one is to deal with people on a large scale & say what one thinks, how can one avoid melancholy? I don't admit to being hopeless though – only the spectacle is a profoundly strange one; & as the current answers don't do, one has to grope for a new one; & the process of discarding the old, when one is by no means certain what to put in their place, is a sad one. (*D1*, p. 259)

Woolf's comments perfectly capture the hesitancy and confusion of much of *Night and Day*, a novel which, like its protagonists, barely trusts itself to celebrate its own happy ending, is not even sure that it really is happy. The elusiveness of its characterisation – E. M. Forster complained that 'none of the characters in N. & D. is lovable' – works against any notion that the solutions it proposes are reliable or long-lasting (*D1*, p. 310). Indeed for her next novel Woolf turned not to *Night and Day* but to the experimental short stories she had been writing alongside it, as her stylistic model. The caution and the classicism of *Night and Day* were left far behind.

Her project in *Jacob's Room*, at least as she describes it in her diary, was primarily formal and stylistic. Her aim was twofold: to write a novel about a character to whose inner life we rarely have access; and to experiment with gendering the narrative voice as feminine. The two goals were related, of course: the narrator herself describes her difference from Jacob as one determined largely by gender: 'whether we know what was in his mind is another question. Granted ten years' seniority and a difference of sex, fear of him comes first; this is swallowed up by a desire to help.'[45] *Jacob's Room* gives up, as if in despair, on the project of imagining the forms which female autonomy might take: this narrator serves Jacob even as she observes him. It is in *Jacob's Room* that Woolf tries to reflect on the conditions of the narrative voice itself: what it means to speak for a silent other; and whether that speech is inevitably a form of displacement and destruction (hence, perhaps, the nihilistically satirical tone of much of *Jacob's Room*). The novel is also, of course, a reflection on the speech of the bereaved. Sara Ruddick has persuasively argued that like *The Waves*, *Jacob's Room* is a 'tribute' to Woolf's brother Thoby, who died in 1906 from a fever contracted, like Rachel Vinrace's, during a trip abroad.[46] In what voice can Woolf remember the dead? In whose voice can she engage with fictional forms of living?

Woolf had already tried structuring a story around the thoughts of an observing and interpreting mind in the stories 'An Unwritten Novel' and 'The Mark on the Wall', and she saw these as the seeds of *Jacob's Room*: 'conceive mark on the wall, K[ew]. G[ardens]. & unwritten novel taking hands & dancing in unity. What the unity shall be I have yet to discover: the theme is a blank to me; but I see immense possibilities in the form I hit upon more or less by chance 2 weeks ago' (*D*2, p. 14). One of the frustrations of the novel, indeed, is that its theme is its form. It tells the story of the short life of Jacob Flanders, his childhood in Scarborough, his university years in Cambridge, his friendship with Bonamy and dalliances with women, a trip to Greece, during which he falls in love, and finally his death in the First World War. But most of the main events of the novel occur obliquely, just outside our range of vision, and the narrative sequence is choppy, fragmented, discontinuous. Leonard Woolf found it disconcerting (although remarkable): 'he says that the people are ghosts', wrote Woolf in her diary: 'he says it is very strange: I have no philosophy of life he says; my people are puppets, moved hither & thither by fate' (*D*2, p. 186). Jacob has no identifiable voice, and the narrative voice is undercut all the time by its own uncertainties. *Jacob's Room* takes as its formal and philosophical grounding the idea that voice is unstable and dynamic, and experiments with the kind of novel that can be built on that assumption – an assumption which, as Woolf constantly remarked, was directly at odds with the aesthetics of her Edwardian predecessors.[47] As Woolf said defensively over and over again in her letters, 'it has *some* merit, but its [*sic*] too much of an experiment'.[48] Such comments are a far cry from the excitement of the diary entry with which I opened: 'I have found out how to begin (at 40) to say something in my own voice' (D2, p. 186). If this *was* her 'own voice', it was, on her own admission, preliminary and tentative.

The novel opens with Betty Flanders, Jacob's mother, writing a letter on the beach, and pausing to look through tear-filled eyes at the bay and the lighthouse: 'the entire bay quivered; the lighthouse wobbled; and she had the illusion that the mast of Mr Connor's little yacht was bending like a wax candle in the sun' (p. 3). At its outset the world of the novel threatens to dissolve into the tears of women (Betty is writing about the death of her husband). Betty's point of view is followed by a series of sections written from the perspective of one woman after another: Mrs Jarvis, Mrs Norman, Mrs Plumer, Mrs Pascoe. Even when the women cede to an apparently impersonal narrator, after Jacob moves to the masculine environs of Trinity College, the narrator eventually reveals herself, as we have seen, to be a woman. In Sara Ruddick's words, the narrator's vision is 'the natural extension of that of Betty Flanders'.[49] Of course, none of the women who want Jacob – his mother, Clara, Florinda, even married Sandra with whom he is in love – ever succeed in possessing him, so that the voices in the novel are always unsatisfied and unanswered.

The book then is focused through a specifically female yearning: through women's tears. Rachel Bowlby sees this as a comment on the exile of women from the realities and the authority of masculine worlds. 'The novel of a young man's development is told from the point of view of the woman as outsider: outsider both to the institutionalised stages through which the youth passes, and to the conventions according to which they are presented as natural.'[50] But, as I suggested above, *Jacob's Room* also has broader concerns with the language of mourning and with the hopelessness of voice, and especially of apostrophe, that figure so beloved of the Victorian women poets from whom Woolf took some of her inspiration. From the beginning the novel is full of unanswered calls: '"Ja – cob! Ja – cob!" Archer shouted' (p. 4). 'The voice had an extraordinary sadness. Pure from all body, pure from all passion, going out into the world, solitary, unanswered, breaking against rocks – so it sounded' (p. 5). Right away the novel announces the failure of voices to animate either their interlocutors or their speakers. Woolf wanted to know what would happen if she deliberately imagined voices free of the bodily contexts with which we are so used to identify them. Hence, as Rachel Bowlby has commented, the book's obsession with letters.[51] Even Betty's words at the opening of the novel are not spoken but written. Voices stray wildly from the bodies that might have secured them.

But in spite of its concentration on the sexual politics of narration – a female voice speaking for a young and virile man – *Jacob's Room* is much less certain than the earlier novels about the sexual politics of voice. At times it suggests that no voice – male or female – is stable or reliably interlocutory:

> It seems then that men and women are equally at fault. It seems that a profound, impartial, and absolutely just opinion of our fellow-creatures is utterly unknown. Either we are men, or we are women. Either we are cold, or we are sentimental. Either we are young, or growing old. In any case life is but a procession of shadows, and God knows why it is that we embrace them so eagerly, and see them depart with such anguish, being shadows. (pp. 95–6)

Men's and women's voices alike drift in a world of phantoms, their own specificity rendered irrelevant by the spectral nature of their world. But at other times it is specifically women's voices – and the voice of the mother in particular – which are seen as displaced and ignored. One of Betty's letters lies on the table unopened while Jacob makes love to Florinda in the room next door. 'If the pale blue envelope lying by the biscuit-box had the feelings of a mother, the heart was torn by the little creak, the sudden stir . . . My son, my son – such would be her cry' (p. 124).[52] The cry of the letter echoes her little son Archer's cry on the beach at the opening. The empty apostrophe expresses simultaneously a general, and a specifically feminine, predicament.

Sexual difference itself then, one of the bodily differences that voices mark, is compromised by the novel's exploration of apostrophe. Sex, as Jacob first encounters it, is both obscene and uncannily silent. He stumbles on 'an enormous man and woman' lying on the beach, 'stretched motionless', their 'large red faces lying on the bandanna handkerchiefs [staring] up at Jacob' (p. 7). This proto-Oedipal scene serves only to confuse Jacob's perceptions of bodies and of substance: he runs away in horror and mistakes a rock for his nurse (p. 7). Seeing male and female anatomies at such close quarters throws Jacob's world into crisis: far from helping him to understand the organisation of the world, the sight of the huge bodies upsets him so much that immediately afterwards he cannot even distinguish between the animate and inanimate. Indeed in this novel it is often objects, not bodies, that speak most eloquently: in Jacob's room after his death: 'listless is the air in an empty room, just swelling the curtain; the flowers in the jar shift. One fibre in the wicker armchair creaks, though no one sits there' (p. 247). Sex tells one nothing that one needs to know about the world.

Jacob's Room, then, continues the preoccupation of the two earlier novels with the difficult negotiation of voice. But what had been, in *The Voyage Out* and *Night and Day*, a proto-feminist concern, becomes, in

Jacob's Room, a concern about the ontology of voice itself, an exploration of the unreliability of voice as a figure for identity. The paradox is the same for both Virginia Woolf and, decades later, for Roland Barthes: voices at once seem to speak the 'grain' of the body that produces them ('my own voice', as Woolf would call it), and to float free of all grounding in the material world: to be essentially, in Barthes's word, 'hallucination'. We might call this the paradox of voice itself, a paradox which Woolf, constantly working on her own definitive literary 'voice', and yet constantly afraid of auditory hallucination, experienced even more acutely than most. It is important that we recognise that her early fiction, far from being 'apprentice work', addresses one of the foundations of fiction-writing and of subjectivity itself: the assumption and elaboration of voice. It has been hard to recognise because the conclusions these novels come to are so uncomfortable and run so counter to all the assumptions with which we continue to approach the figure of literary and other 'voices'. In these early novels Woolf shows us what an unstable, seductive metaphor – and phenomenon – 'voice' is.

NOTES

I am grateful to the following people for their help with the writing of this chapter: Elizabeth Barnes, P. A. Skantze, and the members of the First Draft Club, especially Michael Szalay, John Whittier-Ferguson, Yopie Prins, Tobin Siebers and Jill Greenblatt.

1 Janis M. Paul, *The Victorian Heritage of Virginia Woolf: The External World in her Novels* (Norman, Oklahoma: Pilgrim, 1987), p. 51. Sue Roe, in *Writing and Gender: Virginia Woolf's Writing Practice* (New York: St Martin's, 1990), discusses all the early novels together in one chapter called 'Virginia Woolf's Writing Practice'; and such major works as Rachel Bowlby, *Virginia Woolf: Feminist Destinations* (Oxford: Blackwell, 1988), Makiko Minow-Pinkney, *Virginia Woolf and the Problem of the Subject* (Brighton: Harvester, 1987) and Alex Zwerdling, *Virginia Woolf and the Real World* (Berkeley: University of California Press, 1986) do not have separate chapters on *The Voyage Out* and *Night and Day*.

2 Virginia Woolf, *ROO*, 1929, repr. in *A Room of One's Own and Three Guineas*, ed. Morag Shiach (Oxford: World's Classics, 1992), pp. 99, 101.

3 Virginia Blain, 'Narrative Voice and the Female Perspective in Virginia Woolf's Early Novels', in *Virginia Woolf: New Critical Essays*, ed. Patricia Clements and Isobel Grundy (London: Vision, 1983), pp. 115–36; p. 118.

4 See, for example, Sigmund Freud, 'On Narcissism: An Introduction', 1914, in *General Psychological Theory: Papers on Metapsychology*, ed. Philip Rieff (New York: Collier, 1963); and Jacques Lacan, 'The Mirror Stage as Formative of the Function of the I as Revealed in Psychoanalytic Experience', 1949, in *Ecrits: A Selection*, trans. Alan Sheridan (New York: Norton, 1977).

5 See, for example, the section on 'Slips of the Tongue' in Sigmund Freud, *The Psychopathology of Everyday Life*, 1901, trans. Alan Tyson, ed. Angela Richards, *Penguin Freud Library*, 5 (Harmondsworth: Penguin, 1975), pp. 94–152.

6 Virginia Woolf, 'I Am Christina Rossetti', 1930, repr. in *Virginia Woolf: Women and Writing*, ed. Michèle Barrett (London: Women's Press, 1979), pp. 161–8; p. 164. The quote is from Mary F. Sandars, *Life of Christina Rossetti* (London: Hutchinson, 1930).

7 For further discussion of this issue, see Yopie Prins, *Victorian Sappho: Declining a Name* (Princeton University Press, 1999).

8 Virginia Woolf, *VO*, 1915, ed. Lorna Sage (Oxford: World's Classics, 1992), pp. 249, 239, 207. All further references will be to this edition.

9 Virginia Woolf, *O*, 1928, ed. Rachel Bowlby (Oxford: World's Classics, 1992), p. 298.

10 See, for example, Virginia Woolf, *TL*, 1927, ed. Margaret Drabble (Oxford: World's Classics, 1992), p. 123; and *ROO*, p. 70: 'there would always have been that assertion – you cannot do this, you are incapable of doing that – to protest against, to overcome'.

11 Virginia Woolf, *ND*, ed. Suzanne Raitt (Oxford: World's Classics, 1992), p. 106. All further references will be to this edition.

12 Louie Mayer, 1970, in *Virginia Woolf: Interviews and Recollections*, ed. J. H. Stape (London: Macmillan, 1995), p. 171.

13 Virginia Woolf, 'Old Bloomsbury', 1922 [?], in *Moments of Being: Unpublished Autobiographical Writings*, ed. Jeanne Schulkind, 1976 (repr. London: Triad/Granada, 1978), p. 186.

14 Leonard Woolf, 'Virginia Woolf: Writer and Personality', in Stape, ed., *Virginia Woolf: Interviews and Recollections*, p. 6. Quentin Bell also refers to this episode in *Virginia Woolf: A Biography*, 1972 (repr. London: Hogarth, 1982), 1, pp. 89–90.

15 Hermione Lee, *Virginia Woolf* (London: Chatto and Windus, 1996), p. 196.

16 *Ibid.*, pp. 196–7.

17 See Woolf, *MB*, p. 107.

18 See Roland Barthes, 'The Grain of the Voice', in *Image Music Text*, trans. and ed. Stephen Heath (London: Fontana, 1977).

19 Sue Roe, *Writing and Gender*, p. 21.

20 See Peter Jacobs, '"The Second Violin Tuning in the Ante-room": Virginia Woolf and Music', in *The Multiple Muses of Virginia Woolf*, ed. Diane F. Gillespie (Columbia and London: University of Missouri, 1993), pp. 227–60; p. 238.

21 Virginia Woolf, 'A Sketch of the Past', 1939–40, *MB*, p. 94.

22 *Ibid.*

23 Virginia Woolf to Leonard Woolf, 18 March 1941, quoted in Quentin Bell, *Virginia Woolf*, 2, p. 226.

24 Susan Stanford Friedman argues that, like Rachel, Woolf was trying in *VO* to make her own transition into an identity and a life as a writer. 'The story of Rachel's failed *Bildung* relates to Woolf's efforts to make her own development a success. Her numerous revisions engaged Woolf in a "writing cure" in which the transferential scene of writing gradually constitutes a new subjectivity.' See

Susan Stanford Friedman, 'Spatialisation, Narrative Theory, and Virginia Woolf's *The Voyage Out*', in *Ambiguous Discourse: Feminist Narratology and British Women Writers*, ed. Kathy Mezei (Chapel Hill: University of North Carolina Press, 1996), pp. 109–36, 127. Friedman ignores the fact that as she was working on the novel Woolf was also undergoing another *Bildung* much like Rachel's own: her courtship and engagement to Leonard Woolf.

25 Quentin Bell, *Virginia Woolf*, 1, p. 126; and Leonard Woolf, 'Virginia Woolf: Writer and Personality', p. 150. See also Louise A. DeSalvo, *Virginia Woolf's First Voyage: A Novel in the Making* (Totowa, New Jersey: Rowman and Littlefield, 1980), p. 9. Louise DeSalvo describes her work on all the manuscript versions of *VO* in the introduction to her edition of the earliest complete extant version, composed 1909–10. See Virginia Woolf, *Melymbrosia: An Early Version of 'The Voyage Out'*, ed. Louise A. DeSalvo (New York Public Library, 1982).

26 See Quentin Bell, *Virginia Woolf*, 1, p. 125.

27 DeSalvo, *Virginia Woolf's First Voyage*, p. x.

28 Woolf, *ROO*, p. 145. See 'Mr Bennett and Mrs Brown', 1923, 2nd edn. 1924, in Virginia Woolf, *A Woman's Essays*, ed. Rachel Bowlby (Harmondsworth: Penguin, 1992), pp. 69–87.

29 The piano becomes a privileged means of self-expression in a number of Edwardian novels. In E. M. Forster's *A Room with a View*, for example, which Woolf reviewed while she was working on *VO*, Lucy Honeychurch uses the piano to excite and play out her own passions: 'like every true performer, she was intoxicated by the mere feel of the notes: they were fingers caressing her own; and by touch, not by sound alone, did she come to her desire' (1908; repr. Harmondsworth: Penguin, 1978), p. 51. Gwenda in May Sinclair's *The Three Sisters* (1914) also plays the piano both to challenge her father and to release her own frustrations.

30 'Sir, a woman's preaching is like a dog's walking on his hinder legs. It is not done well; but you are surprised to find it done at all.' See *Boswell's Life of Johnson*, 1787 (repr. Oxford University Press, 1946), I, p. 309.

31 Barthes, 'The Grain of the Voice', *Image Music Text*, p. 182.

32 *Ibid.*, p. 181.

33 *Ibid.*, pp. 188–9.

34 *Ibid.*, p. 184.

35 Christine Froula, 'Out of the Chrysalis: Female Initiation and Female Authority in Virginia Woolf's *The Voyage Out*', *Tulsa Studies in Women's Literature*, 5, No. 1 (Spring 1986), pp. 63–90; p. 85.

36 *Ibid.*, p. 68, p. 63.

37 Josef Breuer and Sigmund Freud, 'On the Psychical Mechanism of Hysterical Phenomena: Preliminary Commentary', 1893, in *Studies on Hysteria*, 1893–5, trans. James and Alix Strachey, ed. Angela Richards, *Penguin Freud Library*, 3 (Harmondsworth: Penguin, 1974), p. 58.

38 Louise A. DeSalvo, 'Virginia, Virginius, Virginity', in *Faith of a (Woman) Writer*, ed. Alice Kessler-Harris and William McBrien (New York: Greenwood, 1988), pp. 179–89; p. 188.

39 Lee, *Virginia Woolf*, p. 327; *D*5, p. 17.

40 E. M. Forster, 'The Early Novels of Virginia Woolf', 1925, in *Abinger Harvest* (London: Edward Arnold, 1936), pp. 106–15, p. 108.

41 See Jane Marcus, 'Enchanted Organ, Magic Bells: *Night and Day* as a Comic Opera', in *Virginia Woolf and the Languages of Patriarchy* (Bloomington: University of Indiana Press, 1987).

42 Virginia Woolf based Mrs Hilbery on novelist Anny Thackeray Ritchie, sister of her father Leslie Stephen's first wife. Anny Ritchie seems to have had all of Mrs Hilbery's inconsequentiality and love of the random. See Joanne P. Zuckerman, 'Anne Thackeray Ritchie as the Model for Mrs Hilbery in Virginia Woolf's *Night and Day*', *Virginia Woolf Quarterly*, 1 (1973), pp. 32–46.

43 Marcus, 'Enchanted Organ', p. 27.

44 *L*1, p. 502. See Lee, *Virginia Woolf*, p. 336, for further discussion of this issue.

45 Virginia Woolf, *JR*, 1922, ed. Lorna Sage (Oxford: World's Classics, 1992), p. 128. All further references will be to this edition.

46 Sara Ruddick, 'Private Brother, Public World', in *New Feminist Essays on Virginia Woolf*, ed. Jane Marcus (London: Macmillan, 1981), pp. 185–215; p. 186.

47 See note 32.

48 *L*2, p. 573. See also pp. 546 and 591.

49 Ruddick, 'Private Brother, Public World', p. 198.

50 Bowlby, *Virginia Woolf: Feminist Destinations*, p. 112.

51 *Ibid.*, p. 116.

52 Betty's words are an echo of David's lament at the death of his mutinous son Absalom in the Bible: 'O Absalom, my son, my son' (2 Sam. 18: 33). Here Woolf reimagines it as a maternal, rather than a paternal, expression of grief.

3

SUSAN DICK

Literary realism in *Mrs Dalloway*, *To the Lighthouse*, *Orlando* and *The Waves*

On Monday 26 January 1920, Virginia Woolf recorded in her diary that she had 'arrived at some idea of a new form for a new novel'. The 'theme' was 'a blank' to her, but the form had immense potential: 'Suppose one thing should open out of another – as in An Unwritten Novel – only not for 10 pages but 200 or so – doesn't that give the looseness & lightness I want' (*D2*, pp. 13–14). In Woolf's short story 'An Unwritten Novel', the narrator, imagining the life story of a stranger sitting across from her in a train, strains against both the conventions of realist fiction and, behind these, the demands of life itself. 'Life imposes her laws; life blocks the way', she writes after conceding that she must include a commercial traveller named Moggridge in her story.[1] Life also finally proves her wrong, for the woman does not fit the story created for her. Nonetheless, the narrator concludes on a high note: she has celebrated a vision of life, which is much more than a narration of mere facts.

'An Unwritten Novel' reflects two of Woolf's firmest assumptions about how the realist novel needed to be reformed. First, novelists must be selective. The mid-Victorian novelists, she wrote in a 1910 review, 'left out nothing that they knew how to say. Our ambition,' she added provocatively, 'is to put in nothing that need not be there.'[2] Second, the choices novelists make should evolve from a shift of focus so that 'life' is conveyed not only in its external aspect, but as it is experienced. Taking on the 'materialists' Arnold Bennett, John Galsworthy and H. G. Wells in her essay 'Modern Novels' (1919), she asserted that 'the proper stuff for fiction' was the myriad impressions received by the mind 'exposed to the ordinary course of life' (*E3*, p. 33).

The novel that grew out of these thoughts was *Jacob's Room* (1922). Two narrative voices and perspectives intermingle in this book. One is the omniscient narrator Woolf had employed in her first two novels, *The Voyage Out* (1915) and *Night and Day* (1919). This impersonal narrator shares the narration with a second who has all the limitations of any single point of view: 'the observer is choked with observations', the second narrator says, 'we must choose . . . wherever I seat myself, I die in exile'.[3] These two narrators tell Jacob's story episodically and in fragments. Woolf was aware that the elimination of the 'scaffolding' and 'bricks' of a conventional plot (D3, p. 13) and the 'effort of breaking with strict representation' in *Jacob's Room* would be 'unsettling'. But if her novel was at times 'obscure' and the characters 'shadowy', it was not the fault of the 'method', she told a correspondent, but of her 'ignorance of how to use it psychologically'. 'Next time,' she wrote in another letter, 'I shall stick like a leech to my hero or heroine' (L2, p. 588; L6, p. 501). She took her own advice and began to write 'Mrs Dalloway in Bond Street', the short story that soon 'branched' into the book which became *Mrs Dalloway* (1925) (D2, p. 207).

In order to use her method psychologically, Woolf needed to shift the focus from the mind of the narrator to the minds of the characters. While she had long recognised the fragmented structure of 'the flight of the mind',[4] it was only during the writing of *Mrs Dalloway* that she found a way to use that as the basis for the creation of character. She recorded this important discovery on 30 August 1923: 'I should say a good deal about The Hours, & my discovery; how I dig out beautiful caves behind my characters; . . . The idea is that the caves shall connect, & each comes to daylight at the present moment' (D2, p. 263). Later she refers to this as her 'tunnelling process, by which,' she adds, 'I tell the past by instalments, as I have need of it' (D2, p. 272). Woolf's early notion that nothing should be included in the novel that 'need not be there' also lies behind this discovery. She had found a method of creating character that imitated the selective process by which we know and recollect ourselves, one another, and our world.

The structure Woolf developed for her novel was important to her portrayal of this process. Instead of covering several months or years as she had done in her previous novels, Woolf restricts the time of the narrative to a single day. This may reflect her desire in this book 'to be more close to the fact than Jacob' (D2, pp. 207–8). Time measured by the clock moves ahead ceaselessly and audibly as the narrative progresses. The contrast in the narrative between what Woolf in *Orlando* calls 'time on the clock and time in the mind',[5] can be linked to a tension she frequently wrote of in her diary during this period: that between the reality of the observable world and the intangible reality she knew to exist elsewhere. 'I daresay its true, however, that I haven't that "reality" gift', she wrote after recalling Arnold Bennett's harsh review of *Jacob's Room*. 'I insubstantise, wilfully to some extent, distrusting reality – its cheapness . . . Have I the power of conveying the true reality? Or do I write essays about myself?' (*D*2, p. 248). Although they existed in a hierarchy for Woolf, the two realities of 'fact' and 'vision', as she sometimes called them, were clearly interdependent. The writing of *Mrs Dalloway* sharpened her focus on this interdependence and on the ways it could be portrayed in fiction. The reality Woolf claimed to distrust appears in her middle novels in her treatment of historical, political, and social forces (now recognised as playing a central role) but just as interesting are the representations of details of everyday reality in them and the functions these details perform.

Throughout *Mrs Dalloway* the focus continually shifts from the external world to the minds of the characters perceiving it. As a result, the details which ground the narrative in observable reality often emerge more slowly than they do when presented by an omniscient narrator. The setting is, however, established immediately. The London streets and landmarks are among the real, as opposed to the fictional, facts in the narrative. Readers may follow Clarissa Dalloway's route and the routes of several other characters on a map of the city.[6] The verisimilitude of the setting adds solidity to the characters, who are very much a part of it. Clarissa even believes that 'somehow in the streets of London, on the ebb and flow of things, here, there, she survived' (*Mrs D*, p. 9).

Although the events in the narrative take place on a specific date, that fact is disclosed more slowly than is the setting. As she walks along the street, Clarissa thinks, 'For it was the middle of June. The War was over' (p. 6). A few pages later the narrator tells us it is Wednesday (p. 15). Later still, Peter Walsh's thoughts about all that has changed during the five years he has been away reveal that it is 1923 (p. 55). By naming a specific year, Woolf turns what could have been a fictional fact into a real one. She never discloses the date, but references to Gold Cup Day at Ascot and to the results of the cricket matches enable readers to discover that the actual date of these fictional events is 20 June (*Mrs D*: note 6). Similarly, a little digging reveals that the unnamed Prime Minister at the Dalloways' party is Stanley Baldwin (*Mrs D*: note 13).

The most complex element in Woolf's lexicon of facts is the representation of time. 'I foresee, to return to The Hours,' she wrote on 19 June 1923, 'that this is going to be the devil of a struggle. The design is so queer & so masterful. I'm always having to wrench my substance to fit it' (*D*2, p. 249). Under the heading 'Fuller plan' in some early notes she wrote, 'Hours: 10. 11. 12. 1. 2. 3. 4. 5. 6. 7. 8. 9. 10. 11. 12. 1. 2.' Eleven o'clock strikes. This is the aeroplane hour. wh. covers both Septimus and Rezia in Regents Park. & Clarissas reflections which lead to 12 o'clock: interview with specialist'.[7] The eventual change of title from 'The Hours' to *Mrs Dalloway* reflects not only the new depth that Woolf's tunnelling process enabled her to give her central character, but also the loosening of the tight chronological structure she had at first planned to use. Her design involves moving the characters through the streets of London while also timing their movements in a way that will create the impression of disparate events occurring simultaneously. This design is further complicated by the continual shifts from an omniscient perspective to one tied to a particular character, shifts that often take us from 'actual time' into 'mind time',[8] two modes which are not, as our own experience tells us, measured on the same scale.

In terms of representational realism the first twenty pages of *Mrs Dalloway* seem to me the most complex that Woolf ever wrote. As Clarissa waits to cross Victoria Street at the beginning of her walk, she thinks about the sound of Big Ben chiming the hour and then seems actually to hear it. She does not specify the time, but later events indicate that it must be ten o'clock. The narrator accompanies her to the flower shop and then uses the sound of an 'official car' backfiring, which Clarissa hears, to shift the focus to Rezia and Septimus Warren Smith, whose attention is also drawn to the car. This is the first in a series of moments in the narrative that link Clarissa with Septimus, whom she never meets and who is intended, Woolf said in her 1928 Introduction to the book, to be Clarissa's 'double' (*Mrs D: Appendix c,* p. 198). The narrator returns briefly to Clarissa who is standing at the corner of Brook Street waiting to cross (p. 15) and then adopts an expansive view. We see the crowd waiting at Buckingham Palace, hoping for a glimpse of the Queen, and then a sky-writer whose message the people on the Mall try to decipher. Soon after the appearance of the plane, the narrator, looking at the sky, tells us the time: 'in this extraordinary silence and peace, in this pallor, in this purity, bells struck eleven times' (p. 18). The official car arrives at the palace and the plane flies west over Green Park, then north over Piccadilly, Regent Street, and Regent's Park, where Rezia and Septimus see it. 'Look, look,' Rezia says (p. 18). From there it heads east as far as Greenwich and then turns west again. We last see it flying over St Paul's and Ludgate Circus (p. 23).

Its appearance over Ludgate Circus appears to coincide with Clarissa's arrival home, announced in the next paragraph. 'What are they looking at?' she asks the maid who opens the door. Her question has several functions. It suggests, as John Sutherland convincingly argues, that Clarissa has not walked home, but has taken a taxi, from which she could not see the plane.[9] It also indicates that she arrives home when the sky-writer is flying not over Ludgate Circus, which is some distance from the part of London she is in, but over Buckingham Palace and Green Park, near Clarissa's probable route home. We know from the narrator's description of the bells that the plane was in this vicinity shortly after eleven o'clock. Her question also reminds us of Rezia's admonition to Septimus to look at the plane, thus linking him again with Clarissa. Woolf's careful description of the flight of the plane over London functions, like the journey of the official car, as a structural device enabling her to present scenes which are happening simultaneously. As Clarissa arrives home, some of the events we have just read about are also occurring. After moving steadily ahead in time, the narrative here pauses and loops back.

In the next scene, Clarissa has already dealt with some domestic matters and begun to mend her dress when Peter Walsh arrives unexpectedly and she thinks, 'it was outrageous to be interrupted at eleven o'clock on the morning of the day when she was giving a party' (p. 32). Clarissa's reference to the time is probably meant to be general rather than specific, since no chiming clock confirms it and since Peter's visit, which ends as clocks strike eleven-thirty (p. 37), could easily fit into fifteen or twenty minutes. Much of the scene takes place within their minds and, while their thoughts fill several pages, they do not necessarily take much actual time. This is one of many points in the book when time seems suspended as the focus shifts from external to internal events.

Peter notes the sounds of Big Ben and St Margaret's chiming the half-hour as he leaves. When he reaches Trafalgar Square, a walk of at least five minutes, he refers vaguely to the time (much as Clarissa had) when he reflects on 'the strangeness of standing alone, alive, unknown, at half-past eleven in Trafalgar Square' (p. 40). He walks up Regent Street to Regent's Park, where he finds a seat, smokes part of a cigar, falls asleep, dreams, then wakes and recalls the summer at Bourton that Clarissa has also thought about. Leaving the park he passes Rezia and Septimus just as a clock strikes a quarter to twelve (p. 54). This is the only point in the novel when the representation of actual time seems at odds with events. Woolf wants Peter to see the Smiths since his misperception of them as a young couple having a lovers' spat is deeply ironic. Also his association with Clarissa, whom he had loved and lost when they were young, again links her to Septimus. The time also needs to be a quarter to twelve since the Smiths have an appointment at noon with Sir William Bradshaw on nearby Harley Street.

From this point on, Woolf is more selective in her representation of time. As the clocks strike noon, 'the Warren Smiths walked down Harley Street' and Clarissa lays 'her green dress on her bed' (p. 71). At one-thirty, having seen Bradshaw, they are back on Harley Street and Hugh Whitbread is nearing Lady Bruton's house where he and Richard Dalloway will have lunch. Big Ben strikes three as Richard returns home and then strikes the half hour moments after Elizabeth Dalloway and Doris Kilman leave for the Army and Navy Stores (p. 95). Rezia hears a clock striking six just after Septimus kills himself (p. 112) and Peter, who has heard the ambulance responding to this event, arrives at his hotel to find a letter from Clarissa. 'To get that letter to him by six o'clock she must have sat down and written it directly he left her, stamped it; sent somebody to the post', Peter thinks, thus reminding us that Clarissa's activities between eleven-thirty and three are unnarrated (p. 115). The 'leaden circles' of Big Ben are heard once more, near the end of the party. 'The young man had killed himself,' Clarissa thinks, 'but she did not pity him; with the clock striking the hour, one, two, three' (p. 138). In the first draft, the clock goes on striking until it reaches twelve, but in the final version the exact time at the close of the book, like that at the beginning, is not given.

While the narrator generally confirms the characters' thoughts about time and place, verification is sometimes withheld when it comes to other facts. Facts are slippery things, the narrative implies, and any single point of view is potentially unreliable. Also, since much of what we learn about most of the characters comes from their thoughts and perceptions we always need to take into account the source of a fact. For instance, whether Elizabeth's dress is pink, as Ellie Henderson and Richard see it (pp. 126, 144), or red, which is what Sally Seton sees (p. 140), depends upon who is looking.

Age is an important fact in *Mrs Dalloway*. Clarissa, Sally and Peter all assert their vitality in the face of increasing age. 'She was not old yet', Clarissa thinks. 'She had just broken into her fifty-second year' (p. 29). Sally is 'fifty-five, in body,' she later tells Peter, 'but her heart was like a girl's of twenty' (p. 143). Unlike the ages of Clarissa and Sally, that of Peter, whose engagement to the twenty-four-year-old Daisy has brought him back to London, is a slippery fact. When he tells Clarissa of his engagement she thinks, 'he's six months older than I am!', which would make him fifty-one or fifty-two, an age consistent with his thought a moment earlier that he 'was only just past fifty' (pp. 34–5). A bit later he twice thinks of himself as fifty-three (pp. 57, 60), yet when he compares himself to Hugh Whitbread, who is fifty-five (p. 78), Peter thinks he is two years older than Hugh (p. 57). Finally, when he tells Sally he is 'fifty-two to be precise' (p. 143) we cannot be sure whether he is shaving a year off his age or Woolf has made a mistake. With the exception of Richard, whose age is not mentioned, the ages of the other main characters are given just once and from reliable points of view.

Woolf often uses the characters' perceptions of themselves and one another as the source of information about their appearance. This method is highly economical, for while we are being told about a character's appearance, we are also learning about the perceiving character. Some characters have a much greater visual presence in the novel than others. In contrast to Peter, for example, whose appearance is noted by Clarissa, Rezia, Septimus, his fellow diners at his hotel, Ellie Henderson, Sally Seton, the narrator, and Peter himself, Richard's appearance is described only once, by the narrator (p. 87). All the main characters, except Richard and Septimus, reflect at some point on what they look like. One sign of the disintegration of Septimus' sanity may be the absence in his thoughts of any sense of his appearance or the impression it makes on others.

Physical appearance is part of the surface of life, the visible world of facts that in Woolf's fiction can be a source of stability. Both Clarissa and Peter celebrate their place in this world: both enjoy dressing well, eating well, walking in London, and gossiping at parties. As he sets out for Clarissa's party, Peter describes the sense of reality they share: 'For this is the truth about our soul, he thought, our self, who fishlike inhabits deep seas and plies among obscurities . . . suddenly she shoots to the surface and sports on the wind-wrinkled waves; that is, has a positive need to brush, scrape, kindle herself, gossiping' (p. 120). Septimus cannot endure that ascent. 'I leant over the edge of the boat and fell down,' he thinks, '. . . and yet am now alive, but let me rest still, he begged' (p. 53). Part of his role in the book is to show what it is like to be unable to find stability in the familiar world. While she was writing the mad scene in Regent's Park, Woolf noted, 'I find I write it by clinging as tight to fact as I can' (D2, p. 272). In that scene, Rezia urges Septimus to look at things in the park, 'for Dr. Holmes had told her to make him notice real things' (p. 21), but what Septimus sees there are frightening distortions. He knows, however, how the world should look. Later he sits in their flat and slowly surveys the room. 'He began, very cautiously, to open his eyes, to see whether a gramophone was really there. But real things – real things were too exciting.' To his relief, the things he looks at remain stable and themselves. 'None of these things moved. All were still; all were real' (p. 106). Even when Dr Holmes's arrival destroys this stability and Septimus is about to kill himself, he retains a poignant contact with ordinary reality. Could he use his landlady's 'nice clean bread knife with "Bread" carved on the handle,' he wonders. 'Ah, but one mustn't spoil that' (p. 111). Septimus seems most sane as he is about to die.

As he prepares to jump, he thinks, 'He did not want to die. Life was good. The sun hot' (p. 111). Earlier he had recalled a moment when he realised he could no longer enjoy the simple pleasures of life. 'Even taste (Rezia liked ices, chocolates, sweet things) had no relish to him . . . he could not taste, he could not feel' (p. 66). The significance of this loss is highlighted by the food happily consumed by other characters during the meal scenes that also mark the passing hours of this day. Lady Bruton's elegant luncheon, Doris Kilman's comically intense tea with Elizabeth at the Army and Navy Stores, Peter's solitary dinner at his hotel, and the Dalloways' pre-party dinner whose menu is described, all contribute to the detailed depiction of everyday life in *Mrs Dalloway*. Woolf's attention to these and numerous other details of ordinary reality provides the solid base upon which speculations about other dimensions of reality may rest.

The relationship between the two realities is central to *To the Lighthouse* (1927), which Woolf began to plan in the spring of 1925. One of the challenges she faced as she wrote this book was that of transforming a selection of her memories of childhood and especially of her parents, Julia and Leslie Stephen, into a fictional narrative. In her early plans, for example, she foresaw the novel set in St Ives, the Cornish town where the Stephen family spent their summers when she was a child (*D*3, p. 18). Before she began to write, however, she had moved the setting to the fictional village of Finlay in the Isle of Skye. Although a few reviewers complained that the Scottish setting looked decidedly Cornish,[10] most readers are probably untroubled by any lapses in verisimilitude. The remoteness of the island, the lighthouse as a beacon and a goal, and the house as a stabilising centre are the aspects of the setting Woolf wished to stress. Where London is present in detail and as itself in *Mrs Dalloway*, the Isle of Skye functions in a general way as part of the natural world in which human events occur.

Woolf also decided that 'There need be no specification of date' in this book.[11] In contrast again to *Mrs Dalloway*, details concerning the chronological and historical contexts of the action are few. Both Parts I and III take place on unspecified days in September. It is 'past six in the evening' near the opening of Part I (p. 20). The day ends at the beginning of Part II when Augustus Carmichael blows out his candle ('past midnight' in the first English edition, precisely at 'midnight' in the first American edition). It is not yet eight in the morning when Part III opens. As she watches the progress of the sailboat, Lily assumes its occupants will reach the lighthouse by lunch time (p. 163). Just before they land, having eaten their lunch, Mr Ramsay looks 'attentively' at his watch and says 'triumphantly: "Well done!"' (p. 174). But he discloses neither how long the trip has taken nor what time it is.

We know from Lily's thoughts as Part III opens that ten years pass during the brief middle section, 'Time Passes'. Images of destruction, Andrew's death and Carmichael's publishing success are all linked to the First World War, which occurs during these years. By including the war, Woolf not only adds resonance to the narrative, she also moves the historical context of her actual story ahead by about fourteen years. Her mother, the model for Mrs Ramsay, died in 1895. Mrs Ramsay dies early in Part II, which ends ten years later with the restoration of peace in 1919. Thus Woolf has placed Part I not in the Victorian period of her own childhood, but near the end of the Edwardian one, a time when, as she has famously written, 'human character changed' (E3, p. 421).

Woolf also treats another aspect of time, age, more selectively in this book. Through Mrs Ramsay's thoughts we learn that she is fifty (pp. 9, 52), Mr Ramsay 'over sixty' (p. 61), and Minta Doyle twenty-four (p. 53). Lily's thoughts reveal Mr Bankes's age as sixty (p. 42) and her own as thirty-three in Part I and forty-four in Part III (pp. 46, 128). At the opening of the first draft, Lily (there named Sophy) is fifty-five. Woolf's revision enables Lily to relate to Mrs Ramsay as a daughter rather than a contemporary. (Also, at forty-four, Lily is Woolf's age when she wrote *To the Lighthouse*.) In an early note, Woolf wrote, 'The presence of the 8 children; undifferentiated, should be important to bring out a sense of life in opposition to fate – i.e. waves, lighthouse' (*Draft TL*, p. 3). While the children are differentiated to some extent, Woolf follows her original plan by withholding the exact ages of all but the youngest, James, who is six (p. 7). Lily guesses in Part III that Cam is seventeen and James sixteen (p. 128), but no mention is made of the ages of Prue and Andrew, who die so unexpectedly in Part II.

The characters' appearances are also presented more selectively. All we know about Lily's, for example, is that she has 'little Chinese eyes' in a 'little puckered face', wears sensible shoes to paint, and a 'little grey dress' to dinner. 'Everything about her was so small', Mrs Ramsay notes (p. 88). Mr Ramsay finds her 'skimpy', especially in contrast to 'golden-reddish girls' like Minta Doyle, 'who didn't "scrape their hair off"' (p. 84). Her appearance links her to Carmichael, the other artist figure in the book. His 'yellow', 'smoky vague green' eyes (pp. 12, 151) are, like Lily's, unusual among this cast of predominantly blue-eyed characters. His yellow slippers and yellow-streaked beard and moustache give him both a comic and an exotic air, much as Lily's Chinese eyes and puckered face give her. The link between them is recognised by Mrs Ramsay when she thinks, echoing Peter Walsh, 'And to everybody there was always this sense of unlimited resources . . . one after another, she, Lily, Augustus Carmichael, must feel, our apparitions, the things you know us by, are simply childish. Beneath it is all dark, it is all spreading, it is unfathomably deep; but now and again we rise to the surface and that is what you see us by' (p. 55).

What the other characters see Mrs Ramsay by is her beauty, a quality we must take on trust since we are told scarcely anything specific about her appearance. When she looks in the mirror, she sees 'her hair grey, her cheek sunk, at fifty' (p. 9). To William Bankes she is 'Greek, straight, blue-eyed' (p. 28), to Charles Tansley, 'the most beautiful person' he has ever seen (p. 16), and to Mr Ramsay, 'the beauty of the world' who is 'lovelier now than ever' (pp. 34, 57). Lily sees her beauty, too, but does not attempt to reproduce it in her painting. To see only Mrs Ramsay's beauty is to simplify. 'Beauty had this penalty', Lily thinks, ' – it came too readily, came too completely. It stilled life – froze it' (p. 151). Lily focuses instead on articles of clothing – Mrs Ramsay's crumpled glove, an old fur coat, a deer-stalker's hat – which are animated by her personality, much as Mr Ramsay's boots are by his. To these the narrator adds the green shawl Mrs Ramsay wears to dinner and then drapes over the sheep's skull, and the grey cloak left behind in the house, both of which become emblems of her sheltering presence.

We see Mr Ramsay a little more clearly. He is 'lean as a knife', has 'little blue eyes', and a 'magnificent head' (pp. 8, 34). At dinner he looks 'astonishingly young' to Mrs Ramsay, who has earlier noted that his arm is still 'thin and hard' like a young man's (pp. 84, 61). Cam notes his 'great forehead and his great nose' as he sits bareheaded in the boat (p. 172). The attention paid by the narrator to his clothing as they are about to land reflects the close scrutiny Cam and James are giving to every move he makes. Their final vision of him as larger than life – seeming to be saying there is no God as he leaps into space – is thus firmly grounded, like his feet when he lands on the rock, in ordinary reality.

Like their appearances, the characters' pasts are also disclosed highly selectively. This is especially interesting in the case of the Ramsays and it marks one of the major contrasts between the realistic treatment of characters in this novel and in *Mrs Dalloway*. The narrator even makes a point of not telling us about Mrs Ramsay's past (p. 27). Mr Ramsay could answer the narrator's questions but, like his wife, he never thinks in specific terms about either his past or hers. Linked to this silence is the absence of first names for the Ramsays. An important and subtle aspect of the realism in both of these novels is the care Woolf takes to use the form of address for a character which is appropriate to the context in which it appears. Woolf was writing about people who, like herself, were scrupulous about using proper forms of address. 'Will he become "Tom"?' she wondered of T. S. Eliot after she had known him nearly two years (*D2*, p. 100). The opening line of *Mrs Dalloway* – 'Mrs Dalloway said she would buy the flowers herself' – reports what she has said to her maid and thus refers to her in the form of address the maid would use. Her first name appears as soon as the narrator reports her thoughts: 'And then, thought Clarissa Dalloway, what a morning – ' (p. 5). When she thinks about herself and when Peter and Richard think about her, she is 'Clarissa' (and sometimes to Richard 'his wife'). When Hugh Whitbread calls her by her first name, the narrator comments on the fact, saying he does so 'rather extravagantly, for they had known each other as children'. We notice that she answers him as 'Mrs Dalloway' (p. 7). She, too, is sensitive to the identities associated with her names. 'She had the oddest sense of being herself invisible; unseen; unknown;' she thinks in a passage that will be echoed by Mrs Ramsay, 'this being Mrs Dalloway; not even Clarissa any more; this being Mrs Richard Dalloway' (p. 10).

In eliminating the Ramsays' first names, Woolf was not only following the formality of the time and giving herself an interesting technical challenge, she was also creating some distance between the reader and the characters. At one point quite early in the first draft, she experimented with giving Mr Ramsay the first name 'Rhoderick'. Each time she wrote it – three times when Mrs Ramsay is thinking about him and once when he is thinking about himself – she crossed it out (*Draft TL*, pp. 60–2). A few pages before this, Woolf added 'happier' to the book inscription in which Mrs Ramsay is compared to Helen of Troy (*Draft TL*, p. 54), a revision that could indicate that Mrs Ramsay's name is also Helen. This is pure speculation, but it may help to highlight the effect that omitting first names has on our sense of both these characters. Had they been Helen and Rhoderick Ramsay, they would not have been the same characters. Their function as in some ways representational figures – Lily sees them, for example, as 'symbols of marriage, husband and wife' (p. 63) – is enhanced by the omission of their first names.

While the design of *To the Lighthouse* is less rigid than that used in *Mrs Dalloway*, Woolf has nonetheless an extremely complex realistic surface to deal with. In Part I the activities of sixteen characters need to be organised. The central event, the dinner scene, takes place in chapter seventeen. Before that, the characters are busy doing ordinary things: walking, talking, reading, knitting, painting, playing cricket. The narrator presents these activities with great economy, choosing details which give each scene concreteness without overshadowing the inner dramas in which the characters are also engaged. In Part I, as in Part III, where there are fewer characters and events, she often links their activities to other matters she wishes to explore. For instance, Mrs Ramsay's knitting reflects her role as the creative centre of the house and family, the one who makes it 'real', as she assures her husband while 'flashing her needles' (p. 35).

In the wonderful dinner scene, the realistic details, such as the look of the dining-room, the seating arrangement of the fourteen diners, the glances and words exchanged and the food served are all presented in a way that makes them contribute to the unspoken monologues and dialogues taking place. 'It is always helpful when reading her,' E. M. Forster noted of Woolf, 'to look out the passages describing eating. They are invariably good.'[12] The comedy of the scene should not be overlooked. Unvoiced discord mounts during the soup course, culminates in Carmichael's request for more soup, then dissipates with the lighting of the candles and the eating of the triumphant Bœuf en Daube. The change in atmosphere enables Mrs Ramsay to consider what is being achieved during this ordinary event: 'Of such moments, she thought, the thing is made that endures' (p. 89). Mrs Ramsay is experiencing a moment of heightened consciousness, a perception of 'reality', which Woolf called a 'moment of being'.[13] Late in Part III, Lily will discover that she seeks to achieve in art what Mrs Ramsay achieved in life, a moment when the ordinary and the extraordinary are perceived as one (p. 170).

The harmonies achieved at the end of Part I are broken in Part II where the house and natural world move into the foreground and the characters' lives go on elsewhere. In the first draft, news of the Ramsays comes only through the thoughts of Mrs McNab. At some point late in the writing of the book, Woolf decided to supplement these muddled reports with the bracketed passages that announce the deaths of Mrs Ramsay, Prue and Andrew, along with other facts. Elsewhere in the novel she uses parentheses to create 'the sense of reading the two things at the same time' (D3, p. 106) and that is the effect she creates here, too. But the use of distinctive square brackets in 'Time Passes' adds another dimension by emphasising visually the disconnection between the foreground and the background of the narrative, a disconnection further enhanced by the contrast between the poetic style of the surrounding narrative and the plain, even trite, prose of the interjections.

As she was nearing the end of the first draft of the book, Woolf asked herself what the 'stock criticism' of it would be: 'Sentimental? Victorian?' (D3, p. 107). The deaths of a much-loved wife and mother, of a young bride and of a young man in battle would in a Victorian novel evoke many a tear. Woolf's decision to announce these deaths in the way she does reflects a desire not only to avoid, but to debunk, sentimentality. She cut from the final proofs a long passage in which James recalls the 'unreal' atmosphere of oppressive mourning following his mother's death (TL, Appendix B, pp. 207–8). She did not exclude grief from the novel, for it drives the action of Part III, but she presents the devastating deaths first of all as blunt facts which are, as Mr Ramsay says of all such facts, 'uncompromising' (p. 8).

For Mr Ramsay, the reality of facts and solid objects is the truth. Andrew tells Lily that his father's books are about '"Subject and object and the nature of reality . . . Think of a kitchen table then",' he adds, '"when you're not there"' (p. 23). For Lily, however, truth and reality are not only in appearances, but also 'at the back' of them (p. 135). The world around her dissolves into 'a pool of thought, a deep basin of reality' as she confronts fully her grief for Mrs Ramsay (p. 152). Her realisation that the artist's vision is a fusion of the ordinary and the extraordinary unites on a theoretical level the perceptions of reality enacted by Mr and Mrs Ramsay. Lily needs the scene around her as she stands on the lawn painting *and* the scenes she imagines and remembers. Each is a gateway to a perception of reality, for reality is both the solid world and the intangible one behind it.

The lack of specificity about time and place in *To the Lighthouse*, the limited amount of information given about the characters' ages, appearances, and histories, the creation of characters who function as types as well as individuals and the bracketing of facts within the poetic prose of 'Time Passes' all foreshadow the highly selective treatment of realistic detail in *The Waves* (1933), which Woolf foresaw writing soon after she had finished *To the Lighthouse* (*D*3, p. 131). Before tackling that book, however, Woolf felt she needed to take a 'writers holiday' (*D*3, p. 177). That holiday was *Orlando: A Biography* (1928). The idea for this book came to her suddenly and developed quickly. It would be a fantasy, a satire, an escapade; it would be 'half laughing, half serious: with great splashes of exaggeration'; Vita Sackville-West would be Orlando, 'only with a change about from one sex to another' (*D*3, pp. 131, 168, 161). She began writing it in October 1927, and published it almost precisely a year later. In contrast to *To the Lighthouse*, where she made highly selective use of the factual basis of her story, she drew extensively in this book on historical facts and on real-life models and events. Vita Sackville-West, whom she was seeing often, was a constant source of both information and inspiration. 'I am writing Orlando half in a mock style very clear & plain, so that people will understand every word', she wrote. 'But the balance between truth & fantasy must be careful. It is based on Vita, Violet Trefusis, Lord Lascelles, Knole &c' (*D*3, p. 162).

The balance between truth and fantasy in *Orlando* has from the time of publication led to questions of genre. When booksellers insisted on placing it among the biographies, a less popular genre than the novel, Woolf wrote, 'I doubt therefore that we shall do more than cover expenses – a high price to pay for the fun of calling it a biography' (*D*3, p. 198). (In fact, it sold extremely well.) Yet Woolf did not think of it as a novel either. 'Anyhow I'm glad to be quit this time of writing "a novel"; & hope never to be accused of it again', she wrote in May 1928 (*D*3, p. 185). A few months earlier she had added to a similar remark, 'I shall invent a new name for them' (D3, p. 176), echoing a comment she made while planning *To the Lighthouse* (when the name she suggested was 'elegy' [D3, p. 34]) and anticipating the quest for terms that would accompany her early thoughts about *The Waves*.

In casting the narrator in the role of biographer, Woolf restricts the narrative perspective of *Orlando* to 'the firm, if rather narrow, ground of ascertained truth' (p. 120). The narrator repeatedly acknowledges the limitation of this perspective, especially when the subject of the biography is a writer: 'every secret of a writer's soul, every experience of his life, every quality of his mind is written large in his works,' the biographer asserts, 'yet we require critics to explain the one and biographers to expound the other. That time hangs heavy on people's hands is the only explanation of the monstrous growth' (pp. 189–90). To the biographer, 'thought and imagination' are 'of no importance whatsoever' (p. 241). Thus 'life' in *Orlando* is primarily the external reality of the 'materialists' whom Woolf derided in 'Modern Novels' (E3, p. 32). The activities of Orlando's daily life, along with the people and places Orlando encounters are all rendered with a realist's attention to detail. The narrative makes clear the delight Woolf took in abandoning psychological realism for a time to write 'exteriorly' (D3, p. 209). Many of the descriptive passages serve Woolf's satirical intentions. The nineteenth century, for example, begins with a dramatic change in the weather: 'Rain fell frequently, but only in fitful gusts, which were no sooner over than they began again' (p. 205). Not only furnishings, diet, dress, and vegetation are affected by the gloom. 'Men felt the chill in their hearts; the damp in their minds' (p. 207). Warmth, bright skies, and brilliant colours return with the twentieth century (pp. 266–8).

Besides describing the places Orlando goes, such as London and Turkey, and the stately home Orlando lives in (which was firmly based on the Sackville family home, Knole), Woolf has Orlando encounter historical figures, including Queen Elizabeth I, Alexander Pope and even Shakespeare, although the latter is only fully named in the index. The index, preface and illustrations further contribute to the 'truth' side of the equation in this mock-biography. In the fulsome preface, Woolf thanks all her friends, both living and dead, who helped her write the book. Among these is 'my niece Miss Angelica Bell, for a service which none but she could have rendered' (p. 13). Angelica posed in fancy dress for the portrait of 'The Russian Princess as a Child', one of the eight illustrations placed at the centre of the book. Woolf omitted from the preface any reference to Vita Sackville-West, who helped her most and to whom she dedicated the book. Also unacknowledged are the three photographs of Vita used to illustrate Orlando's appearance in the eighteenth, nineteenth and twentieth centuries.

Time as measured by clock and calendar is kept in the foreground in *Orlando*, but this is done in a way that tends to mock such chronological verisimilitude. 'The occasion was Tuesday, the 16th of June 1712', the narrator states, fixing precisely in time the moment when Orlando confides to her spaniel Pippin that she has become disillusioned with high society (p. 177). Once, the narrator even names the date on which the passage we are reading is being written (p. 73). Woolf's final joke with chronology comes at the conclusion when the story of Orlando's life ends at the stroke of midnight, 11 October 1928, the date on which *Orlando* was published (p. 295).

Within this carefully and playfully chronicled narrative structure, Woolf tells the story of someone whose life extravagantly defies the effects of time. Orlando is sixteen when the book begins in the sixteenth century (p. 15) and thirty-six when it ends in the twentieth (p. 279). Other characters also enjoy fantastic longevity. Mrs Grimsditch, Orlando's housekeeper, manages Orlando's household from the sixteenth into the eighteenth centuries. The disreputable Nick Greene, who lampoons Orlando in the eighteenth century, meets her again in the nineteenth as Sir Nicholas Greene, a portly, prosperous, respectable and influential critic (pp. 248–9). Woolf must have enjoyed taking this holiday from death. 'The true length of a person's life, whatever the *Dictionary of National Biography* may say,' the narrator observes near the end of the book, 'is always a matter of dispute' (p. 275). A mere account of years lived does not necessarily add up to the true length of a person's life. This is as close as the narrator comes to commenting on Orlando's mysterious longevity.

Orlando also seems to take her long life for granted. Late in the book, in a passage that looks forward to *The Waves*, she surveys the multiplicity of selves within her and makes no comment on the great length of time they span (p. 278). Nor does she pause to reflect on the other extraordinary aspect of her past, the fact that many of the selves she remembers are male. Orlando's change of sex is, of course, the other fantastic element in the book that Woolf sought to balance with 'truth'. 'It is enough for us to state the simple fact,' the narrator says, wisely making no effort to explain this inexplicable event, 'Orlando was a man till the age of thirty; when he became a woman and has remained so ever since' (p. 128). While Orlando is a man, Woolf adopts the distanced perspective of the satirist, whose 'sympathies are not deeply engaged', as she noted in 'Phases of Fiction' (1929), the long essay she was working on while she wrote *Orlando*.[14] The narrator even claims to have no gender, for biographers, like historians, enjoy immunity 'from any sex whatever' (p. 199). Yet once Orlando becomes a woman, the distance between her and the narrator narrows and the narrator sees things more from a woman's point of view. In a passage that anticipates *A Room of One's Own* (1929), for example, the narrator proposes to 'leave it to the gentlemen to prove, as they are very fond of doing,' that it is impossible for a woman to enjoy 'the society of her own sex' (p. 199). 'Sometimes women do like women', Woolf will soon observe in *A Room of One's Own*.[15]

In addition, a perception of the reality behind appearances, which has no place in the first part of the book, begins to be hinted at near the end. In one late passage, the narrator describes Orlando's impressions as she arrives home. 'All this, the trees, deer, and turf, she observed with the greatest satisfaction as if her mind had become a fluid that flowed round things and enclosed them completely.' Her words to her servant, though 'of no beauty, interest, or significance themselves', were 'now so plumped out with meaning that they fell like ripe nuts from a tree, and proved that when the shrivelled skin of the ordinary is stuffed out with meaning it satisfies the senses amazingly' (p. 283). In a closely related passage in *A Room of One's Own*, Woolf describes this meaning as 'what remains over when the skin of the day has been cast into the hedge' and calls it 'reality' (*ROO*, p. 166).

During the final stages of composition Woolf had some doubts about *Orlando* and worried that it was 'freakish & unequal' (*D*3, p. 184), but in the end she judged it a 'very quick brilliant book . . . Orlando taught me how to write a direct sentence', she added; 'taught me continuity & narrative, & how to keep the realities at bay. But I purposely avoided of course any other difficulty. I never got down to my depths & made shapes square up, as I did in The Lighthouse' (*D*3, p. 203). She now turned her attention again to the 'very serious, mystical poetical work' she had foreseen after completing *To the Lighthouse* (*D*3, p. 131). Woolf's diary comments make clear her intention to do something in this book she had not done before. In sharp contrast to *Orlando*, this work would be 'Away from facts: free; yet concentrated; prose yet poetry; a novel & a play' (*D*3, p. 128). She called it a 'playpoem' and even an autobiography, although she also said that the childhood depicted must not be hers (*D*3, pp. 139, 203, 229, 236). She would 'do away with exact place & time'(*D*3, p. 230) and 'eliminate all detail; all fact' (*L*4, p. 381). She termed the narrative method she eventually settled on 'a series of dramatic soliloquies' (*D*3, p. 312) and declared she was 'not trying to tell a story' and not writing to a plot, but rather to a rhythm (*D*3, pp. 229, 316). In this book there must be, she wrote, 'great freedom from "reality." . . . Well all this is of course,' she added, 'the "real" life' (*D*3, p. 236).

As we have seen, both Peter Walsh and Mrs Ramsay reflect on the two domains of the soul, the ordinary world of appearances and the other region in which we dwell invisible and in which, as Mrs Ramsay thinks, 'the range of experience seemed limitless' (p. 55). Woolf's earlier books are narrated from the perspective of the ordinary world. The glimpses some of the characters have of the reality behind it are intense but fleeting. In *The Waves* Woolf gives the narration to six speakers who are continually open to this other reality. We can borrow Woolf's notion of the multiple selves that make up the individual and say that the self in the foreground of *The Waves*, the self that speaks there, is the one that is most receptive to a perception of the reality behind appearances. 'That the novel changed,' Woolf wrote in her notes for *The Waves*, 'when the perspective changed'.[16]

What made this book so difficult to write and makes it so demanding to read is this radical shift of perspective. Woolf worried as she worked on the first draft, which she began in 1929, that the 'interesting things' in the book were not 'firmly based . . . here's my interesting thing; & there's no quite solid table on which to put it' (*D3*, p. 264). The interludes which precede each of the nine sections may have grown out of this concern. They were 'essential', she wrote, 'so as to bridge & also give a background – the sea; insensitive nature' (*D3*, p. 285). She was satisfied with the dramatic soliloquies but wondered if they could be read consecutively (*D3*, p. 312). She noted on the back of one page of the manuscript, 'The author would be glad if the following pages were read not as a novel' (*Draft W*, p. 582v). Instead of eliminating facts and realistic details in *The Waves*, Woolf eliminates the familiar fictional context in which we expect to find them. Until Bernard's summing up in the final section, the speakers narrate their experiences as perceptions and reflections occurring as they are being narrated. Memory again plays a large part in the narrative, for the speakers frequently recall events in their lives, but the narration itself moves forward in a continuous present. Many of the sorts of details one would find in a conventional novel that link characters and events to the material world are present in *The Waves*. 'I hate the smell of pine and linoleum. I hate the wind-bitten shrubs and the sanitary tiles', Susan says, for example, during her first night at school.[17] There is, however, no elaboration of such passages. We see Susan's life at school and at home, as we see the lives of the others, in brief, vivid scenes. The transitions a narrator would make as the narrative moves from speaker to speaker and from scene to scene, like the momentum created by a plot, are absent. This is perhaps why Woolf wondered if the soliloquies could be read consecutively.

The six speakers are not conventional characters. Jinny, Rhoda, Susan, Bernard, Louis, and Neville have no surnames. They live in ordinary reality – they go to school, have relationships, homes, and jobs, they shop, take trains, travel, eat out and so on – but the point of view from which they perceive life and the 'purebred prose' they speak (L4, p. 381) make even the most mundane activity seem latent with a larger significance. They have a physical presence in the book, for they are all deeply aware of their bodies, but in contrast to *Mrs Dalloway*, *To the Lighthouse* and especially *Orlando*, their features and their clothing are rarely described. The balance of three female and three male speakers, the similarities among their voices, the close bond uniting them and the ways they both resemble and differ from one another, have led many readers to see them as aspects of a single individual, a reading Woolf herself endorsed (L4, pp. 381, 397). Yet to view the six only as caricatures of personality traits is to oversimplify Woolf's treatment of them. Like the Lighthouse, nothing in *The Waves* is simply one thing (*TL*, p. 158).

The time-frame in this book is less specific than in the three previous narratives. The movement of the sun across the sky in the interludes follows the progress of a day. The seasonal changes described there suggest a yearly cycle, though this is not followed rigidly. In the final interlude, along with the rotten apples that suggest winter, elm trees are seen 'in full summer foliage' (p. 154), as if in defiance of naturalistic realism. The cyclical time of the natural world in the interludes is juxtaposed with the linear time that shapes the speakers' lives. They are young children at the opening; Bernard is 'elderly' at the close (p. 155). When Woolf told Ethel Smyth that she was writing to a rhythm rather than to a plot, she acknowledged that this method was 'completely opposed to the tradition of fiction and I am casting about all the time for some rope to throw to the reader' (L4, p. 204). Among the realistic details that act as helpful ropes are the references to the speakers' ages. Woolf is not as precise here in her treatment of this fictional fact as she is in the earlier books, but it is significant that she sometimes saw the need to fix the speakers in a familiar chronological context at all.

In the third section, Susan says she is 'not twenty yet' (p. 62) and Rhoda that she is 'not yet twenty-one' (p. 67). Age is one of the 'details of the individual life' that Rhoda 'hates' and Susan, by contrast, simply accepts. Jinny states her age in the sixth section while boasting of the path she has followed: '(I have lived my life, I must tell you, all these years, and I am now past thirty, perilously, like a mountain goat leaping from crag to crag)' (p. 112). Like the other male speakers, Bernard never mentions his age, but he does state the only precise age given in the book, that of Percival at the time of his death: '(for he was twenty-five and should have lived to be eighty')' (p. 98). The use of parentheses to enclose all the ages except Rhoda's recalls the bracketing of facts in 'Time Passes'.

Thus we do not know how many years pass in the book. Nor are we told the historical context of the narrative. Jinny's mention of the portrait of Queen Alexandra, wife of Edward VII, hanging in her school (p. 14) places their childhood in the Edwardian period, but only in Bernard's comment 'An army marches across Europe' (p. 160) is any specific allusion made to the First World War, which would have occurred during their lifetimes. Their focus is on the events of their own lives, many of which are not realistic occurrences but phases of consciousness that have no counterpart in the world's history or in ordinary action.

The locations of the boarding-school the speakers attend as children and of the seashore, house and garden described in the interludes are not given. 'They had been educated on the east coast or on the south coast,' Bernard says of the girls' school Jinny, Rhoda and Susan attend, implying that its precise location is of no importance (p. 161). Susan's time at a finishing school somewhere in Switzerland (p. 61) is one of many periods in their lives that occurs outside the range of the narrative. Neither the public school Bernard, Louis and Neville attend nor the university where Bernard and Neville are students is named. All but Susan, however, whose home is somewhere in Lincolnshire (p. 174), spend most of their adult lives in a place Woolf makes no effort to obscure, London, 'the centre', Neville says, 'of the civilised world' (p. 45). As in *Mrs Dalloway* and *Orlando*, streets and landmarks are named, and even the sounds of the city evoked, making London function in this book, as in the earlier ones, as a verifiable realistic setting for a fictional world. London is perhaps the strongest rope Woolf throws her reader. Like the many other realistic details named, the speakers' references to the city reflect their sense of themselves as grounded in a shared, solid world.

Woolf's use of realistic details in *The Waves* can be illustrated in a specific scene, the farewell dinner for Percival, which takes place at a French restaurant in London. This and the reunion dinner at Hampton Court are the only extended scenes involving all six speakers. At times they hear and address one another, thus introducing some dialogue into the narrative. They also provide us with a few rare glimpses of themselves as they comment on each other's appearance. These comments, along with the dialogue and the references to the tables, chairs, waiters, other diners, and especially Neville's Keatsian description of the taste of the food (p. 87), ground the scene in a familiar setting. The realistic context which remains sketchy much of the time thus comes closer to the surface in this scene.

Its progress recalls that of the dinner scene in *To the Lighthouse*. Initially the speakers are ill at ease. As they talk, however, they recover the sense of community they had as children. This union in turn enables each to move in thought beyond the present event, much as Mrs Ramsay does when the tensions around her table are gone. The stability this sense of union brings becomes part of the 'moment of being' each experiences as the elements in the scene around them take on heightened significance. Louis says, for example, 'The roar of London . . . is round us. Motor-cars, vans, omni-buses pass and repass continuously. All are merged in one turning wheel of single sound. All separate sounds – wheels, bells, the cries of drunkards, of merry-makers – are churned into one sound, steel blue, circular' (p. 85). In *The Waves* Woolf goes behind the depiction of this experience as an event of consciousness to portray in much greater detail than in her previous books the contents of these moments. Neville says of his experience, to give another example, 'Happiness is in it, . . . and the quiet of ordinary things. A table, a chair, a book with a paper-knife stuck between the pages' (p. 91). One of the titles she considered using for the book was 'Moments of Being' (*Draft W*, p. 1).

In her 'private shorthand' Woolf contrasted these moments of being when one is conscious of reality to the 'moments of non-being' in which they are embedded, the soon forgotten mundane events of an ordinary day ('A Sketch of the Past', *MB*, p. 70). She associated 'non-being' with conventional realism. Near the end of the farewell dinner, Bernard adopts the realist's manner to describe 'the handsome young man in the grey suit' calling for the bill. 'That is the truth,' Bernard then says; 'that is the fact, but beyond it all is darkness and conjecture' (p. 91). A realistic description, like the biographer's account of Bernard's life which he makes up later (p. 168), offers only an external view. In this book, Woolf absorbs that perspective, which focuses on what can be known through observation, into a more inclusive one that explores everything that crowds into consciousness. She does this in part by making the moment of being and the scene that contains it the central unit in the narrative. As the farewell dinner illustrates, one aspect of the rhythm that replaces the plot is the continual shift of attention inward and outward which builds toward and then away from moments of being.

Four of the six speakers say little about the activities Woolf associates with 'non-being'. The high value Bernard places on the comfort of a daily routine – 'Something always has to be done next', he says. 'Tuesday follows Monday; Wednesday Tuesday' (p. 170) – becomes his refrain, but he says nothing about what he does with such regularity. When he, Neville, Jinny or Rhoda speak of doing ordinary things it is because these activities have become memorable and have thus shaped themselves into scenes. By contrast, Susan's 'life of natural happiness' with her husband and children on the farm is described in some detail, for it reflects her integration with the rhythms of the natural world. Louis, who also says quite a lot about his daily life and his work as an agent in what seems to be a shipping company, is in some ways Susan's opposite. Through ordinary activity he is seeking to fix his place in the world and thus stabilise his fluid sense of self. 'I, who would wish to feel close over me the protective waves of the ordinary', he says while eating alone in a restaurant near his office in the Strand (p. 59).

Percival, the silent young man whose death stands at the centre of the narrative, also lacks the realistic presence of a conventional character. We see him in glimpses, through the eyes and imaginations of the others, who seem smitten more by the idea of him than by the actual person. His death, however, enters the narrative with the impact of an event in a conventional novel. Although it occurs offstage, both Neville and Bernard imagine it so vividly that it becomes a scene for the reader, too. Percival's death is a fact, like the deaths of Septimus, Mrs Ramsay, Prue, and Andrew, which the survivors must accommodate to their experience of life.

There is another death in *The Waves* which also occurs offstage, but it is announced without fanfare and goes unmourned within the narrative. 'While he brushed the fluff from my coat,' Bernard says of his hairdresser, 'I took pains to assure myself of his identity, and then, swinging my stick, I went into the Strand, and evoked to serve as opposite to myself the figure of Rhoda, always so furtive, always with fear in her eyes, always seeking some pillar in the desert, to find which she had gone; she had killed herself' (p. 182). The reader whose attention has momentarily lapsed might well miss this announcement. Rhoda slips out of the narrative almost unobserved. In contrast to Percival's death, which dominates the fifth section, Rhoda's receives no elaboration. We never learn how, when or where she killed herself. The treatment of her death is consistent with her role in the book, for Rhoda's hold on ordinary reality is far more tenuous than that of the other speakers and her desire to escape from it into another reality far stronger. By the time she is an adult, she has come to court rather than resist her sense of being distanced from 'the real world' (p. 27) the others live in. 'Yet there are moments when the walls of the mind grow thin', she says in one of her last soliloquies; 'when nothing is unabsorbed, and I could fancy that we might blow so vast a bubble that the sun might set and rise in it and we might take the blue of midday and the black of midnight and be cast off and escape from here and now' (p. 145).

From this perspective, death is not the enemy to be fought, as Bernard declares at the end, but a vision to be embraced, an escape into the other reality behind appearances. In an early note for *Mrs Dalloway*, Woolf wondered if death could be 'the reality' ('Hours', p. 425). From Rhoda's point of view, the answer would be yes.

The two views of death portrayed in *The Waves* encapsulate Woolf's complex attitude toward reality. As we move from *Mrs Dalloway* to *To the Lighthouse* to *The Waves* we see her distancing herself more and more from what she called the 'appalling narrative business of the realist: getting on from lunch to dinner' (*D*3, p. 209). While she took a break from that progression in *Orlando*, the success of that book, the relative ease with which she wrote it and the pleasure Woolf habitually took in externality, played their parts in the composition of *The Waves*. Even in this book, in which she moves furthest away from writing 'exteriorly', she could not abandon material reality, for it is an integral part of the other, more profound, reality she wished to explore. Rhoda's vision of a moment when 'nothing is unabsorbed' expresses Woolf's desire to 'saturate every atom' (*D*3, p. 209), to include the ordinary within her vision of the extraordinary. In each of these books, Woolf's interesting things always rest upon a very solid table.

NOTES

1 *CSF*, ed. Susan Dick (London: Hogarth, 1989), p. 118.
2 *E1*, ed. Andrew McNeillie (London: Hogarth, 1986–94), p. 341.
3 *JR* (London: Hogarth, 1976), pp. 67–8.
4 *EJ*, ed. Mitchell A. Leaska (London: Hogarth, 1990), p. 393.
5 *O* (London: Hogarth, 1928; 1970), p. 91.
6 D. Daiches and John Flower, 'Virginia Woolf's London' (New York & London: Paddington Press, 1979), pp. 82ff; *Mrs D*, ed. Morris Beja (Oxford: Shakespeare Head Press, 1996), pp. xxxiv–xxxv. All further references will be to this edition.
7 *Hours*, ed. Helen M. Wussow (New York: Pace University Press, 1996), p. 416.
8 *BA* (London: Hogarth, 1941, repr. 1969), p. 13.
9 John Sutherland, 'Clarissa's Invisible Taxi', in *Can Jane Eyre Be Happy?* (Oxford University Press, 1997), p. 222.
10 *TL*, ed. Susan Dick (Oxford: Shakespeare Head Press, 1992), p. xx.
11 *Draft TL*, ed. Susan Dick (University of Toronto Press, 1982), p. 2.
12 E. M. Forster, *Virginia Woolf* (Cambridge University Press, 1942), p. 18.
13 See 'A Sketch of the Past', *MB*, ed. Jeanne Schulkind (London: Hogarth, 1985), pp. 70–2; 142.
14 *CE2*, ed. L. Woolf (London: Chatto & Windus, 1966–7), p. 90.
15 *ROO* (London: Hogarth, 1929; 1974), p. 123.
16 *Draft W*, ed. J. W. Graham (University of Toronto Press, 1976), p. 765.
17 *W*, ed. James M. Haule and Philip H. Smith (Oxford: Shakespeare Head Press, 1993), p. 21.

4

JULIA BRIGGS

The novels of the 1930s and the impact of history

> 'Were they like that?' Isa asked abruptly. . .
> 'The Victorians,' Mrs Swithin mused. 'I don't believe,' she said with her
> odd little smile, 'that there ever were such people. Only you and me and
> William dressed differently.'
> 'You don't believe in history,' said William.[1]

Virginia Woolf's fiction explores the nature of the human condition: what makes up our consciousness when we are alone and when we are with others, how we live in time, and to what extent our natures are determined by the accidents of gender, class and historical moment. In her novels, the Great War (as it was always referred to, until the Second World War) was the defining moment, the line that separated the past from the present, always seen as an abyss or a watershed. *Jacob's Room* (1922) portrays middle-class English society before the war; *Mrs Dalloway* (1925) portrays it after the war. *To the Lighthouse* (1927) contrasts the two, separating them from one another with the 'Time Passes' section. Woolf began *To the Lighthouse* with the intention of exploring who her parents had been, but in the process of recording them she relocated them in a post-war perspective, seeing them through the affectionate yet critical gaze of a modern young woman, Lily Briscoe, who is painting a portrait of Mrs Ramsay. The effect of Lily's viewpoint in the novel was to begin to isolate and set in perspective the elements that made up the Ramsays' (and the Stephens') cultural consciousness, so that Woolf could see in what ways their particular historical moment had determined who her parents were, as well as what they believed and how they behaved.

The family life of the Ramsays is presented in 'The Window' section as the norm, but by the time 'Time has Passed' and we reach 'The Lighthouse' section, the children have grown up and the nature of the family has changed: they no longer regard their father as a harsh unpredictable god, but as human and fallible, like themselves. The Victorian ideal of marriage

72

which Mrs Ramsay had so enthusiastically promoted is now interrogated by other narratives, such as that of the open marriage of Paul and Minta Rayley, which Lily Briscoe imagines herself describing to Mrs Ramsay as part of their disagreement on the nature and significance of marriage.[2]

Recognising the value system that governed her parents' assumptions enabled Woolf to see them more clearly within the context of their times, and, to some extent as a product of them. The question of who the Victorians were was, in any case, one that increasingly interested post-war society, in the process of defining its own comparative sophistication. Lytton Strachey's *Eminent Victorians* (1918) and *Queen Victoria* (1921) had encouraged a tendency to be amused at their expense, to make fun of their cant and clutter. Catching up something of this tone, Woolf composed a hilarious satire on Victorian ideals of romance, love and marriage in the form of a play, written to be performed by and for her family and friends: in *Freshwater* (1923),[3] her great-aunt Julia Margaret Cameron is trying to photograph Tennyson, while G. F. Watts is trying to paint his child-bride Ellen Terry and she is trying to elope with John Craig. But it was not until the end of the 1920s that Woolf began to think more seriously about the comedy and tragedy of Victorian life. *Orlando* (1928) is a romp through English literary history, defining 'the spirit of the age' in a series of quick, broad strokes as a background for the hero/ine, who reflects and reacts against the changing times.

In *Orlando*, Woolf characterises the Victorian age in terms of a dark and spreading cloud, and a creeping damp which is at once a source of growth and fecundity but also of a general depression and debilitation. It is an age characterised by excess and incongruity, with its oddest features piled up to form a gigantic trophy that ranges from the sublime to the ridiculous, from crystal palaces to sponge-bag trousers.[4] The age is further characterised by its repressive and excessive respect for marriage and family life: 'Couples trudged and plodded in the middle of the road indissolubly linked together.'[5]

A more affectionate account of Victorian romance occurs in the first chapter of *A Room of One's Own*. Recalling the lost hum of excitement between the sexes, Woolf identified 'what men hummed at luncheon parties before the war' as the lover's song from Tennyson's *Maud*, as he awaits her in the garden ('She is coming, my dove, my dear'); what women hummed was Christina Rossetti's poem 'A Birthday' ('My heart is like a singing bird / Whose nest is in a water'd shoot'). She goes on to observe that 'the illusion which inspired Tennyson and Christina Rossetti to sing so passionately about the coming of their loves is far rarer now than then', but cannot decide whether this should occasion regret or relief.[6]

Woolf's exploration of the differences in outlook between the Ramsays and Lily Briscoe, between her parents and herself, was further developed in her writings of the 1930s. In a lecture read to the National Society for Women's Service on 21 January 1931 (a lecture which was also to provide the starting-point for *The Years* and *Three Guineas*, as her diary entry for the previous day records), Woolf analysed and rejected the Victorian ideal of womanhood, labelling it 'the Angel in the House', after Coventry Patmore's poem celebrating domestic love.[7] In 1931 she began work on a second mock-biography, *Flush* (1933),[8] an account of the most appealing of all Victorian love affairs, that between the poets, Elizabeth Barrett and Robert Browning – a relationship which served as the model for many late Victorian passions. Woolf deflates its quasi-mythical power by observing it from the resentful angle of Elizabeth Barrett's pet spaniel (Flush). The nature and workings of the Victorian family are also central to *The Years* (1937), a novel that explores women's changing roles in the half-century from Woolf's birth in 1882. *Between the Acts* (1941) engages with a wider sweep of history, and a darker threat, yet even here the village pageant culminates in an ideal Victorian domestic scene: '"Oh but it was beautiful," Mrs. Lynn Jones protested. Home she meant; the lamplit room; the ruby curtains; and Papa reading aloud.'[9]

The fiction of the 1930s begins, however, with a novel that questions the whole concept of historical determination by enquiring what aspects of human nature might lie beyond it, what might be permanent in human experience beyond the succession of Mondays and Tuesdays, beyond daily events, both personal and historical. This novel was *The Waves* (1931), whose seeds lay also in the writing of *To the Lighthouse* (1927), which it at once echoed and answered (though the publication of *Orlando* and *A Room of One's Own* intervened). In her working notebook, Woolf described the structure of *To the Lighthouse* as if it were a letter H, 'Two blocks joined by a corridor',[10] in which the uprights, the first and third sections, recorded a day in the lives of the family on holiday, although substantial changes took place between the two. The horizontal bar corresponds to the shorter 'Time Passes' section, a dark fantasia of the unconscious, which Woolf found the most challenging and exciting part of the book to write. In it, the group unconscious, the dreaming selves of the night, wander bodilessly down to the seashore where there are storms and 'a purplish stain upon the bland surface of the sea as if something had boiled and bled'.[11] Ten years that include the Great War itself are thus compressed into the passage of a single night.

The success of this experiment encouraged Woolf to develop her new technique further. She envisaged her next book (at this stage she thought of it as *The Moths*) as 'abstract mystical eyeless'[12] – in other words, it was to rework some of the features of 'Time Passes', which she had earlier described as 'the most difficult abstract piece of writing – . . . all eyeless & featureless with nothing to cling to'.[13] Woolf used the word 'eyeless' as a kind of shorthand to herself, holding together a number of related senses: it partly stood for the kind of inexplicable and pitiless fatality that is manifested in Percival's death. Within the novel Bernard recognises this, challenging it as whatever 'is abstract, facing me eyeless at the end of the avenue, in the sky'.[14] A further sense, derived from its homonym, 'I-less', was of the absence of or detachment from the self (itself one possible consequence of deep shock or grief). 'I am not concerned with the single life but with lives together', she had reminded herself, in the course of composing the first draft.[15] All these senses had also been present in the 'Time Passes' section of *To the Lighthouse*.

The Moths, or *The Waves*, as it was to become, was not only to be mystical and eyeless, but also abstract: in it, Woolf extended the critique of realism made in her earlier essays (especially 'Mr Bennett and Mrs Brown') and fictional practice. She was developing a style which, in its abstraction, its 'eyelessness', allowed her to ignore or close her eyes to the accumulated objects and circumstances with which the Edwardian novelists had over-loaded their writings, the suburban 'crusts and cruets, frills and ferns' (as satirised in her short story 'An Unwritten Novel'). By being 'I-less', Woolf could avoid the outworn conventions of character-drawing, although writing 'the life of anybody'[16] created another set of problems: not only when 'anybody' had lived (and whether that made a difference) but who she – or he – was. The first draft became increasingly focused upon six characters who borrowed characteristics from her friends, as well as from her sense of herself: Louis, the outsider, picked up traits from Tom (T. S.) Eliot, and the social discomfort he displayed; Neville was at least partly inspired by Lytton Strachey, while Susan's rootedness, her sense of place and passionate, possessive love of her children reflected aspects of Virginia's sister Vanessa. From an early stage, it became clear that the central characters belonged to a particular social class, since Woolf could not 'hear' the voices of Florrie the kitchen maid, or Albert 'whose father was a cowman'[17] as she could the characters of her own class. The voices began to dominate, and to resolve themselves into a series of soliloquies. Woolf was excited by the dramatic nature of her text, describing it as a 'playpoem'.[18]

The voices spoke in sequence against a background of everyday objects, a set for living that consisted of a room, plates, cups, table napkins, a flower pot – a still life such as her sister Vanessa Bell or Duncan Grant might have painted. Instead, she painted them in words which recorded the changing sunlight as it crept across their several surfaces and forms, defining their nature. In 1917, Woolf had written an experimental short story, 'Kew Gardens',[19] in which pairs of voices rose and fell against the background of a flower-bed. The bed was populated by small insects and snails, moving in a different rhythm among the leaves and stones, a world of nature such as is seldom perceived except by very small children, a world without people – 'not oneself but something in the universe that one's left with'.[20] Such observed movement implies an observer, although the narrative style resists the notion of individual consciousness, so that the paragraphs describing the flower-bed are, in some sense, both eyeless and 'I-less'. In November 1927, when Woolf had set *The Moths* aside to work on *Orlando*, the Hogarth Press reissued 'Kew Gardens' in a new edition with extra illustrations by Vanessa Bell. Its particular combination of disembodied dialogues, alternating with a garden world of nature, made its own contribution to *The Waves*. But in her search for what human beings have in common, Woolf substituted soliloquy, the interior voice of drama, for dialogue. The effect of setting the voices against a nature emptied of human presence was to isolate and simplify them. They appeared as if silhouetted against an imaginary skyline, an image Woolf herself used as she completed the first draft: 'I think it possible that I have got my statues against the sky.'[21]

Yet Woolf was as interested in what her characters had in common as in their isolated forms. Even at the egotistical stage of the nursery, they exist largely in interaction: when Jinny kisses Louis, Bernard attempts to console the weeping Susan. Escaping together, they glimpse the different world and time of Elvedon, where archetypal gardeners forever sweep the leaves and a lady sits writing between the two long windows. Later the children share their experiences of school and, for two of the boys, university. The central episodes of the book consist of communal occasions: the farewell dinner before Percival leaves for India, and the reunion supper at Hampton Court, creating eddies of movement and reflection within the characters. Woolf was always fascinated by the relation of the individual to the group. Mourning, above all other experiences, is suffered both communally and individually, and is celebrated as such in the final chapters of *The Voyage Out*, *Jacob's Room* and *Mrs Dalloway*.

The Waves aspired to the condition of poetry or drama, yet unlike most drama, it uses speech not to differentiate the speakers, but to unite them through a common style, even though each reverts to private sequences of imagery. Their mode of speech is characterised by the use of simple verb tenses, especially the present tense: '"I burn, I shiver," said Jinny'.[22] Such verb tenses are more often used in poetry than in common speech.[23] Compound tenses such as the continuous present ('I am burning, I am shivering') are more usual in conversation or writing. One effect of this is to detach the characters from their desires and actions so that, as James Naremore has observed, their voices 'seem to inhabit a kind of spirit realm from which, in a sad, rather world-weary tone, they comment on their time-bound selves below'.[24]

The novel searches for the fundamental things in human existence: the nature of human love; our need for and fear of one another; our shared experience of our world, of death and of the implacable indifference of nature; our use of imaginative sympathy both to relate to one another and to tell stories about one another. Bernard, as the artist, uses this ability instinctively, responding from the first to Susan, and eventually feeling that in some sense he includes the others within himself, though at the same time he shares their sense of being part of 'the body of the complete human being whom we have failed to be, but at the same time, cannot forget'.[25] It is possible to read the characters as six different versions of a single self. Among them, similarities are as significant as differences, and are not tied to gender: Jinny and Neville are linked through their restless desire for new lovers, new encounters, while Bernard and Susan are linked by their desire to create and perpetuate, and their search for roots; Rhoda and Louis are tormented by a sense of social inadequacy and of alienation. One result of the focus on what is shared, and what is fundamental, is a sense of the monolithic, the statuesque that is potentially at odds with the movement of the novel through time. The book is poetic in its simplifications and repetitions, but also shares in the immediacy, the absence of process, of lyric poetry. It forms a sustained meditation, and the element of time, which had run so markedly through Woolf's earlier fiction, is here strangely suspended. Bernard displays the greatest versatility, acting out different roles, recording the responses of the others, and so narrating his own story and sometimes theirs. Yet in the final section he turns against the significant story, the meaningful sequence, the conventional conclusion, preferring the little language of lovers, 'a rushing stream of broken dreams, nursery rhymes, street cries, half-finished sentences and sights'.[26]

Bernard's comprehensive rejection of master narratives suggests that *The Waves* does not so much dissolve history as redefine it. Its simplifications demand a different kind of history, perhaps on an altogether vaster scale. Louis envisages huge tracts of time, either entirely dwarfing the significance of his own life, or perhaps offering an obscure consolation for it: ' "But listen", said Louis, "to the world moving through abysses of infinite space. It roars; the lighted strip of history is past and our Kings and Queens; we are gone; our civilisation; the Nile; and all life." '[27] But if the novel reaches beyond narrowing particularities, there is much that defines the speakers' experiences as contemporary, as Susan Dick's chapter in this volume brings out: the boys attend a public school; the girls' (Edwardian) classroom displays a portrait of Queen Alexandra.[28] The social life of restaurants, private visits and parties belongs as decisively to the twentieth century as does the underground or the gilt chair on which Jinny perches. Yet for readers at the end of the twentieth century, the central story of Percival's life and death, exemplary as it is, serves to locate the book at a particular moment in world history, that moment when the British Empire and the ideals that glorified and disguised the nature of its economic basis were beginning to crumble. Percival has been educated in the best traditions of Thomas Arnold to excel at games, to be one of the 'boasting boys', to be a natural leader: 'Look at us trooping after him, his faithful servants' says Louis.[29] One purpose of such an education was to send him overseas to take up the so-called 'white man's burden', that is, to govern the empire. But the race that he runs is cut short when his horse stumbles, and he is thrown to his death.

Since she had begun writing, Woolf had shown her impatience with a particular kind of history, history as the 'lives of great men', of heroes and hero-worship: it was part of an imaginary quarrel that she had with her father about the *Dictionary of National Biography*, with its emphasis on the lives of men of action, and its indifference to the lives of the obscure and of women; part of a larger argument on behalf of social rather than political history. Percival's qualities as a leader make him loved; he is a hero; in India 'the multitude cluster round him, regarding him as if he were – what indeed he is – a God'.[30] Jane Marcus has pointed out the way in which Percival's fall anticipates the end of empire, and with it the end of its white mythologies.[31] By the late 1920s, the success of Mussolini's fascist regime in Italy, accompanied by such slogans as 'Believe! Obey! Fight!' and 'War is to the male what childbearing is to the female!', gave warning of where such hero-worship might lead. In his book *Quack, Quack!* Leonard Woolf showed how Thomas Carlyle's writings on hero-worship had provided 'the "philosophy" of dictatorship, "strong" government, and violence'[32] that had laid a path for Hitler and Mussolini. The rise of fascist politics in the 1930s gave new urgency to questions about the meaning and outcomes of history, and in Woolf's last two novels these take centre-stage, although they use antithetical techniques to arrive at their analyses. Both *The Years* (1937) and *Between the Acts* (1941) focus upon historical change, its nature and significance, as Woolf had experienced it during her lifetime. Both explore the problems that Woolf had first posed in *Orlando*, where she used fashion as a figure for wider cultural change: '[clothes] change our view of the world and the world's view of us . . . there is much to support the view that it is clothes that wear us, and not we them'.[33]

To read *Between the Acts* is to realise just how serious the questions posed comparatively light-heartedly in *Orlando* would eventually become: is there anything fixed or constant in human nature, anything that might stop a nation becoming a war-machine or a machine dedicated to mass murder? The pageant in *Between the Acts*, with its many costume changes, invites a reconsideration of these questions within a desperately, yet also comically, foreshortened scenario, for the pageant is performed on an afternoon in June 1939, a matter of weeks only before England declared war on Germany on 3 September for the second time in twenty-five years. 'Scraps and fragments [of conversation] reached Miss La Trobe . . . "D'you think people change? Their clothes, of course . . . But I meant ourselves . . . Clearing out a cupboard, I found my father's old top hat . . . But ourselves – do we change?"'[34] *Between the Acts* adapts a way of writing with amused affection about domestic or village life that was popular during the 1930s (and was practised by E. M. Delafield, 'Jan Struther' and E. F. Benson, for example) to interrogate the significance of history, portraying English middle-class society on the eve of war, much as she had done in the penultimate chapter of *Jacob's Room*, but in greater depth. *The Years*, before it, had examined history as process, using the lives of an extended family, not unrecognisably different from Woolf's own, to show how social structures and behaviour had altered since the 1880s. Her investigation had begun somewhat formally, since the early drafts alternated fiction with discursive analyses of the meaning of the events portrayed in the fiction.

The Years opens with an examination of the hidden underside of Victorian family life, a subject glanced at in *Freshwater*, and examined rather more seriously in *Flush* (1933). Here the spaniel's easy intimacy with his mistress gives him insights into the oppressive tensions that lurk beneath the surface of family life (in discussing the 'infantile fixation' that characterises the patriarch, Woolf later claimed that 'The case of Mr. Barrett of Wimpole Street is, perhaps, the most famous and the best authenticated').[35] A rather different but equally sinister aspect of Victorian life is revealed when Flush is stolen from his mistress and taken to a thieves' den in Whitechapel to await the payment of his ransom. But whereas *Flush* leaves the implications of the society it portrays to be picked up by the reader, the earliest version of *The Years* is explicitly didactic. It takes up where Woolf's lecture 'Professions for Women' had left off, being couched as a series of lectures addressed to the young women of the 1930s to show them how much women's lives had already changed – as it were, Lily

Briscoe's reminiscences of the Ramsay family for the sake of the next generation. Fiction is here used to recreate the lives of the mothers and grandmothers of her audience, its purpose becoming apparent in the discursive analyses that follow. Woolf depicts the frustration and disappointment of young girls whose opportunities to exercise their talents, or to meet and mix with young men, were severely limited; the shock of life in the slums for a young middle-class woman practising philanthropy; the Colonel's secret love affair as his wife slowly dies at home and, perhaps most disturbingly, the 10-year-old Rose's encounter with a sexual exhibitionist in a street near her home.

The third essay of The Pargiters (as the first draft was entitled when published) examines Rose's experience. It is of a type at once common, yet traditionally excluded from fiction, and even Woolf herself softens it a little by categorising it under 'aspects of love – of street love, common love, of the kind of passion which pressing on the walls of Abercorn Terrace made it impossible for the Pargiter girls to walk in the West End alone, or to go out after dark unless they had a maid or a brother with them'.[36] Woolf's discussion shows how Rose's encounter has aroused both her fear and her curiosity, and how both must be concealed with the same furtiveness and silence that had previously excluded such incidents from fiction. Mitchell Leaska, in his edition of The Pargiters, has pointed out the way in which the very name of the family denotes whitewashing or concealment, since pargeting involves placing a layer of decorative plaster over an external surface, a kind of literal cover-up.[37]

The Years records the gradual release of its closely constrained young women into freedom and even self-determination as the Victorian patriarchs, like so many dinosaurs, die out. In middle age the heroine, Eleanor, is finally released from her duties to her father and delightedly takes possession of her own life at last, free to travel to India, to lunch or dine where and with whom she likes. Part of the novel's initial purpose had been to urge the young women of the 1930s that they must continue to 'knock on the door', that they must never forget what women had already achieved, nor come to take it for granted. Peggy, the bitter young woman doctor, goes with her aunt Eleanor to the party that is the culmination of the final section, 'The Present Day', and their friendship itself further mirrors Woolf's intention of conveying to a younger generation the sense of exhilaration felt by women like Eleanor and Kitty within the novel, who have finally discovered the pleasures of freedom, of living their own lives.

The Years documents the Pargiters' progression from the oppressive atmosphere of life at Abercorn Terrace to a much more open existence in which individual brothers, sisters and cousins live alone but visit one another to discuss the past and the present. In the 'Present Day' episode, the huge family reunion is oddly consolidated by the presence of the outsider, Nicholas Pomjalowsky, who is no relation, is foreign, homosexual and yet is loved and accepted by Sara, Maggie and Eleanor as one of themselves. *The Years* echoes and enlarges upon the movement first outlined in *To the Lighthouse*, from the warmth and oppression of Edwardian family life as depicted in 'The Window', to the much more open relationships of post-war society shown in 'The Lighthouse', where individuals interact with tolerance, and even warmth, yet do not want to sacrifice their identities or their personal satisfactions to the larger group.

Both in *To the Lighthouse* and *The Years*, the First World War lies across the centre of the book, as the great divide between past and present, though the transition is marked rather differently in *The Years*. Kitty gives a party in the spring of 1914, and at the end of it catches the overnight train back to her country home in the north. The journey itself is used to convey something of the experience of historical change:

> There was a perpetual faint vibration. She seemed to be passing from one world to another; this was the moment of transition . . .
>
> The years changed things; destroyed things; heaped things up – worries and bothers; here they were again. Fragments of talk kept coming back to her; sights came before her. . . All their clothes are the same, she thought; all their lives are the same. And which is right? she thought, turning restlessly on her shelf. Which is wrong? She turned again.
>
> The train rushed on. The sound had deepened; it had become a continuous roar. How could she sleep? How could she prevent herself from thinking? . . . *Now* where are we? she said to herself. Where is the train at this moment? *Now*, she murmured, shutting her eyes, . . . And she resigned herself to the charge of the train, whose roar now became dulled and distant.[38]

Woolf, writing at great pressure, creates a powerful pun on 'charge': Kitty is helpless in the charge of the train, like a child in the charge of her nurse, while the train itself charges in a headlong rush through time and space. It travels faster than she wishes, as do our lives in time, but she must resign herself to its momentum.

The war brings changes: the old patriarch, Abel Pargiter, dies, freeing his daughter Eleanor from her long self-sacrifice. Her active interest in the deficiencies of her society, in administration and the law have been evident from the first, and she is eager to discuss them with her brother Martin, who, although he has received a formal education as a lawyer, lacks his sister's commitment. With Colonel Pargiter's death, the family house is finally shut up and the aged retainer Crosby retires to Richmond, taking with her the family dog, a large, smelly old animal who 'ought to have been put down long ago'[39] – the remains of a family life that nobody wants. The Victorian household with its intimate but increasingly uneasy relations with the servants on whom it depended is now replaced by single lives or unconventional marriages, such as that of Maggie and Renny, which Eleanor, with a momentary pang of envy, recognises as happy.[40] During the 1917 section an air raid takes place as Eleanor, Sara, Nicholas, Maggie and Renny discuss over dinner the brave new world that will dawn when the war is over. New freedoms have been promised particularly for women (many of whom would be granted the vote in 1918); yet enjoying freedom and independence is not always as easy as it seems.

The discussions of the new world hoped for after the war highlight the problems that Woolf encountered in the course of writing this novel. She had begun it in the voice of the lecturer addressing an audience of young women, and in the earliest draft, fiction and opinion, in the form of essays, had co-existed. Events on the world stage during the 1930s increasingly persuaded Woolf of the urgency of her critique of patriarchy. At the end of 1936, the year in which the Spanish Civil War broke out, she wrote an article for the communist newspaper The Daily Worker on why the artist had to adopt a political position, concluding that the status of the artist and of art itself was now under threat ('Why Art Today Follows Politics').[41] Her critique was eventually delivered in the form of Three Guineas (1938), yet even here the text is troubled by her anxiety at expressing anger in print, as well as by her recognition of the problems that anger brought with it: anger at the oppression of women was problematic in itself, since there was no point in responding to men's unconsidered (and possibly uncon-scious) anger with women with further aggression, no point in women becoming what they were fighting. Woolf was by instinct a pacifist. By a further and darker parallel, how was England to fight Hitler without losing its higher moral ground, without meeting weapons with weapons? This question became peculiarly pressing once it was known that Hitler was systematically persecuting the German Jews, and what the cost of non-intervention might mean for them. Both questions trouble the arguments of Three Guineas.

In a key passage in Three Guineas, Woolf links the oppression of patriarchy with that of the fascist dictators, a passage widely dismissed as nonsense when she wrote it, but now widely accepted as serious analysis: 'The whole iniquity of dictatorship, whether in Oxford or Cambridge, in Whitehall or Downing Street, against Jews or against women, in England, or in Germany, in Italy or in Spain is now apparent to you.'[42] The Jews, whose situation she here links with women, are a disturbing presence in her last two novels. In *The Years*, the Jew is represented as the repulsive other, the stranger who shares Sara's bath and drives her to consider taking a job to avoid his unpleasant physical proximity, yet at the same time he is also Nicholas, first supposed by Eleanor to be 'Russian, Polish, Jewish?',[43] but inside out, because hated instead of loved. This passage in the 'Present Day' section,[44] a reminder of the Jews' unwelcome and disruptive presence in the *laissez-faire* politics of the 1930s, has often been misread. It is always a mistake to assume that Woolf automatically endorsed the positions expressed even by apparently 'sympathetic' characters within her fiction. Percival's links with her brother Thoby or her own with Sara (who here voices her disgust with Abramson) do not make their positions morally or politically acceptable – and the same is true of Clarissa Dalloway, both in *Mrs Dalloway* and as she had appeared earlier in *The Voyage Out*. *Three Guineas* finds some compensation for women's exclusion from power in the fact that, as outsiders, they are peculiarly well placed to offer an informed critique of their society. *The Years* also sets a value on the position of the outsider: as a category, it includes not only North and Sara, but also Nicholas and Mr Abramson, the Jew in the bath.

In writing *The Years* Woolf found herself caught up in something of the double bind that had affected *A Room of One's Own*, and was characteristic of her work more generally. The novel offers a critique of the notion of history as the lives of great men, as well as of the narrative values that it generated, stories in which will and intention determine action and event, but to avoid these pitfalls Woolf also had to reduce the weight of her own opinions within the text, as well as the motivation of her characters and the clear outlines of their individual lives. The novel was 'dangerously near propaganda'[45] and she had consciously to prevent it from becoming didactic, or turning into a sermon, as she kept reminding herself: '[T]here are to be millions of ideas but no preaching – history, politics, feminism, art, literature – in short a summing up of all I know, feel, laugh at, despise, like, admire hate & so on'.[46]

Writing *The Years* became a struggle to retain her initial purpose of teaching, while not appearing to do so, and her commitment to a conception of history and historical fact as fundamentally arbitrary: its title changed from 'The Pargiters' to 'Here and Now', from 'Ordinary People' to 'The Caravan' to 'Other People's Houses' and sometimes it was just 'the nameless book'.[47] Woolf invested all her intensest beliefs and ideas about society in it, only to decide that she must pull her punches: that as fiction, it should not have a palpable design upon the reader but should rather whisper its truths – it was ultimately to do so through a series of highly charged allusions to particular topical events. The process of revision involved massive cutting, reducing the force of some of the characters (Elvira became Sara, the plainer and shorter name reflecting further parings), and abandoning a number of discussions on topics such as the motives of social workers or the use of birth-control devices, which would have interested modern readers. Its renunciation of conventional narrative structures is celebrated by Rachel Blau DuPlessis: 'The art of the book – to look déshabillé, uncrafted, a little dim – sustains the final picture of the unclosed, never fully measured capacities of time, people, history.'[48]

'How tired I am of stories, how tired I am of phrases that come down beautifully with all their feet on the ground!', Bernard had complained at the end of *The Waves*.[49] *The Years* resisted doing so to the last: the climax of the family party in the 'Present Day' section comes when the caretaker's children sing an incomprehensible song:

> [T]hey had made this hideous noise. The contrast between their faces and their voices was astonishing; it was impossible to find one word for the whole. 'Beautiful?' [Eleanor] said with a note of interrogation, turning to Maggie.
> 'Extraordinarily,' said Maggie.
> But Eleanor was not sure that they were thinking of the same thing.[50]

These are the voices of the next generation, the children who, in a world of social justice, should inherit the earth. Though their upper-middle-class audience listen attentively – and we as readers mentally listen to the syllables as they are written on the page – they can make no more sense than we can of what they hear. *The Years* is a novel that recognises that experience may teach us nothing, and that class, like race or gender, creates barriers which are not easily surmountable, even though individuals long for and believe in the possibility of a world where such barriers no longer exist.

The Years ends with an incomprehensible song in an unrecognisable language, yet it has rhythm and rhyme, primitive aspects of language that became increasingly fascinating to Woolf. In *Between the Acts*, the rhymes and rhythms embedded in the matrix of the language become part of Isa's consciousness, just as they had been part of Sara's in *The Years*, although for both of them the words that romantically sing in their ears are at odds with their prosaic everyday lives. The heavy implication of language in history and historical process is centrally dramatised through the village pageant which makes up the novel's central action. Pageants of English history seem to have been popular in the late 1930s, both in fact and fiction: E. M. Forster put on 'The Abinger Pageant' in 1934 and 'England's Pleasant Land' in 1938, while E. F. Benson's provincial lady, Lucia, had elaborate plans for a village fête whose climax would be Queen Elizabeth's visit to Drake's *Golden Hind*.[51] The pageant at Pointz Hall provides the opportunity to create a potted history of the English language written in a series of parodies, in a distant echo of Joyce's 'Oxen of the Sun' chapter in *Ulysses*. The pageant reduces English history to a sequence of familiar, and therefore essentially comic, plots; within it, history becomes identified with its usual modes of representation, its several stylised discourses.

A preoccupation with the history of the English language is part of the novel's wider sense of how history is experienced, and even of what nationalism, washed clean of all its sinister associations, might one day come to mean. Woolf's very last, unfinished writings were plans for the opening chapter of a common history of literature that was to begin with a celebration of the importance of 'Anon',[52] the unidentified poet whose appeal lay partly in the absence of determining circumstances: anon has no gender, no individuality, no defining position in society to leak into the poetry – it is the nearest that literature can come to the voice of us all, the voice of community. As such, it has obvious links with the songs, verses and merging choric voices of *Between the Acts*, in which Woolf had intended to reject 'I' in favour of 'we': 'we all life, all art, all waifs & strays'.[53] 'Anon' holds together a concept of sharing, of mutuality that *Between the Acts* had sought to create, both in terms of the voices evoked within the pageant, and the voices of the audience as they respond to it. The new history that Woolf planned to write would decentre or even deconstruct the male histories of identity, authority and authorship, histories of the biographies of great men, the histories coloured by Carlylean hero-worship that had led to the rise of the great fascist dictators Hitler and Mussolini, men whose personal fantasies of destruction and revenge now threatened the future of civilisation itself.

Both *The Years* and *Between the Acts* are centrally concerned with history and the meaning of history and its impact on lives, but they use antithetical methods of approaching their material and therefore produce very different effects. Both are concerned with social change, its causes and meaning, especially as Woolf had experienced it during her lifetime, and both take up the question of whether human nature alters or whether, at some fundamental level, we remain the same, the question posed in the epigraph. But *The Years* is written in the form of a family chronicle (like Galsworthy's *Forsyte Saga* or Walpole's *Herries Chronicle*), strung out over fifty years, while *Between the Acts* uses the equally popular fictional model of an episode of village life, revising and compressing the family chronicle and centuries of English history miraculously and effortlessly into the events of a single day. The novel, with its 'insubstantial pageant', is Woolf's version of *The Tempest*,[54] 'our island history', constructed within tightly observed unities of time and place, a snapshot of English village life on the eve of a war that Woolf herself did not survive, a war that lent a desperate urgency to the need to learn the lessons of history, but gave no indication of where to begin. Many, perhaps all, of the old immunities, confidences and assumptions were now under threat.

As Gillian Beer has shown,[55] the invention of the aeroplane, more than any other single factor, called in question England's island status. Mrs Swithin, reading (probably H. G. Wells's) *Outline of History* conjures up visions of an England in which dinosaurs blunder through primeval thickets of fern, but which is not yet England, since it is still joined to the continent,[56] as it is once again, in terms of the threat of German military power. Giles alone recognises, with a sense of impotent fury, that the view that has not changed since Figgis's Guide Book (1833) would be annhilated beneath aerial bombardment: 'At any moment guns would rake that land into furrows; planes splinter Bolney Minster into smithereens and blast the Folly. He, too, loved the view.'[57] It is primarily through Giles's consciousness that we are made aware of a Europe 'bristling with guns, poised with planes'. He is possessed by irrational anger against his family ('old fogies'), against William Dodge for his homosexuality, against Mrs Manresa for her lust (or for the lust she arouses in him) and against his own cowardice, an anger that finds expression in his stamping on the horrible snake that is trying to swallow a toad[58] – an image that is as complex as it is elusive, but must surely suggest Hitler's greed to swallow Europe, as well as the moral and political impasses that his greed would lead to.

Giles' anger that no one else seems to recognise the doom he cannot forget is part of Woolf's wider questioning as to what was the nature of reality, the nature of experience, a questioning evident in the way she had enclosed the deaths of Prue, Andrew and Mrs Ramsay in *To the Lighthouse*, and now given a further twist by the looming war. In August 1938, some six months into her final novel, she wrote:

> Hitler has his million men now under arms. Is it only summer manœuvres or – ? Harold [Nicolson] broadcasting in his man of the world manner hints it may be war. That is the complete ruin not only of civilisation, in Europe, but of our last lap. Quentin conscripted &c. One ceases to think about it – thats all. Goes on discussing the new room, new chair, new books. What else can a gnat on a blade of grass do? And I would like to write P[ointz] H[all].: & other things.[59]

'Pointz Hall', later *Between the Acts*, is marked by the recognition of the emerging plot of history that would soon interrupt and change the life of anybody and everyone. Woolf's quarrel with conventional plots characterises all her fiction: she was justifiably wary of the kinds of messages they carried, having recognised from the outset the heavy burden of social pressure within the plots of love and romance. The village pageant, with its welter of genres, plots and outmoded master-narratives, invites us to apply the technical terms of art to the nature of experience:

> There was such a medley of things going on . . . that she could make nothing of it.
>
> Did the plot matter? She shifted and looked over her right shoulder. The plot was only there to beget emotion. There were only two emotions: love; and hate . . .
>
> Don't bother about the plot; the plot's nothing.[60]

If Giles is only too familiar with the plot of hate, Isa reads only the plot of love – over her right shoulder is Rupert Haines, the gentleman farmer whom she hardly knows yet with whom she has fallen in love. The constricting limitations of these two plots strike her forcibly as the novel draws to its close:

> Love and hate – how they tore her asunder! Surely it was time someone invented a new plot, or that the author came out from the bushes . . .
>
> Here Candish came in. He brought the second post on a silver salver.[61]

Isa fails to recognise the new plot, while Giles can see little else. In the final lines, the narrative turns to gesture towards the acts of darkness between which the interlude of the novel is framed. In 1937, Woolf had answered a letter from Stephen Spender about *The Years* by explaining 'I think action generally unreal. Its the thing we do in the dark that is more real; the thing we do because people's eyes are on us seems to me histrionic, small boyish.'[62] Theatrical metaphors dominate this novel, and it ends with the words, 'the curtains rose': the play that has remained suspended, unperformed all the way through the book, the story of the quarrel of Giles and Isa, is about to begin. In fact, Giles and Isa have so far not addressed a single word to one another, and Woolf has deliberately avoided giving us 'their' story, avoided the usual concern with heterosexual couples, their loving and fighting. Now that they are alone together, the narrative seems to slip back to the oldest, most atavistic plot of all: 'Before they slept, they must fight; after they had fought, they would embrace . . . But first they must fight as the dog fox fights with the vixen, in the heart of darkness, in the fields of night.'[63] Finally, night engulfs the couple and the house: 'It was night before roads were made, or houses. It was the night that dwellers in caves had watched from some high place among the rocks.'[64] Finally, the plots of love and war come together, since it is the primitive and uncomprehended impulses of love and hate within the individual that nurture the seeds of war. And finally all history is swallowed up – 'Our English past – one inch of light'[65] is extinguished in a moment that identifies the present simultaneously with an unimaginably distant past, and with the anarchy to come.

Between the Acts is Woolf's most consistently underestimated novel: it brings together the rhythms and passions of language and the body with the historical specificity of a moment of national crisis. Composed during her long labours on the biography of Roger Fry and under the shadow of the coming war it yet retains a Yeatsian 'Gaiety transfiguring all that dread'.[66] It followed her 'interminable struggle' with *The Years*, flying out apparently effortlessly from beneath its weight, and following closely and inevitably on *Three Guineas* in its demonstration that 'the public and the private worlds are inseparably connected; that the tyrannies and servilities of the one are the tyrannies and servilities of the other':[67] domestic fear and hatred are intimately connected with the anger that leads to war. Yet with the artist's instinct for balance, these dark leitmotifs are set in a highly specific and even comic genre of country-house and village-life fiction. *The Waves*, *The Years* and *Between the Acts* form a second arc in Woolf's work comparable to that created by *Jacob's Room*, *Mrs Dalloway* and *To the Lighthouse*, with *Between the Acts* challenging *To the Lighthouse* by its combination of the familiar and the profound, its concern with design and chaos, with cultural assumptions and the relation of the artist to her materials. And *Between the Acts* inherits and redefines the arguments concerning historical determination that *To the Lighthouse* had initiated.

NOTES

1 *BA* (London: Hogarth, 1941); ed. Gillian Beer (Harmondsworth: Penguin, 1992), p. 104.
2 *TL* (London: Hogarth, 1927), ed. Stella McNichol with an introduction by Hermione Lee (Harmondsworth: Penguin, 1992), pp. 187–9.
3 *Freshwater: A Comedy*, ed. Lucio P. Ruotolo (New York: Harcourt Brace Jovanovich, 1976).
4 *O* (London: Hogarth, 1928), ed. Brenda Lyons with an introduction by Sandra Gilbert (Harmondsworth: Penguin, 1993), p. 160. Rachel Bowlby discusses this passage in *Virginia Woolf: Feminist Destinations and Further Essays on Virginia Woolf* (Oxford: Basil Blackwell, 1988) second rev. edition (Edinburgh University Press, 1997), p. 104.
5 *O*, p. 166. Woolf was probably remembering the lines from *Epipsychidion*, where Shelley writes of

> the beaten road
> Which those poor slaves with weary footsteps tread,
> Who travel to their home among the dead
> By the broad highway of the world, and so

With one chained friend, perhaps a jealous foe,
The dreariest and the longest journey go.   (lines 154–9)

E. M. Forster had taken the title of his novel, *The Longest Journey* (1906), from this passage.

6 *ROO* and *TG* (London: Hogarth, 1929, 1938); ed. Michèle Barrett (Harmondsworth: Penguin, 1993), pp. 11, 13–14.

7 *D*, vol. 4 (1931–5), ed. Anne Olivier Bell, assisted by Andrew McNeillie (London: Hogarth, 1982), p. 6. 'Professions for Women' was first published in *The Death of the Moth* (London: Hogarth, 1942), and is reprinted as Appendix 2 in *ROO* and *TG*, pp. 356–61.

8 *Flush* (London: Hogarth, 1933).

9 *BA*, p. 103.

10 *Draft TL*, ed. Susan Dick (London: Hogarth, 1983), Appendix A, p. 47.

11 *TL*, p. 146.

12 *D3*, p. 203.

13 *D3*, p. 76.

14 *W* (London: Hogarth, 1931); ed. Kate Flint (Harmondsworth: Penguin, 1992), p. 116.

15 *Draft W*, ed. J. W. Graham (University of Toronto Press, 1976), p. 42.

16 *Ibid.*, p. 1.

17 *Ibid.*, p. 67.

18 *D3*, p. 203.

19 'Kew Gardens', 'An Unwritten Novel' in Virginia Woolf, *Selected Short Stories*, ed. Sandra Kemp (Harmondsworth: Penguin, 1993).

20 *D3*, p. 113.

21 *Ibid.*, p. 300.

22 *W*, p. 7.

23 Compare, for example, 'The New Year waits, breathes, waits, whispers in darkness. / While the labourer kicks off a muddy boot and stretches his hand to the fire' (T. S. Eliot, *Murder in the Cathedral*, part I, lines 12–13).

24 James Naremore, *The World Without a Self: Virginia Woolf and the Novel* (New Haven: Yale University Press, 1973), p. 173.

25 *W*, p. 213.

26 *Ibid.*, p. 196.

27 *Ibid.*, p. 173.

28 *Ibid.*, p. 16.

29 *Ibid.*, p. 26.

30 *Ibid.*, p. 102.

31 Jane Marcus, 'Britannia Rules *The Waves*' in *Decolonising Tradition: New Views of Twentieth-Century 'British' Literary Canons*, ed. Karen R. Lawrence (Urbana: University of Illinois Press, 1992).

32 Leonard Woolf, *Quack, Quack!* (London: Hogarth, 1935), p. 130.

33 *O*, pp. 131–2.

34 *BA*, pp. 73–4.

35 *ROO* and *TG*, p. 258.

36 *The Pargiters: the Novel-Essay Portion of 'The Years'*, ed. Michell A. Leaska (London: Hogarth, 1978), p. 50.

37 *Ibid.*, p. xiv.

38 Y (London: Hogarth, 1937), ed. Jeri Johnson (Harmondsworth: 1998), pp. 198–9.
39 *Ibid.*, p. 161.
40 *Ibid.*, p. 219.
41 *The Moment and Other Essays* (London: Hogarth, 1947); reprinted in Virginia Woolf, *The Crowded Dance of Modern Life*, ed. Rachel Bowlby (Harmondsworth: Penguin, 1993).
42 *ROO* and *TG*, p. 228.
43 *Y*, p. 206.
44 *Ibid.*, pp. 248–51.
45 *D*4, p. 300.
46 *Ibid.*, p. 152; see also pp. 145, 281.
47 *Ibid.*, pp. 6, fn. 8, 129, 176, 245, 266, 271, 274, 279, 335.
48 Rachel Blau DuPlessis, *Writing Beyond the Ending: Narrative Strategies of Twentieth-Century Women Writers* (Bloomington: Indiana University Press, 1985), p. 166.
49 *W*, p. 183.
50 *Y*, p. 315.
51 'The Abinger Pageant' appears in *Abinger Harvest* (London: Edward Arnold, 1936); for 'England's Pleasant Land' see *D*5, p. 156, fn. 5; for Lucia's fête see E. F. Benson, *Mapp and Lucia* (London: Hodder and Stoughton, 1935).
52 Edited by Brenda R. Silver in *The Gender of Modernism: A Critical Anthology*, ed. Bonnie Kime Scott (Bloomington: Indiana University Press, 1990), pp. 679–96).
53 *D*5, p. 135.
54 *BA*, p. 128: 'Sitting in the shell of the room she watched the pageant fade.' Compare Prospero's 'And like this insubstantial pageant faded', *The Tempest*, IV. I. 179.
55 Gillian Beer, *Viginia Woolf: The Common Ground* (Edinburgh University Press, 1996), pp. 149–78.
56 *BA*, p. 8.
57 *Ibid.*, p. 34.
58 *Ibid.*, p. 61.
59 *D*5, p. 162.
60 *BA*, p. 56.
61 *Ibid.*, pp. 127–8.
62 *L*6, p. 122.
63 *BA*, p. 129.
64 *Ibid.*, p. 130.
65 *W*, p. 174.
66 W. B. Yeats, 'Lapis Lazuli', *Last Poems* (1939).
67 *ROO* and *TG*, p. 270.

5

HERMIONE LEE

Virginia Woolf's essays

The conversation Virginia Woolf has been having with her readers for nearly a hundred years now (her first publication was in 1904) has gone on changing, as conversations do. As a pioneer of reader-response theory, Virginia Woolf was extremely interested in the two-way dialogue between readers and writers. Books change their readers; they teach you how to read them. But readers also change books: 'Undoubtedly all writers are immensely influenced by the people who read them.'[1] Writers must adapt to changing conditions. Books alter as they are re-read: 'Even things in a book-case change if they are alive; we find ourselves wanting to meet them again; we find them altered' ('The Modern Essay', 1922, 1925, *E*4, p. 220). They are read differently by different generations: 'In 1930 we shall miss a great deal that was obvious to 1655; we shall see some things that the eighteenth century ignored.' Readers, therefore, need always to be aware of themselves not as isolated individuals, but as part of 'a long succession of readers',[2] joining in the conversation.

In the dialogue between Woolf and her readers, a great variety of different Virginia Woolfs have come into being. A recent reincarnation (or 'renaissance') has been of Woolf as an essayist. Not that her writing of essays and journalism, which spanned her whole publishing career, has ever been ignored. But in recent years this aspect of her work has been read in new ways.

Her reputation as a writer of non-fiction has fluctuated greatly. Virginia Woolf the essayist moved, in her lifetime and after it, from anonymous obscurity, to high fame and a large readership, to relative neglect. She wrote 'over a million words' of reviews, journalism and essays (*E*1, p. ix), but only a small part of this prodigious achievement has been attended to with the same intensity as her fiction or her book-length feminist essays. Yet the history of her essay-writing was at all points intimately bound up with her work as a novelist and her thinking about women, politics and society.

For the first ten years of her life as a published writer she made money entirely from her journalism, which was largely anonymous. She cut her teeth rapidly and greedily on a great mixture of books, and perseveringly turned herself into a professional through the discipline of regular reviewing (mainly for *The Times Literary Supplement*). But she also struggled against editorial pressures, an inhibiting sense of a male tradition of essay-writing (her father's tradition), and a feeling of censored self-consciousness as a woman writer.

Her development into the kind of novelist she wanted to be, in the 1910s and 1920s, was worked out in large part through the essays of that period – reviews of individual writers, and more discursive, synthesising considerations of 'modern' writing. (At the same time she and Leonard Woolf were forging an influential literary partnership at the Hogarth Press, from 1917, and with Leonard's editorship of the *Nation*'s literary pages from 1923.)

Twenty years' worth of professional non-fiction writing went into *The Common Reader*, which began as her 'Reading book', and which was being devised and shaped between the publication of *Jacob's Room* and of *Mrs Dalloway* (which came out three weeks after *The Common Reader*) in 1925. All through the 1920s she produced a huge output of essays and reviews, commanding increasingly large fees (especially after the success of *Orlando* in 1928) and writing for a greater variety of outlets, including the major American magazines and literary pages. Her essays continued to be closely interconnected with her fiction, and would be so for the rest of her life.

By the end of 1925 she was thinking about (and taking notes for) a book 'for the H. P. . . . . about fiction' (*D3*, p. 50). For most of 1926 she wrote *To the Lighthouse* instead, but in the autumn of 1926 she started to plan the 'book on literature' again, and worked on it throughout 1927, while publishing essays on reading and writing called 'Poetry, Fiction & the Future' (revised as 'The Narrow Bridge of Art'), 'An Essay in Criticism' and 'Is Fiction an Art?' (revised as 'The Art of Fiction'). She worked at her fiction book, 'Phases of Fiction' and a long essay on Hardy, while she was writing *Orlando* in 1928 and *A Room of One's Own* in 1929. Eventually 'Phases' was published not as a book but as three long essays in the *Bookman*, in the early summer of 1929. These essays on the history of literature and on reading were closely connected to *Orlando* and *A Room of One's Own*.

In the 1930s this pattern of interconnection between essays and fiction continued. *The Waves* kept pace with the reading for the second *Common Reader*, published in 1932, *The Years* and *Three Guineas* with much writing on the relation between art and politics, *Roger Fry* with an essay on

'The Art of Biography' and with her own memoir-writing, and *Between the Acts* with a third projected book on the history of reading and of English literature, with the emphasis on anonymity and communality.

Her preoccupation with audience, access and the market is reflected in the strategies she adopted for her non-fiction. Through newspapers and magazines, her essays and journalism reached a much larger audience than her novels did in the 1920s, '30s and '40s. And they were deliberately written to be accessible, entertaining and uncondescending for the varied audience of non-specialist general readers she wished to identify with. The marketing of the two *Common Reader* volumes in cheap Pelican paperbacks, the first for 6d in 1938, the 'Second Series' for 9d in 1944, both with print runs of 50,000, reflected the popular demand for her essays.[3]

But her feelings about the market-place, and about the side of the mind she used for non-fiction, were very mixed. She was eager for (and needed) her own money: she never ceased to relish the fact that she was a professional writer who earned her income. But she had a horror of identifying herself with 'Grub Street' or with professional journalism. She was caught between 'writing as a job and writing as art'.[4] It worried her that *The Common Reader* was 'a book too highly praised' (*D*3, p. 33). The planned book on literary history, 'Phases of Fiction', became very burdensome to her. Revising her essays for *The Common Reader: Second Series* felt like 'drudgery'; she told herself she was doing it 'by way of proving my credentials' (*D*4, p. 115; *D*4, p. 77). Her antipathy to the 'intellectual harlotry' of reviewing (a phrase from *Three Guineas*), and to the censorship, corruption and hierarchies of the professional literary world, hardened up in her later years and became ever more involved with her critique of a capitalist male-dominated society. Many of the essays of the 1930s and of 1940 incorporated these views: 'Letter to a Young Poet', 'Thoughts on Peace in an Air Raid', 'Why?', 'Royalty', 'Why Art Today Follows Politics', 'The Leaning Tower', 'Reviewing'. Her political reading of the literary market-place was an essential part of her feminism.

Yet the politics of Woolf's essays have taken some time to be fully responded to. In her lifetime, she was highly praised and respected as a sensitive, cultured critic of 'brilliance and integrity'.[5] After her death, her reputation was husbanded by Leonard Woolf's policy of issuing, at regular intervals, a series of selections of her uncollected essays and journalism (and of her stories and diaries): *The Death of the Moth* (1942), *The Moment* (1947), *The Captain's Death Bed* (1950), *Granite and Rainbow* (1958), *Contemporary Writers* (1965). These culminated in his four-volume selection, incomplete, unannotated and unchronological (but at the time invaluable) of what he called her 'Collected Essays', published in 1966 and 1967.

After Leonard Woolf's death in 1969, there was a further trickle, through the 1970s, of selected non-fiction volumes (accompanied by the two-volume Quentin Bell biography, and the editions of the diaries and letters): *The London Scene* (1975), her autobiographical writings, *Moments of Being* (1976, revised in 1986), *Books and Portraits* (1977), *Women & Writing* (1979). In that forty-year period, Virginia Woolf as an essayist was patchily read and unevenly responded to. Not until 1986, forty-five years after her death, did the great project of a complete, fully annotated, chronological edition of her essays begin, under the masterly editorship of Andrew McNeillie, of which four volumes are published and two volumes are still to come. Woolf's temporary emergence from copyright in 1992 also allowed for two Penguin selections of her essays, edited by Rachel Bowlby.

The scattered and gradual publishing history of the non-fiction has made it hard to see these writings as a whole, in their full significance, and in their relation to her better-known work. The essays have had a peculiarly mixed posthumous life. Praise for them came to be a subtle way of denigrating the fiction: it is quite often maintained by readers out of sympathy with Woolf that she is a better writer of essays than she is of novels.[6] By contrast, the very popularity of the essays in her lifetime has made them, for some readers, harder to admire than the fiction. The accessibility, the affability and charm of the essays can seem less interesting than the more challenging and complex texture of the novels.

And piecemeal publishing has made for selective readings. While Woolf was under discussion mainly as a modernist, with the emphasis falling on the 1919–27 period, her manifestos on fiction, such as 'Mr Bennett and Mrs Brown', or 'The Narrow Bridge of Art', were used to elucidate what she was doing in her own novels. Even so, her standing as a modernist literary critic fell much below that of – say – Eliot's, and her lightness of touch meant that her essays 'never acquired credibility within the mainstream critical establishment'. When feminist and Marxist readings turned more to the work of the late 1920s and 1930s, *A Room of One's Own* and (to a lesser extent) *Three Guineas* became prioritised reading, and much more attention was paid to her essays on women's memoirs, letters and diaries, on the lives of women and of the 'obscure'. But her stylish, formal, at first sight conventional-looking appreciations of male authors – Gibbon, Montaigne, Boswell, Hardy, James – were harder for her feminist admirers to deal with, and great tracts of her essay-writing fell into 'benign neglect'.[7] Michèle Barrett, introducing her timely and influential selection, *Women &*

Writing, in 1979, observed that Woolf's 'critical essays have been some-what neglected since her death'.[8]

More recently, growing interest in Woolf's rethinkings of an extraor-dinary range of intellectual issues – history, science, evolutionary theory, psychoanalysis, technology, consumerism, painting – combined with the new map of her writing provided by the collected *Essays*, has moved the reading of her essays into a much more central position in Woolf studies.[9] Their use largely as ammunition for ideological approaches, or as back-ground data for the novels, has shifted towards an interest in the strategies, thought-processes and textures of the essays themselves. They are being re-read, now, as crucial parts in the great complex web of Woolf's criss-crossing between novels, stories, diaries, letters, notebooks, reviews, sketches, essays, story-essays, essay-novels: a huge lifelong conversation on paper which only now is beginning to be seen and understood in its entirety.

Woolf's absorption in women's lives and writing, her passion for entering into domestic detail and for recovering hidden histories, her quest for female forebears, has become essential to considerations of her work as an essayist. Her feminist agenda has long been linked to her interest in history and biography (Bowlby, p. 84). More recently, increasing emphasis has been placed on Woolf's reading through the body and reading as a woman.[10] And the many essays on dead white males, which had been something of an embarrassment to earlier feminist readers, are now being revalued as quests for female inspiration within a patriarchal tradition. Juliet Dusinberre's book on Woolf's Renaissance essays shows her 'con-structing for women a place in a male-dominated record', reading the great male Renaissance writers (Montaigne, Donne, Bunyan, Pepys) as outsiders, writers out of tune with their times. Dusinberre (pp. 2, 62, 177) sees the essays on the Elizabethans as quests for cultural ancestors who might provide 'an alternative tradition'.

In such revaluations of Woolf as historian, critic, and (in Gillian Beer's phrase) as 'quasi-biographer', the essays' tactics of apparently loose, spontaneous form, of interruptive open-endedness, have been found very alluring. In resisting definitiveness, closure and opinionated certainties, Woolf's literary criticism is seen to 'disclaim authority'. The essays' wandering structures, their 'speculative and hesitant' refusals to lay down the law, create a form of subversion.[11]

Woolf's anti-authoritarian tactics in her essays are closely connected to her recommendations for a democratic literary community. Given the prolonged class emphasis (dating from the 1930s) on Woolf as an elitist, narcissistic or neurotically individualistic writer, her passionate desire for a shared, common ground of communication between readers and writers has taken some time to be recognised. Though new readings of the novels have been placing great emphasis on communal memory, shared histories, group dynamics, struggles with traditions and women's lives, and though *A Room of One's Own* and (more problematically) *Three Guineas* have long been valued for their arguments against dictatorship, repression and conformity, the politics of her literary essays have not been so fully understood. Yet they are intensely interested in breaking down hierarchies, validating ordinary lives and encouraging readers to follow their own judgements. Woolf finds all kinds of excuses to strike this note, whether she is talking about isolated geniuses ('still the best artistic work is done by people who mix easily with their fellows') ('Melodious Meditations', 1917, *E*2, p. 81), academic analysts ('Where the ordinary reader is concerned, it is his feeling, not the reason he gives for his feeling, that is of interest') ('Pure English', 1920, *E*3, p. 235) or a great writer like Montaigne who believes that 'we must dread any eccentricity or refinement which cuts us off from our fellow-beings . . . to communicate is our chief business' ('Montaigne', 1924, 1925, *E*4, p. 76).

Attention is now being paid to Woolf's 'fascination with communities', her quarrel with the protectionism of the literary market and her dislike of the cultural power structures which get in the way of the reader's conversation with her book. This new emphasis is summed up in the title of Gillian Beer's 1996 book on Woolf, *The Common Ground*. In all her work, Beer says, Woolf 'strained across genre, attempted to break through – or disturb – the limits of the essay, the novel, the biography, to touch realities denied by accepted forms' (Beer, 1996, pp. 48, 77). Though her essays are so affably user-friendly, they are as iconoclastic in their disruption of genre as in their arguments.

Though Woolf's essays do their best to resist categories, they do fall, to an extent, into distinct areas. A large part of her non-fiction consists (especially in her early years) of reviews of contemporary work. These were often quite short, and responded to a mixed bag of fiction, anthologies, memoirs, editions, biographies, critical books, poetry and essays. In those contemporary reviews she sometimes gave high praise to very transient titles, or had difficulties – notably in the case of Joyce – with work she found unsympathetic. Some of her readings were skewed by rivalry, friendship or temperament.[12] But she herself was acutely aware of the 'crimes of criticism' perpetrated by reviewers writing about the living ('How it Strikes a Contemporary', 1923, *E*3, p. 354).

She felt more secure, and had more room and perspective for considera-tion, in her longer, individual critical essays (many of them revised for the two *Common Readers*) on authors from the past. These were usually constructed from several sources – a new edition of the works, a memoir, a collection of letters, a new biography. Her numerous essays on little-known 'Lives' (often, though not always, of women) might work in a similar way, as a narrative synthesised from several sources.

In these longer essays (which she increasingly distinguished from, and preferred to, the journalism of contemporary reviewing) there were recur-ring, lifelong themes. These would emerge from books she was sent for review, but they were also things she repeatedly chose herself to write about. In her reading of literary history, certain authors persisted as key figures: Defoe, Boswell, Sterne, Austen, Coleridge, De Quincey, George Eliot, Barrett Browning, Christina Rossetti, Meredith, Gissing, James, Hardy, Conrad. Certain periods and cultural movements spoke to her more than any others: classical Greece, the Elizabethans, the eighteenth century, the Romantics, nineteenth-century Russian fiction. And there were certain subjects – essay-writing itself, painting, women's lives, biography, memoirs, and letters – which she never exhausted.

Her enormous range of reading fed into her more theoretical pieces on fiction, which were, for a time, her best-known essays: manifestos on contemporary reading and writing, on the literary market, on patronage and audience, on modern forms. These aesthetic debates were always politically charged, and took the form increasingly in the 1930s of polemical essays on war, women, capitalism and politics in art. But Woolf was never an exclusively literary essayist. She loved writing on houses, architecture, streets, the country, radio, cinema, aquariums, mushrooming, flying, opera, exhibitions, painting, travel, shops. These might be short pieces or long meditations: on the eclipse, on London, on an evening drive, on laughter or illness, on reading itself.

But to categorise these writings is an unstable operation. Everywhere you look there is cross-fertilisation, overlap and the dissolving of divisions. Essays turn into fictions, fictions into essays; criticisms of others or readings of modern fictions may be commentaries on her own processes; recommen-dations of how to read may be demonstrations of how to write. There is an attractive example of this in the much-revised essay 'How Should One Read a Book?'

The essay was first given as a lecture to schoolgirls in January 1926, revised for the *Yale Review* in October 1926 and again in 1932 for the second *Common Reader*.[13] The essay is on the ideal relation between reader and writer, on how best to understand how different writers work and on the pleasure of reading. It is closely linked to her work at the Press: the writer is imagined as a kind of mental compositor, and the reader is invited to think of the book not as a fixed object, but as a process. It is bound up with the writing of *To the Lighthouse* (a fragment of the lecture is written in the manuscript of the novel) and mirrors her dealings with structure and composition in that book. And the evolution of the essay illustrates how she likes, not only to read a book, but to tell a story.

As in 'Street Haunting' (Bowlby, pp. 191–219), this essay figures reading as a strolling or sauntering through city streets. She shows how three different writers – Defoe, Auden, Hardy – deal with 'life', by imagining each of them encountering a beggar in the street. In her draft of the essay, she illustrated this with a long anecdote about three middle-class women, called Mary, Elizabeth and Helen, each of whom gives seven shillings and sixpence to a plausible beggar called Eliza Pett, who has told them she needs to catch the last train home to Bedford. 'Mary' wants to describe this event, but 'she did not know what to leave out'. This introduces Defoe, the novelist who *does* know what to leave out, and a passage follows on *Robinson Crusoe*. Then 'sober' Mary throws down her pen, and Elizabeth picks it up. She is a 'chatterbox': 'If she went to a party, she would always come back & tell you, word for word, what someone had said, & imitate their way of saying it.' She tries to write down how people talk – like Jane Austen in *Emma*. Then the third girl, Helen, takes up the story. She is neither 'observant nor methodical', but she gets 'very vivid ideas, or visions, or impressions'. Eliza Pett seems to her 'like a tree against the sky in winter'. But it is very difficult to communicate that: 'Women are not trees; the Tottenham Court Road is not the world.' To write like that you have to be Thomas Hardy.

The fairy-tale structure of the three women, representing three novelists, each with a story to tell (rather like the three 'Marys' who appear in *A Room of One's Own*, or the three begging letters in *Three Guineas*) is buried in the final version of 'How Should One Read a Book?', leaving just a trace behind.[14] But the essay has emerged from a story which is itself an exploratory refusal to choose between different species: fantasy or fact, realism or romance, essay or fiction.

The overlap between essays and fiction is pervasive. The idea of the essay is very important to *Jacob's Room*, whose novel-biography provides an alternative to the sort of historical essays Jacob is writing on great men, and which contains within it set-piece essays – on letter-writing, on Greece, on the British library – which interrupt and develop the fictional story. *Orlando* is a series of brilliant essays on history, fashions, literary periods and sexuality, and is closely connected to her 'fiction' book, to the shape of many of her biographical essays and to a political piece such as 'Thunder at Wembley', which dismantles the great Empire exhibition of 1924 in an absurd, chaotic, *Orlando*-esque storm. *The Years* was planned as an essay-novel, alternating political diagnoses of middle-class British family life with the story of the Pargiters. And her thoughts about fiction in the novel are reflected at the time of *The Years* in the major essays she was writing on Goldsmith, Turgenev and Sickert. Her essays, too, as well as being some-times like fictions, often read like diaries or letters (Dusinberre, pp. 74, 101, 122). Towards the end of her writing life Woolf became increasingly impatient with all genre distinctions: 'I am doubtful if I shall ever write another novel . . . Were I another person, I would say to myself, Please write criticism; biography; invent a new form for both; also write some completely unformal fiction: short: & poetry. . .' (*D*5, p. 91).

In her essays on single figures, Woolf was writing an inextricable mixture of criticism, history and biography. And she brought her critical mini-biographies as close to fiction as she could through a bold, inventive, subtle process of synthesising and scene-making. This sort of critical essay was the opposite of the 'sweeping and sterile' literary criticism she disliked, which generalised, laid down the law and shut the door in the reader's face ('Patmore's Criticism', 1921, *E*3, p. 310). Temperamentally and politically, she set herself against the kind of (usually male) reading which set out to establish, define and conclusively sum up everything about a writer:

> Critics of Henley's persuasion are, indeed, inspired by a colossal ambition. First they will know the facts; next they will elicit from them whatever is relevant to their purpose; finally, having created the man, set him in his proper surroundings, supplied him with aunts and uncles, followed his wanderings, named his lodgings, and indicated precisely how far and at what points wine, women, heredity, poverty, disease and a taste for opium have laid hands upon his art, they will then from this elevation soar above the accidental and the temporal and exhibit his work as it appears in the eye of eternity. They are biographers, psychologists, novelists, and moralists; to crown all they can do the critic's business – analyse the work to its elements and rate them at their proper worth. Such being the aim it is natural that few live to achieve it. ('Henley's Criticism', 1921, *E*3, p. 285)

The very opposite of this approach is taken in the long essay (or fiction, or memoir?) called 'Reading', written in 1919 but not published in her life-time. Here she works her way into the idea of an empathetic reading of the past, of books as a linked historical procession, and of reading as a curious mixture of association, memory, dreaming and responsiveness, through the images of a woman reading by the window of an Elizabethan house, and of children catching moths in a wood at night.

The essay takes an odd rambling trajectory through ideas of reading. It is an evocation of English history imagined through books, and so anticipates the pageants of English history in *Orlando* and *Between the Acts*. It is a meditation on how different moods require different kinds of reading. It compares the modern reader with the reader of the past, suggesting that individualism has replaced community. And it is a semi-autobiographical fiction which engenders various metaphors, all centring on the old English house and its grounds, for the act of reading. Its slipping, dreamy motion between reading and history, place and childhood memory suggests how she perceives reading as at once personal and impersonal, self-transforming and self-abnegating.

The scene-making of 'Reading' is at the heart of her critical method. She is above all interested in how a book works on the reader's feelings. Arguing with Percy Lubbock's formalist critical approach in *The Craft of Fiction* in 1922, she maintains that the 'book itself' is not 'form which you see, but emotion which you feel' ('On Re-reading Novels', 1922, *E3*, p. 340). Her tactics for analysis are always to re-experience and so transmit that emotion, very often by lingering on the atmosphere of a particular scene.

> Perhaps it is the silence that first impresses us. Everything at Bly is so profoundly quiet. The twitter of birds at dawn, the far-away cries of children, faint footsteps in the distance stir it but leave it unbroken. It accumulates; it weighs us down; it makes us strangely apprehensive of noise. At last the house and garden die out beneath it. 'I can hear again, as I write, the intense hush in which the sounds of evening dropped. The rooks stopped cawing in the golden sky, and the friendly hour lost for the unspeakable minute all its voice.' It is unspeakable. We know that the man who stands on the tower staring down at the governess beneath is evil. Some unutterable obscenity has come to the surface. It tries to get in; it tries to get at something. The exquisite little beings who lie innocently asleep must at all costs be protected. But the horror grows . . . We are afraid of something, unnamed, of something, perhaps, in ourselves. In short, we turn on the light.
>
> ('Henry James's Ghost Stories', 1921, *E3*, p. 325)

What is not explicit in James's *The Turn of the Screw*, the sexual threat to the children – powerfully registered in Woolf's reading of the story, perhaps for personal reasons – comes home to us through this evocative recapitulation of his scene-making. There is a more benign example of the same process in her affectionate reading of *Mansfield Park*, where she is explaining how Jane Austen's 'impeccable sense of human values' can quietly fill an 'ordinary act of kindness' with 'meaning':

> Here is nothing out of the way; it is midday in Northamptonshire; a dull young man is talking to a rather weakly young woman on the stairs as they go up to dress for dinner, with housemaids passing. But, from triviality, from commonplace, their words become suddenly full of meaning, and the moment for both one of the most memorable in their lives. It fills itself; it shines; it glows; it hangs before us, deep, trembling, serene for a second; next, the housemaid passes, and this drop, in which all the happiness of life has collected, gently subsides again to become part of the ebb and flow of ordinary existence. ('Jane Austen', 1925, *E4*, p. 152)

This is far from being a closely analytical piece of criticism. You have to know the novel and the scene she is talking about for it to have its full effect. There is no attempt to explain the technical devices which create the emotion; quite the reverse, it is left as a mystery: 'their words become suddenly full of meaning'. She gets at the emotional atmosphere of the writing through a highly Woolfian (rather than Austenesque) image.

Often, she will devise an image for the experience of reading which takes the form of a physical space, a sphere of cohabitation in which subject and critic, author and reader, are fused together across time. So in writing about Mme de Sévigné's letters, she provides an image which fits her subject's historical context, but which also brings her to us as a living figure. At the same time, a subtly coercive use of 'we' breaks down potential barriers between this image-making critic and *her* readers:

> The fourteen volumes of her letters enclose a vast open space, like one of her own great woods; the rides are crisscrossed with the intricate shadows of branches, figures roam down the glades, pass from sun to shadow, are lost to sight, appear again, but never sit down in fixed attitudes to compose a group. Thus we live in her presence . . . ('Madame de Sévigné', 1942, *CE3*, p. 66)

Sometimes the image leaks or drifts over from being a description of the texture or quality of the writing to a description of what it feels like to read it, so that there is no perceptible distinction between the text and 'our' response to it. So George Eliot's work 'procures' for us a 'delicious warmth and release of spirit'.

> As one comes back to the books after years of absence they pour out, even against our expectation, the same store of energy and heat, so that we want more than anything to idle in the warmth as in the sun beating down from the red orchard wall. ('George Eliot', 1925, *E4*, p. 174)

That evocative, scenic, sensual form of criticism is part of a larger agenda. What Woolf does in her essays is what she likes in, and recommends for, the writing of fiction. Her radicalising programme to undo what she saw as the heavy-weight materialism, the over-stuffing, the literal detail and the thick plotting of the English novel is embodied in her critical preference for indirection and suggestion. She wants fiction to shift the emphasis, as in Chekhov's stories, where 'the emphasis is laid upon such unexpected places that at first it seems as if there were no emphasis at all' ('Modern Novels', 1919, E3, p. 35). She very often talks about strategies of omission and allusion when she is making technical recommendations for fiction-writing. In Turgenev, for instance, 'the individual never dominates; many other things seem to be going on at the same time' ('The Novels of Turgenev', 1933, CE1, p. 251). In Meredith, description is always through synecdoche and ellipsis: 'Let us suppose that he has to describe a tea party; he will begin by destroying everything by which it is easy to recognise a tea party – chairs, tables, cups, and the rest; he will represent the scene merely by a ring on a finger and a plume passing the window' ('On Re-Reading Meredith', 1918, E2, p. 274). At the time when she is most immersed in the Russian writers, this is how she thinks it should be done:

> If we want to describe a summer evening, the way to do it is to set people talking in a room with their backs to the window, and then, as they talk about something else, let someone half turn her head and say, 'A fine evening', when (if they have been talking about the right things) the summer evening is visible to anyone who reads the page, and is for ever remembered as of quite exceptional beauty.   ('Mr Kipling's Notebook', 1920, E3, p. 239)

Her critical and historical essays are full of those half-turns of the head. But looking aslant, lightening the fabric, throwing in odd details, can be risky play. At times she goes so fast and skates so dexterously and glances sideways at so much stuff that she edges into a kind of surrealistic narrative in which history is all strangeness. (She loves weird lists, for instance.) It is an odd paradox in her essays that while she is all the time trying for an empathetic breaking-down of time barriers between past and present lives, she is also fascinated by the alien otherness of history. So, in her extra-ordinary essay on the Edgeworths, she jumps from the minor figures hardly anyone notices in eighteenth- and nineteenth-century memoirs, dogged by obsession or desire for fame, to the equally odd character of Maria Edgeworth's father Richard:

> And in the whole world there is probably but one person who looks up for a moment and tries to interpret the menacing face, the furious beckoning fist, before, in the multitude of human affairs, fragments of faces, echoes of voices, flying coat-tails, and bonnet strings disappearing down the shrubbery walks, one's attention is distracted for ever. What is that enormous wheel, for example, careering downhill in Berkshire in the eighteenth century? It runs faster and

faster; suddenly a youth jumps out from within; next moment it leaps over the edge of a chalk pit and is dashed to smithereens. This is Edgeworth's doing – Richard Lovell Edgeworth, we mean, the portentous bore.

And so the essay, loosely based on Richard Edgeworth's memoirs, careers onwards into the life-story of the 'portentous bore', at once risking and warning against the danger of improvising from historical facts ('It is so difficult to refrain from making scenes which, if the past could be recalled, might perhaps be found lacking in accuracy'), ending up in a bizarre encounter between Richard Edgeworth, a mad clergyman and his daughter, and running out in a flurry of rhetorical questions: 'Who was she? And why was the house in this state of litter and decay? Why was the front door locked?' ('The Lives of the Obscure: 1. Taylors and Edgeworths', 1925, *E4*, pp. 121–2, 124). The wheel of invention risks every moment being 'dashed to smithereens' on the reader's impatience, disbelief or desire for dates and facts. What saves the wheel from crashing is the brilliant complicity the essay's voice sets up with the reader.

In 'On Being Ill', Woolf fantasises heaven as a place for conversation: Pepys is there, we might have 'interviews with celebrated people on tufts of thyme', and 'soon fall into gossip about such of our friends as have stayed in Hell' (1926, *E4*, p. 323). Conversation was to have concluded *The Waves* and to have formed the frame-structure of the first *Common Reader* (Beer, 1996, pp. 64, 70; *D2*, p. 261). She tried out conversation as a form for essays in 'A Talk about Memoirs' in 1920 (*E3*, pp. 180–4), in 'A Conversation about Conrad' in 1923 (*E3*, pp. 376–9), and in her first, cancelled introduction to *The Common Reader*, 'Byron & Mr Briggs', drafted in 1922, in which characters from her own novels talk about literature (*E3*, pp. 473–99). And she used the strategy again in her essay on Sickert, first published in 1934 as 'A Conversation about Art', which lures the reader into a dinner-party conversation about painting and writing, and incorporates a commentary on talk as a (risky) narrative method:

> Though talk is a common habit and much enjoyed, those who try to record it are aware that it runs hither and thither, seldom sticks to the point, abounds in exaggeration and inaccuracy, and has frequent stretches of extreme dullness. ('Walter Sickert', 1934, *CE2*, p. 233)

One of her most daring and inventive essays, 'Miss Ormerod' (a fine example of a twentieth-century woman writer excavating the obscure life of a nineteenth-century woman scientist) moves in and out of conversation, as though we are overhearing and piecing together the fragments of a life-story.

'Miss Ormerod' (very loosely improvised, Andrew McNeillie tells us, from the 1904 memoir and letters of Eleanor Ormerod, Economic Entomologist) starts in the Gloucestershire family home of the Ormerods in 1835, where a small girl is left alone observing some grubs, and tries unsuccessfully to tell her parents about them. She is interrupted by a rapid time-shift, *Orlando*-style, to 1852, and the capture of a locust in the streets of Chepstow. Local gossip is heard about the earnest Miss Ormerod, only interested in beetles. Cut to the family talking in the library in 1862, where Eleanor's ruminations on the incubation period for turkeys interrupts her father at his prayers, who shortly dies: 'Oh, graves in country churchyards' (says the narrator in our ear, taking us aside) ' – respectable burials – mature old gentlemen – D.C.L., L.L.D., F.R.S., F.S.A. – lots of letters come after your names, but lots of women are buried with you!' Cut to a voice, presumably Eleanor's, mulling on the Hessian Fly and the uses of Paris Green (the insecticide which she pioneered), and to a conversation between a lady painter in Penzance and a market-gardener whose business was saved by Miss Ormerod's book on 'Injurious Insects'. Cut to Miss Ormerod, 'no longer young', talking to herself about sparrows and flour infestation, and then to a conversation with her Doctor, which illustrates, without comment, her pragmatism, her modesty, and her latent influence: 'I do believe all good work is done in concert', she says to him, while he jokingly suggests that the farmers of England set up a statue to her as a pagan Goddess. A conversation is overheard between a couple reading Miss Ormerod's obituary on 20 July 1901. Cut back to Miss Ormerod talking to her sister about her work on sparrows as a pest, and the animosity this has aroused in the British sparrow-loving establishment; the death of the sister; the fading away of Miss Ormerod, done in callous headline style, with dashes; and the narrator's voice, ironically taking leave: 'That is life, so they say.'

This is early Woolf at her most brilliant, teasing and inventive, telling us under these glancing surface voices about the efforts of women scientists in the nineteenth century to professionalise themselves against patriarchal pressures, and about the gap between conventional biography and the inner life. It is written just before the breakthrough that moved her on from *Night and Day*, via 'An Unwritten Novel', to *Jacob's Room*, whose methods it prefigures. But such has been the relative neglect of Woolf's essays that this remarkable piece of work failed to find its rightful place in the English edition of *The Common Reader*, alongside two other 'Lives of the Obscure', until 1984.[15]

Even when conversation is not used as a narrative strategy, the idea of the talking voice dominates her reconstruction of literary history. Over and over again in her essays she will make up her subjects through the sound of their voices: Hazlitt telling us 'exactly what he thinks' in his conversational prose ('William Hazlitt', 1930, 1932, CE1, p. 155); Meredith whose 'manner of speaking . . . much resembled his manner of writing' ('Small Talk about Meredith', 1919, E3, p. 8); Addison whose best essays preserve 'the very cadence of easy yet exquisitely modulated conversation' ('Addison', 1919, 1925, E4, p. 113); Mary Wollstonecraft, a living presence still since 'we hear her voice and trace her influence even now among the living' ('Mary Wollstonecraft', 1929, 1932, CE3, p. 199); Mme de Sévigné, whose talking voice is so audible that 'we live in her presence. We are very little conscious of a disturbing medium between us – that she is living, after all, by means of written words' ('Madame de Sévigné', 1942, CE3, p. 68).

In her late essay on Coleridge (whose voice, like de Sévigné's, provided refuge and pleasure for her in war-time), his voice is metamorphosed into an aura, a penumbra, 'so that as we enter his radius he seems not a man, but a swarm, a cloud, a buzz of words, darting this way and that, clustering, quivering, and hanging suspended'. Her essay on his writings unravels a whole stream of images for the voice – bee-swarm, rain-drop, breaking walls, ripe fruit, smoke-screen, hypnotic fumes – in re-enactment of the 'perpetually pullulating ideas' that swarmed through Coleridge's mind ('The Man at the Gate', 1940, CE3, pp. 217, 220). The stopping of the voice (this essay was written towards the end of 1940) is a form of death.

Coleridge's voice fills her with pleasure, and pleasure is what she wants from reading.[16] The first *Common Reader* was planned as a testimony to 'the great fun & pleasure my habit of reading has given me' (D2, p. 259; E3, p. xviii). It began by suggesting that the common readers' relation to their reading could allow for 'affection, laughter and argument': a pleasurable conversation with their book ('The Common Reader', 1925, E4, p. 19). Laughter is an essential ingredient in this pleasure. 'The Value of Laughter' was the title of one of her earliest thematic essays, and a great part of Woolf's essays – more than her novels – is taken up with her pleasure in laughing and making us laugh. 'Dr Burney's Evening Party' is one example out of hundreds, but perhaps the best, of a sustained comic set-piece on a disastrous soirée given for Dr Johnson, where attempts at conversation went terribly wrong (1929, 1932, CE3, pp. 132–46).

And, as a narrative strategy, talk *can* go wrong. There are many voices in Woolf's essays, Coleridge's among them, whose voices reel hopelessly out of control 'to the verge of incoherence', and who end up not having conversations but talking to themselves, as people do (and as she did) in the streets, 'dreaming, gesticulating, often muttering a few words aloud' ('The Man at the Gate', p. 219; 'Street Haunting', 1927, E4, p. 488).

The communication of 'fun & pleasure' through a narrative voice which tries to come as close as possible to conversational speech ran the risk, she knew, of being too meandering, fanciful, random; of being all surface; of being all self. When she looked back in 1929 at a discursive piece of 1923 about criticism, 'How it Strikes a Contemporary', in which the idea of 'random talk' plays an important part, she very much disliked its 'looseness', its 'wobble & diffusity & breathlessness' (E3, p. 360; D3, p. 235). But she also had a horror of the suave, urbane 'man of letters' style of Gosse or J. C. Squire, 'smooth, rotund, demure and irreproachable', essays as mere polished surface ('Imitative Essays', 1918, E2, p. 249). And she loathed the kind of essay that said 'I' all the time. Right from the beginning of her essay-writing career, in 1905, she set herself against 'the unclothed egoism' of many of the essayists of her time ('The Decay of Essay-Writing', 1905, E1, p. 27). As with her fiction, she wanted her criticism to express deep feeling, but not to be personal. But if essays were to be like conversation, to communicate pleasure and to entertain, did that mean they had also to be depthless and uncentred? The negotiation in her essay-writing between personality and surface is analogous to the struggle in her fiction between autobiography and the formal shaping of her materials.

There is, in fact, much personal material detectable in the essays, but it never takes the form of confession. Traces of her own life lie under the surface: as when she writes on the short and glorious life of Sidney soon after her brother Thoby's early death; on the incompatibility of the Carlyles just after she has turned down Lytton Strachey's proposal; on Gissing's unflinchingly melancholy view of human relationships at the time when she was deciding whether to marry Leonard Woolf; or on illness weakening one's resistance to love, when she was starting her relationship with Vita Sackville-West. Sometimes deep private feelings rise up to the surface of the essay, as when, in 'Hours in a Library' (1916, E2, p. 56), she speaks poignantly about the reading lists of a self-educated twenty-year-old, and of her memory of childhood reading.

Virginia Woolf's essays can be read as the autobiography of a reader, full of personal emotion and intimacy. But her life as a reader always takes the colour of what she is reading or arguing with. She does not speak about herself directly. She never refers to herself in her essays as a novelist, or to her life as Virginia Woolf, or to her personal relations with anyone she is writing about. She speaks from the ground of the literary, the historical, and the cultural, not the personal. Yet her character, her experience and her voice come very close to us.

When she talks about reading De Quincey in 1926, she says the scenes in his *Autobiographical Sketches* do 'compose an autobiography of a kind', yet we learn very little about him from them, 'only what De Quincey wished us to know'. 'Nevertheless there grows upon us a curious sense of intimacy', even though he is always 'self-possessed, secretive and composed' ('Impassioned Prose', 1926, *E*4, pp. 366–7). This is something like the experience of reading Woolf's essays, at once so free, light and conversational, so artful and composed and so full of strong feeling.

There is a peculiar image she sometimes uses of the essay as a veil, or curtain. It can be an image for intimacy: 'A good essay . . . must draw its curtain round us, but it must be a curtain that shuts us in, not out' ('The Modern Essay', 1925, *E*4, p. 224). Or it can be an image for something more mysterious, a transparent veil of style that half reveals, half conceals the writer. Montaigne's essays allow us to hear 'the very pulse and rhythm of the soul, beating day after day, year after year, through a veil which, as time goes on, fines itself almost to transparency' ('Montaigne', 1925, *E*4, p. 78). The image is used again for Hazlitt: 'Soon, so thin is the veil of the essay as Hazlitt wore it, his very look comes before us' ('William Hazlitt', 1930, *CE*1, p. 155). Under the transparent veil we can see the 'very look', 'the beating soul', the essential self of the writer. But there has to be a veil, or there is no essay, no conversation, no art, just feeling and opinion and personality. In 'The Modern Essay' (*E*4, p. 221), she identifies this as the vital paradox and challenge for the essay-writer: 'Never to be yourself and yet always.'

NOTES

1 'Reading', 1919, Andrew McNeillie (ed.), *E* (London: Hogarth Press, 1986), vol. 2, p. 157.
2 'The Countess of Pembroke's Arcadia', Leonard Woolf (ed.), *CE* (London: Chatto & Windus, 1996–7), vol. 1, p. 19.
3 See Michael Kaufmann, 'A Modernism of One's Own', in Beth Carole Rosenberg and Jeanne Dubino (eds.), *Virginia Woolf and the Essay* (New York: St Martin's Press, 1997), p. 137 (hereafter *VWE*); John Mepham, *Virginia Woolf: A Literary Life* (Basingstoke and London: Macmillan, 1991), pp. 131, 193; Juliet Dusinberre, *Virginia Woolf's Renaissance* (London and Basingstoke: Macmillan, 1997), p. 192 (hereafter Dusinberre).
4 Rachel Bowlby, *Feminist Destinations & Further Essays on Virginia Woolf* (Edinburgh University Press, 1997), p. 224 (hereafter Bowlby); Alex Zwerdling, *Virginia Woolf and the Real World* (Berkeley, Los Angeles, London: University of California Press, 1986), pp. 108–9.

5 Robin Majumdar and Allen McLaurin (eds.), *Virginia Woolf: The Critical Heritage* (London: Routledge & Kegan Paul, 1975), p. 151.

6 See *E*3, p. xx, note 51.

7 Sally Greene, 'Entering Woolf's Renaissance Imagery', and Michael Kaufmann, 'A Modernism of One's Own', in *VWE*, pp. 81, 137ff; Dusinberre, 1997, p. 15.

8 Michèle Barrett, *Virginia Woolf: Women & Writing* (London: The Women's Press, 1979), p. 2.

9 See 'Bibliography', Hermione Lee, *Virginia Woolf* (London: Chatto & Windus, 1996).

10 Gillian Beer, *Virginia Woolf: The Common Ground* (Edinburgh University Press, 1996) (hereafter Beer), p. 104; Dusinberre, 1997, ch. 7.

11 Dusinberre, pp. 14, 85; L. Low, 'Refusing to Hit Back', *VWE*, p. 267; Bowlby, p. 228.

12 See Peter F. Alexander, *Leonard and Virginia Woolf: A Literary Partnership* (Hemel Hempstead: Harvester Wheatsheaf, 1992), for a harsh treatment of this; also Cheryl Mares, 'The Burning Ground of the Present', *VWE*, p. 117.

13 See Beth R. Daugherty, 'Readin', Writin' and Revisin': Virginia Woolf's "How Should One Read a Book?"', *VWE*, pp. 160–78, for the changes between the three versions.

14 Mss in 'Articles, Essays, Fictions and Reviews 1925–1941', Virginia Woolf Manuscripts, Henry W. and Albert A. Berg Collection, New York Public Library. *E*4, pp. 388–99, reprints the first published version of the essay from the *Yale Review*, 1926. *CE*, pp. 1–11, reprints the much-revised version from *The Common Reader: Second Series*.

15 *E*4, pp. 131–45. Planned as part of a series on 'Eccentrics' for the *Athenaeum* in 1919 (*D*1, 30 Mar 1919, p. 260), 'Miss Ormerod' was not published until 1924 in the *Dial*, and not included in an English edition of *CR* until 1984. Andrew McNeillie (ed.), *The Common Reader* (London: Hogarth Press, 1984), introduction; *E*4, pp. xiii, xxv, 144.

16 See Michael Kaufmann, *VWE*, p. 140; Anne E. Fernald, 'Pleasure and Belief in "Phases of Fiction"', *VWE*, pp. 194–5; Bowlby, p. 222; Lee, ch. 23.

6

SUSAN SELLERS

Virginia Woolf's diaries and letters

'From the chuckle & the babble to the rhapsody'
(*D*4, p. 4)

Virginia Woolf kept an almost daily diary throughout her life and wrote many thousands of letters. The first extant journal dates from 1897 when Woolf was fourteen and the diaries continue, with interruptions, until her suicide in 1941. Her earliest surviving letter was written in 1888, and she maintained a regular correspondence right up to her death, sometimes writing six letters a day.[1] The diaries and letters are now published in twelve volumes and form a substantial part of her *œuvre*.[2] They have been hailed as works of genius. Quentin Bell, in his introduction to the mature diaries, describes them as a 'masterpiece', and reviewers of both the diaries and the letters have been equally laudatory.[3] Yet, despite the accolades, the tendency has been to scour the diaries and letters for the insights they afford into Woolf's writing, or – in the wake of the seemingly endless fascination with Bloomsbury – into Woolf herself. They are rarely read in their own right.[4]

Considering the diaries and letters as distinct and intrinsically worthwhile works of art raises interesting questions. What is their relationship to Woolf's other writing – her fiction and criticism? How does one read a personal diary, or a letter intended for its addressee? What reading strategies might be appropriate for such material? Can Woolf's views expressed in her diaries be taken in evidence when reading her fiction? Does the fact that she signs her letters mean that they are true? In this chapter, I explore these and other questions, and suggest that postmodern theory offers a rewarding frame from which to review the genres. In particular, I argue that recent French feminist accounts of human subjectivity and writing provide dynamic routes into the diaries and letters, and intimate their accomplishment of the new form for which Woolf was searching throughout her career.

'There's no knowing what won't interest old Virginia' (D2, p. 117)

Bloomsbury gossip. Madness. Lesbianism. Suicide. It is not difficult to see why the more uncommon aspects of Woolf's life have lured readers to her diaries and letters. Yet those in search of the real Virginia often emerge disappointed. Her recurrent illness is marked more by omission than comment;[5] there are no references to her impending suicide in her diaries, and only the briefest mention in her final letters to her husband and sister.[6] She discusses the major events of her day only in passing;[7] and we must turn to Vita Sackville-West's journal rather than to Woolf's for an account of their affair.[8]

There are, of course, compensations, such as the lively depictions of the people Woolf meets and the events she attends.[9] For those seeking to compile a portrait of the author there are glimpses into her relationships, and the occasional expression of her views on war, feminism, marriage, religion.[10] The majority of the diaries and letters, however, are devoted to rather different preoccupations. There is Woolf's detailed reporting of the minutiae of living.[11] We have her work plans, her thoughts on the books she is reading, her reactions to other writers.[12] There is the constant anxiety over the reception of her work;[13] and the apparently insoluble dilemma of her need for stimulus and her requirement for solitude in order to write.[14]

Critics wishing to spice their studies with illustrative quotations fare rather better than seekers after the real Virginia. Traditionally, in so far as it has taken account of them at all, Woolf scholarship has raided the diaries and correspondence for illuminating or supporting statements about Woolf's writing. Again, it is easy to sympathise with the temptation. The diaries give an unparalleled insight into Woolf's development and methods as a writer. We are given her plans for her various novels,[15] her thoughts as she works at them,[16] the compositional problems she encounters,[17] and her reactions to them once they are finished.[18] She describes the 'rapture' of inspiration,[19] and the 'torture' of revision.[20] We can trace her incessant search for 'a new form' for her novels in which 'one thing should open out of another . . . & enclose everything, everything' (D2, p. 13). Occasionally we may detect the genesis of an incident in the fiction, such as the sight of a 'snake eating a toad: it had half the toad in, half out' which recurs in *Between the Acts*.[21]

The editor of the letters, Nigel Nicolson, argues that they have little to say about Woolf as a writer (L3, p. xv). He quotes her comment to Jacques Raverat: 'I'm terrifically egotistic about my writing, think practically of nothing else, and so, partly from conceit, partly shyness, sensitiveness, what you choose, never mention it' to justify his claim (*L3*, p. 130). Nicolson's assessment is unfounded, however, and the letters provide valuable information about Woolf's writing. She replies to observations about her work,[22] and now and again describes the piece she is engaged on[23] or comments on her novels.[24] She offers criticism to young writers,[25] and outlines her view of literature.[26] She compares her fictional to her critical writing,[27] and delineates her determination to 're-form the novel' into a new, inclusive shape.[28]

'But the truth is – no, I dont think I know the truth' (*D2*, p. 285)

Despite the dividends of reading the diaries and letters in this way, it will be the contention of this chapter that such an approach is problematic. To extract from them those sections which discuss the writing or Woolf's view of art distorts their essence and arguably misses their achievement. There are also difficulties with a reading which wishes to discover an authentic Virginia. One of Woolf's purposes in keeping a diary was as a training-ground for her art.[29] 'This is an attempt at the concise, historic style', she noted as she described the impact of the war on supplies in 1918 (*D1*, p. 100); there are practice dialogues, occasional trials for novels and notes for her lectures.[30] Thus Woolf is less concerned with 'truth' than with the play and possibilities of writing. Memory similarly twists the accuracy of her accounts. 'Its impossible to remember a week at a stretch, which I must confess would be my task if I were to pretend to be accurate' she observed in an early diary (*D1*, p. 82). Endeavours to trace the truth about the author are also frustrated by frequent contradictions.[31] Such inconsistencies and distortions are paralleled in the letters, which are slanted towards their addressee. Woolf complimented Vera Brittain on her biography of her friend Winifred Holtby, for example, but then wrote to Ethel Smyth condemning not only the book but its subject as well (*L6*, pp. 378–9); and she sent almost daily letters to Violet Dickinson following her brother Thoby's death in which she maintained the fiction of his recovery so as to speed Dickinson's own convalescence (*L1*, pp. 247–64).

The diaries and letters offer more than a glimpse into Woolf's view of writing or personal life. They contain many of the elements we look for in a work of art. There is narrative, drama, even poetry in a significant number of the letters, and the diaries are far from being a prosaic recording of the day's events. At one point in the diaries Woolf expressly rejected the listing of what had occurred as 'too flat' (*D4*, p. 147); her descriptions are often powerfully written, evocative and witty, as when she pronounced a party given by Ethel Smyth to have been 'a ghastly frizzly frying pan affair' (*D3*,

p. 65), or portrayed their secretary, Bernadette Murphy, as 'an ill-conditioned mongrel woman, of no charm, a Bohemian scallywag, something like Irish stew to look at' (D3, p. 10). That she is consciously thinking of the quality of the writing is shown in her occasional interjections. 'I've said that partly for the sake of the m's', she noted, after depicting Mary Hutchinson as having 'much of the mute meretricious fille de joie' about her (D2, p. 28), and she upbraided herself for an ugly internal rhyme: '(how I hate that clash)' (D5, p. 306). In her correspondence she repeated conversations she had had or overheard as dialogue (see L2, p. 200), invented a scenario around her sister Vanessa's imagined reaction (L3, p. 375) and even wrote in the form of a newspaper (L2, p. 288).

The tendency in traditional readings of Woolf has been to band the diaries and letters together.[32] There are reasons for doing so. 'I mean I scribble to you as I scribble in my diary', Woolf wrote to Ethel Smyth (L6, p. 453), and she now and again attributed a gap in her diaries to the fact that she had written letters 'which drained up some of the things I should have said here'.[33] The diaries and letters also occasionally repeat or extend each other.[34] Nevertheless, to group them together is to ignore the differences between them. While the diaries were intended for Woolf's own perusal the letters were written to communicate with others.[35] Occasionally the diaries are in shorthand,[36] which sometimes becomes a list of books read or people seen,[37] and there are notes on the progress of work,[38] schedules,[39] even financial accounts.[40] The letters had a different function. 'You will probably suffer from many long, and diffuse, egoistical, ill written, disconnected, delightful letters, because solitary as I am, and fertile as a tea pot, it becomes necessary to empty the brew on someone' Woolf admitted to Violet Dickinson (L1, p. 308), and she justified a letter to her brother Thoby with 'I dont get anybody to argue with me now, and feel the want.'[41] The need for conversation orients the letters towards their addressees. Thus, there is a distinction between a letter written for a friend such as Ethel Smyth and one intended to raise money or settle work plans. A case in point is Woolf's correspondence to her sister, Vanessa Bell. Woolf wrote, 'I always keep a sort of pouch of gossip for you in my mind' and her sister's predilection is amply catered for in her letters (L2, p. 104). There are changes in the tone and content of the letters Woolf wrote to individuals over time.[42] Although there are indications that Woolf composed her letters as freely as she wrote her diary, any liberties in the correspondence are swiftly followed by an apology.[43] The diaries and letters also occasionally contradict each other, as is shown in the series of melancholy diary entries relating the revision of Jacob's Room and Woolf's lively, upbeat letters of the time.[44]

'What in the world should I like more than letters – daily letters,
long letters . . .?' (L6, p. 68)

'Death will be very dull', Woolf confided to her diary, 'There are no letters
in the grave' (D4, p. 273). This leads us to the question: how did Woolf
view her diaries and letters? She charged Ethel Smyth, 'never see a pillar
box without dropping a letter in' (L4, p. 211) and urged her nephew
Quentin Bell, 'please write a full and indiscreet account of your amorous
adventures . . . or I shall be forced to invent one' (L5, p. 373). Woolf also
enjoyed other people's correspondence.[45] 'Letters and memoirs are my
delight – how much better than novels!' she wrote to Violet Dickinson, and
she advised Ethel Smyth to quote letters in her book as 'they often shed a
whole cuttle fish bag of suggestion'.[46] Ironically, Woolf often asserted her
hatred for letter-writing. 'If you knew the misery it is to me to sit down to a
writing table and begin a letter' she complained to Violet Dickinson (L1,
p. 298), and to Saxon Sydney-Turner she insisted 'how much I *hate* and
detest writing letters' (L3, p. 515). While some of her protestations must be
seen as a pose, the evidence seems to confirm her comment to Stephen
Spender that 'I love getting letters, but I hate answering them' (L5, p. 314).
Part of her avowed aversion to letter-writing appears to derive from her
disillusion with the possibility of communication. 'I shake these brief notes
onto the page, like – what can I think of – only lice – instead of distilling
the few simple and sweet and deep and limpid remarks which one would
like to send to Spain in a letter', she wrote to Gerald Brenan, adding
'suppose one could really communicate, how exciting it would be'.[47] To
Jacques Raverat she exposed the simplifications and 'convenient mask'
which letter-writing inevitably produced,[48] urging instead for an end to 'all
superfluities'.[49] This is reflected in the kind of letters Woolf preferred. She
implored Ethel Smyth to include 'everything' in her letters (L4, p. 211) and
praised her 'charming' letter 'that jumped and tumbled and wandered in
and out of corners'.[50] She petitioned Hugh Walpole to write her 'a real life
letter' (L6, p. 387) and thanked Margaret Llewelyn Davies for her 'bunch
. . . that creates a whole world' (L6, p. 305). This potential for letters to
convey 'real life' is a point to which I shall return.

'A natural growth of mine' (D1, p. 150)

Whereas replying to letters was often a troublesome duty, Woolf viewed
her diary as a chance to 'uncramp' (D5, p. 80). She turned to it as a
confidante,[51] called it 'my long suffering & . . . tolerant diary' (D1,
p. 296), her 'benignant page' (D2, p. 208). It supplied an antidote to 'dry'

criticism (D4, p. 70) and the ardours of revision,[52] and provided a 'more terrestrial soil' than fiction (D2, p. 195). She often wrote it to 'soothe' herself (D3, p. 155) or to fill in odd moments of time.[53] It offered a place where she could get rid of 'fidgets' (D2, p. 120) and scribble without 'reflection'.[54] Sometimes it was written as a 'treat' (D5, p. 126), in time 'stolen' from more laborious work (D5, p. 161). In it she recorded her 'ups & downs' as she waited for reviews of a book (D5, p. 64). Woolf also appears to have viewed her diary as a means of preserving what 'will soon be gone forever' (D4, p. 94). She often reproached herself for her lapses in writing, which resulted in 'life [being] allowed to waste like a tap left running'.[55] In a lengthy note on her reactions to rereading her diaries Woolf pondered: 'What sort of diary should I like mine to be? Something loose knit, & yet not slovenly, so elastic that it will embrace any thing, solemn, slight or beautiful that comes into my mind' (D1, p. 266). This desire connects to her predilection for letters that 'create . . . a whole world'.

'Who's going to read all this scribble?' (D5, p. 269)

I would like to argue the case in this chapter for considering the diaries and letters as distinct works of art, on a parallel with, rather than as adjuncts to, Woolf's fiction and criticism. There are, however, difficulties with such an approach. Neither the diaries nor the letters present a homogenous body of writing. Anne Olivier Bell begins her five-volume edition of the diaries in 1915, thereby excluding the earlier extant journals. A number of the early diaries are missing, and there are omissions in the later ones.[56] This is an even more serious impediment when we turn to the letters, where what remains depends on the whim of the addressee and his or her descendants. The diaries are not published as they appear in the notebooks but in chronological sequence.[57] This, rather than classification by theme or recipient, is similarly the order for the published correspondence. There are letters and even a page of the diaries in Leonard Woolf's hand, thus complicating the question of authorship.[58] Both the letters and the diaries require extensive annotation explaining cryptic allusions or the identity of people referred to. In her diaries Woolf often made a shorthand note to herself recalling a scene, person or incident which would remain obscure without editorial comment. The same is true of the letters, which draw on private codes and shared intimacies between sender and receiver. This brings us to the issue of trespass. What right have we to read letters addressed to 'Todger' (L1, p. 64), 'Cresty' (L1, p. 76) and 'Toadlebinks' (L1, p. 159) when they are so clearly not intended for our perusal? Are we justified in reading a set of essentially private journals at all?

The most consistent use Woolf appeared to anticipate for her diaries was as a record for her memoirs.[59] She also imagined herself rereading them for her own amusement.[60] And yet there is evidence in the diaries that she was writing with a reader in view. 'Do I ever write, even here, for my own eye?' she wondered (D5, p. 107), and she opened an entry with a note on Kipling's death and King George V's illness 'forced by a sense of what is expected by the public' (D5, p. 8). She lamented the fact that while she and many of her friends kept a journal 'we daren't trust each other to read our books' (D1, p. 95). Together with Samuel Koteliansky she translated and published fragments from Chekhov's private notebooks – a decision for which she was criticised.[61] Her diaries were one of the few items she salvaged from the bomb-site of her London home (D5, p. 331), and she scrupulously recopied or pasted in entries not written in her actual notebooks.[62] However, while she stated categorically that she did not intend full publication,[63] she did consider that Leonard might make 'a little book' from them though 'the body' would be burned (D3, p. 67). She noted after rereading some of her diaries: 'I confess that the rough & random style of it, often so ungrammatical, & crying for a word altered, afflicted me somewhat' (D1, p. 266). This would seem to suggest that Woolf's resistance to full publication derived from a belief that the diaries needed the same thorough condensation and revision as her fiction and criticism.

Woolf's suicide note to Leonard contained the instruction 'will you destroy all my papers' (L6, p. 487), and there are other instances in the letters that indicate her intention to prohibit their publication. When Violet Dickinson presented her with two bound typescript volumes of her early correspondence she implored: 'all I beg of you is dont let anybody else read those letters' (L6, p. 90), and she entreated Vanessa to burn her letters (L1, p. 366) and not circulate them (L3, p. 368). In a similar vein, she informed Ethel Smyth that she would prefer her letters not to be shown or quoted from as she did not consider them sufficiently well written.[64] There is also evidence, however, to support the opposing view. Woolf pressed for the publication of Dora Carrington's letters after her death (L5, p. 106), and compiled a posthumous volume of her nephew Julian's correspondence: 'nothing seemed to me too private' (L6, p. 245). She described her biography of Roger Fry as 'an amalgamation of all his letters', and her only misgiving about such a method appears to have been her fear that they will be 'of no interest . . . except to his half dozen devotees' (L6, p. 381). At Margaret Llewelyn Davis' request she wrote an introduction to a book that contained private letters without knowing whether the authors wanted 'to appear in print' or not (L4, p. 192). Woolf admitted that one of her 'perversities' was a 'dislike of personal appearances' (L5, p. 89), and she was furious when she discovered that the photographer Giselle Freund planned to exhibit a series of portraits she had reluctantly agreed to on condition that they remained private.[65] Her sensitivity on this point may explain her disinclination for her correspondence to be published during her lifetime at least, a supposition which is given credence by her comment to Ethel Smyth: 'lets leave the letters till we're both dead . . . and let posterity, if there is one, burn or not'.[66]

The evidence therefore appears to indicate that Woolf was averse to the full circulation of her diaries and letters during her lifetime because she believed they were insufficiently crafted and because of her sensitivity to public exposure. The question of their posthumous publication, however, is less certain.

It is possible to justify the publication of the diaries and letters on the grounds of Woolf's feminism. As essays such as *A Room of One's Own* make clear, Woolf was acutely aware of the need for female role-models. She encouraged Ethel Smyth, for example, to write her autobiography since 'there's never been a womans autobiography' (*L6*, p. 453). Her reaction to the publication of Katherine Mansfield's journal similarly furnishes a claim in support of their circulation. In a review of Mansfield's work written shortly after Mansfield's death, Woolf suggested of the journal: 'nothing could be more fragmentary; nothing more private'.[67] And yet Woolf implicitly defended its appearance in a manner that sheds light on how we may view the publication of her own diaries and letters: 'she is a writer; a born writer. Everything she feels and hears and sees is not fragmentary and separate; it belongs together as writing'.[68]

'How difficult it is to collect oneself into one Virginia' (*L4*, p. 397)

Postmodern theory offers a rewarding frame from which to read Woolf's diaries and letters. It has taught us to think differently about the nature of the 'I', which we can no longer assume refers in any straightforward sense to the person who spoke or wrote it. It thus becomes impossible to treat the diaries and letters as the expressions of a coherent self, and we must negotiate instead with a linguistic construct that has only a tenuous relation to its producer. Woolf herself recognised that the self is not static but multiple, dynamic, constantly shifting. 'We're splinters & mosaics; not, as they used to hold, immaculate, monolithic, consistent wholes', she wrote in her diary.[69] Julia Kristeva's description of a 'subject-in-process' – a subject that is endlessly in the process of becoming while subject to the conditions of language – furnishes a useful model.[70] In this light, any endeavour to trace through the writing the truth about the author or her views becomes suspect. Instead, postmodern theory prompts us to concern ourselves with the 'I' as it figures in the text, linking Woolf's diaries and letters to her search for a new form for writing 'corresponding . . . to the dimensions of the human being' (D4, p. 347).

Postmodern theory has also taught us to think differently about writing. An understanding of the mechanisms of language complicates decisions about intention and truth, and the shattering of our belief in linguistic transparency has forced the recognition that buried within writing are alternative possibilities that necessarily disrupt any attempt to fix or define its text. Traditional preoccupations with the author and her views thus give place to an engagement with the multifarious operations of the work itself.

In this chapter I would like to argue for a reading of Woolf's diaries and letters which considers them as writing. The diaries are not simple statements of fact, just as the letters comprise far more than straightforward reporting or unembroidered disclosure. They contain all the ingredients we look for in writing, from the spinning of a narrative, the presentation of characters, description, argument, humour, drama, catastrophe, to complex linguistic configurations such as metaphor and semantic play. Hélène Cixous has delineated a *feminine writing* which refuses the false conventions of omniscient perspective, order, consistency, and definitive summations of people and plot. I believe that this model offers a fruitful context from which to approach the diaries and letters, and to consider to what extent they achieve the new form for writing Woolf so incessantly sought.[71]

'What a discovery that would be – a system that did not shut out' (D4, p. 127)

Throughout her career, Woolf dreamed of a new form for her writing. 'I want to put practically everything in' (D3, p. 210), she wrote of *The Waves*, 'to give the moment whole; whatever it includes'.[72] Her quest extended to her critical writing.[73] She gave her aim in writing her diary as summing up 'the whole of life' (D4, p. 134), and she urged Ethel Smyth to write her 'letters about everything'.[74] She pleaded with Jacques Raverat to make his autobiography 'the waste paper basket, conduit pipe, cesspool, treasure house, and larder and pantry and drawing and dining bed room of your existence. Write about everything, without order, or care' (L3, p. 145). Yet Woolf was too conscious a writer to allow such freedoms to predominate in her own published work; she substantially revised even the most experimental of her novels to amend what she perceived as faults in their structure, balance, tone and the quality of the prose. The uncorrected writing of the diaries and letters may thus come closer to the inclusive ideal Woolf envisioned: 'something swifter & lighter & more colloquial & yet intense: more to the point & less composed; more fluid & following the flight' (D5, p. 298).

For Hélène Cixous, feminine writing strives to avoid a masculine position of mastery which reduces and controls the limitless range of possibilities for its own ends, and seeks, instead, to incorporate everything.[75] It is a writing of the other rather than the self, working to abandon those configurations which utilise or obliterate others and dedicating itself to their faithful recording.[76] Cixous's stress on fidelity to the other is echoed in Woolf's diaries and letters. 'I was trying to get at something about the thing itself before its made into anything', Woolf intimated to Vita Sackville-West, and she stressed that the writer must curb her facility with words and 'stand outside with one's hands folded, until the thing has made itself visible'.[77] She observed to Violet Dickinson: 'my brain . . . floats in blue air; where there are circling clouds, soft sunbeams of elastic gold, and fairy gossamers – things that cant be cut – that must be tenderly enclosed, and expressed in a globe of exquisitely coloured words. At the mere prick of steel they vanish.'[78] In a similar vein, she objected to D. H. Lawrence's letters for their insistent 'philosophy', adding: 'art is being rid of all preaching: things in themselves: the sentence in itself beautiful' (D4, p. 126).

One of the questions the diaries and to some extent the letters raise is the viciousness of their portraits of others. Woolf is uninhibited in her depictions of the weak-spots and foibles of the people she knew, and her descriptions make for stimulating reading. Critics have usually explained the ferociousness of Woolf's accounts by pointing out that they are often a response to other people's selfishness, and are generally modified or reversed by subsequent reports.[79] Since Woolf did not intend her diaries or correspondence for full-scale publication it can also be argued that her portrayals are the products of frustration rather than an unwarranted annihilation of the other. Viewed in this way, they become the expression of what is outlawed from social intercourse – the things we feel, but are conditioned not to say.

It is also important to note that the other is treated differently in the diaries and correspondence. While the letters are generally less savage in their presentations of the people Woolf knew, there is a greater degree of seduction as the 'I' endeavours to ingratiate itself with or control the reactions of its interlocutor.[80] In this sense, it is possible to argue that Woolf's diaries, with their relative unconcern with the self's public image, offer the more complete illustration of feminine writing.

'To adventure & discover, & allow no rigid poses: to be supple & naked to the truth' (D4, p. 252)

Cixous suggests that the first step towards a feminine mode of writing is stringent work on the self, and Woolf's diaries and letters demonstrate this process.[81] 'Always shave off the expected, dictated attitude; & find whats under it', Woolf noted in her diary (D5, p. 205). To be an artist 'one must cease to be Mary', she observed (D4, p. 231), and she chafed against reviewers whose verdicts inhibited her progress: 'I wish I need never read about myself, or think about myself, anyhow till its done, but look firmly at my object & think only of expressing it.'[82] She related to John Lehmann that her aim in *The Waves* had been 'to eliminate . . . myself',[83] and in a letter to Ethel Smyth argued: 'I believe unconsciousness, and complete anonymity to be the only conditions . . . in which I can write'.[84] Woolf's progress in this respect can be charted in the gradual eradication of the 'I' from her fiction, in favour, in the later novels, of a multiple, all-embracing 'we': '"I" rejected: "We" substituted . . . composed of . . . all life, all art, all waifs & strays.'[85]

Feminine writing does not, however, mean the negation or obliteration of the self, since this would merely reverse the destructive hierarchy of relations between subject and other. Instead, feminine writing recognises that there is no universal or neutral truth, and that one's perspective is necessarily filtered through one's needs, desires, questions, prejudices and fears. This awareness is mirrored in the form of the diaries and letters, where a consistent, omniscient overview is absent. For Cixous, such a position places considerable onus on the writer to achieve self-knowledge, a point that is made by Woolf: 'I dont think you can get your words to come till youre almost unconscious; and unconsciousness only comes when youve been beaten and broken and gone through every sort of grinding mill' (L5, p. 408). The diaries in particular can be viewed as an endeavour to assuage and comprehend the self.

The speed at which the diaries and letters were written evokes Cixous's insistence that feminine writing must be free.[86] Woolf described how her diary was written at a 'rapid haphazard gallop', 'rather faster than the fastest typewriting', and 'if I stopped & took thought, it would never be written at all'.[87] The same appears to have been true of her letters.[88] Replying to Clive Bell's query as to whether she liked his letters she intimated 'you think more pains are needed than I do', and urged him to 'put your style at the gallop' (L1, p. 362). To Gerald Brenan she defined letter-writing as 'a mere tossing of omelettes . . . if they break and squash, can't be helped' (L3, p. 80). 'I dont think I've ever taken more time than it takes to form a word in writing to you', she confessed to Ethel Smyth (*L6*, p. 439), and to Pernel Strachey: 'I can only write, letters that is, if I don't read them: once think and I destroy' (*L3*, p. 63). This is in marked contrast to her published writings which were painstakingly redrafted and rewritten. She reworked some scenes of *The Years* so that 'hardly a line of the original is left' (*D4*, p. 266), and many of the sentences of *Roger Fry* were 're-written a dozen times'.[89] Her diaries and letters offered a welcome release from such 'strain':[90] she told Ethel Smyth that she could not rewrite a letter because it would be 'stale' (*L6*, p. 78) and she frequently turned to her diary with 'relief' at being able 'to write a free sentence here' (*D5*, p. 190).

Woolf's diaries and letters also indicate how she followed the rhythms and flows of writing itself.[91] Cixous argues that the feminine writer must be attentive to the play of writing, and actively incorporate its myriad possibilities. For Cixous, the multiple and heterogeneous suggestions thus produced challenge the rule of linear logic, objective viewpoint and the single, self-referential meaning decreed. This position is echoed by Woolf. 'All books now seem to me surrounded by a circle of invisible censors' (*D5*, p. 229) she noted, and she warned herself as she reread her diaries 'not to play the part of the censor'.[92]

Feminine writing involves constant endeavour, since the writer must strive to prevent her language from altering or destroying her subject. Woolf observed in her diary: 'I was telling myself the story of our visit to the Hardys & I began to compose it . . . But the actual event was different' (*D3*, p. 102), and she outlined her writing as follows: 'I shall see a light in the depths of the sea, and stealthily approach – for one's sentences are only an approximation, a net one flings over some sea pearl which may vanish; and if one brings it up it wont be anything like what it was when I saw it, under the sea'.[93] Feminine writing also requires the taking of risks. 'I have to some extent forced myself to break every mould & find a fresh form of being, that is of expression, for everything I feel & think' Woolf observed (*D4*, p. 233). The word 'being' is especially striking in this passage, recalling both the aliveness of feminine writing and Woolf's quest for a new form.

An important aspect of Cixous's account of feminine writing is its inscription of what is repressed within history and culture. 'Writing 'give[s] us . . . back our dead alive', Cixous suggests,[94] and Woolf's diaries in particular contain reminders of those she lost.[95] Feminine writing similarly gives voice to what is painful or taboo. Woolf wrote of sanitary towels, the menopause, diarrhoea, incest, homosexuality and rape in her diaries and letters; she recounted a dream in which she passionately kissed her niece, and reported a conversation in a ladies' lavatory.[96] Encompassing what is painful may in turn inflict pain on the reader. Cixous quotes Kafka's aphorism that 'a book must be the axe for the frozen sea inside us',[97] and this is paralleled in Woolf's reflection: 'how can one weight and sharpen dialogue till each sentence tears its way like a harpoon and grapples with the shingles at the bottom of the reader's soul?' (L3, p. 36).

Recalling Cixous's descriptions of feminine writing, Woolf endorsed the crucial role played by the body and the unconscious. 'How tremendously important unconsciousness is when one writes', she recorded in her diary,[98] and 'what a little I can get down with my pen of what is so vivid to my eyes, & not only to my eyes: also to some nervous fibre or fan like membrane in my spine' (D3, p. 191). She delineated the different bodily 'symptoms' her various books produced (D4, p. 143), and her diary-writing in particular was constantly interrupted by physical sensations.[99] Even an imperfect nib could inhibit the corporal process of writing, and Woolf was vehemently opposed to the typewriter (L3, p. 507).

Cixous suggests that writing requires a corresponding attitude of femininity from the reader if it is to be brought alive, and Woolf's diaries and letters document her awareness of this.[100] 'When one reads the mind is like an aeroplane propeller invisibly quick and unconscious' she noted (D5, p. 151), and 'heaven must be one continuous unexhausted reading. Its a disembodied trance-like intense rapture' comparable to 'flying.'[101]

Finally, feminine writing has radical implications for genre. The feminine writer's endeavour to give voice to the other explodes conventional notions of character as a stable, coherent entity whose behaviour can be predicted and made use of. Similarly, in Woolf's diaries and letters, we have an incessant panoply of recurring and disappearing figures, contradictory, complex and necessarily viewed through the desiring and various self. The feminine writer's duty to be all-embracing prevents the adoption of traditional literary structures; while even the most experimental of Woolf's fictions exhibits careful composition her diaries and letters involve no such arrangement. The experience of reading is one of immersion: we are plunged into recollections, feelings, plans, flashes of insight, questions, thoughts – 'life itself going on' (D3, p. 229). The diaries and letters thus offer themselves as writings which refuse mastery and artificial order to embody, instead, 'the texture of the ordinary day' (D2, p. 298).

'Writing must be formal', Woolf reminded herself as she reread her diary (D2, p. 321), and although she contemplated transferring the freedom of her diary and letter-writing to her fiction and criticism the censor in her remained strong.[102] Her plan for *The Years*, for example, 'to take in everything' dwindled as she painstakingly wrote and rewrote each page

(*D*4, p. 129), while her diaries and letters were spared such revisions.[103] And yet the shadow of the censor threatened even here. Woolf frequently reproached herself for the poor quality of her letters. 'This is vilely written', she lamented to Emma Vaughan,[104] and she told Vita Sackville-West, 'I would write a draft if I could, of my letters; and so tidy them and compact them.'[105] 'This diary writing does not count as writing', she insisted,[106] and an unplanned internal rhyme is followed by the comment '(if I were writing I should have to remove either lies or eyes)'.[107] This returns us to the issue of trespass, and opens an alternative aesthetic to the one propounded by Hélène Cixous. We may feel that Woolf is right, that many of her letters are frankly boring, and it is a Herculean task to wade through every entry of the diaries. The answer seems to be to read in a new way, allowing ourselves to skim and ponder as we acknowledge our predilections and needs.

'The singing of the real world' (*D*3, p. 260)

Early in her diaries Woolf wrote:

> There looms ahead of me the shadow of some kind of form which a diary might attain to. I might in the course of time learn what it is that one can make of this loose, drifting material of life; finding another use for it than the use I put it to, so much more consciously & scrupulously, in fiction.
>
> (*D*1, p. 266)

While neither her diaries nor her letters met Woolf's strict standards, and were consequently dismissed by her from full-scale publication, it is my contention that they may be productively viewed in the context of postmodern theories of writing. With their inclusiveness and fidelity to the disorder and flow of real life, they embrace both the dross and the poetry – the babble and the rhapsody – and point to the accomplishment of that new form for writing for which Woolf was searching throughout her career.

NOTES

1 See *L*2, p. 522.
2 The early diaries are published as *EJ*, ed. Mitchell A. Leaska (London: Hogarth, 1990).
3 See the 'Introduction' to *D*1, p. xiii. The backcovers of the Penguin edition cite a representative range of reviewers' comments.
4 There are, of course, exceptions. Linda Anderson's 'Virginia Woolf: "In the Shadow of the Letter 'I'"' in *Women and Autobiography in the Twentieth Century: Remembered Futures*, ed. Linda Anderson (Hemel Hempstead:

Prentice Hall/Harvester Wheatsheaf, 1997), pp. 42–75, and Catharine R. Stimpson's 'The Female Sociograph: The Theater of Virginia Woolf's Letters' in *The Female Autograph*, ed. Domna C. Stanton (The University of Chicago Press, 1984), pp. 168–79, are refreshing attempts to review the diaries and letters in the context of female autobiography.

5 For examples of the latter, see $D2$, p. 125, $D3$, p. 110, $D3$, p. 112.

6 This is particularly noteworthy in the light of evidence that Woolf tried to commit suicide some days before she finally succeeded. See $L6$, pp. 489–91.

7 See, for example, her comment on the General Strike of 1926: 'I suppose all pages devoted to the Strike will be skipped, when I read over this book. Oh that dull old chapter, I shall say. Excitements about what are called real things are always unutterably transitory' ($D3$, p. 85).

8 See $L1$, p. xxi.

9 See, for example, $L1$, p. 38, $L3$, p. 163; $D3$, p. 96, $D3$, p. 329.

10 See, for example, $D1$, p. 138, $D3$, p. 52, $D3$, p. 316, $D4$, p. 297; $L1$, p. 41, $L5$, p. 321, $L6$, p. 379.

11 While this is most obviously true of the diaries, the letters also reflect this. See, for example, the series of letters written to Vanessa Bell concerning Woolf's endeavours to find her domestic help ($L2$, pp. 318–21).

12 See $D1$, p. 178, $D2$, p. 188, $D2$, p. 208, $D3$, p. 7, $D4$, p. 157; $L1$, p. 45, $L2$, p. 205, $L2$, p. 525, $L2$, p. 548; EJ, p. 275; also note 16 below.

13 See the cluster of diary entries charting 'the temperature' ($D3$, p. 16) of public reaction each time one of her books appears.

14 This is a persistent theme of the diaries and is also frequently alluded to in the letters (see $L3$, p. 244, $L4$, p. 200, $L4$, p. 222, $L4$, p. 318).

15 See $D2$, p. 207, $D3$, p. 18, $D3$, p. 36, $D3$, p. 229, $D3$, p. 236.

16 See $D2$, p. 323, $D3$, p. 275, $D3$, p. 285, $D3$, p. 339, $D4$, p. 152, $D4$, p. 173, $D4$, p. 221.

17 Examples are $D3$, p. 106, $D3$, p. 264, $D3$, p. 343, $D4$, p. 161.

18 See $D1$, p. 259, $D2$, p. 199, $D5$, p. 75.

19 $D3$, p. 161, see also $D2$, p. 248, $D3$, p. 59.

20 $D5$, p. 262, see also $D5$, p. 222 and below.

21 $D4$, p. 338. Another example is her account of her cousin Harry Stephen whose obsessive playing with 'an enormous pocket knife' foreshadows Peter Walsh in *Mrs D.* ($D1$, p. 151).

22 $L1$, p. 382, $L2$, p. 588, $L3$, p. 3, $L4$, p. 231, $L4$, p. 397.

23 See $L4$, p. 354.

24 $L2$, p. 400, $L3$, p. 385, $L4$, p. 231, $L6$, p. 116.

25 See $L1$, p. 362.

26 Examples are $L2$, p. 598, $L3$, p. 135, $L4$, p. 66.

27 See $L4$, p. 195.

28 $L1$, p. 356, see also $L2$, p. 82.

29 See $D1$, p. 266, $D2$, p. 319, $D2$, p. 320, $D3$, p. 293, $D5$, p. 26, $D5$, p. 95, $D5$, p. 290, also EJ, particularly the 'Warboys' and the 1903 journals, pp. 135–213.

30 See $D2$, p. 252, also $D2$, p. 86, $D3$, p. 326, $D4$, p. 67, $D4$, p. 69, $D4$, p. 212, $D4$, p. 240, $D5$, p. 266.

31 For example, the diaries and letters reveal both Woolf's longing to have children

and her view of motherhood as 'destructive and limiting' (see D_3, p. 241, D_3, p. 254, D_5, p. 106 and L_3, p. 366).

32 As I have been asked to do in this chapter.

33 D_1, p. 106, see also D_3, p. 194, D_5, p. 25, D_5, p. 179.

34 See, for example, D_2, p. 143 and L_2, p. 493.

35 Though see her comments to Violet Dickinson L_1, p. 114 and L_1, p. 147, and below.

36 See D_4, p. 18, D_4, p. 162, D_4, p. 336, D_5, pp. 337–8.

37 See D_4, p. 15, D_4, p. 122, D_4, p. 200, D_4, p. 346.

38 Examples are D_4, p. 35, D_5, p. 55.

39 See D_4, p. 308, EJ, p. 317.

40 See, for example, D_5, p. 120, D_5, p. 192, EJ, p. 358.

41 L_1, p. 77, see also L_1, p. 79, L_1, p. 144, L_6, p. 152 and D_3, p. 302.

42 It is noteworthy that in her diary Woolf acknowledged the changing relationship one has to one's correspondents as circumstances and perceptions change. See D_1, p. 121, also D_1, p. 235.

43 See, for example, L_1, p. 273 and below.

44 D_2, p. 72 and L_2, p. 441.

45 See, as an illustration, her positive reaction to Jane Austen's letters (L_5, p. 127).

46 L_5, p. 354; see also her request to Molly MacCarthy to write a second book 'made entirely of letters' (L_2, p. 276) and her advice to read letters to the beginning writer Ling Su-Hua (L_6, p. 222).

47 L_4, p. 97, see also her comments to Ethel Smyth, 'how I hate writing and the futility of all human intercourse has never seemed to me greater' (L_4, p. 382) and Vita Sackville-West, 'this letter writing business is such a fraud' (L_6, p. 225).

48 'The difficulty of writing letters is, for one thing, that one has to simplify so much, and hasn't the courage to dwell on the small catastrophes which are of such huge interest to oneself; and thus has to put on a kind of unreal personality; which, when I write to you for example, whom I've not seen these 11 years, becomes inevitably jocular. I suppose joviality is a convenient mask' (L_3, p. 136).

49 *Ibid.*

50 L_6, p. 311; see also Woolf's description of 'perhaps the most brilliant' of her own letters as 'full of scandal, confidences, self reproach, remorse, revelation, together with character sketches' (L_4, p. 308) and her comment to R. C. Trevelyan that what she enjoyed in his published letters was being able 'to trace the character of the writer, the peculiar humour and idiosyncracy [*sic*] of his mind' (L_6, p. 348).

51 D_3, p. 239, also D_5, p. 334.

52 See D_5, p. 244, also D_4, p. 14 and D_4, p. 286.

53 D_1, p. 134, D_2, p. 53, D_3, p. 195.

54 D_3, p. 35, see also D_2, p. 252, D_4, p. 40, D_4, p. 318, D_5, p. 320.

55 D_1, p. 239, see also D_2, p. 138, D_2, p. 141, D_2, p. 176, D_3, p. 6.

56 For instance no journal survives for the period from December 1897 to August 1899 and the notebook in which Woolf kept a record of her French journey is lost (D_5, p. 219). The omissions in the later journals are often due to ill health (and see, for example, L_2, p. 32).

57 Woolf would sometimes fill the end of an old notebook rather than continue in sequence.

58 See D_1, p. 74.
59 D_1, p. 234, D_3, p. 58, D_3, p. 125, D_5, p. 61, D_5, p. 181, D_5, p. 222, D_5, p. 235, D_5, p. 269, D_5, p. 332.
60 D_2, p. 24, D_4, p. 24, D_5, p. 227, D_5, p. 352. There are also passages in the diaries where she has done just this, see, for example, D_4, p. 167, D_5, p. 204.
61 See D_2, p. 123.
62 See D_1, p. 233.
63 See D_5, p. 162, D_5, p. 266.
64 L_4, p. 217, see also L_5, p. 236.
65 L_6, p. 351, see also D_5, p. 220 and her letter arguing for personal privacy to *The New Statesman* (L_5, pp. 237–80).
66 L_6, p. 272, see also her comment to Ottoline Morrell: 'I'm only anxious that we shall all figure truthfully for the sake of literature' (L_6, p. 511).
67 'A Terribly Sensitive Mind', in CE_1 (London: Hogarth, 1966), p. 356.
68 *Ibid.*
69 D_2, p. 314, see also D_3, p. 12, D_4, p. 329; L_4, p. 188, L_5, p. 445.
70 See my discussion in *Language and Sexual Difference: Feminist Writing in France* (Basingstoke: Macmillan, 1991), pp. 48–52.
71 For a full account of Cixous's view of feminine writing see my discussion in *Hélène Cixous: Authorship, Autobiography and Love* (Cambridge: Polity Press, 1996), pp. 1–23.
72 D_3, p. 209. Her search is reflected in her endeavour to find a new name for her fiction: 'I have an idea that I will invent a new name for my books to supplant "novel". A new – . . . But what?' (D_3, p. 34), see also D_3, p. 203, D_3, p. 229, D_4, p. 129.
73 See D_5, p. 298.
74 L_4, p. 211, see also L_1, p. 282, L_4, p. 215 and L_5, p. 346 where she describes the most effective letters as 'a haul of live water, with crabs and sand in it, out of the real sea'.
75 See Woolf's comment on her plans for *Jacob's Room* – the first of her experimental novels – that it is to 'enclose everything, everything' (D_2, p. 13).
76 See, for example, Cixous's delineation of the feminine writer in *Vivre l'orange* (Paris: des femmes, 1979): 'there are women who speak to watch over and save, not to catch, with voices almost invisible, attentive and precise like virtuoso fingers, and swift as birds' beaks, but not to seize and mean, voices to remain near by things, as their luminous shadow, to reflect and protect the things that are ever as delicate as the newly-born' (p. 8, translation by Sarah Cornell and Ann Liddle).
77 L_3, p. 321, see also L_3, p. 432.
78 L_1, p. 320. Similarly, Woolf informed Clive Bell that what she hoped to give in her writing was 'the feel of running water' (L_1, p. 308); she likened the writing mind to a 'cauldron, which must bubble as richly as possible before its poured & stilled & hardened' (D_4, p. 96); and recorded with pleasure that *The Waves* 'is alive: because it has not crushed the thing I wanted to say' (D_3, p. 298).
79 See, for example, Anne Olivier Bell's 'Preface' to D_2, pp. viii–ix.
80 Good examples are the letters Woolf wrote to Ethel Smyth on 8 and 13 October 1931 (L_4, pp. 388–9).
81 Cixous gives a full account of this apprenticeship in her essay 'De la scène de

l'Inconscient à la scène de l'Histoire', in *Hélène Cixous: Chemins d'une écriture*, eds. Françoise Van Rossum-Guyon and Myriam Diaz-Diocaretz (Amsterdam: Rodopi, and Saint Denis: Presses Universitaires de Vincennes, 1990).

82 *D*4, p. 289, see also her comment: 'I think writing, my writing, is a species of mediumship. I become the person' (*D*5, p. 101).

83 *L*4, p. 381, see also *L*5, p. 193, *L*5, p. 195.

84 *L*5, p. 239, see also *L*5, p. 242.

85 *D*5, p. 135, the citation refers to *Between the Acts*.

86 See, for example, Cixous's essay 'Sorties' in *The Newly Born Woman*, translated by Betsy Wing (Minneapolis: University of Minnesota Press, and Manchester University Press, 1986).

87 *D*1, pp. 233–4, see also *D*1, p. 266, *D*2, p. 250.

88 See *L*1, p. 29, *L*3, p. 247, *L*3, p. 254, *L*4, p. 332.

89 *D*5, p. 197, see also *D*5, p. 261 for an example of her rewriting of *Roger Fry* and *L*3, p. 474.

90 *D*4, p. 306. Woolf's use of the word 'architecting' is interesting in this passage and echoes her comments elsewhere that her revision was a question of 'my craft not my creation' (*D*5, p. 4).

91 See, for example, *D*2, p. 322, *D*3, p. 276, *D*3, p. 316; *L*4, p. 204.

92 *D*1, p. 266, see also her condemnation of her 'soul' for 'framing all these judgments, & saying as she sits by the fire, this is not to my liking, this is second rate, this vulgar; this nice, sincere, & so on. And how should my soul know?' (*D*2, p. 236).

93 *L*4, p. 223, see also *L*3, p. 529.

94 Cixous, *Three Steps on the Ladder of Writing*, trans. by Sarah Cornell and Susan Sellers (New York: Columbia University Press, 1993), p. 12.

95 See, for example, *D*2, p. 190, *D*2, p. 300, *D*3, p. 208, *D*3, p. 317, *D*5, p. 85. Cixous's concern here is similarly paralleled in Woolf's desire to preserve what is transient: see *D*2, p. 311, *D*3, p. 209, *D*4, p. 94 and above.

96 See *L*5, p. 417; *D*5, p. 357.

97 Cixous, *Three Steps on the Ladder of Writing*, p. 17.

98 *D*4, p. 186, see also *L*5, p. 422.

99 See, as an example, *D*2, p. 307.

100 See Cixous's thoughts on this subject in 'Conversations' in *Writing Differences: Readings from the Seminar of Hélène Cixous*, ed. Susan Sellers (Milton Keynes: The Open University Press, 1988), pp. 141–54.

101 *L*5, p. 319, see also *L*5, p. 140; *D*2, p. 133, *D*3, p. 270.

102 See, for example, *D*2, p. 312, *D*4, p. 199 and above.

103 See *D*4, p. 141.

104 *L*1, p. 29, see also *L*1, p. 102, *L*1, p. 109, *L*4, p. 217.

105 *L*3, p. 247, see also *L*1, p. 309, *L*1, p. 361.

106 *D*1, p. 233, see also *D*1, p. 266, *D*5, p. 335.

107 *D*5, pp. 256–7, see also Woolf's account of how, even when she is not writing, 'my mind is hard at work (in my absence) arranging, editing, bringing forward, eliminating' (*D*4, p. 100).

7

MARIA DiBATTISTA

Virginia Woolf and the language of authorship

Words

In 1915, under the terms of the National Registration Act, Virginia Woolf was registered by her husband Leonard as an 'author'.[1] This official classification seems straightforward enough. The literary vocation of Virginia Woolf seems a public fact, now as then, to which we might hardly give a second thought, especially given the avalanche of work on her literary ideas, politics, psychology, autobiographical and critical writings that began with Quentin Bell's 1972 biography of his aunt and gathered force and momentum with the publication of her complete diaries, letters and collected essays. In truth, everything about Virginia Woolf, author, is in danger of becoming benignly familiar to common readers as well as professional critics – her life, her critical precepts, her feminist politics, the distinctive rhythms of her prose.

Yet, just when we believe Woolf is securely enshrined in the niche ('modern author, female') assigned to her, we encounter, as we do in a radio address entitled 'Craftsmanship', a writer whose relationship to words strikes us as either so advanced or so primitive as to confound any settled view we might have of her. Woolf begins this talk, part of a series devoted to the theme 'Why Words Fail Us', by confessing to a limited knowledge of her subject: 'Now we know little that is certain about words,' she disingenuously remarks, 'but this we do know – words never make anything that is useful; and words are the only things that tell the truth and nothing but the truth.'[2] This is an extraordinary claim and we hardly know how to credit it. First, there is the questionable assertion, which Woolf treats as incontrovertible fact, that words never make anything useful. But of course they do – they are used to make inventories, manuals and guides, contracts, treaties, to name only a few of the useful forms words may take, as Woolf elsewhere openly acknowledges.[3] We can only surmise that she is deliberately exaggerating both the total uselessness and the absolute truth-value of words in order to dramatise a rather more reasonable and subtle point – namely, that words do not fail us; we fail them. Perhaps such a judgement also underlies her claim that words always tell the truth and nothing but the truth. She speaks in legal terms, as if words themselves were perpetually 'under oath'. It is we, she insinuates, who lie and deceive and employ words for fraudulent ends.

Not everyone believes words have no useful function to perform or uses them with such strict regard for truth. Only authors do. No one exemplifies this dictum better than Woolf herself. In assessing what was singular and impracticable, even iconoclastic about her relationship to words, it is worth recalling, first of all, the etymological origin of authorship in *augere*, to increase. An author is a creator, then, in the sense that writing *adds* something to our store of information about the world, enlarges the range of experience allotted to us and expands our sense of what words can mean and what they can do when liberated from the utilitarian purposes to which we commonly enlist them.

Certainly no one could accuse Woolf of making words perform any practical work.[4] The language of authorship for her is a distinctly literary language that pays slight court to the common usages of life. It is in fact surprising how little of her feeling for words is aroused by the colloquial-isms and neologisms peculiar to modern times. Her fictional language remains relatively unaffected either by the slang heard in the streets or the specialised jargon of scientific or social elites. Although she does not flinch before lewd realities, obscene words are not part of her vocabulary, as they are, for example, of that garrulous marvel of modern fiction, Molly Bloom. Nor does Woolf adapt the terminology being spawned by the 'new' physics, as D. H. Lawrence did the language of electromagnetism, to express her vision of reality. Perhaps most surprising, given her repeated declarations that modern fiction is rightly concerned in illuminating the 'dark places of psychology', is the relatively traditional language Woolf uses in her own representations of the mind, what it contains and what it produces. Woolf speaks of the mind's sensations and impressions in ways that make her more conversant with Hume and Locke than with modern psychologists and their talk of libido and drives. Even Woolf's use of the word 'atoms' in her famous description of how little pellets of perception fall upon the mind like an 'incessant shower'[5] is one that Democritus, the fifth-century philosopher who gave the word its modern meaning, might have under-stood. While she was certainly aware of psychoanalysis and reviewed the newest instances of Freudian fiction (the title of one of her reviews),[6] she avoided radically assimilating its language to her own. Her characters may exhibit the *symptoms* of the mental afflictions that preoccupy modern psychology, but neither they nor the narrator make explicit reference to the diagnostic *nomenclature* of psychoanalysis. Words like hysteria, complex, repression, trauma, melancholia, fetishism, cathexis are either absent or rarely encountered in her fiction, and even then, as Hermione Lee observes, only in the late work of the 1930s. Perhaps Woolf found these words too clinically 'useful'; perhaps she was not convinced of their truth-value. Whatever her reasons, Woolf, who, as Lee also remarks, was caught between 'competing narratives of mental illness – Darwinian, moralistic, Freudian', preferred to create 'an original language of her own . . . which could explain her illness to her and give it value'.[7]

Virginia Woolf, author, might thus justly be characterised as a radical conservative in practising her craft. The most obvious sign of her linguistic conservatism is that, unlike Joyce, she never played too freely with the material form of words. Perhaps she feared that their truth-content might leak out if words were broken up into their component parts or if their letters were rearranged to form anagrams or neologisms in the jocular style of free-wheeling modernists. Certainly she never contemplated *inventing* a language, as Joyce did in *Finnegans Wake*, that would amalgamate all known forms of expression from the litter/letter of post-Babelian humanity. Nor on a more modest scale does she indulge in word-play of the kind that entrances and amuses. The pun hardly appears in her fiction, whereas for a writer like Beckett, who once affirmed 'In the beginning was the pun',[8] there could be no authorship without this initial doubleness and potential duplicity at the very heart of language, which dates to the beginning of the world.

Only once did Woolf stage the kind of word-play in which *Ulysses* displays its irreverent modernism – in the sky-writing sequence of *Mrs Dalloway*:

> Dropping dead down, the aeroplane soared straight up, curved in a loop, raced, sank, rose, and whatever it did, wherever it went, out fluttered behind it a thick ruffled bar of white smoke which curled and wreathed upon the sky in letters. But what letters? A C was it? an E, then an L? Only for a moment did they lie still; then they moved and melted and were rubbed out up in the sky, and the aeroplane shot further away and again, in a fresh space of sky began writing a K, an E, a Y perhaps? (p. 29)

The 'K E (Y?)' to this enigmatic script, as it transpires, proves to be nothing more lofty than an advertisement. Woolf doubtless intended a sly jab at the dream entertained by Joyce's imaginative hero, the ad-man Leopold Bloom, whose habitual 'final meditations' before retiring to bed centre on 'some one sole unique advertisement to cause passers to stop in wonder, a poster novelty with all extraneous accretions excluded, reduced to its simplest and most efficient terms not exceeding the span of casual vision and congruous with the velocity of modern life.'[9] The novelty of sky-writing,[10] aside from its unusual choice for a pen, is that words are no sooner formed than they dissolve. Though it might satisfy Bloom's criteria of being consonant with the velocity of modern life, the simple, efficient and wondrous message written on air proves to be not only an instantaneous, but a radically unstable one. While ground-gazers stutter out the letters, the plane, using the sky as its parchment, is transformed into a vehicle for ethereal authorship, 'the symbol of something which has soared beyond seeking and questing and knocking of words together and has become all spirit, disembodied, ghostly' (p. 42).

Woolf would later return to more homely ground to dramatise how language might be used *before* the seeking and questing and knocking of words together. Here, for example, is a pedestrian scene from *Between the Acts*, a novel urgently concerned with recovering a primordial relation to words:

> The nurses after breakfast were trundling the perambulator up and down the terrace; and as they trundled they were talking – not shaping pellets of information or handing ideas from one to another, but rolling words, like sweets on their tongues; which, as they thinned to transparency, gave off pink, green, and sweetness.[11]

The custodians of the young are also conservators and curators of what we might classify as a form of ur-language, language before it becomes devoted to practical ends, like recording information or transmitting ideas. The nurses are not 'coining' words into expressive shapes, as Woolf speculates the people of Babel did in the beginning, 'taking . . . pain in one hand, and a lump of pure sound in the other'.[12] On the contrary, their talk conveys nothing of substance. Their words are verbal confections that, as they liquefy, release their sweetness and colour. No meaning is 'released' by the increasingly transparent nuggets of sound they roll off their tongues, yet they contain a reality as palpable, as nutritive for the mind, hungry for sensations, as any words graven in tablets of indigestible stone.

These last examples suggest that Virginia Woolf's relationship with words was never secure, nor was it even healthy, if health is measured by a commonsensical determination to let words retain the meanings and practical uses, some of them actually quite nuanced and refined, they have in common parlance. I will be devoting the major portion of this chapter to enumerating the ways Woolf helped create the syntax and rhythms of modern prose, but we cannot understand, much less appreciate, how much

Woolf extended the boundaries of modern writing unless we remark how much she was willing to forgo, as well as preserve, in making her unique representations of the world. An irony confronts us, then, at the outset of any consideration of the literary language fashioned by Virginia Woolf, the author of novels, essays, political tracts, one biography (two, if you count *Flush* and why shouldn't we?) and many abbreviated literary portraits, including the partial self-portraits collected in *Moments of Being*. The irony, which has the potential of ripening into a paradox, is this: Virginia Woolf is a writer who increased our sense of what writing is by taking away as much as she bestowed.

Voices

Nowhere does this irony resonate more plangently than in the pages of Erich Auerbach's magisterial history of realism in western literature, *Mimesis*. When Auerbach, marooned in Turkey during the Second World War, sought a work representative of the modernist 'epoch', he chose *To the Lighthouse*. At the time it must have seemed an odd, even eccentric choice. Indeed his initial effort to describe what arrests his attention as 'new' in Woolf's prose style suggests that he selected Woolf's novel for what was in fact anomalous in her rendering of reality. In the course of summarising the events and motifs represented in a passage he has extracted for analysis, he suddenly comes upon a phrase, unremarkable in itself, that confounds him. It is a phrase describing Mrs Ramsay in a certain mood and in a certain light: 'Never did anybody look so sad.' Auerbach, as if taken aback, almost blurts out the question that opens the following paragraph: 'Who is speaking in this paragraph?' His question is not a rhetorical one, although it may appear to be. He poses this question as if in finding an answer he might unlock the mystery of narrative speech itself, by which not only human beings, but entire societies and even worlds are predicated and brought to life.

Auerbach is beginning to feel, somewhat urgently, the absence of the familiar, reassuring presence who has accompanied him as he read through western literature from its founding texts, the Bible and Homer's *Odyssey*, to the modern realist works of Cervantes, Stendhal and Flaubert – the figure of the author. He tentatively concludes that while it is Virginia Woolf, the author, speaking, 'she does not seem to bear in mind that she is the author and hence ought to know how matters stand with her characters'. Struck by the uncertainty with which the author conveys the impressions and feelings that fill the consciousness of her characters, Auerbach openly wonders at the 'doubtful, obscure suppositions' that replace the objective certainties of the traditional narrator who presents and interprets his characters with robust confidence. Could these suppositious musings about a woman looking so sad originate in a non-human order? Are these speakers not 'human beings at all but spirits between heaven and earth, nameless spirits capable of penetrating the depths of the human soul, capable too of knowing something about it, but not of attaining clarity as to what is in process there, with the result that what they report has a doubtful ring, comparable in a way to those "certain airs, detached from the body of the wind" which in a later passage move about the house at night "questioning and wondering?"'[13]

In passages such as the one that perplexes Auerbach, Woolf extended modern authorship to the verge where the distinct 'voice of the author' – let us call it the voice of the narrative person, whether young or old, male or female, well- or ill-educated – merges with and is absorbed into a language 'voiced' by no one we can easily identify, much less locate. Late in her life, Woolf thought that authors might be divided into two kinds: the ventriloquists and the soliloquists.[14] Woolf's own progress as an author might be charted as a series of attempts to orchestrate the two kinds of literary performance not harmonically, but in counterpoint. Her fictions are structured by alternating currents of poetic soliloquy and novelistic impersonation. The strange consonance Woolf makes of their fundamental differences helps explain the peculiar effect of Woolf's narrative voice, at once so intimate and confiding, yet capable of cool, even savagely ironic detachment.[15]

Let us first parse the ventriloquist's mode of authorship, one rooted in the common language of the people. It is as a ventriloquist that Woolf is most conscious of her ties to tradition; it is as a ventriloquist, we might say, that she offered her famous maxim on the language of masterpieces in *A Room of One's Own*: 'For masterpieces are not single and solitary births; they are the outcome of many years of thinking in common, of thinking by the body of the people, so that the experience of the mass is behind the single voice.'[16] Like all great originals, Woolf returned to a traditional form to embody the experience of the mass: the chorus, steeped in convention, suspicious of moral renegades and wary of any radical departure from the established order of things. The voice of the chorus is thus not to be confused with the voice of mass or popular culture. It is not the voice of the crowd or of the faceless masses. Her fiction shares little of the literary naturalist's 'lowbrow' fascination with the pungent, often racy language and entertainments spawned by and for mass culture. What unites the chorus and shapes their common language are the shared values that emerge out of a long and common experience of living and thinking together, not the tastes bred by the fashions of the lively but fugitive moment. This choric voice begins sounding in *Mrs Dalloway*, dissolves in the lyric meditations of *The Waves*, is revived in *The Years*, only to be fragmented and dispersed into the 'stray voices, voices without bodies, symbolical voices' (p. 151) that sound, alternately stentorian and muffled, throughout *Between the Acts*. This last was the novel in which Woolf set out to test the limits of her negative capability, not so much by suspending, as rejecting entirely 'the damned egotistical self' (*D2*, p. 14) she discerned and disliked in the writing of Joyce and Dorothy Richardson, two pioneers in the 'stream-of-consciousness' technique that tracked the mind's undifferentiated flow of thoughts and sensations.

Woolf, for her part, was busy devising a form supple enough to allow her to write indiscriminately about 'anything that comes into my head', while avoiding the shoals of egotism on which, to her mind, so much modern writing foundered. Her diary records her determination to discuss all literature

> in connection with real little incongruous living humor: & anything that comes into my head; but 'I' rejected: 'We' substituted: to whom at the end there shall be an invocation? 'We' . . . composed of many different things . . . we all life, all art, all waifs & strays – a rambling capricious but somehow unified whole – the present state of my mind? (*D5*, p. 135)

The novelist's rambling, capricious mind, so attuned to the 'many different things' that combine to form the plural 'We,' seems especially susceptible to having its own stray thoughts swept along by the irresistible currents of collective emotion. Woolf's prose is frequently infected by the contagion of group feeling, which alters the rhythm and accelerates the momentum of her sentences. We can see such contagion at work in Woolf's description of the royal cavalcade in *Mrs Dalloway*. As it makes its way through London, the car 'bestowed emotion, vainly, upon commoners out for a drive'. The word 'vainly', placed at a strategic juncture in the sentence, makes us pause before committing ourselves to the emotion slowly gathering momentum in the streets. By introducing this slight 'hitch' in the onward motion of the caravan (and, of course, of the sentence that describes its passing), she alerts us to the limits, as well as the waywardness of the emotion aroused by the regalia of royalty (which itself may be judged a vanity in the biblical sense). The emotion, when it is finally allowed its unconstrained expression, takes the infectious form of rumour. The narrator accordingly begins to trace, quickly and nimbly, the associative chain that links all those commoners who

> let rumour accumulate in their veins and thrill the nerves in their thighs at the thought of Royalty looking at them; the Queen bowing; the Prince saluting;

at the thought of the heavenly life divinely bestowed upon Kings; of the equerries and deep curtsies; of the Queen's old doll's house; of Princess Mary married to an Englishman, and the Prince – ah! the Prince! who took wonderfully, they said, after old King Edward, but was ever so much slimmer.

(pp. 20–1)

The thoughts and words represented here are not those of an homogenised mass, but of a highly differentiated, yet amiably communicative 'we'. Individual responses, while still audible, are subsumed into a continuous train of thought that moves in comic synchrony with the motor car. The narrator exults in this demonstration that thought, especially as it transmits itself from mind to excited mind, can move so quickly – and so far! From the streets it transports itself to the private chambers where the Queen keeps her old doll's house; once there it ranges freely and not all that illogically from the venerable conception of society and state embodied in the divine right and existence of kings to the more mundane fascination with generational fluctuations in the royal avoirdupois.

This exuberant rush of communal fantasy is given an extra lift by that gratified exclamation – ah! – that temporarily arrests the flow of associations, an effect so captivating, yet so odd that we might be forgiven for wondering if it is not excitement itself crying out in the thrill of the moment. Or perhaps we are hearing the voice of rumour that has accumulated long enough in the veins of the onlookers and now must release that little yelp of surprised and satisfied delight. Joyce will make such exclamatory sounds parts of the dramatis personae in the hallucinatory drama staged in 'Circe', the Nighttown episode of *Ulysses*. 'The Hue and Cry' along with 'The Call' and 'The Answer' are personified and given speaking parts, as are 'The Echo' and 'Chimes'. But Woolf's tactic is at once more subtle and more strange. The 'ah' uttered here is not meant to signal, as Joyce's auditory hallucinations do, a schizophrenic breakdown in narration. Woolf is out to capture something at large in the human world but audible only to the novelistic inner ear, like 'the unheard rhythm of their own wild hearts' (p. 65) to which only the narrator of *Between the Acts* is attuned.

At other times the ventriloquiser's language seems to issue not from the body of the people but, as Auerbach first surmised, from the non-human world that pre-dated and will outlast us. In such moments 'I' is rejected in order that, literally it would seem, the divinities who shape our ends can be heard. Here, for example, is what the god of rain sounds like, as translated by the narrator of *The Years*:

the god of rain, if there were a god, was thinking, Let it not be restricted to the very wise, the very great, but let all breathing kind, the munchers and the chewers, the ignorant, the unhappy, those who toil in the furnace making innumerable copies of the same pot, those who bore red hot minds through contorted letters and also Mrs Jones in the alley, share my bounty.   (p. 48)

The itemising language of the catalogue combines with the memorialising strains of litany to enlist 'all breathing kind' who might benefit from the rain god's cooling ministrations, from the foundry workers toiling at their mechanical reproductions, to the scholars who labour singly to straighten what is contorted in human 'letters', to Mrs Jones in the alley. The odd humour[17] that suggests to Woolf the possibility of adapting liturgical forms to the novel's more secular devotions may also account for the somewhat antiquated diction of the passage, notably in her conspicuous use of the word 'toil' to describe the work of turning out mass-produced articles like pots. In writing about divine rather than human dispensations, Woolf avoids the word labour, with its unhappy associations to the contentious world of political economy where capital and labour are never on easy terms. Toil, with its alternate meaning of weave, evokes a less industrialised world of piecework, crafts and guilds.

Woolf playfully elaborates here the aesthetic she first articulated in *Mrs Dalloway*, through which meaning is built up, like Rezia's sewing, by first one thing then another. Such images, quaint as they appear in the industrialised world of giant mills and foundries, offer modest, but real instances of unalienated labour in whose products we can still see the distinct imprint of the artist's hand. Many commentators have noted and praised the richly detailed and democratic weave that results from Woolf's humble aesthetic in which no one person or thing necessarily takes precedence over another. Still, we should take note of any pronounced irregularities in the textual weave, audible as well as visible traces of Woolf's determination to work in the idiosyncratic category, like this one about munchers and chewers, into her narrative fabric. Such irregularities are signs of authorial generosity as well as caprice; they hold the promise that anything or anyone, even Mrs Jones in the alley, might eventually be accommodated in the community envisioned by the 'capacious' novelistic mind. Indeed, Woolf's predilection for waifs and strays ensures that the 'We' she hopes to invoke in her fictions will not, in the end, consist, like the royal or editorial we, of a plurality of one, but will resound with the voice of multitudes, of plebeian as well as high-born life.

This sounds all very egalitarian and admirably selfless. Yet there are private risks as well as public benefits in rejecting the authorial 'I' to embrace an all-encompassing, itinerant 'We'. Woolf herself was constantly aware of them, as Gillian Beer has shrewdly noted:

'We' is an elastic pronoun, stretching in numbers and through time. Its population ranges from the exclusive pair of lovers, now, to the whole past of human history. It can welcome or rebuff the hearer. It can also colonise. Virginia Woolf saw clearly that 'we' may be coercive and treacherous. It invites in the individual, the subset, the excluded, who once inside may find themselves vanished with an alien group claiming on their behalf things of no benefit or relevance to themselves'.[18]

Beer primarily has in mind the coercive force of the patriotic 'we' or the 'we' complacently adopted by 'male writers to speak in universals which cover (in many senses) the experience also of women'.[19] But just as menacing is the 'we' that is the outcome of many years of thinking in common. Necessary and admirable as it is to find a common language that transcends the parochial identifications of gender, class and nation, such language may leave the solitary soul, 'the thing . . . that mattered',[20] without a language of its own, stranded and bereft in the land of soliloquy.

Woolf understood that the nominative 'I' was as elastic, if less crowded a pronoun, as 'We'. It certainly was a more brittle psychological and linguistic construction in her fiction. She could lambast, as she does in *A Room of One's Own*, the sterile egotism perpetuated by the male mantra 'I, I, I' without underestimating the intrinsic fragility of the first-person singular. Reading her, we can often see the 'I' breaking up before us on the page, most spectacularly in the language of Septimus Smith, the mad visionary of *Mrs Dalloway*. But his pathology represents a special case, symptomatic as it is of the trauma inflicted by the First World War and of the burden of prophecy itself, to which Septimus alludes in remonstrating with 'the unseen' voice summoning him 'to renew society', protesting that 'he did not want it . . . putting from him with a wave of his hand that eternal suffering, that eternal loneliness' (p. 27). Less sensational, but equally unnerving are Woolf's representations of identity decomposing on the very threshold of non-being. Witness, in *The Years*, the distress of the dying Mrs Pargiter on awaking from a fretful sleep:

> 'Where am I?' She was frightened and bewildered, as she often was on waking. She raised her hand; she seemed to appeal for help. For a moment Delia was bewildered too. Where was she? 'Here, Mama! Here!' she said wildly. 'Here, in your own room.'[21]

Mrs Pargiter's speech functions here as a tepid form of echo-location. She weakly emits words in order to determine, by the way they rebound, the material perimeters of her world, now shrunk to a deathbed. But the principle, once established, gathers force and adherents, as we see when Delia is momentarily caught up in the general bewilderment of the phrase, 'Where am I?' Later she will pick up the burden of this refrain when, relieved from her death-watch by an attending nurse, she finds herself outside the close confines of the sickroom:

> Where am I? She asked herself, staring at a white jug stained pink by the setting sun. For a moment she seemed to be in some borderland between life and death. Where am I? She repeated, looking at the pink jug, for it all looked strange. Then she heard water rushing and feet thudding on the floor above.
>
> (p. 25)

In such jarring moments of disassociated perception, objects begin to shed their customary aspect. Words no longer serve as names for things, indicators of reality. They assume a contrary, frightening power to defamiliarise the ordinary world we had (erroneously) thought thoroughly tamed by habit and the rule of reason. The comic-grotesque way Delia re-enters reality, summoned by the rush of water and thud of feet presumably coming from the water-closet upstairs, enhances rather than diffuses the trance-like states when the self seems adrift in a world suddenly grown strange.

Never does the interplay between the rippled surface of Woolf's narrative syntax, in which the ventriloquising narrator navigates nimbly from mind to mind, fact to associated fact, and the 'deep structure' of her narrative grammar attain more subtle counterpoint than in the opening of her last novel, *Between the Acts*. We know that there is an author present and presumably available to us, since the novel begins on a matter-of-fact, even banal note: 'It was a summer's night and they were talking, in the big room with the window open to the garden, about the cesspool.' The discrepancy between the natural beauty of the novel's setting and the coarse matter under discussion is reinforced by the narrator's mordant description of one conversant, a Mrs Haines, as 'a goose-faced woman with eyes protruding as if they saw something to gobble in the gutter'. The mirror the narrator is holding up to human nature initially exhibits the ungainly reflection of Mrs Haines' goose-faced countenance. It is the same mirror – 'malicious; observant; expectant; expository' – as the broken mirror held up in the last act of the pageant to capture the 'reality' of 'present day'. By 1939, we thus are prompted to conjecture, modern fiction no longer could represent life as a 'luminous halo, a semi-transparent envelope surrounding us from the beginning of consciousness to the end'.[22] That vision of human possibility belongs to 1919. To the observant and expository author of 1939, reality – in this instance, the character of Mrs Haines – takes the form of malicious, yet not inaccurate caricature. Mrs Haines's goose-face is as much moral fact as her unseemly proclivity to 'gobble in the gutter'. Even music has lost its power to make 'us see the hidden, join the broken' (p. 120). The broken, jagged tune that provides the disconcerting musical accompaniment to the pageant's final act only reinforces satire's impertinent cackle: 'What a cackle, a cacophony! Nothing ended. So abrupt. And corrupt. Such an outrage; such an insult! And not plain. Very up to date, all the same. What is her game?' (p. 183). 'We', the audience that the ventriloquiser purports to speak for as well as to, is here, rather generously I think, given her chance to blurt out her objections to what is neither plain nor complementary, yet admittedly 'up to date all the same' in modernist writing. 'We' are allowed to complain about the incompleteness and the abruptness of modern art, protest against its focus on the litter, 'the orts, scraps and fragments' of reality (the caves of *Mrs Dalloway* have degenerated into cesspools and gutters) rather than on luminous and enveloping wholes.

Such passages confirm how committed Woolf remained to the realist ethics propounded in *To the Lighthouse*; she remained faithful to the last in her reporting of 'facts uncompromising' which, as *To The Lighthouse* advises, has little regard for common feelings. But Woolf was equally determined to counter the sharp, incisive tongue of an observant, arguably malicious modernism with her own visionary utterances. To respond to and oppose the fractious language of the present time she devised a language released from the duties of exposition, a language capable of translating the real into a sphere where it is no longer subject to the contaminations of the transient and splintered moment. The dialogue between these two languages, the ventriloquist tethered to the present, the soliloquist anchored in the timeless realm of her own sensations and imaginings, is as much a part of the 'action' in a novel by Virginia Woolf as the giving of a party, the leap from a window, the journey to a lighthouse or the putting on of a pageant.

We can hear the subtle interplay between Woolf's ventriloquising and soliloquising voices in the quiet, but deeply resonant, opening of *Between the Acts*. The opening mood abruptly changes when a bird interrupts the human chatter:

> A bird chuckled outside. 'A nightingale?' asked Mrs Haines. No, nightingales didn't come so far north. It was a daylight bird, chuckling over the substance and succulence of the day, over worms, snails, grit, even in sleep. (p. 3)

The narrator presumably knows the difference between a chirp and a chuckle, but is availing herself of the novelist's licence to render non-human life anthropomorphically, just as a few moments before she had exposed the animal voracity lurking in Mrs Haines famished-seeming eyes. Mrs Haines wonders if the bird sound she hears belongs to the nightingale, arguably the most poetic of birds, as Woolf herself noted in the first typescript of the novel, describing the nightingale as 'the amorous, the expressive'.[23] Another voice, this one unidentified, but still belonging to a character within the novel, replies with something akin to a naturalist's certainty that nightingales do not migrate so far north. Then still another voice intervenes, a voice unlike all the others we have heard, a voice that belongs to no one and situated nowhere that we readers can discern, not even by echo-location. Presumably we are hearing the voice of the narrator, but the narrator no longer speaking as a narrator but, as it were, to herself. The word 'succulence' marks off this sentence as decidedly different from the banal talk in which it makes its surprising, somewhat obtrusive appearance. Succulence is a poetic word; there is nothing 'conversational' about it. Even if a bird could speak, we would hardly expect it to exhibit a gourmet's appreciation for the savouriness of worms and grit. Woolf rightly edited out the editorial comment in the original draft that would have made clear that the dream belonged to a bird. Either the bird or the word succulence had to go. Predictably, impractically perhaps, the word won out.

Even in such minimal acts of authorship, we can see how much Woolf added to her representations by suspending us in incertitude. Editing generally works to clarify the action or sense; here the revised and final version makes matters less clear. This revision is in keeping with Woolf's growing determination to resist saying 'I am this or I am that', thus granting the authorial self more latitude, but also potentially making it more isolated from its kind, more unsure that its impressions will hold good for others. Woolf's resolve to represent the world from the point of view of incertitude gives her sentences their peculiar character. A crisis of confidence lurks at the edge of every Woolfean sentence, begetting the suspense we feel in following her sinuous sentences through the many detours, self-interruptions and self-questionings that threaten to derail her thought and her narrative altogether; it accounts for the relief that is ours when internal doubts and external distractions are overcome, when the disparate emotions that often contend for place and primacy in the entanglements of her syntax are eventually sorted out and the sentence, often as riddled with typographical as it is riven with emotional division, finally completes itself. Here the uncertainty attaches to the fate of the narrative voice itself, which seems in danger of disappearing altogether into the dreamscapes of the musing mind where cesspools metamorphose easily, thanks to the unopposable logic of dreams, into sumptuous avian repasts.

Silence

As these examples suggest, Woolf did not so much violate as tamper with the narrative grammar of persons, by which the 'I' that reports and records remains distinctly separate from, if commendably responsive to, the 'voice' of individual characters or even communal opinion represented within the novel itself. No writer of English fiction, with the possible exception of D. H. Lawrence, was more versatile in experimenting with the lyric potentials of narration, by which the subjective voice speaks without any distinct hope, often without even real care, that its language will be heard, much less understood by an audience. This is the possibility entertained by Lily Briscoe when she thinks to herself that her paintings will be hung in attics; this is the actual hope of the playwright La Trobe who, fearful that 'Reality [is] too strong' for her audience, dreams of writing 'a play without an audience, *the* play' (p. 180). Voice, however, is a more gregarious, less solitary faculty than vision – language, unlike paint, belongs to everyone and is more deeply connected to our nature as social beings, longing to communicate. To think of the unseen painting is one thing; to contemplate the unheard voice or unread page or unattended play is to approach a disassociated state of consciousness akin to autism. Woolf presents us with an icon for such art in *Between the Acts* in the picture of a lady that hangs opposite a portrait of a garrulous ancestor at the top of the stairs in Pointz Hall:

> He was a talk producer, that ancestor. But the lady was a picture. In her yellow robe, leaning, with a pillar to support her, a silver arrow in her hand, and a feather in her hair, she led the eye up, down, from the curve to the straight, through glades of greenery and shades of silver, dun and rose into silence. The room was empty.
>
> Empty, empty, empty; silent, silent, silent. The room was a shell, singing of what was before time was; a vase stood in the heart of the house, alabaster, smooth, cold, holding the still, distilled essence of emptiness, silence.   (p. 37)

It is hard to determine, after we have followed the lady garbed in yellow 'through' the looking glass presented in and by this picture, whether the empty room at journey's end is inside or outside the picture. A tomb-like quiet overcomes the narrative; nothing resounds within this silent interior except the verbal echo of 'still' in 'distilled', an echo which gives the 'essence' of silence an auditory, if not material density, as heavy, let us say, as anti-matter is purported to be. This internal echo helps dispel the stupefying effect of the incantatory repetition 'empty, empty, empty, silent, silent, silent'. The silence condensed and deposited in this shell of a room is a silence that pre-existed the Creation, originating before time and space. It may even be a Silence that prefigures the emptiness awaiting at the other side of time, when the universe as we know it will have been extinguished. The soliloquist's dream of abiding, like Mr Ramsay, in 'some moon country uninhabited by men' is here realised in its purest, yet most dreadfully inhuman form.

In the section marked *Silence* in the earlier typescript of *Pointz Hall*, Woolf interrogates the nameless visionary presence who seeks such a silent world: 'Who noted the silence, the emptiness? What name is to be given to the presence which notes that a room is empty? This presence requires a name for without a name what has an existence? And how can silence or emptiness be noted by that which has not existence . . .'[24] The observant presence here is not a ghost, for even a ghost may be said to have had an existence. Only a name confers existence, and the Woolf who promoted the writerly ideology of anonymity has reached a cul-de-sac, trapped in the vacant ante-chamber of narrative being.

This was not always the case. Woolf's fascination with silence links the beginning of her writing with its end, but at first this fascination was confined to the traditionally novelistic sphere of human rather than primordial nature. By revisiting her beginning, we can better assess what she was either forced or willing to relinquish to attain this nameless presence. She had proclaimed in her first novel, *The Voyage Out*, a desire to write about 'Silence . . . the things people don't say' (p. 262). 'Just consider,' proclaims the aspiring novelist Terence Hewet,

> it's the beginning of the twentieth century, and until a few years ago no woman had ever come out by herself and said things at all. There it was going on in the background for all those thousands of years, this curious silent unrepresented life. Of course we're always writing about women – abusing them, or jeering at them, or worshiping them; but it never comes from women themselves. I believe we still don't know in the least how they live, or what they feel, or what they do precisely. (p. 258)

Excavating the hidden, unexpressed life of women is now a commonplace of feminist criticism, although we may still marvel at the exacting standard Woolf establishes through that adverb 'precisely', with its demand for the unmitigated and factual truth. Finding a language precise as well as voluble enough to express what has been consigned to silence by the 'horrible domestic tradition', by the internalised codes imposed by chastity, by 'the entire tea-table training' inculcated at Hyde Park Gate, was to preoccupy her for a lifetime.[25]

It had to be, inescapably, the language of indoors. The language of interiors is the language of modernism, as Woolf signalled when she had her transhistorical (as well as transsexual) heroine Orlando usher in the twentieth century by going indoors. Her gesture symbolises the inward turn of narrative that Woolf advocated in such landmark essays as 'Modern

Fiction' and 'Mr Bennett and Mrs Brown'. It also signified Orlando's felt need, as a woman writer, to retreat into 'a room of one's own', the autonomous space where a woman might speak without fear of censure, where she might harness for public and artistic ends the 'complex force of femininity' silently lavished on interiors:

> For women have sat indoors all these millions of years, so that by this time the very walls are permeated by their creative force, which has, indeed, so overcharged the capacity of bricks and mortar that it must needs harness itself to pens and brushes and business and politics. But this creative power differs greatly from the creative power of men. And one must conclude that it would be a thousand pities if it were hindered or wasted, for it was won by centuries of the most drastic discipline, and there is nothing to take its place. It would be a thousand pities if women wrote like men, or lived like men, or looked like men . . .[26]

Woolf's respect for the drastic discipline that is the woman writer's most conspicuous inheritance from her creative female forbears underlies her conviction that woman's language, shaped in confinement, allows her 'to say a great many things which would be inaudible if one marched straight up and spoke out'.[27] Yet we can also detect in her writing a growing restlessness with such prolonged imaginative confinement, a restlessness that surfaces, for example, in the exuberant opening of *Mrs Dalloway*, the novel in which Woolf's modernity and her heroine make exhilarating contact with the out-of-doors:

> What a lark! What a plunge! For so it had always seemed to her, when, with a little squeak of the hinges, which she could hear now, she had burst open the French windows and plunged at Bourton into the open air. How fresh, how calm, stiller than this of course, the air was in the early morning; like the flap of a wave; the kiss of a wave; chill and sharp and yet (for a girl of eighteen as she then was) solemn, feeling as she did, standing there at the open window, that something awful was about to happen . . .   (p. 3)

A profusion of parentheses, exclamation points and semi-colons at once reflect and subdue the manic gaiety of this verbal and existential plunge into the open air. Woolf's singular use of the semi-colon will become an habitual, indeed symptomatic feature of her prose. By its aid she is able to regulate the excited rush of perceptions that threaten to outrun her powers of expression. Yet such syntactically and typographically elaborate sentences may also represent an anxiety formation, a linguistic anodyne to overcome the agoraphobia instilled by all those years of confinement indoors. Perhaps this explains the heroine's ominous premonition that something awful was about to happen and the inordinately heavy time symbolism of the novel that is always reminding us as well as its characters of the 'leaden' tolling of the bells.

A similar dread overcomes Mrs Ramsay in *To the Lighthouse* when, in the midst of her domestic crooning, she is suddenly roused by an unidentifiable rustle of wind or burst of sound 'that like a ghostly roll of drums remorseless beat the measure of life'. The rhythm of a Woolfean sentence is calculated to counter the monotony of this remorseless beat by which life measures and doles out life. Words fashioned to counter that rhythm can even turn failure into an opportunity for a human – that is ephemeral – success. If you doubt the power of words to accomplish so much, consider this exchange, when Mr Ramsay, nearly speechless with anxiety, demands comfort from his wife:

> He was a failure, he repeated. Well, look then, feel then. Flashing her needles, glancing round about her, out of the window, into the room, at James himself, she assured him, beyond a shadow of a doubt, by her laugh, her poise, her competence (as a nurse carrying a light across a dark room assures a fractious child), that it was real; the house was full; the garden blowing.   (p. 60)

This intimate exchange between husband and wife is played out in silence. Indeed the entire passage describes the intense desire to obliterate a word – failure – in which the entire misery and persistent anxiety of Mr Ramsay's existence has deposited itself. It is by outward signs, the language of gesture, that Mrs Ramsay communicates her own inward agitation as she prepares to reply to this mute appeal. The flashing needles communicate their point and fire to the glance she darts impatiently, a little wildly, out of the window. Her gaze then returns indoors, back to James. Her silent glance traces an entire circuit of relations between what lies outside and beyond the window (where we might glimpse how the sea is eating up the very ground we stand on) and the room in which the entire complex force of femininity has asserted itself (symbolised and priding itself in James, both the fruit of love and hostage to time). Yet we should also notice that there seems to be a third silent partner to this complex interchange. Who is it, after all, who commands 'Well, look then, feel then.' To whom are these words directed? All we can know for certain is that the imperative to feel must be obeyed. Even the words on the page seem to obey it. The agitated language that captures the flash and flow of charged glances eventually subsides; the 'sentence' recovers its composure and utters, in a serene and stately measure, the humanly enabling conviction that 'it was real'.

Whatever the uncertainties and indeterminacies that plague Woolf's sentences, they work to provide the best possible assurance anyone can receive – the assurance of reality. Such assurances, by their nature, can only be temporary. They seldom come in the forms nor in the manner we expect. But the making of them is the primary burden of the language of Virginia Woolf. These assurances constitute her finest work in her life as an author.

NOTES

1 Woolf did not register herself since, as Hermione Lee notes, 'she was in the dark cupboard of her mental illness, and did not emerge until the autumn of that year'. But 1915 did see the publication, delayed by war, of her first major effort as an author, *The Voyage Out*. See Hermione Lee, *Virginia Woolf* (New York: Alfred A. Knopf, 1997), p. 322.

2 Virginia Woolf, 'Craftsmanship', *The Death of the Moth* (London: Hogarth, 1981), p. 126.

3 'Prose,' she matter-of-factly admits in 'The Narrow Bridge of Art', 'has taken all the dirty work on to her own shoulders; has answered letters, paid bills, written articles, made speeches, served the needs of businessmen, shopkeepers, lawyers, soldiers, peasants.' See *CE4*, ed. Leonard Woolf (London: Chatto and Windus, 1967), p. 223.

4 Of course, the *ideological* impact of her writing is undeniable, especially in such polemic works as *TG*. But Woolf never forges manifestos to be acted on, never issues guidelines or provides instructions to be followed to the letter.

5 Virginia Woolf, 'Modern Fiction', *The Common Reader* (New York: Harcourt, Brace and World, 1925) p. 154.

6 The book under review is J. D. Beresford's *An Imperfect Mother*. See *The Essays of Virginia Woolf*, 4, edited by Andrew W. McNeillie (San Diego and New York: Harcourt, Brace and Jovanovich, 1988) pp. 195–97.

7 See Hermione Lee's excellent discussion of Virginia Woolf and the language of madness in her *Virginia Woolf*, p. 187.

8 Samuel Beckett, *Murphy* (New York: Grove Press, 1957), p. 65.

9 James Joyce, *Ulysses* (New York: Random House, 1986), p. 592.

10 Elaine Showalter insightfully remarks on how sky-writing, a 'brand-new phenomenon when Woolf was composing her novel' is used by Woolf as a 'cinematic linking device'. See her 'Introduction', *Mrs. D* (London: Penguin Books, 1992), pp. xxiii–xxiv.

11 Virginia Woolf, *BA* (New York: Harcourt, Brace and Jovanovich, 1969), p. 10. All further references to the novels will be to this edition.

12 'On Being Ill', *CE*, p. 11.

13 Erich Auerbach, *Mimesis* (Princeton University Press, 1991), p. 532.

14 'Divisions of novelists into ventriloquists: soliloquists', Virginia Woolf, 'Notes for Reading at Random', ed. Brenda Silver, *Twentieth Century Literature* 25, No. 3/4, Fall/Winter 1979, p. 374.

15 Detachment, but not indifference. The one pose Woolf was never desirous of mastering was the godly impassivity that the aloof creator Stephen Dedalus holds up as a model for his own writerly aspirations, one that would mimic 'the God of creation . . . invisible, refined out of existence, indifferent, paring his fingernails'. James Joyce, *A Portrait of the Artist as a Young Man* (New York: Penguin World Classics, 1993), p. 233.

16 Virginia Woolf, *ROO* (New York and London: Harcourt, Brace and Jovanovich, 1957), pp. 68–9.

17 The word 'humour' is freighted with associations for the English mind. In its original sense it denoted the various moistures of the body that accounted for the dominant types of human temperament – sanguine (blood), melancholy (black bile), phlegmatic (phlegm), choleric (choler). This sense survives in our speaking of someone as good or ill-humoured, but for the literary-minded, Ben Jonson's 'humour' characters, comic eccentrics whose inflexibility originates in moral as much as bodily imbalances, give a special piquancy to the phrase, 'odd humour'.

18 Gillian Beer, 'The Body of the People in Virginia Woolf', in *Women Reading Women's Writing*, ed. Sue Roe (Brighton: The Harvester Press, 1987), p. 87.

19 *Ibid.*

20 *Mrs. D*, p. 202.

21 Virginia Woolf, *Y* (New York: Harcourt, Brace and Jovanovich, 1965), p. 23. All further references will be to this edition and cited in the text.

22 'Modern Fiction', p. 154.

23 Virginia Woolf, *Pointz Hall*, ed. Mitchell A. Leaska (New York: University Publications, 1983) p. 34.

24 *Ibid.*, p. 61.

25 'A Sketch of the Past' in *MB* (London: Hogarth, 1982), p. 129.

26 *ROO*, p. 91.

27 'A Sketch of the Past', p. 129.

8

MICHAEL WHITWORTH

Virginia Woolf and modernism

Away and away the aeroplane shot, till it was nothing but a bright spark; an aspiration; a concentration; a symbol (so it seemed to Mr. Bentley, vigorously rolling his strip of turf at Greenwich) of man's soul; of his determination, thought Mr. Bentley, sweeping round the cedar tree, to get outside his body, beyond his house, by means of thought, Einstein, speculation, mathematics, the Mendelian theory . . .

(*Mrs D*, p. 30)[1]

The aeroplane scene in *Mrs Dalloway* combines many of the perspectives relevant to Virginia Woolf's modernism: intellectual, technological, social, and literary. As 'Einstein' suggests, modernist literature responded to radical intellectual developments in philosophy and science. In 1911, as Leonard Woolf recalled, 'Freud and Rutherford and Einstein' had begun 'to revolutionise our knowledge of our own minds and of the universe'.[2] The late nineteenth-century philosophical work of Friedrich Nietzsche and Henri Bergson was equally significant. As the aeroplane suggests, modernism was also a response to technological innovation, particularly in the urban environment. As the setting in Greenwich suggests, it explored the nature of time. The distinction between psychological time and clock time, the *durée* and *temps* of Bergson's philosophy, underlies the modernist experiments with time and narrative form. Psychology and anthropology encouraged explorations of prehistorical time, and of primitive and mythic ideas of time. The aeroplane's evanescent sky-writing raises other issues: of reading and interpretation; of the transitory nature of modernist beauty; and, in the way that the spectacle unites a disparate group of characters, the nature of the crowd in the urban environment.

The sky-writing also recalls Hely's sandwich-board men in Joyce's *Ulysses* (1922): as well as responding to their intellectual and social environment, modernist writers responded to each other's works. Though their experiments in literary form were primarily intended to represent and question the experience of modernity, they secondarily addressed the experience of reading other texts. This is important in the case of Woolf. Although, along with Eliot and *The Waste Land* (1922), Joyce and *Ulysses*, Pound and *The Cantos* (1917 onwards), Woolf can be seen as an important exemplar of High Modernism, the role of exemplar is inappropriately passive. Although the term 'modernism' had been applied to literature as early as 1908, it gained widespread currency only after the Second World War as a convenient label for university courses.[3] Woolf thought of herself as one of the 'moderns', as part of a more fluid grouping, encompassing thinkers and literary journalists as well as writers and artists. The moderns existed as a web of affiliations, not as a coherent artistic movement. Woolf was acutely aware of the dangers inherent in generalisation and, in exploring her modernism, we need to acknowledge her differences from, as well as her similarities to, a generalised 'modernism'. The strand of late-Victorian aestheticism in her modernist thinking kept her at a critical distance from the aesthetic preferences of many of her modernist contemporaries, which were rooted in metaphors of sculptural 'hardness' and 'dryness'. Woolf also maintained a critical distance from the politics which corresponded to these metaphors, a politics of authoritarianism and exaggerated masculinity.

There is another significant tension between the terms 'modernism' and 'modernity'. The relationship between the two terms has conventionally been seen as antagonistic: though modernist writing is dominated by the experience of the metropolis, of technological innovation and the accelerated pace of modern life, it satirises and rejects the phenomena of 'bourgeois' modernity in favour of 'tradition', primitivism and myth. Even if this model of antagonism were completely true for Eliot and Joyce, it would need to be treated sceptically in relation to Woolf. Even as her novels register the psychological stresses of urban life, they celebrate its fertile possibilities. Although Woolf explores the same problems as her contemporaries, and adopts the familiar dichotomies of modernist thought, she diverges from them in many respects.

I

Of the influential thinkers mentioned above, Woolf met only Freud. She never met, and may never have read, Einstein, Bergson, Nietzsche or Rutherford. Yet her novels apparently respond to their works and employ their ideas. Leonard Woolf doubted that she had ever read Bergson or attended his lectures, and he was certain that she had never read her sister-in-law's book on the philosopher.[4] One may reply that Bergsonism was part of the intellectual atmosphere of the years from 1910 to 1912, as Einstein was to be in the years from 1919 to 1930. But the idea of an all-pervading 'intellectual atmosphere' easily obscures the partisan affiliations of modernist sub-cultures, their specific patterns of ignorance and knowledge, and the material means by which knowledge is disseminated. The biographical and bibliographical contexts of Woolf's career indicate how she was able to encounter these thinkers indirectly. Moreover, they suggest that her identity as one of the 'moderns' was sustained by the proximity of other moderns, socially and textually.

Woolf's diaries suggest that conversations in Bloomsbury were wide-ranging, moving from the intellectual to the intimate, and crossing the acknowledged boundaries of the disciplines. In 1930 Woolf records an evening spent with David Cecil, Lytton Strachey and Clive Bell, shortly after the publication of Sir James Jeans's best-selling popular science book *The Mysterious Universe*: 'Talk about the riddle of the universe (Jeans' book) whether it will be known; not by us; found out suddenly: about rhythm in prose' (*D3*, p. 337). It is momentarily unclear whether the riddle of cosmology or composition has been 'found out suddenly'. Similarly, in May 1932, on holiday with Roger Fry and his sister, Woolf describes Leonard 'discussing prison reform with Marjorie, informing Roger about the break up of the atom' (*D4*, p. 96). Woolf's fluid syntax indicates the ease with which borders could be crossed. Such conversational acquaintance with ideas creates fragmentary, unsystematic knowledge, but, for these very reasons, is all the more valuable to the literary artist. The systematic treatise can stifle rather than stimulate.

There were many people in Bloomsbury and on its fringes who could introduce such topics of conversation. Roger Fry had studied science, and remained open to influences from a wide range of sources (*RF*, p. 116). Bertrand Russell was equally comfortable in the realms of mathematics, politics, philosophy and the new physics, about which he wrote two compact accounts, *The ABC of Atoms* (1923) and *The ABC of Relativity* (1925). Less central to Woolf's circle, but as intellectually significant, were C. P. Sanger and Sydney Waterlow. A barrister by profession, the polymathic Sanger had co-translated a work on the new physics, and reviewed many scientific books.[5] Waterlow worked intermittently as a diplomat, but also wrote on philosophical topics including, before the war, the work of Henri Bergson.

Woolf's sense of modernity was further shaped by other groups which overlapped with Bloomsbury. Lady Ottoline Morrell combined the roles of society hostess and patron of the arts, allowing writers, artists and philosophers to mingle at both 44 Bedford Square in Bloomsbury and Garsington Manor near Oxford. Among those who adopted Garsington as their meeting-place were Aldous Huxley, T. S. Eliot and the modernist painter Mark Gertler; it was also, during the war, a refuge for conscientious objectors. Over and above the potential it created for discussing particular ideas, Garsington reinforced its habitués' sense of belonging to a progressive cultural movement. Intersecting with the Garsington circle was one which formed around the literary weekly *The Athenaeum* under the editorship of John Middleton Murry between 1919 and 1921. This circle included Eliot, Huxley and occasionally Waterlow; also central were Samuel Solomonovitch Koteliansky, a translator of Russian fiction, and J. W. N. Sullivan, an important interpreter of the new physics and its implications for art and philosophy. Though Woolf was often contemptuous of this 'underworld' of literary journalism, it created a further context for the discussion of innovative ideas (*D2*, p. 52). Woolf was particularly close to Katherine Mansfield, though Mansfield's work often precipitated Woolf's doubts about the emotional dryness of her novels (*D2*, pp. 161, 248).

Woolf's modernity was sustained not only by personal contacts, but by her publishing context. Literary journals and publishing houses create imaginary communities, geographically disparate, but possessing some degree of cultural or ideological agreement. Journals like *The Athenaeum* and *The Times Literary Supplement* also displayed a surprising heterogeneity of content. In reading *The Athenaeum* one could move from Eliot reviewing a literary work to Sullivan discussing the implications of Einstein's theory to Fry on aesthetics.[6] Heterogeneous journals reproduced some of the cross-disciplinary qualities of a Bloomsbury conversation, and this potential was at a maximum for a reader like Woolf, who relished the possibility of reading in a non-linear, free-associative way.

Many critics have noted the importance of the 'little magazines' to the development of modernism: small in circulation, often short-lived, even when underwritten by wealthy benefactors, they published experimental writings and reviewed new works.[7] Joyce's *A Portrait of the Artist as a Young Man* was serialised in *The Egoist*, and parts of *Ulysses* appeared in *The Little Review*; *The Waste Land* first appeared in Eliot's own *Criterion*, and in the USA in *The Dial*. Some magazines, such as Wyndham Lewis's *Blast*, with striking typography, were works of modernist art in themselves. However, Woolf generally contributed to journals that were less stridently avant-garde: *The Athenaeum*, though it defined itself in opposition to the traditionalist *London Mercury*, was itself conservative in appearance and moderate in its tone; *The Criterion*, in which 'Character in Fiction' appeared, resembled a respectable academic review more closely than its modernist predecessors.

Important though literary journalism was, the Hogarth Press was Woolf's crucial publishing context. Her first two novels had been published by her half-brother Gerald Duckworth. Woolf was disheartened at the prospect of her work being 'pawed & snored over' by a man who had sexually abused her as a child, and who, 'pampered' and 'overfed', represented the complacent Club man in her demonology (D1, pp. 129, 261). Moreover, as Laura Marcus suggests, the Duckworth firm represented for Woolf an audience that was 'Victorian, conventional, anti-experimentation'; its publishing decisions were determined in part by the requirements of Mudie's circulating library (D1, p. 261).[8] Owning the Hogarth Press liberated Woolf's experimentalism. Its first publication, 'The Mark on the Wall', was her first sustained experiment in literary form. As Woolf wrote to David Garnett, who had admired this piece, the 'greatest mercy' of owning the Press was 'to be able to do what one likes – no editors, or publishers, and only people to read who more or less like that sort of thing' (L2, p. 167). She and Leonard were also able to publish other works by innovative contemporaries. Although they were unable to take on *Ulysses*, they published *The Waste Land*, the works of Freud and the most influential anthologies of the early 1930s, *New Signatures* (1932) and *New Country* (1933). The powerful intellectual developments that made modernism a pan-European phenomenon were sustained at a local level by material institutions like the Hogarth Press.

The liberating effect of the Press highlights some of the paradoxes inherent in modernism's relation to the material circumstances of publishing. Modernist writers positioned themselves in opposition to the masses and popular readerships; their works, in their quest for aesthetic autonomy, tried to resist commodification.[9] Woolf's contempt for Mudie's is entirely typical: she was repelled not only by its subscribers, 'pallid and respectable', but by the sight of books borrowed in bulk, ranged 'like bales of stuff upon a drapers shelves – only with out the solid merit of good wool' (D1, pp. 61, 166). The prospect of such commodification left her sickened of reading and disinclined to write. Yet the experimental works which she wrote with such a sense of liberty were also commodities, in their own way. They differed from the 'bales of stuff' at Mudie's only in physical appearance and, more crucially, in the fact that Leonard and Virginia controlled their production.

2

By defining herself as 'a modern', Woolf concealed her many affiliations with nineteenth-century writers. The strategy of rejecting the Victorian and Edwardian literary heritage is a defining feature of modernism, adopted not only by individual writers, but by the modernist reviews. Some rejected it vigorously, like *Blast*, which in its opening manifesto directed rhetorical 'blasts' at the 'years 1837 to 1900'; others, more subtly, rejected the physical format and the lengthy reviews of the Victorian quarterlies. A generational divide had developed before the First World War, highlighted by reactions to playwrights like Ibsen and Shaw, to Roger Fry's post-impressionist exhibitions, or to sculptors like Jacob Epstein.[10] The war accentuated the divide. For the many male modernists who were non-combatants, the war provoked a compensatory exaggeration of an already aggressive rhetoric. However, Woolf's self-definition as modernist falls inevitably along different lines, as does the Victorian heritage which she tried to conceal.

In the essay 'Modern Novels' (1919), although Woolf distinguishes between the generations, she is more concerned to emphasise the differences between the 'materialist' and the 'modern' approaches. It is only in 'On Re-reading Novels' (1922) and 'Mr Bennett and Mrs Brown' (1923) that her distinction between the 'Edwardian' and the 'Georgian' generations appears.[11] Moreover, that Woolf identifies 1910 as the watershed, and not 1900, betrays a certain ambivalence about the Victorian novelists. In 'Mr Bennett and Mrs Brown' Woolf praises the 'astonishing vividness and reality' of Victorian characterisation, contrasting it with the Edwardian concentration on 'things in general' (E3, pp. 385–7). Yet in 'Character in Fiction' she conflates the two generations, using the 'Victorian cook' to symbolise the Edwardians (E3, p. 422).

In rejecting Victorian 'materialism', Woolf is rejecting the Victorian idea of reality itself. This marks her experimental work from the outset. In 'The Mark on the Wall' (1917), the narrator identifies a whole range of Victoriana, such as 'mahogany sideboards and . . . Landseer prints', as having once been 'the standard thing, the real thing' (CSF, p. 86). In her diary, too, Woolf satirises the 'Orderly solidity' of her elderly cousin's dining-room (D2, p. 235). 'Materialism' suggests hard science as well as soft furnishings, and, for many, the most striking scientific development of the early twentieth century was Rutherford's discovery that the atom was 'porous'; 'all that we regard as most solid' turned out to be 'tiny specks floating in void'.[12] Woolf rejects science when it manifests itself in the authoritarian form of Holmes's and Bradshaw's materialism, but she alludes clearly to the new-found porosity of matter in The Years and Between the Acts, and more mutedly in earlier works. In doing so, she asserts her modernity of outlook. Throughout her fiction and criticism, Woolf expresses a preference for a reality which is semi-transparent, combining the solidity of granite and the evanescence of rainbow. Though many critics have seen in modernism an irrationalist rejection of science in favour of myth, in the case of Woolf at least, the situation is more complex.

Woolf's satire on Victorianism simplifies it, and to some extent this vitiates her arguments. Wyndham Lewis wrote scornfully that 'the late Mr. Bennett' was a soft target, 'a dead horse' dragging 'a dead issue'. [13] As John Carey has argued, Woolf fails to appreciate much of what Bennett was trying to achieve through his 'materialist' descriptions.[14] More importantly, the caricature of materialism presented by 'Character in Fiction' looms so large that it threatens to obscure Woolf's real debts to the Victorians.

Woolf was particularly indebted to the Victorian non-fictional prose writers. She borrowed selectively, suppressing the pompous, the sage-like and the patriarchal in their writing, and simultaneously recovering their particularity, their non-linearity and their fragmentariness. The examples of Carlyle and Ruskin suggested to Woolf the possibility of an 'impassioned prose' which would address the feelings and imagination without taking on the 'overdressed' appearance of the prose poem (E4, p. 361). In Ruskin, Woolf found a man who combined 'the austerity of the puritan, and the sensuous susceptibility of the artist' (E4, p. 503). Though Woolf alludes to the puritan Ruskin in Night and Day (p. 9) as one of the oppressive 'great dead', the hyper-aesthetic Ruskin resembles Woolf in many respects.[15] There may also be a concealed intellectual debt to the Victorian sages, and, beyond them, to the Romantics, in Woolf's recurrent distinction between mechanical and rhythmic modes of thought. The distinction between the mechanical and some non-mechanical other – be it organicism, hellenism or gothicism – was central to the thought of Carlyle and Arnold, and was significant in that of Ruskin. Woolf reproduces this opposition most clearly in the distinction between the materialist Edwardians and the 'spiritualist' Georgians, between the linear-thinking Mr Ramsay and his laterally thinking wife, and between the mechanically minded Holmes and Bradshaw and the non-mechanical Septimus and Clarissa.

Pater's theories of art and perception, as presented in the 'Conclusion' to The Renaissance (1867) and Marius the Epicurean (1885), had strongly influenced the British aestheticist writers of the 1890s and were important to Woolf. While his contemporaries maintained a belief that the real world contained real objects and real people which it was the writer's duty to depict as accurately as possible, Pater saw reality as being in a constant state of flux. Its apparent solidity was merely an illusion created by language: 'That clear, perpetual outline of face and limb is but an image of ours, under which we group them – a design in a web, the actual threads of which pass out beyond it.'[16] The mind received a series of disconnected impressions – like Woolf's 'shower of atoms' – which it grouped as best it could into isolated 'moments'. In the Paterian world, the 'susceptibility' to impressions exhibited by Peter Walsh is a positive virtue, bringing the perceiver closer to reality. Though Woolf's 'moments of vision' resemble Joyce's 'epiphanies', Pater is the more significant ancestor. Moreover, Pater's view of the self significantly anticipates Woolf's: for Pater, the self is fluid, maintaining harmony with the unstable external world through a 'constantly renewed mobility of character'.[17]

Perry Meisel has suggested that Woolf was frustrated by Pater's influence, feeling that she had 'inherited modernism rather than created it herself'.[18] However, Woolf developed Pater's ideas of perception and art in important respects. Pater's type of a physical sensation is an 'exquisite' moment of 'delicious recoil from the flood of water in summer heat' (Pater, *Renaissance*, p. 186); he emphasises sensations of beauty and pleasure, and implies a classical and pastoral landscape. Though Clarissa, at the start of *Mrs Dalloway*, 'plunges' into sensations as if into the sea, the sensations are urban. The reader is forced to revise his or her ideas of beauty and pleasure. Moreover, Clarissa plunges simultaneously into London in the present, and the early morning air at Bourton in her memory. For Pater, consciousness is the perceptual consciousness of the present moment, in a world where time is infinitely divisible into a series of isolated slices. For Woolf it is a more complex mixture of memory and perception, in a world where the shredding and slicing of clock time is challenged by the complex intermingling of past and present.

3

> In people's eyes, in the swing, tramp, and trudge; in the bellow and the uproar; the carriages, motor cars, omnibuses, vans, sandwich men shuffling and swinging; brass bands; barrel organs; in the triumph and the jingle and the strange high singing of some aeroplane overhead was what she loved; life; London; this moment of June. (*Mrs D*, p. 4)

Clarissa's 'plunge' into the city is not Woolf's, and the celebratory force of plunging is later qualified by Septimus's plunge through an open window, but, nevertheless, throughout Woolf's work the city is associated with life and love; the rhyme and alliteration of this passage reshape the city's shower of atoms into a rhythmical form. While bourgeois and aesthetic modernity are distinct in Woolf's work, they are not as 'irreducibly hostile' as they are for other modernists (Calinescu, *Five Faces*, p. 41). Such hostility as Woolf directs towards modernity is not directed specifically at city life.

T. S. Eliot dwells on the sordid details of the city, its 'grimy scraps' and 'dull canal'; moreover, when he finds beauty within the city, such as the 'Inexplicable splendour of Ionian white and gold' in St Magnus Martyr, it is entirely isolated, a fragment of the past which has miraculously survived.[19] Woolf's narrators and focalisers do not dwell on sordidness, and they present beauty not as something existing in spite of urban life, but as emerging from its energy and motion. Louis shares many characteristics with Eliot (G. Beer, *Common Ground*, pp. 87–8), and, sitting in the eating-shop, he notes as Eliot might have done the 'steam from a tea-urn' and the 'meaty, vapourish smell'; he is patronising about the 'little men' at the next table, 'prehensile like monkeys'; he is troubled by the crowds that constantly pass (*W*, pp. 68–70). Yet from this scene emerges a sense of order: the hats of the crowd 'bob up and down'; the door opens and shuts repeatedly. Louis is 'conscious of flux, of disorder; of annihilation and despair', yet he also feels 'the rhythm of the eating house . . . eddying in and out, round and round'; he admires the rhythms with which the waitresses deal out the plates of food, and even admires the 'little men' for accommodating the rhythms of their speech to the rhythm of the waitresses. This glimpse of rhythmic order within the urban scene is very different from Eliot's images of 'weeping multitudes' drooping in eating-houses (Eliot, *Poems and Plays*, p. 45). Nor is this attitude unique to *The Waves*: in her essays on London, Woolf finds 'æsthetic delight' in the rhythmical movement of the cranes at the docks ('The London Scene', p. 11).

While Woolf celebrates forms of rhythmical order which seem to emerge from chaos itself, she directs her most forceful satire at imposed systems of order, whether the 'real and standard things' of Victorian life, the social hierarchies contained in Whitaker's Table of Precedency, or Mr Ramsay's idea of thought progressing from A to Z. These systems of order are all based either on ideas of linearity, or of hierarchy, the Victorian 'pyramidal accumulation' (*Mrs D*, p. 178). Woolf extends her rejection of these systems to literary aesthetics, criticising 'Bennett, Galsworthy and so on' for adhering to a 'formal railway line of sentence' (*L3*, p. 135), and praising the fictitious Mary Carmichael for breaking both the sentence and the sequence (*ROO*, p. 81). The breaking of sequence, and the adoption of what Joseph Frank called 'spatial form', is common to many modernist works. The reader is encouraged to interpret the works as if every word and image were simultaneously present. However, the term 'spatial form' is Frank's: Woolf described her formal innovations in her own particular language.

The phrase about the 'railway line' of sentence might suggest that in rejecting linearity, Woolf rejects technological modernity. In *The Waves* Bernard makes a similar association, likening a 'sound like the knocking of railway trucks' to 'the happy concatenation of one event following another in our lives. Knock, knock, knock. Must, must, must. Must go, must sleep, must wake, must get up' (*W*, p. 180). These skeletal narratives suggest the 'appalling narrative business of the realist: getting on from lunch to dinner' (*D3*, p. 209). Although Bernard appreciates their consolatory value more than Woolf, they indicate failed, unadventurous lives. However, technological modernity is not Woolf's real target. Bernard also associates the 'happy concatenation' with the 'small shopkeepers' and then with the 'boasting boys'. Woolf repeatedly associates linearity and measurement with the shopkeeping classes: both Sir William Bradshaw and Charles Tansley are the sons of grocers; elsewhere she ridicules the idea that gifts of mind and character 'can be weighed like sugar and butter' (*ROO*, p. 104). Moreover, she repeatedly associates linearity and regimentation with the exclusively male world of the public schools, the army and the empire. These associations link Woolf's rejection of linear form with her critique of patriarchy.

Technological modernity transformed perceptions of narrative and subjectivity. Woolf's representations of technology suggest that it anticipated her narrative innovations. Her fragmentary narrative syntax is anticipated by the experience of fast travel: for the narrator of 'The Mark on the Wall', the experience of being 'torn asunder' from the previous occupants of her house in mid-conversation resembles that of train travel (*CSF*, p. 83). Orlando's car journey out of London tears language asunder, slicing up a motto over a porch ('Amor Vincit Omnia', which becomes 'Amor Vin – '), and the name over an undertaker's business. Speed affects interpretation and identity: 'Nothing could be seen whole or read from start to finish. What was seen begun – like two friends starting to meet each other across the street – was never seen ended'; the 'process of motoring fast' resembles 'the chopping up small of identity' (*O*, p. 212). In her alignment of modernity and the machine, Woolf curiously and unexpectedly resembles the Italian Futurists, who celebrated the car, the train and the aeroplane; curiously, as she would certainly have felt uncomfortable with their pro-war, pro-fascist posturing.[20]

The attitudes of modernist writers to the present shaped their attitudes to the past. Social order and psychic integration were usually located in some pre-lapsarian era: for T. S. Eliot, the era of the metaphysical poets, before the 'dissociation of sensibility';[21] for Yeats, the era of Byzantium; for Pound, early in his career, that of the Provençal troubadours. The order of the past often manifested itself in the form of myth. Many modernist writers adopted what Eliot christened 'the mythic method' as a means 'of controlling, of ordering, of giving a shape and a significance to the immense panorama of futility and anarchy which is contemporary history' (Eliot, *Prose*, p. 177). Yeats employed his personal myths of gyres and cyclical history; Eliot employed the fertility myths of *The Waste Land*. Beyond literature, Nietzsche's use of the Apollonian and Dionysian, Freud's use of the Oedipus myth or Stravinsky's use of fertility myth in *Sacre du Printemps* (1913) seem to spring from the same source. All implicitly cast doubt on modern society's ability to control its own destiny, implying that we are powerless to resist these long-established narratives and patterns.

How did Woolf respond to mythic modernism? She was certainly aware of it, having read *Ulysses* and argued with Eliot about its value. From her first experimental work to her last, Woolf punctuates her narratives with glimpses of prehistory: the mark on the wall resembles at one moment 'a smooth tumulus like those barrows on the South Downs' (*CSF*, p. 86); in *Between the Acts* Mrs Swithin imagines 'rhododendron forests' in Piccadilly (*BA*, p. 8). However, prehistory and myth are not identical. Those allusions which apparently refer to fertility rites – the beggar-woman in *Mrs Dalloway* (pp. 88–90), or Septimus as the 'destroyer of crops' (p. 163) – are isolated, and cannot easily be forced into the pattern of mythic modernism. Woolf is not, as Carey argues, simply 'eliminating' beggars in a 'primitivist cosmetic haze' (*Intellectuals*, p. 37). One may attribute the mythicising representation of the beggar-woman to Peter or to the narrator – the text is ambiguous to this extent – but not to Woolf. She, through Rezia, presents her clearly and humanely, without myth: 'Poor old woman'. The 'primitivist haze', particularly if one attributes it to Peter, may indicate Woolf's dissatisfaction with the modernism of her contemporaries, and its dangerous potential to blur real political issues. Woolf's primeval glimpses do not provide a narrative, or even an interpretative framework. Rather, they function as interrogatives, questioning not only 'civilisation' but also mythic modernism, without providing any answers.

While Woolf does not privilege primeval time, in several works she idealises her characters' childhoods or early lives. The defining characteristics of the six characters in *The Waves* are determined from childhood onwards: Louis's fixation with punctuality, time and sequence is fixed from the moment he hears the church bells; his relationship with Rhoda, and their later dialogues, are anticipated in the way that he completes her third sentence. The novel's narrative is also structured around the idea of an original, mythic unity which is shattered by the death of Percival; literally and metaphorically, a myth of the fall. In *Mrs Dalloway*, Bourton has a similar mythic value. It is represented as a time of fluid sexual categories and flexible social roles, a time of idealism before the characters made their irrevocable choices. Although in the Bourton scenes some mention is made of historically specific topics, such as women's rights, generally speaking Bourton exists outside history, in sharp contrast to the contemporary scenes in London. But although Bourton acquires a mythic quality, it does not shape or control contemporary history.

Eliot took Joyce's *Ulysses* to exemplify the mythic method, but he underplayed Joyce's sense of the comic discrepancies between myth and contemporary history, between Odysseus the Homeric hero, and Leopold Bloom the advertising salesman. Without this ironic gap, the mythic representation of modern life implies a conservative view of history in which the lives of every generation are fundamentally the same. Such a view was advanced by T. E. Hulme, who wrote in 1912 that 'man' is 'an extraordinarily fixed and limited animal whose nature is absolutely constant' and that it is only by 'tradition and organisation that anything decent can be got out of him' (Hulme, *Writings*, p. 61). In aesthetic terms, the mythic method provided such organisation. Though the complexities of Woolf's politics cannot be adequately summarised in this chapter, her position was more liberal and progressive than those of many modernist contemporaries. In consequence, she did not consistently present the past as being more orderly than the present. Though Bourton is idyllic, and harboured from the brute realities of history, it is not more orderly than the London of 1923: at Bourton, subjectivity and sexuality are not policed, and time is not mechanically divided. Rather than neatly contrasting order and disorder, in *Mrs Dalloway* Woolf presents two different forms of chaos. In *To the Lighthouse*, the summers before the First World War, which were afterwards widely idealised, are shown by Woolf to contain suppressed violence between the generations, and, in Tansley's attitude to women artists, between the sexes.[22] Woolf's scepticism about the orderliness of the past is accentuated by her focus on women's history. *The Years*, though acknowledging the threat of fascism, views history as a narrative of increasing freedom. Although Woolf does not couple social and technological progress as the Edwardians did, her imagery of doors opening and barriers dissolving is a progressive, not a reactionary, modernism. In *Between the Acts* Woolf develops *To the Lighthouse*'s critique of the pre-war idyll. Again, the tranquillity of the British summer is seen to contain suppressed tension and violence. Moreover, the very idea of the nation is seen to be a myth, constructed through narratives such as the pageant, which Miss La Trobe subversively reworks. In place of the tableau of Britannia and the flag, the villagers are presented with the image of themselves. Myth here is seen not so much as the means of reintegrating the shattered psyche or social order, but as the very grounds of subjectivity itself. With regard to national myths at least, Woolf seems to have anticipated political critiques of mythic modernism.[23]

Urban life is characterised by the spectacle of the crowd, and the fascination of modernists with order and disorder is related to their reactions to the urban crowd. Modernist representations of the crowd are usually contemptuous, betraying occasionally an underlying fear of engulf-ment: Lawrence's Ursula sees Londoners as 'unliving, spectral people', and the crowds in *The Waste Land* are similarly etiolated.[24] The crowd is not purely a literary interest: it had become an important area of sociological and psychological investigation in the late nineteenth and early twentieth centuries, in works such as Gustave Le Bon's *Psychologie des foules* (1895), Wilfred Trotter's *Instincts of the Herd in Peace and War* (1916), and Freud's *Group Psychology and the Analysis of the Ego* (1921). In Britain in this period, the working classes became increasingly organised: the Inde-pendent Labour Party was formed in 1893, and the first Labour MPs were elected in 1906. If modernist writers pictured the masses as disorganised, devitalised or as a threat to aesthetic and political order, this was more a compensatory reaction than an accurate depiction.

Woolf's personal snobbery, and the many caustic remarks in her diaries, mark her out as standing aloof from the masses. It is on the basis of her self-conscious elitism that John Carey, in his influential polemic *The Intellectuals and the Masses*, groups her with T. S. Eliot, D. H. Lawrence and Pound. However, Carey conflates several distinct phenomena: Woolf's personal snobbery with her literary output; distaste for the working-class crowds with distaste for lower-middle-class individuals; and Bloomsbury snobbery with Nietzschean individualism. Woolf's response to *Ulysses* as an 'illiterate, underbred book . . . the book of a self taught working man' (*D2*, p. 189) indicates how far her social outlook could distort her judgement as a critic; but this is a response to an individual, not a crowd. In her diary Woolf describes a crowd on Hampstead Heath, and reveals her and Leonard's reaction: 'the crowd at close quarters is detestable; it smells; it sticks' and is 'a tepid mass of flesh scarcely organised into human life'. But her reaction transmutes:

> But they looked well dressed & well fed; & at a distance among the canary coloured swings & roundabouts they had the look of a picture. It was a summers day – in the sun at least; we could sit on a mound & look at the little distant trickle of human beings eddying round the chief centres of gaiety & filing over the heath & spotted upon its humps. Very little noise they made; the large aeroplane that came flying so steadily over head made more noise than the whole crowd of us. Why do I say 'us'? I never for a moment felt myself one of 'them'. (*D1*, pp. 267–8)

When Woolf considers the crowd from a distance, in artistic terms, it becomes beautiful. Unlike Lawrence, who describes 'the masses' as nause-ating black beetles, Woolf sees them as almost inanimate objects. Her narrators and characters tend to view things similarly: the 'eddies' of the crowds on Hampstead Heath recall the 'eddies' of the dance in *The Voyage Out*, from which Helen and Rachel were similarly detached (*VO*, p. 139); the impersonality of the perception recalls the 'dissolving and combining pattern of black particles', which is Ralph's agitated perception of the street crowds (*ND*, p. 193). While this impersonality may be ethically question-able, it differs greatly from Lawrence's response. Notably, the strength of Woolf's aesthetic attraction to the crowds causes her momentarily to identify with them.

The French school of writing known as 'unanimism' was concerned with the 'group', and the idea that all members of a group shared a common consciousness or, in the literal meaning of 'unanimous', one spirit or mind. It was often defined in contradistinction to the 'virile' or individualist school of modernism, one that drew inspiration from Nietzsche's idea of the *übermensch* (literally, 'overman' or 'superman').[25] British writers who might have been alarmed by the 'crowd' warmed briefly to the idea of the 'group' in the years from 1913 to 1919, though many ultimately rejected it as incompatible with their individualist philosophy. Woolf was more sympathetic than many of her contemporaries, and the influence was longer-lasting. Jules Romains, the most important figure in the school, had developed the idea from the poetry of Whitman, the philosophy of Bergson, and from an experiment in communal living.[26] He expounded it in the essay 'Réflexions', translated in 1913 by Ezra Pound, and put it into practice in poetry, a play and a novel, *Mort de Quelqu'un* (1911), translated in 1914 by Woolf's friends Sydney Waterlow and Desmond MacCarthy as *Death of a Nobody*. Leonard Woolf explained Romains's ideas in 1913, emphasising that he was not interested in characters as individuals but as part of the group; he was interested in the 'consciousness of the group in addition to that of the individual' (*E2*, p. 17).[27] For Romains, the individual consciousness is not spatially restricted to the body, but extends beyond it as an intangible field of force. Each being 'exists a great deal in one place, rather less in others, and further on, a second being commences before the first has left off . . . Everything over-crosses, coincides and cohabits.'[28]

While Pound was dismissively vague about unanimism, describing it as 'the adoration of the group unit or something of that sort',[29] Woolf was more sympathetic. As Leonard Woolf described it, *Mort de Quelqu'un* suggested the possibility of a novel in which there were 'no "characters", no humour, no plot' (*E2*, p. 16). Its narrative begins with the death of a retired engine driver, Godard, who lives alone, and it follows the news of his death spreading across France, touching and involving individuals who had never known him. The novel ends with the extended reflections of a young man who had passed Godard's funeral cortège a year earlier. In *Mrs Dalloway*, the 'nobody' is Septimus. While Woolf's novel is less concerned with the spreading of news, it retains many of Romains's images of mysterious interconnection: webs, filaments and spreading ripples. The crowd scenes which focus on the backfiring car and the aeroplane are also unanimist in their spirit. The early title of *The Waves*, 'the life of anybody', hints at a more optimistic rewriting of 'the death of a nobody';[30] Bernard's concluding soliloquy parallels that of the young man in *Mort de Quelqu'un*. However, in the final version Woolf is more pessimistic than Romains: the death of Percival, the linchpin, threatens the group consciousness. For Woolf, unanimism overcomes the solipsism which was an inherent danger of Paterian aesthetics: the 'stream of consciousness' can refer to the group's consciousness as much as the individual's. For many other modernists, the collective consciousness grew only from knowledge of 'tradition', or 'race consciousness'.[31] Mystical and idealistic though it may be, unanimism offered an alternative, in which strangers could be united in their experience of the moment.

Like her modernist contemporaries, Woolf believed that changes in the modern world had changed subjectivity itself. What Lawrence described in 1914 as the 'old stable ego' of character, and the coherent moral order which sustained it, no longer existed.[32] However, there was no universal agreement about the new form of human subjectivity, and once again Woolf differs from many of her contemporaries. In the letter cited above, Lawrence declares his intention to explore the inhuman will, a 'deeper' self than ordinary feelings. Broadly speaking, Lawrence's distinction between human feelings and the inhuman will corresponds to that which T. E. Hulme made between empathy and abstraction. The artist of abstraction, whether 'primitivist' Egyptian or modernist European, sought to present angular and geometrical outlines, eschewing the softness and 'vitality' of the empathist.

Woolf was more inclined to value empathy than her contemporaries, and less inclined to admire 'abstraction'. Yeats drew a sharp distinction between the self and its antithetical mask in *A Vision* (1925); Eliot drew a sharp distinction between Ben Jonson and Shakespeare, suggesting that Jonson's interest in abstraction and surfaces was the more suited to the modern temper. Woolf did not theorise her preferences explicitly, but she seems to have recognised a more fluid relation between the mask and the true self. She subscribes to the Bergsonian idea that 'in each of us there are two different selves'.[33] In one the mental life is 'narrowed down to a point' to focus on a situation of 'imminent danger'; in the other, as in states of reverie, it is diffused.[34] Clarissa Dalloway, drawing her face to a point in front of the mirror, is not in obvious physical danger (*Mrs D*, p. 40); nor was Woolf when, in very similar terms, she resented having to become 'concentrated', drawing upon 'the scattered parts' of her character when Waterlow visited (*D2*, p. 193); but the essential Bergsonian pattern of dilation and contraction underlies Woolf's idea of the self. The similarities between the 'contracted' self and the 'mask' of abstraction are less significant than the differences: while the modes of abstraction and empathy are absolutely distinct, the two Bergsonian selves shade off into each other; and while Woolf recognised the co-existence of the two selves, she valued the 'dilated' self more highly than the 'contracted'.

Woolf's modernism does not conform to any abstract ideal of the movement, nor is it completely idiosyncratic. Her responses to literary and urban modernity often diverge from those of her contemporaries generally, her divergence being influenced by her immediate literary community, by imaginary communities of writers living and dead, and, importantly, by her political outlook. Her decision to revise the genre of family saga in *The Years* was as much political as aesthetic, as were the games she played with conventional biography in *Orlando*. Her lack of sympathy for the Nietzschean and 'classicist' strands of modernism may not have been a conscious political choice, but it had political implications.

Woolf's aestheticisation of the political was and is double-edged. Identifying dominant power interests with abstract ideas such as linearity allowed her to introduce political ideas into her works without the explicit commentary of a narrator, and allowed these ideas (or their anti-types) to inform the very structure of her works. But the very absence of overt commentary means that readers can easily miss, or radically misinterpret, the political aspects of her novels. The question of how to combine politics and modernist aesthetics became more urgent with the crises of the 1930s. Woolf's struggle with the omniscient narratorial voice in the manuscripts of *The Years* (*The Pargiters*) illustrates one side of the problem, and the highly compressed literary and contemporary allusions in *The Years* and *Between the Acts* exemplify the other. There are other problems. The very economy of aestheticisation led Woolf to conflate the shopkeeping and the upper middle classes, presenting both as exponents of linear, mechanical thinking, though their political and cultural ideals were profoundly different. Woolf's modernist scepticism about 'the real standard thing' can be seen as a questioning of the ideological process by which one social group represents its interests as more 'real' or 'natural' than those of any other group; but it can also prevent readers from speaking about the material world in which real lives were lived, without which politics would be meaningless.[35] The mobile Paterian consciousness and the dilating and contracting Bergsonian self are not ideally formed to make a firm stand against anything, but they enable Woolf's texts continually to interrogate the assumptions of her readers and those of modernism.

NOTES

1 All references to Woolf's texts are to the 1992 Penguin editions, with the exception of *The Complete Shorter Fiction*, edited by Susan Dick, revised second edition (London: Hogarth, 1989) and *The Essays of Virginia Woolf*, edited by Andrew McNeillie (London: Hogarth, 1986–94).

2 Leonard Woolf, *Beginning Again* (London: Hogarth, 1964), p. 37. However, Einstein's new theories were not widely discussed in Britain until 1919.

3 Randall Stevenson, *Modernist Fiction: An Introduction* (Hemel Hempstead: Harvester Wheatsheaf, 1992), pp. 1–3; Matei Calinescu, *Five Faces of Modernity* (Durham, NC: Duke University Press, 1987), pp. 80–5.

4 *Letters of Leonard Woolf*, ed. Frederic Spotts (London: Weidenfeld and Nicolson, 1989), pp. 485–6. The book was Karin Stephen's *The Misuse of Mind* (1922).

5 More details of Russell's and Sanger's scientific books may be found in Michael Whitworth, 'The Clothbound Universe', *Publishing History* 40 (1996), pp. 53–82.

6 Linda Hutcheon, *Formalism and the Freudian Aesthetic: the Example of Charles Mauron* (London: Routledge and Kegan Paul, 1984), pp. 52–3.

7 Peter Faulkner, *Modernism* (London: Methuen, 1977), pp. 19–20; Edward Bishop, 'Re:Covering Modernism – Format and Function in the Little Magazines' in *Modernist Writers and the Marketplace*, ed. Ian Willison, Warwick Gould and Warren Chernaik (London: Macmillan, 1996), pp. 287–8.

8 Laura Marcus, 'Virginia Woolf and the Hogarth Press', in *Modernist Writers and the Marketplace*, eds. Willison *et al.*, p. 131.

9 Terry Eagleton, 'Capitalism, Modernism, and Postmodernism', *Modern Criticism and Theory: A Reader*, ed. David Lodge (Harlow: Longman, 1988), p. 392.

10 *The Collected Writings of T. E. Hulme*, ed. Karen Csengeri (Oxford University Press, 1994), pp. 255–62.

11 I have given the titles used in Andrew McNeillie's *Essays of Virginia Woolf*: Woolf revised her essay 'Mr Bennett and Mrs Brown' (1923) under the title 'Character in Fiction' (1924); this revised essay was later reissued by the Hogarth Press as a pamphlet entitled 'Mr Bennett and Mrs Brown': see McNeillie, *Essays* 3, pp. 388 n. 1 and 436 n. 1.

12 A. S. Eddington, *The Nature of the Physical World* (Cambridge University Press, 1928), p. 1.

13 Wyndham Lewis, *Men Without Art* (1934), ed. Seamus Cooney (Santa Rosa, CA: Black Sparrow, 1987), p. 132.

14 John Carey, *The Intellectuals and the Masses: Pride and Prejudice among the Literary Intelligentsia, 1880–1939* (London: Faber and Faber, 1992), pp. 175–6.

15 Gillian Beer, *Virginia Woolf: The Common Ground* (Edinburgh University Press, 1996), p. 100.
16 Walter Pater, *The Renaissance*, ed. Donald L. Hill (Berkeley: University of California Press, 1980), pp. 186–7.
17 Walter Pater, *Marius the Epicurean*, ed. Michael Levey (Harmondsworth: Penguin, 1985), p. 113.
18 Perry Meisel, *The Absent Father: Virginia Woolf and Walter Pater* (New Haven: Yale University Press, 1980), p. 52.
19 T. S. Eliot, *Collected Poems and Plays* (London: Faber and Faber, 1969), pp. 22, 67, 69.
20 Judy Rawson, 'Italian Futurism', in *Modernism: 1890–1930*, ed. Malcolm Bradbury and James McFarlane, pp. 243–58.
21 T. S. Eliot, *Selected Prose*, ed. Frank Kermode (London: Faber and Faber, 1975), p. 64.
22 Paul Fussell, *The Great War and Modern Memory* (Oxford University Press, 1975), pp. 23–4.
23 For this criticism of mythic modernism, see Fredric Jameson, '"Ulysses" in History', *James Joyce and Modern Literature*, ed. W. J. McCormack and Alistair Stead (London: Routledge and Kegan Paul, 1982), pp. 127–8.
24 D. H. Lawrence, *The Rainbow*, ed. Mark Kinkead-Weekes (Cambridge University Press, 1989), p. 342.
25 Herbert Read, 'An Approach to Jules Romains', *Art and Letters* 2, no. 1 (Winter 1918–19), p. 45. See also Patrick Bridgewater, 'English Writers and Nietzsche', in *Nietzsche: Imagery and Thought*, ed. Malcolm Pasley (London: Methuen, 1978), pp. 220–58.
26 P. J. Norrish, 'Romains and L'Abbaye', *Modern Language Review* 52 (1957), pp. 518–25.
27 This review is included in *E2*, but the fourth edition of B. J. Kirkpatrick's bibliography (1997) attributes it to Leonard. However, Virginia was very probably aware of Romains's novel and Leonard's review.
28 Jules Romains, 'Réflexions', tr. Ezra Pound, reprinted in *Instigations of Ezra Pound* (New York: Boni and Liveright, 1920), pp. 81–2.
29 Pound, review of Romains's *Odes et Prières*, *Poetry (Chicago)* II, no. 6 (September 1913), pp. 187–9.
30 *Draft W*, ed. J. W. Graham (London: Hogarth, 1976), Draft 1, p. 1.
31 T. S. Eliot, 'Tradition and the Individual Talent' (1919), *Selected Prose*, ed. Frank Kermode (London: Faber and Faber, 1975), pp. 37–44; Ezra Pound, 'On Technique', *The New Age*, 10 (1911–12), pp. 297–9.
32 *The Collected Letters of D. H. Lawrence*, ed. James T. Boulton *et al.* (Cambridge University Press, 1979–93), 2, pp. 182–3.
33 Sydney Waterlow, 'The Philosophy of Henri Bergson', *Quarterly Review* 430 (1912), p. 159.
34 *Ibid.*, p. 166.
35 For an introduction to 'ideology' in this sense, see Catherine Belsey's *Critical Practice* (London: Methuen, 1980), and for criticism of modernism and the 'real social order', see Eagleton's 'Capitalism, Modernism and Postmodernism'.

9

SUE ROE

The impact of post-impressionism

Ethics and art

When the young Virginia Stephen first began to join in discussions with her brother Thoby Stephen's friends who were just down from Cambridge and making new lives in London – people such as Clive Bell, Lytton Strachey, Maynard Keynes – she had already begun to write. She was trying out descriptions of landscape and anecdotal stories designed to show up elements of colour, light, transpositions in language and human character. She described railway journeys[1] and disasters in duckponds;[2] she made up stories about two young ladies going into the society of university educated people and being shocked by the frankness of the discussion: they discovered that one could discuss politics and philosophy in a charged, energetic way; and that talk was designed to discover things and share ideas, rather than being employed simply to perform the acrobatics of polite society (to amuse, while keeping one's own and the listener's actual views and emotions at bay).[3]

There must have been a significant disparity between the materials she was working with to ply the tools of her trade, and the content of the intellectual discussions to which Thoby Stephen introduced her and her sister Vanessa. The feelings of exclusion called up in her by observing the ease with which educated men communicated with one another never left her. Her writing is split, throughout her *œuvre*, into the kind of writing which makes discoveries through styles of aesthetic charge, and the writings in which she plied her social conscience. In the latter, she usually wrote under strain. *The Years* proved particularly difficult to write; she only wrote with enjoyment about her political anger when she was either being funny, as in *A Room of One's Own* and *Orlando*, or using her aesthetic palette, as in her depiction of Septimus Smith in *Mrs Dalloway*: the novel in which language is stripped and unpeeled, set on fire; her colours are dark and stark, her style is expressionist, showing a mind blown open. The imagery is graphic, intensely visual.

The men – as Virginia Woolf discovered during those early years when Thoby and Vanessa had their evenings at home, and 'Bloomsbury' began to take shape – had been influenced at Cambridge by G. E. Moore. His *Principia Ethica* (1903) challenged prevailing ideas about ethics, fundamentally undermining current ideas about what constituted the notion of good. The implications of this were far-reaching; they broadened out to change the foundation of early-twentieth-century ideas about what constituted civilisation, and civilised behaviour. G. E. Moore advanced the idea that not only was good nothing but itself – immeasurable in terms of other styles of being – but it was indefinable. It had an intrinsic, inner logic and meaning, rather than being a state arrived at by imposing moral judgements. In order to explain this, he used an example which offered a tantalising challenge to philosophers, even while it might not entirely have satisfied art historians. He held that, like 'yellow', 'good' was a simple notion that defied analysis: 'just as you cannot, by any manner of means, explain to anyone who does not already know it, what yellow is, so you cannot explain what good is'. It was, he wrote, 'one of those innumerable objects of thought which are themselves incapable of definition, because they are the ultimate terms by reference to which whatever *is* capable of definition must be defined'.[4] Of course, this begs an enormous question, assuming as it does that yellow may only be perceived as a single, unalterable tone and that pigmentation and light sources are themselves unchangeable states. But the way Moore was using colour here was as a metaphor for unchangeable abstraction. It was this usage that Virginia Woolf would later tease open, incorporating it into her own implicitly interrogative style of experimentation.

The perception of good as irreducible to definition was an entirely radical idea, and contemporary thinkers saw that all sorts of implications for good conduct and right action might be deduced from it. Virginia Woolf has Helen Ambrose read *Principia Ethica* in her first novel, *The Voyage Out*: it explains why she is such an irrational, sensual creature; such a radical thinker (*VO*, p. 65).[5] The Bloomsbury sisters, unchaperoned, witnessed conversations which panned out into jokes about licence, even licentiousness. We all know the story of Lytton Strachey pointing to a stain on Vanessa's dress: 'Semen?'[6] Quite a lot of this remained theoretical. Vanessa's love affair with Roger Fry was a well-guarded secret,[7] as was the parentage of Angelica Garnett.[8] But what could be said seemed to be moving closer to what was actually being felt; and if this was so, writing and painting could take on new responsibilities: both media needed to find new languages for subjective experience; new ways of depicting the rhythms of the inner life.

The other principle on which Moore's ideas were founded was the principle of organic unity. Things mean, in as far as they connect. (Forster's 'only connect' has its source here.) In other words, meaning was relative. Beauty, consciousness, intimacy: all became concepts subject to redefinition, because they could no longer be seen to exist on the basis of preconceived ideas about conduct and morality. Contemplation of beauty was good in and for itself; affection was a good, for its own sake – if it was genuine. The search for truth took on new styles of enquiry and travelled in new philosophical directions. Bloomsbury took up these philosophical ideas and related them to its emerging ideas about art. Through Vanessa, Roger Fry became part of the circle: he knew that since the end of the previous century in France, painters had been thinking in new ways about making an impact in visual form. Vanessa, in the relatively early days of the Slade, was initially still influenced by the English school of painting. But Roger Fry's knowledge and expertise brought French subjectivism to Bloomsbury: it profoundly influenced Vanessa's painting, and, gradually, these ideas filtered into Virginia Woolf's writing.

Visual ideas and personal values evolved together, as Virginia Woolf began the laborious process of producing her first, absurdly ambitious, full-length novel, *The Voyage Out*. While Vanessa was producing new work such as the haunting and mysterious *Studland Beach* (c. 1912)[9] – a painting which perhaps of all her paintings most hauntingly suggests the psychological implications of her experimentation with form – Virginia laboured with the plight of Rachel Vinrace, the heroine under desperate pressure to reveal an inner life which has not yet been formed; and to form it under the weight of the pressure to prove that she is as intellectual as the men she encounters on her voyage out into womanhood, a maiden voyage from which she never returns. The discussion, on this dreadful voyage, all revolves around ideas with which Rachel is largely unfamiliar: people read Greek, discuss Gibbon; and appear to talk nonsense. At the same time, she is being put under pressure by the man she wishes to marry, Terence Hewet, and by his friend St John Hirst, to express her deepest feelings: to shed, in other words, intellectual paraphernalia with which she does not feel furnished in the first place.

The pressure is to connect, reveal, relate. But, as perceived by the men, it is a largely cerebral endeavour. The endeavour itself may be seen as emanating from G. E. Moore: 'Personal affections and aesthetic enjoyments include *all* the greatest, and *by far* the greatest, goods we can imagine.'[10]

What mattered were states of mind, and personal integrity. Aesthetic contemplation and personal affection became the basis of Virginia Woolf's writing in *The Voyage Out*. In that novel, Rachel Vinrace spends a lot of time alone, trying to search within herself to discover the true nature of her reactions to things, and her responses to people. But she cannot embody this search. It was impossible for a good Victorian daughter to shed the profound, educated ignorance which was designed to prevent self-knowledge. Eventually, Rachel becomes broken, deformed, by the endeavour. She develops a highly symbolic fever and becomes delirious, incapable of following a train of thought; floating in and out of consciousness:

> For six days indeed she had been oblivious of the world outside, because it needed all her attention to follow the hot, red, quick, sights which passed incessantly before her eyes . . . the faces . . . were worrying because they distracted her attention and she might miss the clue . . . Now they were among trees and savages, now they were on the sea, now . . . they jumped, now they flew. But just as the crisis was about to happen, something invariably slipped in her brain, so that the whole effort had to begin over again. The heat was suffocating. At last the faces went further away; she fell into a deep pool of sticky water, which eventually closed over her head. She saw nothing.
>
> (*VO*, pp. 321–2)

In Virginia Woolf's second novel, *Night and Day*, the heroine asks 'Why should there be this perpetual disparity between the thought and the action, between the life of solitude and the life of society?' (p. 3). Throughout Woolf's fiction, her heroines – Clara Durrant, Mrs Dalloway, Mrs Ramsay, Isa Oliver – all find different ways of asking the same thing. What Virginia Woolf came to realise, particularly after the First World War, when everyone's social perceptions were changed irrevocably, was that her responsibility as an artist was not to solve this problem, but – in the most resonant, colourful, dynamic ways possible – to depict it. By the time she came to draft *Between the Acts*, she was still grappling with this struggle in the soul, and it eventually tipped her into the mental exhaustion that killed her. In the meantime, she wove it into her writing, finding, as her writing developed, increasingly more experimental and more complex ways of incorporating into her writing style a synaesthesia which began, for her, with the challenge she set herself to see writing initially, at some vital level, as a visual medium.

It was undoubtedly Roger Fry – with a little help from T. S. Eliot,[11] an injection of indignant anger sparked by Katherine Mansfield[12] and the challenge of knowing that James Joyce[13] was, in *Ulysses*, making new, implicitly competing experiments – who radically changed Virginia Woolf's writing, liberating it from the exhaustions of *The Voyage Out* and the frustrations of *Night and Day* into the floods of light and colour we know it by. Fry's exhibitions of post-impressionist paintings at the Grafton Galleries[14] in London in 1910 and 1912–13 included works by Cézanne, Van Gogh and Picasso, and were instrumental in making the British public realise how far the French painters were exceeding them in their experimentation with form. Paintings criticised as being comparable with the daubs of children educated (or failed to educate) the British eye to see rhythms and connections they had not formerly been accustomed to seeing. Virginia Woolf was closely in touch with the art world; it is commonly assumed that when she wrote that 'in or around December 1910, human character changed', she was referring to that first Grafton exhibition. Subjectivism meant that form itself had psychological connotations – Roger Fry argued that 'the graphic arts are the expression of the imaginative life rather than a copy of actual life'. He exemplified this by referring to children who 'never, as we say, "draw from nature", but express, with a delightful freedom and sincerity, the mental images which make up their own imaginative lives'.[15]

Roger Fry was a charismatic lecturer: he lectured on his ideas about post-impressionist theory in which he discussed the power of Primitive forms and the process of training the eye to see forms as opposed to prescribed representations. He made his public aware that they had been educated to see pictures, rather than the world. Those who held that a flash of black and red had nothing to do with a bull in a field had not just seen one; they were thinking, rather, of a bull as depicted in a naturalist painting.[16] The post-impressionists knew that a purple shadow might movingly suggest the form of a seated mother and child, without irreverence.[17] By the time Katherine Mansfield reviewed *Night and Day* and declared disparagingly that she had never thought to look upon its like again – had Virginia Woolf not realised that ideas about the form of the novel had moved on? – Roger Fry had collected together his articles on aesthetics in one volume under the title *Vision and Design* and Virginia Woolf was reading it.[18] She found there – especially in his 'An Essay in Aesthetics' – many of the ideas which would inform her later work. The paradox of post-impressionism was its recognition that subjectivism found expression in surface – this is the principle Lily Briscoe is working on as she paints Mrs Ramsay's portrait in *To the Lighthouse*. The post-impressionists explored the notion that it was the function of art not to imitate but to find equivalents; thus vision and design worked inextricably together, and 'one chief aspect of order in a work of art is unity . . . in a picture this unity is due to a balancing of the attractions of the eye about the central line of the picture' (*Vision and Design*, p. 34). Virginia Woolf, challenged on the matter by Fry, wittily denied that the lighthouse in *To the Lighthouse* had any particular function, except to focus the eye about the central 'line' of her novel. Also collected in *Vision and Design* is Fry's lecture on 'Negro Sculpture'[19] which gave Virginia Woolf pause for thought as she began working on the short stories which led her to *Jacob's Room*: 'Kew Gardens', 'An Unwritten Novel' and 'The Mark on the Wall'. One passage from 'Negro Sculpture' ('in the last sixty years, knowledge and perception have poured upon us so fast that the whole well-ordered system has been blown away, and we stand bare to the blast, scarcely able to snatch a hasty generalisation or two to cover our nakedness for a moment' (*Vision and Design*, p. 86)) finds its echo in 'A Mark on the Wall': 'Why, if one wants to compare life to anything, one must liken it to being blown through the Tube at fifty miles an hour – landing at the other end without a single hairpin . . . Shot out at the feet of God entirely naked!'[20] Realism was getting a shake-up; none of the old prejudices about the construction of a work of art any longer held firm.

One painting Vanessa did at around this time was called *A Conversation (1913–16)*.[21] It depicts three women seated together at a window, with a background motif of a vase of flowers, leaning over, deep in gossipy conversation. Whatever they have to say to each other is so absorbing that the forms are squashed out to follow it: their broad, rounded backs are curved like tulip stems, their small heads reduced in size by comparison: their whole bodies are talking. It is a dynamic, witty presentation of flesh bending to the business of life. Virginia Woolf saw it exhibited at the Omega. This painting, her conversations with and familiarity with the work of painters and writers at the time (she now knew Eliot's *The Waste Land*, Joyce's *Ulysses*, Katherine Mansfield's *Prelude*) and Fry's lectures on aesthetic form stimulated a wealth of new ideas about how to make new experiments in writing. She wrote a short story which, as Vanessa was to point out, was close in its conception and form to *Three Women*: she called the story 'Kew Gardens'. It depicts the flare of colour and light seen by a snail's-eye view from the interior of a flower-bed. As the green stalks, the red, blue and yellow throats of the flowers emerge into 'a straight bar, rough with gold dust', the language of the prose yields up a moving light which travels upwards from the interior of the flowers, out to the prisms reflected by drops of water on inner and outer petals, so that this becomes the light we now, standing back a little, see the whole forms by. This is an ingenious experiment: it enables the narrator to guide the reader's eye through from inner to outer forms in the way Picasso urges in his cubist work;[22] in the way Cézanne trains the eye by guiding our ingestion of subtly graded colour through vertical and horizontal lines.[23] The difference between the painter's brush and the writer's, moreover, is that the writer may, as we travel through the linear compulsion of the sentence, give us nowhere else to look. She seems to have known this and wittily to have taken advantage of it. In this story we may witness the evolution of a technique which was to forcibly and comprehensively alter her view of what was possible, in terms of rendering the organic world in written forms.

Synaesthesia infuses our reading, through a technique which is tactile, transformative, but never suffocates. Through the fibres of this story, Virginia Woolf trickles bits of the imagined conversation of human figures, passing at great height through the flower bed. She tries her hand, as T. S. Eliot did in *The Waste Land*, at working-class voices: 'Nell, Bert, Lot, Cess, Phil, Pa, he says, I says, she says. I says, I says, I says – '/'My Bert, Sis, Bill, Grandad, the old man, sugar / Sugar, flour, kippers, greens, / Sugar, sugar, sugar' (*SSS*, p. 50). The snatches are brief, the political implications, such as they are, do not matter. People are talking intently, both deeply and idly in conversation: there is a kind of organicism in this; a shapely, rhythmical form which connects with the interacting forms of the flowers themselves as they open out into the light. A woman comes to a standstill, like a standing figure in a portrait:

> The ponderous woman looked through the pattern of falling words at the flowers standing cool, firm, and upright in the earth, with a curious expression. She saw them as a sleeper waking from a heavy sleep sees a brass candlestick reflecting the light in an unfamiliar way, and closes his eyes and opens them. (*SSS*, p. 50)

The later languages of *Mrs Dalloway*, the 'Time Passes' section of *To the Lighthouse* and *The Waves* begin here. Later preoccupations, in those novels, with the tensions between civilisation and organicism are also being discovered, through the writing of this story.[24] The mechanised world of city life, the slightly mechanical, slightly organic lilt of the human voice speaking socially, the rhythms of nature, are all fused:

> there was no silence, all the time the motor omnibuses were turning their wheels and changing their gear; like a vast nest of Chinese boxes all of wrought steel turning ceaselessly one within another the city murmured; on the top of which the voices cried aloud and the petals of myriads of flowers flashed their colours into the air. (*SSS*, p. 52)

'Blue and Green'

One of Roger Fry's great talents was a kind of aesthetic agility which enabled him to reconcile within his own vision elements of a wide range of knowledge, acquired through a facility for making connections of the kind

I have outlined above. In a sense we may deem him the most cerebral of Bloomsbury's artists: it was he who gave the lectures, devised the theories, coined the phrase 'post-impressionism'. But one of the many paradoxes of Bloomsbury's vision in its wider sense was that a comprehensive knowledge of the past informed the new. We may see in Duncan Grant's paintings, for instance, a wealth of knowledge and a broad range of influences from the past – particularly the Florentine past.[25] His paintings pick up and play with ideas culled from studying Italian frescoes: we may see in his work echoes particularly of Piero della Francesca. There is nothing new under the sun: the Camden Town artists (Sickert,[26] Gore[27]) investigated the possibility of showing newly intimate relationships between artists and sitters in bedrooms rather than drawing rooms; Duncan Grant drew together ideas from African primitivism and Italian frescoes. Artists work, always, with the human form, still life; the problem of how to light interiors: it was ever thus. What was new was the daring way in which connections now reconciled what in the past would have been thought of as irreconcilable forms; and this became a subtly political issue: the human form now transcended issues of social standing.[28] This, as I have already suggested, seemed harder to achieve in writing, but it was part of what Virginia Woolf was striving for.

While Duncan Grant was bringing a couple of ornate red and gold prayer seats on casters back from his travels to his bedroom at Charleston – anxious, while heralding in the new, not to lose sight of the old – Virginia Woolf toiled with the business of building forms in space, creating colour and evoking light in writing. In a sense therefore she was working as she moved into her new experimental phase with the ancient problems of picture-making. We may see her as she drafts her early short stories, working very loosely with paintings in mind – perhaps not particular ones, but she seems to have been making connections which involved reconciling classical images with the impact of looking at an object and seeing it as if for the first time. This is surely how we must read the two tiny icons 'Blue' and 'Green'. Here, in its entirety, is 'Blue':

> The snub-nosed monster rises to the surface and spouts through his blunt nostrils two columns of water which, fiery-white in the centre, spray off into a fringe of blue beads. Strokes of blue line the black tarpaulin of his hide. Slushing the water through mouth and nostrils he sinks, heavy with water, and the blue closes over him dowsing the polished pebbles of his eyes. Thrown upon the beach he lies, blunt, obese, shedding dry blue scales. Their metallic blue stains the rusty iron on the beach. Blue are the ribs of the wrecked rowing boat. A wave rolls beneath the blue bells. But the cathedral's different, cold, incense laden, faint blue with the veils of madonnas.   (SSS, p. 45)

See how wild and beautiful this image is. A blue whale – or perhaps it is a fish – (or perhaps purely a figment of the imagination: nostrils?) becomes fantastic, through its hugeness, its heaviness, the way it slumps into motionlessness; through these cascading tones of blue the water becomes a 'fringe of blue beads'; his hide is 'strokes of blue'; what closes over him as he sinks down is simply pure colour: 'the blue'. Thrown onto the beach in this conglomeration of dense colour, he sheds 'dry blue scales' and Virginia Woolf pulls us up very close and speeds up time – as she did in 'Kew Gardens' – so that we can actually see this happening. The rusty iron on the beach, stained with monster scales, becomes blue. The ribs of the wrecked rowing boat, included to highlight perspective, become blue. The sea becomes a sea of 'blue bells' (or perhaps bluebells). And we are shown with no preamble (the way Roger Fry would change slides in a lecture, the way Proust wrote by following frame with frame) the next picture which is of a cathedral. It is different: 'cold, incense laden, faint blue with the veils of madonnas'. This is the story of how the Madonna becomes – or may be seen in juxtaposition with – a blue whale. We are the viewers, it is for us to decide the *sense* – or senses – in which the Madonna may also be stroked with blue, shedding blue, stained blue, a sea of blue, veiled with blue.

'Blue' belongs with 'Green'. Virginia Woolf again – in this equally small picture/story – experiments with the depiction of pure colour, inviting us to look and make comparisons. Here is 'Green' in its entirety:

> The pointed fingers of glass hang downwards. The light slides down the glass, and drops a pool of green. All day long the ten fingers of the lustre drop green upon the marble. The feathers of parakeets – their harsh cries – sharp blades of palm trees – green too; green needles glittering in the sun. But the hard glass drips on to the marble; the pools hover above the desert sand; the camels lurch through them; the pools settle on the marble; rushes edge them; weeds clog them; here and there a white blossom; the frog flops over; at night the stars are set there unbroken. Evening comes, and the shadow sweeps the green over the mantle-piece; the ruffled surface of ocean. No ships come; the aimless waves sway beneath the empty sky. It's night; the needles drip blots of blue. The green's out. (*SSS*, p. 44)

Again we are asked to look at a picture and picture a scene. The starting-point seems to be a glass lustre – a Victorian ornament composed of suspended glass prisms – which stands on the mantelpiece. (Virginia Woolf was fascinated by the vulgarity of these objects and joked about her poor taste in interior design in admiring them as she did.)[29] Above the mantel-piece is a painting of parakeets. Here are their cries, evoked through the greenness of their feathers; and now that we can see them, hear them, we can imagine them in their indigenous setting, over desert sand, in stark contrast to this cold marble, hit with hot green, refracted through glass. As the day draws out and the light begins to fade, the green falls into shadow and here are now simply waves of colour; the lustre changes from throwing off green to blue reflections. Virginia Woolf intended 'Blue and Green' to be read together; she draws 'Blue' back into the picture through the medium of the lustre, as its green needles of glass now begin to drip 'blots of blue'. The green's out when the light finally goes out, leaving us with the after-image of 'blots' of blue shadow. Both stories are about looking and about what happens as we look and look: the transition Woolf fictionalised when she had Mrs Ramsay flash her knitting needles and appeal to Mr Ramsay to 'look then, feel then' (*TL*, p. 43).

These stories hark back, moreover, to Virginia Woolf's study of G. E. Moore, and forward into a new style of experimentation with the rendering of his ideas. S. P. Rosenbaum has pointed out that 'Blue' and 'Green' seem to be exercises in the rendering of consciousness.[30] He relates them directly to Moore's essay 'The Refutation of Idealism' (1903), in which Moore again uses colour as a metaphor, this time for consciousness itself:

> The term 'blue' is easy enough to distinguish, but the other element which I have called 'consciousness' – that which sensation of blue has in common with sensation of green – is extremely difficult to fix. That many people fail to distinguish it at all is sufficiently shown by the fact that there are materialists. And, in general, that which makes the sensation of blue a mental fact seems to escape us: it seems, if I may use a metaphor, to be transparent – we look through it and see nothing but the blue; we may be convinced that there *is* something but *what* it is no philosopher, I think, has yet clearly recognised.
>
> (*SSS*, p. 114)

The short stories are small masterpieces, entirely in the spirit of post-impressionism, the movement in painting which experimented with its own classical past, and tried for a new quality of immediacy. What is being introduced here is a range of synaesthetic possibilities now thrown up by a process which combines narrative composition with the practice of *seeing*: it moved Woolf on to the still more complex experiment of 'Kew Gardens', in which she now intersperses with its flashing reds, its play of light upon colour, the drifts of human voices; she could then move further still, into the more sustained and yet more flexible narratives of 'An Unwritten Novel' (which plays again, in a more sustained way, with the role of the imagination in story-telling) and thence into the distortions of 'Solid Objects', 'Moments of Being: "Slater's Pins Have No Points"' and 'Lappin and Lapinova' – with its psychological disorientations, its mock elegance – and on into the emotional chromatics of 'Monday or Tuesday'. That story begins to explore the need to ascertain perspective ('Radiating to a point men's feet and women's feet') and the power of colour ('black or gold-encrusted') to the need to play with language in similar ways: 'Desiring truth, awaiting it, laboriously distilling a few words, for ever desiring . . . for ever desiring truth' (*SSS*, p. 22). The definition of 'truth', like that of 'good', is of course one of philosophy's ancient quests. Here Woolf – more precisely than Moore with his deft but fragile use of colour as metaphor – imagines it in pictorial form: 'From ivory depths words rising shed their blackness, blossom and penetrate. Fallen the book; in the flame, in the smoke, in the momentary sparks – or now voyaging, the marble square pendant, minarets beneath and the Indian seas, while space rushes blue and stars glint – truth?' (*SSS*, p. 22). We may begin then, she seems to say, by plucking a metaphor randomly out of the air and then voyage far, far beyond it: 'Monday or Tuesday' is, at one level, the story of what words do to us; of what we do to words.

They distort us; we distort them. We necessarily distort, because our vision is subjective, and unfixed. Edgar Allan Poe, one of the writers whose work had profoundly influenced the thinking of contemporary painters, had written that were he called upon to define the term 'Art' he would call it 'the reproduction of what the Senses perceive in Nature through the veil of the soul'.[31] And so we are only one step away now from the realm of the supernatural in 'A Haunted House' where 'The wind roars up the avenue. Trees stoop and bend this way and that. Moonbeams splash and spill wildly in the rain. But the beam of the lamp falls straight from the window. The candle burns stiff and still. Wandering through the house, opening the windows, whispering not to wake us, the ghostly couple . . .' (*SSS*, p. 4). At the other pole, set down like stones, immovable as solid objects are words like the ones endlessly rolled around in *The Voyage Out* – here now recurring in the short story, 'A Society': 'What is chastity then? I mean is it good, or is it bad, or is it nothing at all?' (*SSS*, p. 14): horrid, stubborn, uncontingent, unimaginative, morally determined words, which tell a story which keeps breaking up the surface of Virginia Woolf's synaesthetic picture-making, to recur and recur, turning up again in *Night and Day*, *Three Guineas*, *The Years* and even in the interstices of her final attempt to connect the seemingly irreconcilable *Between the Acts*. But the synaesthetic pictures drove her on, appearing for the first time in a full-length novel, in the pictures of loose women and half-lit rooms in *Jacob's Room*: that novel took its cue from the story-telling by hints and guesses of 'An Unwritten Novel' and from the experimentation with perspective which Woolf began in 'Blue and Green', investigated further in 'Kew Gardens' and developed even more fully, incorporating a broader range of ideas, in 'The Mark on the Wall'.

'The Mark on the Wall'

'Perhaps it was the middle of January in the present year that I first looked up and saw the mark on the wall,' begins that story (*SSS*, p. 53), alerting us straight away to the mock-precision, the pseudo-historicism, of the story's method. But there *is* precision, there is history in Woolf's method, here, and she has immediate recourse to it: 'In order to fix a date it is necessary to remember what one saw': again, the mode is pictorial; and the history invoked resides in the history of painting, rather than that of literature. Again, as in 'Blue and Green', the narrator fixes us in the present, then invites us to use our imagination:

> I was smoking a cigarette when I looked up and saw the mark on the wall for the first time. I looked up through the smoke of my cigarette and my eye lodged for a moment upon the burning coals, and that old fancy of the crimson flag flapping from the castle tower came into my mind, and I thought of the cavalcade of red knights riding up the side of the black rock . . . The mark was a small round mark, black upon the white wall, about six or seven inches above the mantelpiece. (*SSS*, p. 53)

We can easily guess the mode or dynamic, if not necessarily the exact content, of the rest of the story: the mark, transformed by the seeing eye of the imagination, enables the imagination to run riot while the story remains, as in 'Monday and Tuesday', in a kind of vorticist suspension, everything 'radiating to a point': in 'The Mark on the Wall' the mark itself, of course, provides that point; and a mark on the wall becomes synonymous with a mark on a canvas. 'Oh! dear me,' intrudes the narrator, 'the mystery of life; The inaccuracy of thought! The ignorance of humanity!' The story turns to the question of 'things lost in one lifetime' and itemises not love, trust, faith, but bird cages, iron hoops, coal scuttles, bagatelle boards. It is an attic or junkshop of a story, perhaps echoing Yeats's rag-and-bone shop of the heart; reminding us, too, of a house's potential to be haunted. We think, we remember, we associate, through solid objects, as the painters know. 'I want to think quietly, calmly, spaciously, never to be interrupted' muses the writer/narrator. Some hope. Dream on, the story tells us. And yet, this practice of looking may, as we have seen before – in 'Monday or Tuesday', in 'Blue and Green' – coexist with something that makes us 'sink deeper and deeper, away from the surface, with its hard separate facts'. Virginia Woolf will explore this more and more fully: in *Jacob's Room*; *Mrs Dalloway*; *To the Lighthouse*; *The Waves*; *Between the Acts*. 'The Mark on the Wall' fuses narrative with treatise, and this is a hint. It mentions 'Whitaker's Table of Precedency'; it mentions Elizabethan nails; Tudor clay pipes; Roman pottery. It mentions Nelson; two Arch-bishops and the Lord High Chancellor. It thinks of trees and insects; sap; ships and rooms. By the end, 'Everything's moving, falling, slipping, vanishing . . . [*sic*] There is a vast upheaval of matter.' The mark on the wall turns out to be a snail, and 'What has it all been about?' War? Conversation? Organic life? At the end, it has all simply gone out, like the fire we started with. To a far greater extent than all the other stories, this story simply muses on images radiating from a point; it free-associates.

It does not, however, associate in order to deduce. Things are things, not symbols, fire goes out, it does not, without intervention, re-kindle. Looking beyond the cigarette, inhaling or exhaling, the writer's eye lodges for a moment on burning coals: the burning conjures crimson, then simply 'red', before it burns itself out. It is an ancient device which we may date back to the fifteenth century and trace back to the repertoire of Hieronymous Bosch, inspired by medieval miniatures or by the idea of hellfires. The aesthetic effects of flames enabled, then, glorious new experimentation with colour, and – out of the experimentation with colour – with psycholo-gical states. Experimentation with violent effects of light became possible; and Leonardo da Vinci himself developed this idea of beginning with firelight in his *Treatise on Painting*: 'The figures which are seen against the fire look dark in the glare of the firelight; and those who stand at the side are half dark and half red, while those who are visible beyond the edges of the flames will be feebly lighted by the ruddy glow against a black background.'[32] Kenneth Clark has identified as characteristic of Leonardo the fact that 'his love of fantastic effects is united with a scientific desire to describe accurately an actual scene' (*Landscape into Art*, pp. 55–6): we may see Virginia Woolf, throughout the short stories, drawing on and echoing this – particularly here in 'The Mark on the Wall'.

Kenneth Clark also observes that in the neo-classicism of the late sixteenth century, 'these fiery disturbances are suppressed . . . From fantastic light we may turn to fantastic form' (*Landscape into Art*, p. 57): the Madonna becomes a blue whale. What Leonardo valued perhaps most highly was, as Kenneth Clark observes, the free play of the imagination (*Landscape into Art*, p. 59). He put this into words in the *Treatise*, and we may juxtapose them with the narrative of 'The Mark on the Wall'. Leonardo would not, he wrote, refrain 'from including among these precepts a new and speculative idea, which although it may seem trivial and almost laughable, is none the less of great value in quickening the spirit of the invention':

> It is this: that you should look at certain walls stained with damp or at stones of uneven colour. If you have to invent some setting you will be able to see in

these the likeness of divine landscapes, adorned with mountains, ruins, rocks, woods, great plains, hills, and valleys in great variety; and then again you will see there battles and strange figures in violent action, expressions of faces and clothes and an infinity of things which you will be able to reduce to their complete and proper forms. In such walls the same thing happens as in the sound of bells, in whose strokes you may find every word which you can imagine.[33]

Later in the *Treatise* Leonardo reverts to the same idea, advising the painter to study, as Kenneth Clark observes, not only marks on walls, but also 'the embers of the fire, or clouds, or mud, or other similar objects from which you will find most admirable ideas . . . because from a confusion of shapes the spirit is quickened to new inventions. But,' [Leonardo] adds, 'first be sure you know all the members of all the things you wish to depict, both the members of animals and the members of landscapes, that is to say, rocks, plants, and so forth'. As Virginia Woolf's story 'The Mark on the Wall' draws to a close, the narrator reflects on what he/she thinks about the sea, and a plank in the sea, and a tree; and 'the tree itself':

first the close dry sensation of being wood; then the grinding of the storm; then the slow, delicious ooze of sap . . . One by one the fibres snap beneath the immense cold pressure of the earth, then the last storm comes and, falling, the highest branches drive deep into the ground again. Even so, life isn't done with; there are a million patient, watchful lives still for a tree, all over the world, in bedrooms, in ships, on the pavement, lining rooms . . . (*SSS*, p. 60)

The tree creates history, and it creates frameworks for the future; it begins in the organic world, and creates interiors. Here is another mystery, teased open throughout Virginia Woolf's fiction: the mystery of the connection between the organic external world, and interiors: the interiors of ships, cities, houses, rooms; of the heart, the mind, and one of the mind's most vibrant manifestations: the imagination, or what we sometimes call the mind's eye.

Strange figures in violent action

At the end of *The Voyage Out*, the novel in which Virginia Woolf's first heroine, Rachel Vinrace, voyages out into the jungle, venturing beyond the civilised world of ideas and social interchange, Rachel becomes reduced – or elevated – into the form of a kind of vestal monster. Her body becomes semi-transparent, expansive, massive, weightless. She can see through walls:

The wave was replaced by the side of a mountain. Her body became a drift of melting snow, above which her knees rose in huge peaked mountains of bare bone . . . everything had become very pale and semi-transparent. Sometimes she could see through the wall in front of her . . . The room also had an odd power of expanding . . . There were immense intervals or chasms, for things still had the power to appear visibly before her . . . But for long spaces of time she would merely lie conscious of her body floating on the top of the bed and her mind driven to some remote corner of her body, or escaped and gone flitting round the room. (VO, pp. 327–8)

The quality of semi-transparency recurs in 'Modern Fiction' in which Virginia Woolf discusses experimentation in writing and the need to find a flexible, more elastic way of constructing a sentence.[34] There she urges us to think, not about the fixed structures of materialism (there are cities, in which houses, in which rooms, in which people) but about the way in which the mind is constantly making choices of perspective. Sickert plays, gently, with this: we look into his paintings and see slices, glimpses of rooms, with mirrors, sometimes in *contre-jour*. Bonnard plays lavishly with walls, mirrors and windows, inviting us to see simultaneously in a number of frames, where we had been used to seeing in a single frame.[35] Braque takes this further, so that we see edges, and tilted frames;[36] Picasso lets us rapidly assemble, as we look quickly, all the different planes constructed by the bones and masses of a face.[37] When he developed the theories collected together in *Vision and Design*, Roger Fry allowed himself to spin off from Clive Bell's claim that art is 'significant form'.[38] Looking at the work of post-impressionists, who played with perspective and juxtaposition to prioritise the effects of colour contrasts over those of light, he was echoing Edgar Allan Poe[39] when he quipped that 'Art is significant deformity'.[40] By now 'deformity' suggested a particular kind of spatial complexity: different from – but still using elements of – the kind of merging that allowed us to see Madonnas in monsters.

When Virginia Woolf showed Rachel's body turning into mountain peaks and her room advancing and retreating, she both drew on the things she had seen and studied, and anticipated her own discoveries. One fundamental way in which post-impressionist painters challenged their classical predecessors was by using composition and form to implicitly question religious belief – for example, as in Duncan Grant's wittily secular *Eve*.[41] The idea of the chaste Madonna is fundamentally challenged by the intellectualism which admits agnosticism. But once that idea is transposed into an agnostic system of values, there seems to be no going back. Sir Leslie Stephen was the kind of Victorian agnostic who remembered the transition from faith to loss of faith, and his daughters inherited at some level that sense of loss.[42] Virginia Woolf weaves it into her writing occasionally, as when Mrs Ramsay finds herself murmuring to herself, 'We are in the hands of the Lord' and has to check herself.[43] Significantly, she leaves us pondering the notion of spiritual faith in her final, uncompleted novel *Between the Acts* through the reflections of her character Lucy Swithin. But intellectualism brought with it, too, a sexual freedom: another notion it seemed impossible to go back on, a dreadful double bind if – as in Virginia Woolf's case – she also found it nearly impossible to acquire.[44] All these elements begin to come together in her writing once she begins to visualise the need for flexible, shifting structures; and to see that she must somehow look, in writing, for solutions to the problem of simultanism.[45] While their immediate predecessors, the impressionist painters, had been content to present life in disconnected, sensual glimpses, the post-impressionists wished to depict a vision of simultaneity which would show the shifting uncertainties within the human psyche which move us from – for example – bliss to despair and back again. Vanessa Bell had hinted at this challenge to fixity when she began to make portraits without faces;[46] Picasso would come to show a multiplicity of dimensions in a single face. Virginia Woolf was working towards a kind of simultanism in *Jacob's Room* by opening out contrasting glimpses, one from another. In 1919 she had reviewed Dorothy Richardson's novel of interior monologue, *Revolving Lights*, and had admired that novelist's method of evoking images and impressions 'one on top of another',[47] an observation which partly contributed to the method of writing *Jacob's Room*. (In *Mrs Dalloway* she would continue the experiment, playing there with the idea of doubling one fluctuating psychic state into two separate, linked characters.)

On the first page of the manuscript of *Jacob's Room*, Virginia Woolf wrote notes to herself about the novel she was beginning to invent. 'I think the main point is that it should be free. Yet what about form? Let us suppose that the Room will hold it together.' She wanted flexibility and containment. She also wanted something else: the kind of sensual impact that she had managed to achieve in the short stories. 'Intensity of life compared with immobility. Experiences. To change style at will.'[48] The room, in *Jacob's Room*, is important as an imagined point from which all lines radiate: Jacob goes out from it, and back into it . . . or does he? Actually, as we learn in the course of that novel, Jacob's room is usually depicted empty. When he is not in it, *it* seems to miss *him*. We – readers, viewers – keep needing to go to it to see if he is there. We need it as a reference point. But Jacob is usually elsewhere. The place he moves out from and ought, if the novel were not a tragedy, to go back to, is home, but we learn in *Jacob's Room* that home is not a space, it is an idea. We construct spaces to represent it, but really it is a psychological space which combines images simultaneously of mother, the beach, brother, a crab in a bucket, woman. As *Jacob's Room* pans out into the final, overall perspective which enables us now to see everything, even the hidden things, we realise that all the interiors we wanted to feel safe in – the college room, the British Museum, the Embassy, the woman's body – are, in some fundamental sense, semi-transparent. They contain what we visualise for them, and what we construct for ourselves. What we – human beings, human forms – really consist of is ever-changing, formless. We are the seers, in control of what is seen, and things only become fixed or offer complete containment once we have decided to select what we see (as Jacob will be forever his mother's innocent son, so long as Mrs Flanders never sees Florinda).[49]

What Virginia Woolf also examined in her fiction, however, was that this kind of freedom is troubling to us. It is troubling in greater or lesser degrees, depending on ephemeral, interior things – character, personality, sexuality – and on external forces: the law, politics, society, civilisation, war. In *Mrs Dalloway* she carried her realisation of the power of juxtaposition right into the interior spaces of mind and bodies, moving on from the constructions within *Jacob's Room* to a starker, more primal picture: we might again see, in the juxtaposition of Mrs Dalloway and the shell-shocked Septimus Smith, the juxtaposition of chaste Madonna and monster, as in 'Blue', if we suspend for a moment issues of moral judgement. There is a sense in which Clarissa and Septimus seem to rise out of one another. Their languages mingle, as here:

> How fresh, how calm, stiller than this of course, the air was in the early morning; like the flap of a wave; the kiss of a wave; chill and sharp and yet (for a girl of eighteen as she then was) solemn, feeling as she did, standing there at the open window, that something awful was about to happen.
>
> (*Mrs D*, p. 3)

> . . . and as, before waking, the voices of birds and the sound of wheels chime and chatter in a queer harmony, grow louder and louder, and the sleeper feels himself drawing to the shores of life, so he felt himself drawing towards life, the sun growing hotter, cries sounding louder, something tremendous about to happen.
>
> (*Mrs D*, p. 75)

Their respective interior monologues seem, at one level, to be mirror images of each other. But the radical difference between them is that Clarissa, though her thoughts transcend the spatial relations which define her, may always return to those spaces, while Septimus can never return.

For Clarissa, it is, and always will be, a question of rooms. When she deserts her own party and goes to look out of her window, seeing the old lady in the house opposite moving about through two panes of glass –

Clarissa's window, and her own – she gazes at her and thinks she can imagine her limitations, through the things she associates with her: 'creeds and prayers and mackintoshes'. But then, she reflects, the 'mystery' of life is in this: that the old lady exists at all, that she moves through space, from her chest of drawers to her dressing-table. 'Did religion solve that? or love?' (*Mrs D*, pp. 139–40). Nothing can 'solve' this feeling of entrapment, except the realisation that we ourselves construct it. But what is there that is outside the human desire to erect such constructions? Septimus can believe that 'Heaven was divinely merciful ... It ... pardoned his weakness. But what was the scientific explanation?' (*Mrs D*, p. 74):

> Why could he see through bodies, see into the future, when dogs will become men? ... Scientifically speaking, the flesh was melted off the world. His body was macerated until only the nerve fibres were left. It was spread like a veil upon a rock.
>
> He lay back in his chair, exhausted but upheld. He lay resting, waiting, before he again interpreted, with effort, with agony, to mankind. He lay very high, on the back of the world. The earth thrilled beneath him. Red flowers grew through his flesh; their stiff leaves rustled by his head. Music began clanging against the rocks up here. It is a motor horn down in the street, he muttered; but up here it cannoned from rock to rock, divided, met in shocks of sound which rose in smooth columns. (*Mrs D*, pp. 74–5)

Septimus can see through bodies, through time, through words: 'Why could he see through bodies?' (*Mrs D*, p. 74); 'The word "time" split its husk; ... and from his lips fell like shells, like shavings from a plane, without his making them, hard, white, imperishable, words, and flew to attach themselves to their places in an ode to Time; an immortal ode to Time. He sang' (*Mrs D*, p. 76). He can do this because in his shell-shocked state he believes himself to be divine: he can see that his role is to interpret to mankind. But what, he asks, along with the Victorian agnostics, was the scientific explanation? The question veers off, like a sharp, white bird through a Braque interior. In *Mrs Dalloway* as in a Braque painting, shrapnel is a haunting presence, though it is never named. Words have forms: they become structures like ears of wheat; shavings from a plane. The plane has now become an instrument, something for shaving wood into flexible curls. What before suggested containment now becomes a way of slicing up, fragmenting or splintering. Sound appears to him in visual structures, rising in smooth columns, but as it does so, the checking process which throughout the speech enables him to check imaginary sensory perceptions with things actually seen, actually heard in the street below, begins to burn itself out.

The song becomes an elegy to 'the boy' (Evans; himself) but now 'he withdraws up into the snows, and roses hang about him – the thick red roses which grow on my bedroom wall, he reminded himself' (*Mrs D*, p. 75). But he cannot actually see them. The style of juxtaposition has changed. What before was imagined and checked against the present is still imagined, but now may only be checked against the past. His memory has been blown up. We may now see something he has not seen: that because he is now imaging in pure symbol – white snow, red roses – there may be things he cannot name: fire, blood. He might see them, but they will be awful, unbearable. He must try not to see them. When he sees Evans again, in his mind's eye, he must see him as a colossus, a 'dead man in a grey suit' as this is the only way he can see that 'no mud was on him; no wounds; he was not changed' (*Mrs D*, p. 76). Not seeing them will be equally unbearable, because somewhere in the recesses of his mind he knows, he has seen, that mud, those wounds: he has the materials to make them in his mind's eye, but he must not:

> I have been dead, and yet am now alive, but let me rest still, he begged (he was talking to himself again – it was awful, awful!) and . . . so he felt himself drawing towards life, the sun growing hotter, cries sounding louder, something tremendous about to happen.
>
> He had only to open his eyes; but a weight was on them; a fear. (*Mrs D*, p. 75)

What is tremendous and awful is to be human, to be able to impact our own knowledge; to know that sometimes we must not see; not to be divine. We construct spaces, and locate ourselves within them, to deal with this lack of omnipotence, this frustrating inability to be omniscient. Our vision shifts, it is semi-transparent; we can never see entirely clearly. We know this; part of what we call sanity consists in knowing it. But when the mind veers off and we know 'madness' our knowledge is unbearable. The partiality of our vision frightens the mad; and it offers the supreme challenge to the artist. The difference is that the artist must select, select; and try to make the part suggest the whole, as Virginia Woolf does even in the tiny story 'Blue'. The civilised among us know that task will feel superhuman; the mad move, in agony, between seeing, and the sudden horror of not being able to see.

Rocks, plants, and so forth

When Mr Bankes in *To the Lighthouse* thinks of Mrs Ramsay, he finds himself musing 'The Graces assembling seemed to have joined hands in meadows of asphodel to compose that face. Yes, he would catch the 10.30 at Euston' (*TL*, p. 34). He lives in a world of trains and timetables; but when he thinks of Mrs Ramsay he sees, in his mind's eye, beauty, and so thinks of the art forms of the past. Accordingly, when he finds himself on the lawn of the Ramsays' summer house with Lily Briscoe (who is painting Mrs Ramsay sitting on the steps with her son James) he is confused by the image appearing on the canvas, and wants scientific explanations:

> Taking out a penknife, Mr Bankes tapped the canvas with the bone handle. What did she wish to indicate by the triangular purple shape, 'just there?' he asked.
>
> It was Mrs Ramsay reading to James, she said. She knew his objection – that no one could tell it for a human shape. But she had made no attempt at likeness, she said. For what reason had she introduced them then? he asked. Why indeed? – except that if there, in that corner, it was bright, here, in this, she felt the need of darkness. Simple, obvious, commonplace, as it was, Mr Bankes was interested. Mother and child then – objects of universal veneration, and in this case the mother was famous for her beauty – might be reduced, he pondered, to a purple shadow without irreverence.
>
> But the picture was not of them, she said. Or, not in his sense. There were other senses, too, in which one might reverence them. By a shadow here and a light there, for instance. Her tribute took that form if, as she vaguely supposed, a picture must be a tribute.   (*TL*, pp. 58–9)

Again here Virginia Woolf juxtaposes classical iconography with the effort of post-impressionism: to construct forms which are equivalent images for, rather than scientific representations of, the things – or figures – seen. In doing so she discovers, and shows, the extent to which the past haunts: in empty rooms, empty houses, phrases: 'We are in the hands of the Lord', 'the Graces assembling'. Perhaps one reason for Lily's difficulty in depicting Mrs Ramsay is that she cannot admit the past into the present: when she eventually finishes the painting, it is because she can finally juxtapose Mrs Ramsay seen with Mrs Ramsay remembered. While paintings incorporate ancient mythologies into new forms, narrative too must find a way of remembering. Right from the start (not only in 'A Haunted House' but back beyond it, through the lost mother in *The Voyage Out*) Virginia Woolf incorporated ghosts into her fiction: the 'fumbling airs' (*TL*, p. 138) we notice when we are consumed by someone's absence; empty rooms, to denote the passing of people, the passage of time.

In *The Waves* she explored this relationship between space and time outwards beyond the triple structure of *To the Lighthouse* into a manifold structure. As the six voices chant 'I see a ring', 'I see a slab of pale yellow', 'I hear a sound', 'I see a globe', 'I see a crimson tassel', 'I hear something stamping' (*W*, p. 5), we are invited to hear and see in simultanism. While the characters go about their business in the material world which they construct and subject to question, the organic world ascertains its own rhythms, which are sustained, come what may. The whole of *The Waves* acts out a struggle between organicism and civilisation, interior and exterior spaces; language and silence. The music of that novel is suggestive of depression: the pressure on language, materialism and the world of civilisation to yield up room to transcend these things; under such pressure, the world seems to keep needing to implode. The languages of Clarissa and Septimus meet and are developed again here. Again the desire is, as it were, to see through a quality of semi-transparency; to walk through walls:

> Now we have fallen through the tree-tops to the earth. The air no longer rolls its long, unhappy, purple waves over us. We touch earth; we tread ground. That is the close-clipped hedge of the ladies' garden. There they walk at noon, with scissors, clipping roses. Now we are in the ringed wood with the wall round it. This is Elvedon. I have seen signposts at the cross-roads with one arm pointing 'To Elvedon'. No one has been there. The ferns smell very strong, and there are red funguses growing beneath them. Now we wake the sleeping daws who have never seen a human form; now we tread on rotten oak apples, red with age and slippery. There is a ring of wall round this wood . . .
> Put your foot on this brick. Look over the wall. That is Elvedon. The lady sits between the two long windows, writing . . . We are the discoverers of an unknown land . . . Look! Do not move. Grasp the ferns tight on the top of the wall.
> (*W*, p. 11)

What is the perspective if the lady sits between two windows? Perhaps she is in a summer house like Virginia Woolf's own, at Monks House. Is it an oblong structure, with a window at each end, or is the looking partial, so that the children look from one angle, then another, and the mind's eye sees in simultanism? In a sense, the lady is inside and they, the onlookers, are outside; but normally we are not able to look over the top of walls into rooms. What separates looking from writing is green: ferns, growing on the top of the wall. Throughout *The Waves* figures move, elastically, from being primal to being civilised selves, from landscape to rooms; and the separations are never absolute, the walls between spaces seem semi-transparent, composed – as the rhythmically juxtaposed seascapes suggest – of something glassy, something blue and green, like windows, water.

In her final novel, *Between the Acts*, Virginia Woolf tried once more to juxtapose artistry with history. In a daring experiment she this time juxtaposes a flawed history with a flawed artistry: the Olivers' house is not really old, it is a mock-structure; and the portraits of ancestors do not really belong to the family. Miss La Trobe's ambition for her pageant is that it will span several centuries, but this plan makes it far too long to be entertaining. Many of the characters feel fake: Isa Oliver has had her children, but cannot write her poetry and she feels inauthentic (*BA*, p. 12).

Her husband is bored and frustrated. He demonstrates as much in an expressionist gesture: he stamps on a snake with a toad in its mouth, 'a monstrous inversion' (BA, p. 61). The word which Isa uses to describe herself to herself is 'abortive' (BA, p. 12). She contemplates her own reflection in triplicate, in front of her three-fold dressing-table mirror, and cannot recognise herself in any version. She has drunk sweet wine, but longs only for water. She imagines it, however, similarly refracted: '"A beaker of cold water, a beaker of cold water"' she repeated and saw water surrounded by walls of shining glass' (BA, p. 42).

Mrs Swithin, the believer, takes William Dodge for a tour of the house. She shows him the bed she was born in. 'But we have other lives, I think, I hope' she murmured. 'We live in others, Mr . . . We live in things' (BA, p. 44). As they walk from room to room, looking at things, we look at them: 'Standing by the cupboard in the corner he saw her reflected in the glass. Cut off from their bodies, their eyes smiled, their bodiless eyes, at their eyes in the glass' (BA, p. 45). As they pass the bookcases on the landing, Mrs Swithin runs her hands over the books: 'Here are the poets from whom we descend by way of the mind' she says (BA, p. 43). But the poetry spoken in Between the Acts is pastiche, as the portraits are not inherited and the stories cannot be told. What William Dodge wants to tell Mrs Swithin is monstrous: he was ridiculed and bullied. But such stories lead nowhere, they are culs-de-sac, dead ends. What Virginia Woolf wanted for this last novel was a story that would run from beginning to end, and transcend its own status as a story. She wanted to make a supernatural reversal: she wanted to make life out of art. This is why Between the Acts could never be finished, why the artist's work is never finished; why one work simply enables us to see through the walls of it, into the next. She looks, in this last novel, through her character Mrs Swithin, for divine likenesses, and seeks to distil characters into their complete and proper forms.

In order to do so she makes Isa monstrous, Giles monstrous, Mrs Manresa monstrous. She has Mrs Swithin take William Dodge into the nursery, but there is no baby in the cradle. The baby is outside, unconnected to its mother; being wheeled about by nurses rolling words in their mouths, like sweets. The baby's mother, Isa, alone in her bedroom 'groped, in the depths of the looking-glass, for a word to fit the infinitely quick vibrations of the aeroplane propeller that she had seen once at dawn at Croydon. Faster, faster, faster, it whizzed, whirred, buzzed, till all the flails became one flail and up soared the plane away and away.' The word she needs would complete the lines of poetry she is trying to compose: '"Where we know not, where we go not, neither know nor care . . . Flying, rushing

through the ambient, incandescent, summer silent . . ." The rhyme was
"air".' Once she finds it, she can pick up the telephone and order fish (BA,
p. 12), a bit like Mr Bankes seeing that 'The Graces assembling seemed to
have joined hands in meadows of asphodel' to compose Mrs Ramsay's face,
and so deciding to catch the 10.30 at Euston.

Lucy Swithin, tired after watching the pageant, gazes into the lily pond:
'her eyes went water searching' (BA, p. 121). Something moves in the
water: 'she had a glimpse of silver – the great carp himself, who came to the
surface so very seldom. They slid on, in and out between the stalks, silver,
pink, gold, splashed, streaked, pied' (BA, p. 121). Fish have faith, she tells
herself, absurdly (BA, p. 121). They do, in her imagination, because it is
she who bequeaths it to them. As the novel draws to its provisional close,
the fish slither in and out between the stalks, and 'the usual sounds
reverberated through the shell; Sands making up the fire; Candish stoking
the boiler.' Isa imagines she can hear the sea; 'sitting in the shell of the
room she watched the pageant fade' in her mind's eye. 'The flowers flashed
before they faded. She watched them flash' (BA, p. 128). With the organic
world visible, alive, present to the senses in this way – more tactile than
bodies or canvases, composed and brought up close by one seeing mind –
the human figures can fall into shadow. Now there is nothing much left
visible in the frame:

> The great square of the open window showed only sky now. It was drained of
> light, severe, stone cold. Shadows fell. Shadows crept over Bartholomew's
> high forehead; over his great nose. He looked leafless, spectral, and his chair
> monumental. As a dog shudders its skin, his skin shuddered.   (BA, p. 129)

The scales of the world are being shed, and Giles and Isa, who by now
have become primal or archetypal – man and woman – are left in silence.
'The window was all sky without colour. The house had lost its shelter. It
was night before roads were made, or houses. It was night that dwellers in
caves had watched from some high place among rocks' (BA, pp. 129–30).
We may see now what the artist begins with, her raw materials: frames,
planes, perspective. Woolf reflects here on the Book of Genesis which
describes the first Creation. Here between the acts of love, war, artistic
creation, she slips the beginning of a scene, and a hint of temporality. We
are invited to realise now that Between the Acts has partly been – that all
Virginia Woolf's work has partly been – about attempts at regeneration
and reparation: the post-impressionist project of reconciling history with
now, through the medium of a primal vision. Words, if they are to
continue being spun and spun into visions of subjectivity, need to keep
reaching back into their points of origination: into silence. François

Mauriac described Virginia Woolf's work as an art form which was 'moving towards silence'[50] and here in her last words of fiction we see her plummeting backwards again, hearing, at the last, the ancient voices of creation. It is the most precarious place imaginable; Virginia Woolf visited and revisited it many, many times. In her final work, she shows her characters reaching into that space, between time present and time past, between creation, recreation and the frustrations of repetition. In a brilliant phantasmagoria, she could drain her own vision, empty it of colour, light, sight, rhythm, sound. How shocking it is, when she suddenly takes it all away. She had brought it all up so close, with her seductive synaesthesia – her crooning, buzzing sounds, her shifting perspectives, her resonant colours, her gentle, shimmering light – that while we were reading it, we thought it was ours, we thought it was real. How reassuring it is when she resumes her narrative each time, and each time brilliantly extends her vision. Art for the post-impressionist is illusory, a complex, complicit conjuring trick on the parts of both artist and viewer, or reader. But the making of art enables us to draw together, in our mind's eye, aspects of our own baffling and insistent multiplicity.

NOTES

1 Monks House Papers, University of Sussex Manuscripts Section: Papers of Virginia Woolf & Related Papers of Leonard Woolf: 'The Penny Steamer', Mss A.23b.

2 Monks House Papers, University of Sussex Manuscripts Section: Papers of Virginia Woolf & Related Papers of Leonard Woolf: 'A Terrible Tragedy in a Duckpond', Mss A.10.

3 Monks House Papers, University of Sussex Manuscripts Section: Papers of Virginia Woolf & Related Papers of Leonard Woolf: 'Phyllis and Rosamund', Mss A.23f.

4 Cf J. K. Johnstone's discussion of G. E. Moore's philosophy, in *The Bloomsbury Group* (London: Secker & Warburg, 1954), p. 21.

5 All Woolf references are to the new Penguin editions, under the general editorship of Julia Briggs (London: Penguin, 1992–8), except where otherwise indicated.

6 This anecdote is related in Hermione Lee, *Virginia Woolf* (London: Chatto and Windus, 1996), p. 243.

7 Virginia Woolf's biography *Roger Fry* (London: Hogarth, 1940) ignores Vanessa Bell's affair with Roger Fry.

8 Angelica Garnett first published the details of her parentage in *Deceived With Kindness* (London: Hogarth, 1984).

9 *Studland Beach, c.* 1912. See Frances Spalding, *Vanessa Bell* (London: Weidenfeld and Nicolson, 1983), pp. 80–1. See also Simon Watney, *English Post-Impressionism* (London: Cassell, 1980), pp. 80–1: 'here, for one of the few times in her life, she painted *away* from nature'.

10 Cf J. K. Johnstone: *The Bloomsbury Group*, p. 24.

11 T. S. Eliot interrupted Virginia Woolf's progress on *JR*: 'He said nothing – but I reflected how what I'm doing is probably being better done by Mr Joyce.' See note 13.

12 Katherine Mansfield reviewed *ND* unfavourably, and told Middleton Murry that it 'reeks of intellectual snobbery' (*L*, ii, p. xix).

13 *D*2, p. 69.

14 The first post-impressionist exhibition opened at the Grafton Galleries in November 1910; the second was in October 1912 to January 1913.

15 Roger Fry, *Vision and Design* (London: Dover, 1998; first published Harmondsworth: Penguin, 1961, 1920), p.15.

16 *Ibid.*, p. 13.

17 Lily Briscoe explains her post-impressionist theories to William Bankes in *TL*, p. 59.

18 *L*2, pp. 385–6, Virginia Woolf to Roger Fry: 'If it didn't look like soliciting more compliments, I would go on to say how much I enjoy reading your articles. Are you getting on with your book?' *Vision and Design* (1920) collected articles previously published in the *Burlington Magazine* and other journals.

19 'Negro Sculpture' in *Vision and Design*, pp. 70–3. Fry was reviewing (in *The Athenaeum*, 1920) an exhibition at the Chelsea Book Club. Virginia Woolf went to see it in April 1920 and could 'dimly see that something in their style might be written' (*L*2, p. 429).

20 Virginia Woolf, *Selected Short Stories* (London: Penguin, 1993), p. 54. Hereafter abbreviated to *SSS*.

21 Vanessa Bell, *A Conversation*, 1913–16. See Frances Spalding, *Vanessa Bell* (London: Weidenfeld and Nicolson, 1983), pp. 144–5.

22 Clive Bell wrote about Picasso in 'Matisse and Picasso' in Clive Bell, *Since Cézanne* (London: Chatto and Windus, 1929; first published 1922), pp. 83–90: 'Picasso . . . is the paramount influence in modern painting' (p. 84).

23 The Bloomsbury painters, especially Roger Fry and Clive Bell, saw Cézanne as a central figure. See Clive Bell, *Since Cézanne*, which contains Bell's essay, 'Since Cézanne', pp. 1–39. It also contains his essay, 'The Douanier Rousseau', pp. 9–56. He there records his famous appreciation that 'Cézanne's ideas on painting are not like ideas at all: they are like sensations; they have the force of sensations', p. 57.

24 I expand on this issue in Sue Roe, 'The Mind in Visual Form: Sketching *The Waves*' in *Q/W/E/R/T/Y: Arts, Littérature et Civilisations du Monde Anglophone* (Pau: Publications de l'Université de Pau, 1995), pp. 241–51.

25 See for example Simon Watney, *English Post-Impressionism* (London: Cassell, 1980), p. 86, with regard to Duncan Grant's fusion of ideas drawn from Florentine frescoes and his responses to contemporary cubism. See also Bernard Denvir, *Post-Impressionism* (London: Thames and Hudson, 1992).

26 Walter Sickert (1860–1942) was a founder of the Camden Town Group of painters who experimented with the play of artificial light on objects and with the human figure in interiors. Virginia Woolf wrote a pamphlet, at Sickert's own request, about the 'stories' suggested by his paintings. It is reprinted in *CE*2, pp. 233–44.

27 Frederick Spencer Gore (1878–1914), first President of the Camden Town Group of painters, was a painter concerned with finding new ways of depicting interiors.

28 See Simon Watney, *English Post-Impressionism* (London: Cassell, 1980), pp. 49–51. The question of democracy related to the painters themselves, who were responding to the politics of the New English Art Club as much as to the politics of British society in general.

29 *L2*, p. 378: 'my taste is very bad . . . And I saw the most lovely piece of glass today – all volutes and spirals, gold-sprinkled and iridescent. Monks House will perhaps be the ugliest house in Sussex'. See *SSS*, pp. 113–14.

30 See S. P. Rosenbaum, 'The Philosophical Realism of Virginia Woolf', in S. P. Rosenbaum (ed.), *English Literature and British Philosophy* (Chicago University Press, 1971), pp. 320–3, quoted in *SSS*, p. 114.

31 See Edgar Allan Poe, 'The Veil of the Soul', in *The Fall of the House of Usher, and Other Writings* (London: Penguin, 1986; first published, 1967), p. 498.

32 Quoted in Kenneth Clark, *Landscape into Art* (London: John Murray, 1997; first published, 1949), p. 80.

33 *Ibid.*, p. 90.

34 Cf. Virginia Woolf, *The Crowded Dance of Modern Life: Selected Essays* vol. 2, ed. Rachel Bowlby (London: Penguin, 1993), p. 8: 'Life is not a series of gig-lamps symmetrically arranged; life is a luminous halo, a semi-transparent envelope . . . Is it not the task of the novelist to convey this varying, this unknown and uncircumscribed spirit?' ('Modern Fiction' is a slightly revised version of 'Modern Novels', first published in *The Times Literary Supplement*, 10 April 1919.)

35 Pierre Bonnard (1867–1947). See Julian Bell, *Bonnard* (London: Phaidon Press, 1994), p. 18: 'mirrors, window frames, scenes within scenes'. Clive Bell, in 'Bonnard', wrote that a picture by Bonnard is 'like a flower, which is beautiful not because it represents . . . something beautiful, but because it is beautiful'. Clive Bell, *Since Cézanne*, pp. 98–104; see p. 99.

36 Braque, a contemporary and friend of Picasso, was injured in the First World War by shrapnel. The sharp, white birds which are a feature of many of his paintings are thought by some to be symbols of peace; others see them as images of fragmentation, with the angular qualities of shrapnel.

37 See, for example, Picasso, *Weeping Woman*, in David Hockney, *Picasso* (Madras and New York: Hanuman Books, 1990), p. 52.

38 See Clive Bell, 'The Artistic Problem', in *Since Cézanne*, p. 40: 'I habitually describe works of art as "significant" rather than "beautiful" forms. For works of art, unlike roses, are the creations and expressions of conscious minds.'

39 Edgar Allan Poe, 'On Imagination', in *The Fall of the House of Usher, and Other Writings*, p. 497: 'The pure imagination chooses, from *either* Beauty *or* Deformity, only the most combinable things hitherto uncombined.'

40 Virginia Woolf quotes Roger Fry, 'Art is significant deformity', in Virginia Woolf, *Roger Fry* (London: Peregrine, 1979; first published, 1940), p. 169.

41 Duncan Grant, *Head of Eve*, c. 1912. See Gillian Naylor (ed.), *Bloomsbury: The Artists, Authors and Designers by Themselves* (London: Octopus, 1990), p. 85.

42 Jane Wheare considers Sir Leslie Stephen's particular brand of agnosticism, and

Virginia Woolf's relation to it, in her introduction to Virginia Woolf, *VO* (London: Penguin, 1992), pp. xvii–xviii.

43 Virginia Woolf, *TL* (London: Penguin, 1992; first published, 1925), p. 70, 'suddenly she added, We are in the hands of the Lord. But instantly she was annoyed with herself for saying that.'

44 See Sue Roe, *Writing and Gender: Virginia Woolf's Writing Practice* (Hemel Hempstead: Harvester/Wheatsheaf, 1990).

45 Simultanism is at the basis of cubism, which post-impressionist artists drew on. David Hockney describes it best, throughout his book *Picasso*, as the nexus of problems inherent in questioning the idea of the fixed viewpoint. Cubism challenged the old idea that the viewer's eye, when looking at a painting, moved through time; instead seeing becomes compatible with the idea of an image produced 'instantly', as in photography. (See note 47 below.)

46 Vanessa Bell painted Virginia Woolf without a face, *Virginia Woolf at Asheham*, *c*. 1910. See Gillian Naylor, *Bloomsbury*, p. 83.

47 (See note 45 above.) Virginia Woolf found a narrative equivalent for simultanism in Dorothy Richardson's long novel *Pilgrimage*, with its interior monologue. She praised her ability to register in the mind of her heroine 'one after another, and one on top of another, words, cries, shouts, notes of a violin' in *Virginia Woolf: Women and Writing*, introduced by Michèle Barrett (London: The Women's Press, 1979), p. 189.

48 The Henry W. and Albert A. Berg Collection, The New York Public Library, Astor, Lenox and Tilden Foundations. Ms of *JR*, p. 1.

49 See Virginia Woolf, *JR* (London: Penguin, 1992; first published, 1922), p. 79, concerning 'the feelings of a mother': 'the heart was torn by the little creak, the sudden stir. Behind the door was the obscene thing.' In the originial ms. her feelings were even stronger. Virginia Woolf deleted from it the line 'Behind the door knives cut human flesh from the bone, or death alights.' She retained 'Surgeons were there with their knives. Something was hinted at that only austere [?] men or women in white capes might see; & having seen would never speak of' (ms., II, p. 5). See *JR*, p. 173.

50 François Mauriac, *Mémoires Intérieurs*, trans. Gerard Hopkins (London: Eyre & Spottiswoode, 1960), p. 101.

10

DAVID BRADSHAW

The socio-political vision of the novels

'The greatest benefit we owe to the artist,' George Eliot once claimed, 'whether painter, poet, or novelist, is the extension of our sympathies.'[1] As richly enlarging as they are tightly controlled, Woolf's novels 'benefit' the reader in just this fashion. But while it has long been agreed that they are geared towards broadening our aesthetic responsiveness – as we read Woolf's novels, we are prompted to question how and why we read fiction and to acknowledge the limitations of our answers – it is only relatively recently that the degree to which her novels seem conceived to extend our ethical and political 'sympathies' has begun to be recognised.[2] An ideological bias, unobtrusive but palpable, is at work, for instance, in *The Voyage Out*, *Jacob's Room*, *To the Lighthouse* and *The Years*, and readers of these novels are challenged to think just as hard about the wider moral, social and political issues which the novels encompass as they are required to come to terms with the writerly goad of the texts. As early as 1908, Woolf noted in her journal that she had grown to 'distrust description' and that she wished to 'write not only with the eye, but with the mind; & discover real things beneath the show',[3] and this was to become her principal aspiration as a novelist. In the same year, Woolf congratulated E. M. Forster for having won her over to what she presumed to be his own position in *A Room With a View*. 'To be able to make one thus a partisan is so much of an achievement, the sense that one sees truth from falsehood is so inspiriting, that it would be right to recommend people to read Mr Forster's book on these accounts alone.'[4] Woolf's own novels have an equally 'partisan' design on the reader, yet it is a measure of her 'achievement' that at no point in any of them do we feel impeded by her point of view, let alone pressurised into adopting it. Woolf's radical critique of 'the fabric of things'[5] is subtly persuasive, never bluntly didactic (as it is, at times, in George Eliot's fiction), and when reading the four novels mentioned above we often feel the reach and intensity of Woolf's socio-political vision, but never the push of her hand.

When the imposing Ridley Ambrose descends from the Strand to the Embankment at the beginning of *The Voyage Out*, beating the air with one arm and with his wife on the other, with a throng of 'small, agitated' clerks scattering before them and 'young lady typists' inconvenienced behind, Woolf brings into focus the nexus of class, culture, gender and power which all her novels, to a greater or lesser degree, will probe. Having freed her arm from her husband's, Helen Ambrose weeps for their absent children before becoming conscious of 'the world she lived in'.[6] She notices the people passing by, the workers, the rich, and 'the poor who were unhappy and rightly malignant. Already, though there was sunlight in the haze, tattered old men and women were nodding off to sleep upon the seats. When one gave up seeing the beauty that clothed things, this was the skeleton beneath.' Woolf's deployment of this striking phrase tells us far more about her socio-political outlook and the polemical thrust of *The Voyage Out* than it does about her interest in chilling the reader's spine. We are urged to see through the thin skin of civilisation which covers society to the armature of poverty and pain which supports it.

Moreover, even though the novel has barely got started, many of Woolf's readers in 1915 would have noted that she makes her 'voyage out' as a novelist by having her characters follow a well-trodden eastwards path. The Ambroses' journey from the Embankment to the benighted quayside of Wapping in London's East End calls to mind the previous transits of numerous social investigators, missionaries and philanthropists, not least because Helen stops to register some of the key sites of 'Outcast London'.[7] General William Booth, for instance, in his widely read *In Darkest England* (1890), had described in poignant detail the homeless hordes which his Salvation Army officers encountered nightly on the Embankment, 'while the recesses of Waterloo and Blackfriars Bridges,' wrote Booth, 'were full of human misery'.[8] That the Embankment at night was a notorious scene of abjection adds bite to Helen's awareness of the 'tattered old men and women' congregating there as the day comes to a close, while Woolf's portrayal of Helen lifting her eyes in distress to 'the arches of Waterloo Bridge and the carts moving across them, like the line of animals in a shooting gallery' (p. 5) takes on a darker significance once we appreciate that the bridge would soon be loaded with 'human misery'.

Similarly, in Chapter Two Rachel Vinrace peers 'into the depth of the sea' and is just able to make out 'the black ribs of wrecked ships . . . [and] smooth green-sided monsters who came by flickering this way and that' (p. 20). A variation on 'the skeleton beneath' theme, Rachel's undersea is most obviously inspired by William Pepper's description of 'white, hairless, blind monsters lying curled on the ridges of sand at the bottom of the sea, which would explode if you brought them to the surface' (p. 16), but all three passages just as readily invoke the proverbial 'Submerged Tenth' or 'Sunken Millions' of *In Darkest England* – that is, the supposed fraction of the population living permanently in poverty – as the fauna and contours of the seabed or the human substructure.[9] Even when Woolf seems to be writing in her most fantastic mode, therefore, her words often resonate with specific socio-political connotations.

Having decided to complete their journey by cab, the Ambroses are soon 'plunged' into the East End:

> It appeared that this was a great manufacturing place, where the people were engaged in making things, as though the West End, with its electric lamps, its vast plate-glass windows all shining yellow . . . was the finished work . . . For some reason it appeared to her as a small golden tassel on the edge of a vast black cloak.　(p. 6)

Helen is amazed at the populousness of their 'gloomy' and alien surroundings and understands 'that after all it is the ordinary thing to be poor, and that London is the city of innumerable poor people'. The shock of 'this discovery' makes her imagine herself 'pacing a circle all the days of her life round Piccadilly Circus' (p. 6), a locality which had long been synonymous with prostitution. Henry Mayhew, in his influential study of *London Labour and the London Poor* (1861–2), refers to 'the circulating harlotry of the Haymarket and Regent Street' (both of which feed into Piccadilly Circus) and Charles Booth, another famous chronicler of London's 'Submerged Tenth' and a friend of Woolf's parents, remarked that 'At the junction of Regent Street and Coventry Street, by Piccadilly Circus, prostitution has its principal market, holding high-change at the hour when the theatres close'.[10] In fact, references to Piccadilly Circus and its prostitutes are so frequent in *The Voyage Out* (e.g., pp. 72, 100, 202, 235), that the narrative seems locked into a kind of stationary orbit around them. In turn, these references interlock with the novel's many examples of genteel women either winding things about themselves, revolving in circles or being confined to circular environments. By describing her women characters turning and curling in these ways, or placing them in circular settings, Woolf continues to allude to the 'skeleton' of prostitution which circulated just beneath the surface of polite society while also highlighting the way in which all England's women, regardless of their circumstances, were then encircled by the oppressive noose of patriarchy.[11] 'London's the place', Terence Hewet tells Rachel further on in the novel when the scene has shifted to Santa Marina. 'They looked together at the carpet, as though London itself were to be seen there lying on the floor, with all its spires and pinnacles pricking through the smoke' (p. 284). These words clearly recall the location of the Ambroses' north London home, situated 'above the pinnacles where the smoke rose in a pointed hill' (p. 5), but Terence's casual comment makes Rachel 'think of the horrors' and the novel about prostitution which she once started but could not finish. Rachel keeps the novel on her table 'as some medieval monk kept a skull, or a crucifix to remind him of the frailty of the body' (p. 284) – to remind them both, in other words, of 'the skeleton beneath'.

No sooner have the Ambroses boarded the *Euphrosyne* than the 'fossilised' (p. 11) Pepper (the social skeleton's ludicrous foil) draws attention to his 'rheumatic' complaint. His self-centredness provokes a barbed retort from Helen, who still has the disturbing 'sight of town and river' (p. 8) in mind. Shortly afterwards, as the ship moves slowly downstream, Helen and Rachel gaze back on the glare of central London:

> There were the lights of the great theatres, the lights of the long streets, lights that indicated huge squares of domestic comfort, lights that hung high in air . . . It seemed dreadful that the town should blaze for ever in the same spot, dreadful at least to people going away to adventure upon the sea, and beholding it as a circumscribed mound, eternally burnt, eternally scarred. From the deck of the ship the great city appeared a crouched and cowardly figure, a sedentary miser. (p. 11)

Four of the most prominent lights which then 'hung high in air' over London were the illuminated dials of Parliament's Big Ben clocktower, lit up by electricity since 1906, while the image of London as a 'circumscribed mound' reinforces our sense of the dreadful confinement of its women and its dispossessed, while also suggesting that the city is a kind of vast burial mound or necropolis, yet again invoking 'the skeleton beneath'. Peeking in from the deck, Helen observes that the men are preoccupied with their cigars and reminiscences: 'Mr Pepper and Mr Ambrose were oblivious of all tumult; they were in Cambridge, and it was probably about the year 1875' (p. 11). Pointedly, Helen and Rachel must make do with a much less comfortable room in which 'a great lamp' swings in the air like the lamps of central London they have just watched in silence. Ironically, it is described as 'the kind of lamp which makes the light of civilisation across dark fields to one walking in the country' (p. 12).

When the *Euphrosyne* drops anchor at Santa Marina, the ship is described as a 'lonely little island', as if England herself has arrived off the coast of South America, and although the remainder of *The Voyage Out* is set there the reader is regularly drawn back to 'Outcast London'. For example, following Richard Dalloway's assault on her during the voyage out, Rachel dreams that she is in 'a long tunnel, which grew so narrow by degrees that she could touch the damp bricks on either side . . . she found herself trapped in it . . . with a little deformed man who squatted on the floor gibbering' (p. 68), just as during her fatal illness Rachel dreams of 'walking through a tunnel under the Thames, where there were little deformed women sitting in archways playing cards, while the bricks of which the wall was made oozed with damp' (p. 313). In both dreams, of course, the projection of London as a 'sedentary miser' is conjured up. More precisely, however, Rachel's night-mares transport the reader back to Wapping, the district in London's East End from where the *Euphrosyne* sets sail. The boatman who rows the Ambroses out to the ship tells them that 'once he had taken many passengers across [the Thames], where now he took scarcely any. He seemed to recall an age when his boat . . . carried delicate feet across to lawns at Rotherhithe' (p. 7), which, between 1843 and 1869, was joined to Wapping on the north bank of the river by the egregiously leaky Thames Tunnel. ' "The very walls were in a cold sweat," wrote *The Times* when it opened', and within no time it had been colonised 'by whores and "tunnel thieves", a new class of criminal who hid in its arches and mugged passers-by beneath the Thames'.[12] Rachel has few options as a woman without means and London's prostitutes and criminalised down-and-outs have none. Her Thames Tunnel dreams underline the fact that they are all victims of the patriarchal oppression which Richard Dalloway personifies.

The contrast between the openings of Empire (for men) and the restric-tions of England (for women and the poor) is brought home in the third chapter of *The Voyage Out* when Dalloway exclaims 'Good Lord, what opportunities there are now for young men!' and his dutiful wife responds by summing up all that England has done, 'our navies, and the people in India and Africa, and how we've gone on century after century, sending out boys from little country villages . . . Think of the light burning over the House, Dick! . . . It's what one means by London' (p. 42). By this point in the novel, of course, the reader knows what Helen and Rachel know about the politics of electrification – that the 'light . . . over the House' also burns and scars London, and that the partial availability of electric power symbolises the inequalities of the capital and England as a whole – and this knowledge ironises Clarissa Dalloway's jingoistic gush. Likewise, just after Richard has told Rachel that he 'can conceive no more exalted aim – to be the citizen of the Empire,' Clarissa interrupts their conversation with a cry of 'Warships, Dick! Over there! Look!' (p. 60). But the ensuing description of the ships underscores how, for Woolf, the Royal Navy and the Empire it helped to control were part and parcel of a larger evil which she was inclined to represent in skeletal terms: '[Clarissa] had sighted two sinister grey vessels, low in the water, and bald as bone, one closely following the other with the look of eyeless beasts seeking their prey' (p. 60).

The Voyage Out warrants close scrutiny because it is still too frequently undervalued and because it is the novel in which the ethical strain of Woolf's fiction is perhaps most 'bald[ly]' exposed. Furthermore, while the socio-political issues it embraces will be raised on many occasions in the novels which follow – the salient problem of the poor, the viciousness of patriarchy and the oppressiveness of the patriarchal family, the unrelenting determinism of the state, the iniquity of empire and the pervasiveness of militarism are all concerns to which Woolf returns again and again – it is almost as if her imaginative investment in the opening chapter of The Voyage Out was so hefty that she felt compelled to remind us of it in the final chapter of the last novel she set in London, The Years.

In February 1920, just before beginning work on Jacob's Room, Woolf re-read The Voyage Out and saw in it 'a direct look ahead of me' (D2, p. 17). Not surprisingly, the two novels have much in common. For instance, returning home from a party in the early hours of the morning, the tipsily elated Jacob observes 'street scavengers'[13] and feels 'well-disposed . . . towards them' (p. 97). The narrator suggests that an innate exhilaration akin to drunkenness ('drums and trumpets' is the term used for it) carries us all along in the face of what would otherwise be the unbearable spectacle of the poor. 'Only, should you turn aside into one of those little bays on Waterloo Bridge to think the matter over,' the narrator continues, 'it will probably seem to you all a muddle – all a mystery' (p. 97). If the reader of Jacob's Room is aware of the 'human misery' those recesses held at night, the meaning of life would undoubtedly seem a bewildering 'muddle'. The narrator continues to gaze on the human traffic crossing Waterloo Bridge. 'It seems as if the poor had gone raiding the town, and now trapesed back to their own quarters . . . On the other hand . . . those girls there, striding hand in hand, shouting out a song, seem to feel neither cold nor shame. They are hatless. They triumph' (p. 97). As with the references to the Embankment, the Thames Tunnel and Piccadilly Circus in The Voyage Out, this passage in Jacob's Room has a real-world correlative in that many of London's West End prostitutes were said to live in the streets which led off either side of the Waterloo Road at the end of Waterloo Bridge.[14] Characteristically, although Woolf's style in this passage is both lyrical and generalised, her words have a specific contextual pitch.

In 1920, nearly two years after the First World War had ended, Woolf complained that her 'generation [was] daily scourged by the bloody war'. (D2, p. 15.) References to the conflict are so ubiquitous in Jacob's Room that it is as if Woolf was so stung by Katherine Mansfield's allegation, in a review,

that *Night and Day* (1919) 'was "unaware of what has been happening"',
that she decided to set down her response to the war on every page of her
third novel.[15] Jacob's untimely death is signalled most plainly in his
surname, Flanders, but it is also foreshadowed in the novel's *memento mori*
theme which picks up and gives impetus to the bone imagery of *The Voyage
Out*. Collectively, the 'old sheep's skull without its jaw' (p. 6) which Jacob
discovers on the beach in Cornwall and which he takes back to his boarding-
house (p. 9); the 'death's-head moth' which the Flanders' maid catches in
their Scarborough kitchen (p. 17); the 'little bones lying on the turf' nearby
(p. 18); Mrs Durrant's 'hawk nose . . . thin as a bleached bone' (pp. 45–6);
the 'Roman skeletons' on the Yorkshire moor (p. 117) and the carved 'ram's
skull' over the doorway of Jacob's lodgings in London (pp. 58, 155), build
up the impression of England as an ossuary or charnel-house first adum-
brated in *The Voyage Out*'s representation of London as a 'circumscribed
mound'. 'But who, save the nerve-worn and sleepless', the narrator asks in
what reads like a direct challenge to the reader to remain mindful of the
wider ramifications of the text, 'or thinkers standing with hands to the eyes
on some crag above the multitude, see things thus in skeleton outline, bare of
flesh? In Surbiton the skeleton is wrapped in flesh' (p. 142). As well as
keeping 'the skeleton beneath' in view, the strewn bones of *Jacob's Room*
also prepare the ground for the permanent absence which Jacob's narrative
fleetingness, his skeletal presence in the novel, portends – just as his absent
corpse at the end is prefigured in the symbolic *rigor mortis* of the two 'lovers'
(p. 6) at the beginning of the novel, 'stretched entirely rigid', 'stretched
motionless' (p. 5), as if they are dead.

Reminiscent of the lights of London which Helen and Rachel observe in
The Voyage Out, London's lamps are said to 'uphold the dark as upon the
points of burning bayonets' (p. 83), while a green clock is 'guarded by
Britannia leaning on her spear' (p. 90); the Houses of Parliament are
depicted as a 'tethered grey fleet of masonry' (p. 151) and Jacob stares
ahead at one point, 'fixed, monolithic like a British Admiral' (p. 145).
England is represented as being on a kind of permanent war footing
through these descriptions, and in one of the novel's many references to the
'Iron Duke', Bonamy is given a 'Wellington nose' (p. 135). Archer Flanders
joins the Royal Navy, Timmy Durrant works in the Admiralty, Captain
Barfoot is 'lame and wanted two fingers on the left hand, having served his
country' (p. 18), and the falling of a tree is described as 'A terrifying volley
of pistol-shots' (p. 25). When a protest march passes down Whitehall,
filling the air with 'whistling and concussions' (p. 151), it is as if the
artillery bombardments of the Western Front have been redirected towards
the seat of power in England.

To Rachel Vinrace, the statesmanly Richard Dalloway 'seemed to come from the humming oily centre of the machine where the polished rods are sliding, and the pistons thumping' (p. 38). This is perceptive, since it is Dalloway's belief that the state is 'a complicated machine' (p. 57) and the individual a mere cog within it. This idea of the State dominated British political thought in the late nineteenth and early twentieth centuries, and Woolf develops her profound opposition to it in *Jacob's Room*. In an arresting passage she travesties the inexorable determinism of mechanised warfare by describing the robotic 'nonchalance' with which 'a dozen young men in the prime of life descend with composed faces into the depths of the sea'. 'Like blocks of tin soldiers,' she continues, 'the army covers the cornfield, moves up the hillside, stops, reels slightly this way and that, and falls flat, save that, through field-glasses, it can be seen that one or two pieces still agitate up and down like fragments of broken match-stick.' Woolf imagines the hollow-headed (p. 151) statesmen and military commanders who preside over this carnage as being 'as smoothly sculpted as the impassive policeman at Ludgate Circus', whose 'face is stiff from force of will' and who, operating like an automaton, brings the buses to a punctual halt. 'It is thus that we live, they say, driven by an unseizable force. They say the novelists never catch it . . .' (pp. 136–7). But Woolf does 'catch it', and in a way which typifies her multiplex vision as a novelist. Her description of the synchronised slaughter of the servicemen forges a connection between the callous indifference of 'the men in clubs and Cabinets' who directed the First World War with an apparently scant regard for human life, and their crude disdain of the novelist 'when they say that character-drawing is a frivolous fireside art, a matter of . . . exquisite outlines enclosing vacancy' (p. 136). Woolf's double-edged rejoinder to those in authority is that if human beings continue to be looked at solely from a distance, 'through field-glasses', as it were, they will neither be grasped by the novelist nor governed with compassion. The conclusion of the novel is doubly ironic, in that Jacob's empty shoes are held out in Jacob's empty room, two especially poignant 'outlines enclosing vacancy', while the gently 'swelling . . . curtain' (p. 155) in Jacob's room half-recalls the gowns of the Cambridge choristers which 'blow out, as though nothing dense and corporeal were within. What sculpted faces, what certainty, authority controlled by piety, although great boots march under the gowns' (p. 24). This reference to the 'sculpted' faces of the choristers reminds us of Rachel Vinrace's sense of a coercive 'force driving through her life' (p. 210) and looks forward to the 'composed faces' of the dead sailors and the 'smoothly sculpted' traffic policeman at Ludgate Circus. In contrast to Dalloway's exaltation of the State, the narrator of

Jacob's Room calls attention to its acutely destructive and dehumanising power.

'Let us think in offices;' Woolf writes in *Three Guineas*, 'in omnibuses; while we are standing in the crowd watching Coronations and Lord Mayor's Shows; let us think as we pass the Cenotaph; and in Whitehall; in the gallery of the House of Commons; in the Law Courts; let us think at baptisms and marriages and funerals. Let us never cease from thinking – what is this "civilisation" in which we find ourselves?'.[16] This fundamental question permeates Woolf's whole output as a novelist and it lies at the heart of *To the Lighthouse*, a text in which the reader is offered a great deal to 'think' about concerning the relationship between civilisation and society. 'Women made civilisation impossible with all their "charm", all their silliness',[17] the prejudiced Charles Tansley believes, while William Bankes doubts 'whether you could have your Darwin and your Titian if it weren't for humble people' like himself and Lily Briscoe (p. 79). The relationship between culture and society is pondered at greater length by Mr Ramsay:

> Does the progress of civilisation depend upon great men? Is the lot of the average human being better now than in the time of the Pharaohs? Is the lot of the average human being, however . . . the criterion by which we judge the measure of civilisation? Possibly not. Possibly the greatest good requires the existence of a slave class. The liftman in the Tube is an eternal necessity.
>
> (pp. 48–9)

The dogma that slavery and civilisation must needs go hand in hand has a long pedigree in European thought, but Mr Ramsay finds the idea 'distasteful' and decides to argue in a forthcoming lecture 'that the world exists for the average human being; that the arts are merely a decoration imposed on the top of human life; they do not express it'.

This seems to be the 'argument' of *To the Lighthouse*, and, as such, the novel may be read as a pre-emptive strike against the elitist position of the art critic and cultural commentator Clive Bell, Woolf's brother-in-law. In the last chapter of *Civilization* (1928) Bell asks:

> an urgent and awkward question: How are the civilizing few to be supplied with the necessary security and leisure save at the expense of the many?
>   The answer is that nohow else can they be supplied: their fellows must support them as they have always done. Civilization requires the existence of a leisured class, and a leisured class requires the existence of slaves.[18]

Civilization had a long gestation and Woolf knew what it was going to assert before it was published. She was deeply sensitive to the real degradation which lay beneath Bell's lofty rhetoric about 'slaves' and she inscribes her opposition to his views in her novel. In 'The Window', for example, the Ramsays and their summer guests (with their relish for tennis and cricket) are provocatively juxtaposed with those around them who must work to survive. The 'attics' of the summer house hold both 'the Swiss girl sobbing for her father who was dying of cancer in a valley of the Grisons, and . . . bats, flannels, straw hats, ink-pots [and] paint-pots' (p. 12). The impedimenta of the leisured class and the distress of the servant are placed side by side in a way which spotlights both the physical well-being and the moral enervation of the island's carefree minority.

In addition, there is a significant gap between the human face of Skye and its literary and painterly representations. Since the fashionable Mr Paunceforte's visit three years previously, all the pictures of the island are like the man in the Panama hat's: 'green and grey, with lemon-coloured sailing-boats, and pink women on the beach' (p. 17). Images of this kind accentuate the island's appeal to the leisured class, while in Paul Rayley's guide book it is written that 'these islands [are] justly celebrated for their park-like prospects and the extent and variety of their marine curiosities' (p. 82). Yet the island which the reader encounters is a place of distinctly limited 'prospects'. Towards the end of 'The Window' we learn that the fishing is bad, unemployment is a fact of life and the islanders are emigrating (p. 102). The first one we come across is mutilated, 'his left arm had been cut off in a reaping machine two years ago' (p. 15), and this accident casts a shadow back on James Ramsay 'cutting out' the picture of a refrigerator 'from the illustrated catalogue of the Army and Navy Stores' (p. 7) at the start of the novel. As James removes the picture his mother imagines him 'all red and ermine on the Bench or directing a stern and momentous enterprise in some crisis of public affairs', but the next boy we read about, the tuberculous son of the lighthouse-keeper, has no such 'future prospects' (p. 7), being 'shut up for a whole month at a time and possibly more in stormy weather, upon a rock the size of a tennis lawn' (pp. 8–9) with his father. As with the juxtaposition of human anguish and *rentier* bric-à-brac in the attics, Woolf's comparison of the lighthouse rock with a tennis lawn is neatly polemical.

The leisured class is personified by the indolent Carmichael, a sometime poet with 'a capacious paunch' (p. 14) who does 'acrostics endlessly' (p. 47) when not sleeping in his deck-chair. Carmichael is described as being 'sunk . . . in a grey-green somnolence which embraced them all . . . a vast and benevolent lethargy of well-wishing' (p. 14), and these words implicate Carmichael and the other summer guests in the distortion of reality for which the island's fashionable painters, with their penchant for a predominantly 'green and grey' palate, are responsible. There is much talk of French things (p. 115) in 'The Window', and Mr Bankes has visited some of the major cultural sites of Europe (p. 79), but 'books were not their line' (p. 117). Mr Ramsay, supposedly a philosopher of some distinction, storms about terrorising his children and guests and torments himself with a simple-mindedly linear model of the intellect, while Lily, stymied by the ignorance of those around her, can make no headway with her painting.

At one point in 'The Window' Mrs Ramsay ruminates on:

> the things she saw with her own eyes, weekly, daily, here or in London, when she visited this widow, or that struggling wife in person with a bag on her arm, and a note-book and pencil . . . in the hope that thus she would cease to be a private woman whose charity was half a sop to her own indignation, half a relief to her own curiosity, and become, what with her untrained mind she greatly admired, an investigator, elucidating the social problem.   (p. 13)

Further on in 'The Window' Mrs Ramsay again ponders 'the eternal problems: suffering; death; the poor. There was always a woman dying of cancer even here' (p. 66), and a few pages after this she wonders 'How could any Lord have made this world? . . . With her mind she had always seized the fact that there is no reason, order, justice: but suffering, death, the poor' (p. 71). But *To the Lighthouse* exposes the insufficiency of her kind of individualistic, Victorian-style philanthropy and sees it as part of the 'vast and benevolent lethargy of well-wishing' in which the leisured class are sunk. As well as the woollen stocking, Mrs Ramsay considers sending to the lighthouse 'a pile of old magazines, and some tobacco, indeed whatever she could find lying about, not really wanted, but only littering the room' (p. 8), and her haphazard (and slightly disgraceful) thoughts underline the comparative futility of such 'good works'.

Watching Mr Ramsay reading, his wife sees him 'weighing, considering, putting this with that as he read' (p. 128), and Woolf's readers need to be no less alert to the pulse and fabric of *To the Lighthouse*. Tuberculosis, for example, haunts the novel. Chronic inflammation of the bones and joints was a common manifestation of TB, and the son of the lighthouse keeper, 'threatened with a tuberculous hip' (p. 8), incarnates a widespread social disease which was particularly virulent among the poor. The earwig in Mr Ramsay's breakfast milk (p. 216) provides further evidence, perhaps, of the island's desperate need for the 'model dairy and a hospital' which Mrs Ramsay would like to build (pp. 64, 112) as a way of combating the threat of bovine tuberculosis being transmitted through dirty milk, while the reason she is anxious to keep 'the windows open and the doors shut' at Elsie's 'poky little house' (p. 18) is almost certainly because she is trying to achieve effective ventilation in response to the airborne TB that appears to have struck down either Elsie herself or one of her children. For the same reason, Mrs Ramsay is annoyed that every door seems to have been left open in her own house. 'That windows should be open, and doors shut – simple as it was, could none of them remember it? She would go into the maids' bedrooms at night and find them sealed like ovens' (p. 33).

The spectre of TB leaves its imprint on the novel in two further ways. First, the grotesque pig's skull 'nailed fast' (p. 124) to the wall of Cam and James's bedroom not only rekindles the concept of 'the skeleton beneath' but also symbolises Mrs Ramsay's fetishisation of TB in that scrofula (from the Latin word for a sow, and so called because the distinctive enlargement of glands in the victim's neck give the face a swollen, pig-like expression), was a common form of the disease. Yet another was 'consumption', characterised by a wasting-away of the body. The erosion or wasting-away of the island (e.g. pp. 20, 50, 220–1, 224), therefore, is analogous to the TB which menaces its inhabitants, particularly its children and old people, while the frequent references to the island's consumption by the sea also recall the description of England in Chapter Two of *The Voyage Out* as 'a shrinking island' (p. 24), and suggest that Skye may be read as a synecdoche for the sickness, both figurative and epidemiological, of the whole country.

The images of labour-saving luxury goods, such as the refrigerator (pp. 7, 19, 69) which James cuts out from the catalogue, are worlds away from the toil and drudgery of Mrs Bast and Mrs McNab, whose lives are 'one long sorrow and trouble' (p. 142). 'Bowed down she was with weariness' (p. 142), Woolf writes of Mrs McNab. 'Time Passes' was written during the class conflict of the General Strike of 1926, and in this section Woolf attempts, symbolically, to reconcile social strife. At the beginning of 'Time Passes' we learn that the island has been metaphorically engulfed – one could 'hardly tell which is the sea and which is the land' (p. 137) – and the darkness and the dampness which envelop the empty house, and the 'swollen sea-moistened woodwork' (p. 138) within it, suggest that TB, and the social malaise it symbolizes, which Mrs Ramsay tried so hard to keep at bay, have finally breached its walls and consumed it. Yet by the time the two women and their various helpers have finished their restoration of the house, they have rescued it, suggestively, from 'the pool of Time' (p. 152). The green shawl, one of 'The Window's' 'thin veils of civilisation' (p. 38) which Mrs Ramsay wraps round the 'horrid' pig's skull (p. 124), gradually slips towards the floor (pp. 142, 145, 150) during 'Time Passes', just as 'the veil on [the] eyes' (p. 154) of the post-war guests is broken at the end of it. In contrast to the 'somnolence' of 'The Window', Lily ends up with her 'eyes opened wide' (p. 155). She is 'Awake!' as 'Time Passes' comes to a close.

By the beginning of 'The Lighthouse', therefore, TB has been banished, 'the fabric of things' has been laid bare, and the house rebuilt. It is also significant that the romantic 'hoary Lighthouse, distant [and] austere' (p. 17) of 'The Window', becomes a real, inhabited structure in the last part of the novel. 'James looked at the Lighthouse. He could see the white-washed rocks; the tower, stark and straight; he could see that it was barred with black and white; he could see windows in it; he could even see washing spread on the rocks to dry. So that was the Lighthouse, was it?' (p. 202). The word 'effort' dominates the first paragraph of the last section of 'The Lighthouse', as if Mrs McNab and Mrs Bast are still at large in the house, and a similar 'effort' enables Lily to imagine Carmichael, standing next to her and looking out to sea, 'spreading his hands over all the weakness and suffering of mankind; she thought he was surveying, tolerantly, compassionately, their final destiny'. This last clause most obviously refers to Mr Ramsay and his children reaching the lighthouse, of course, but 'their' may be just as readily applied to 'mankind'. The key point is that it is a political epiphany which prompts Lily to make her final brush stroke and complete her painting. It is triggered by an almost utopian glimpse of a world based on outreach, sympathy and the elimination of misery. Contrary to what Clive Bell was to argue the following year, civilisation and society need not be antithetical. 'With a sudden intensity, as if she saw it clear for a second, she drew a line there, in the centre . . . Yes, she thought, laying down her brush in extreme fatigue, I have had my vision' (pp. 225–6). In the same way that Lily reduces her insight to its essentials, Woolf does the same, and the reader is left to muse on what both might mean. Lily's bold line may be read in various ways – for instance as signifying the 'dismal flatness' (p. 45) of the Ramsays' marriage; Mr Ramsay's exactingness (p. 63); his being 'as lean as a rake' (p. 152); the 'arid scimitar of the male' (p. 43); or the tree (pp. 92, 111, 191) over which Lily has agonised – but it also denotes the 'dismal flatness' of Mrs McNab's life in particular and the 'weakness and suffering of mankind' in general. In this respect, it is important to note that Lily's grid-like picture is constructed of greens and blues (p. 225), the true colours of the island (p. 17), rather than the false green-grey hues favoured by the modish artists of 'The Window'. Lily's painting succeeds in expressing life as it is, with the centrality of labour acknowledged and incorporated, and, in a visionary way, it symbolises the potential for a shift in the construction of civilisation from one which valorises the works of 'great men' towards one which foregrounds 'the lot of the average human being'.

Although the emphasis of this essay is on Woolf's response to social division and political prejudice, the circle formations in *The Voyage Out*, the bird imagery in *Mrs Dalloway* and the dinner scene in *To the Lighthouse* signify the unity and harmony which she believed to be latent beneath the affliction and fragmentation of her world.[19] In 'A Sketch of the Past', Woolf wrote that it was 'a constant idea of mine; that behind the cotton wool is hidden a pattern; that we – I mean all human beings – are connected with this',[20] and, in turn, the recurring image of a searchlight probing the 'fleecy patch[es]' of the sky in *The Years* seems to express this 'constant idea' of Woolf's.[21] Just as the rain in the '1880' chapter falls 'equally over the mitred and the bareheaded with an impartiality which suggested that the god of rain . . . was thinking Let it not be restricted to the very wise, the very great, but let all breathing kind . . . share my bounty' (p. 46), the expansive circle of 'new combinations' (p. 282) which Pomjalowsky makes with his hollowed hands in the '1917' chapter of *The Years* contrasts with the desire to segregate and expel denoted by the British Union of Fascists' insignia, 'a circle . . . with a jagged line in it' (p. 294), which has been daubed on the doors and windows of an East End street near where Sara Pargiter lives.[22] 'A common interest unites us,' Woolf writes in *Three Guineas*, 'it is one world, one life. How essential it is that we should realize that unity the dead bodies, the ruined houses prove',[23] and in *The Years* this sentiment is encapsulated in Eleanor's quotation from Dante: 'For by so many more there are who say "ours" / So much the more of good doth each possess' (p. 202).

'Justice and Liberty!,' George Orwell wrote in *The Road to Wigan Pier*, '*Those* are the words that have got to ring like a bugle across the world.'[24] Infamously, they did not resound across late 1930s Europe, but they are reiterated in *The Years*, published, like Orwell's book, in 1937. Orwell saw these words as defining 'the essential aims of Socialism'[25] and in Woolf's novel they are linked with the theme of unity symbolised in the searchlight beams and car headlamps (which illuminate the novel's skies and ceilings), and the numerous variations on the figure of 'a dot with strokes raying out round it' (p. 88).[26] Yet by the 'Present Day' chapter, the 'cause of Liberty . . . the cause of Justice' which is so close to the heart of the young Delia (pp. 22, 110) and the Hyde Park socialist (pp. 228–9) is examined more critically by North during Delia's party. 'What do they mean by Justice and Liberty? he asked, all these nice young men with two or three hundred a year. Something's wrong, he thought; there's a gap, a dislocation, between the word and reality' (p. 385). By 1937, with the Second World War drawing ever closer, the visionary optimism which braces *To the Lighthouse* had given way to despair.

It is this pessimism and anxiety which holds sway in *The Years*, a novel in which Woolf stresses the umbilical connection between the fascist oppression of the late 1930s and the tyranny of the patriarchal Victorian family. At the beginning of the '1908' chapter, a merciless wind blows rubbish about the streets. 'Had it any breeding place,' Woolf writes, 'it was in the Isle of Dogs among tin cans lying beside a workhouse drab on the banks of a polluted city.' The wind has 'a joy in destruction' and reveals 'the bare bone' of the city and its inhabitants. It blows about the contents of a dust cart and sends 'old envelopes; twists of hair; papers already blood smeared, yellow smeared, smudged with print' flying about. London's debris is the physical equivalent of the bigotry, xenophobia and general nastiness which characterises the Pargiter family's outlook on life. Abel Pargiter's deformed hand (p. 13) is an apt emblem of his 'deformed' (p. 361) family and 'dislocated' civilisation.

The younger Pargiters are torn between the inveterate intolerance of their backgrounds – North's joining in with Sara's anti-Semitic disgust (p. 322); Peggy's affirmative response to the French writer's contempt for the 'médiocrité de l'univers' (p. 364), for instance – and a more sympathetic outlook on life. During a lull in the music at Delia's party, Peggy listens to the sounds of the London night:

> The far-away sounds, the suggestion they brought in of other worlds, indifferent to this world, of people toiling, grinding, in the heart of darkness, in the depths of night, made her say over Eleanor's words, Happy in this world, happy with living people. But how can one be 'happy'? she asked herself, in a world bursting with misery. On every placard at every street corner was Death; or worse – tyranny; brutality; torture; the fall of civilisation; the end of freedom. (pp. 368–9)

Peggy's thoughts recall those of Helen Ambrose and Rachel Vinrace on the deck of the *Euphrosyne*, and the phrase 'heart of darkness' is used twice (see also p. 391) in this final chapter, reinvoking the *Heart of Darkness*-like first chapter of *The Voyage Out*. Earlier, at the beginning of the '1907' chapter, the drivers of carts bringing fresh fruit and vegetables to the capital are said to see 'through half shut eyes the fiery gauze of the eternally burning city' (p. 124) a phrase which, in turn, brings to mind the eternally burned and blazing Londons of Woolf's first and third novels.

As well as smears and smudges, there are numerous stains in *The Years*, such as the 'dark stain' (p. 17) left by Abel Pargiter's head on a chair in Abercorn Terrace and the stained walls (p. 204) of the house. Sara Pargiter's table-cloth, 'yellowed with some gravy stain' (p. 298), neatly undermines any sense of superiority she may feel over the allegedly unhygienic Abrahamson. Yet the most significant stains, perhaps, are the 'brown stain' on the forehead of Milly in the 'Present Day' chapter and 'the stain like the yolk of egg' in her hair (p. 357). These two stains replicate the 'brown patches' which stain the face of her dying mother in the first chapter of the novel and the 'queer yellow patches' in her hair 'as if some locks had been dipped in the yolk of an egg' (p. 21), and they indicate just how thoroughly the Pargiter offspring have been tainted by the 'abominable system of family life' (p. 212).

If the reader's attention is drawn repeatedly to lights and patterns on the ceilings and skies of *The Years*, we are also asked to look into the novel's many basements. Eleanor is 'ashamed' (p. 206) when she first sees the confined basement in which Crosby, the family servant, has lived for forty years, and the basement-bound Matty Styles squints up at Martin 'from behind the bars of a cage' (p. 142) in the '1908' chapter. Sara may refer to the basement of Renny and Maggie's house as a 'cave of mud and dung' (p. 279), but she only has to spend a short time in it sheltering from the air raid, while there are some characters in the novel who must live underground almost permanently. In particular, the treatment of the two 'frightened' children 'brought up from the basement' (p. 407) at dawn near the end of Delia's party comes across as not just haughty but almost fascistic. The 'distorted sounds' and 'unintelligible words' (p. 408) of the children give voice to what is ordinarily submerged and silent. 'There was something horrible in the noise they made. It was so shrill, so discordant, and so meaningless' (p. 409). 'Cockney accent, I suppose' (p. 409), Patrick says breezily, yet the children's incoherent babble sounds, if anything, like a scrambled allusion to Dante's inclusive vision of mankind. The words 'passo', 'hai', 'Fai', 'Mai', 'Fanno' and 'par' exist in modern Italian as well as Dante's, and this is perhaps why Eleanor half-recognises what the children are saying. Their 'song' also reminds the reader of the 'whining plaint' of the stone-deaf and bed-ridden Mrs Potter, one of Eleanor's tenants, whose 'words ran themselves together into a chant that was half-plaint, half-curse' (p. 95) in the '1891' chapter. Even more powerfully, perhaps, their garbled sounds suggest the biblical 'Confusion of Tongues' (Gen. 11: 1–9) and the idea that the people of the world originally spoke one language and lived together in peace before being scattered and diversified into conflict. *The Years* begins with 'an uncertain spring' and it concludes on an uncertain note. The sun may have risen at the end of the party, and the sky may wear 'an air of extraordinary beauty, simplicity and peace', but the dissonant children and the thirteen smashed glasses (p. 405) overspill the novel's final sentence and convey the profound pessimism Woolf felt at a time when dictators featured in the evening paper (p. 313) on a daily basis.

'He is asking the novelist not only to do many things but some that seem incompatible', Woolf wrote of the Russian novelist Turgenev in an essay of 1933:

> He has to observe facts impartially, yet he must also interpret them. Many novelists do the one; many do the other – we have the photograph and the poem. But few combine the fact and the vision; and the rare quality that we find in Turgenev is the result of this double process.[27]

A similar 'double process' is also at work in Woolf's novels and it is this that makes them such a demanding and rewarding read. In another essay she wrote that 'philosophy should not be separable from fiction' and that a writer's 'view of life . . . should be buried beyond the possibility of exhumation'. Woolf went on to note that in great writers such as Shakespeare, Tolstoy and Austen 'nothing is left unconsumed' whereas with a novelist such as Meredith 'the teaching sticks out from the body of the book'.[28] Embodied with masterly deftness, Woolf's socio-political vision is never protruberant but neither is it missable.

NOTES

1 'The Natural History of German Life', rep. in A. S. Byatt and Nicholas Warren (eds.), *George Eliot, Selected Essays, Poems and Other Writings* (Harmondsworth: Penguin, 1990), pp. 107–39. Quote from p. 110.

2 See, in particular, Gillian Beer, *Virginia Woolf: The Common Ground* (Edinburgh University Press, 1996); Mark Hussey, *The Singing of the Real World: The Philosophy of Virginia Woolf's Fiction* (Ohio State University Press, 1986); Kathy J. Phillips, *Virginia Woolf Against Empire* (University of Tennessee Press, 1994); and Alex Zwerdling, *Virginia Woolf and the Real World* (University of California Press, 1986). Woolf's real-life political activities and affiliations are most easily traced in Hermione Lee's *Virginia Woolf* (London: Chatto and Windus, 1996).

3 Virginia Woolf, *EJ*, ed. Mitchell A. Leaska (London: Hogarth, 1992), p. 384.

4 'A Room with a View', rep. in Andrew McNeillie, ed., *The Essays of Virginia Woolf*, vol. 1 (London: Hogarth, 1986), pp. 221–2. Quote from p. 221.

5 'Character in Fiction', rep. in *E3*, pp. 420–38. Quote from p. 432.

6 Virginia Woolf, *VO*, ed. Jane Wheare (Harmondsworth: Penguin, 1992), p. 5. All further page references are embodied in the text.

7 'In the second half of the nineteenth century, Victorian civilisation felt itself increasingly threatened by "Outcast London"', Gareth Stedman Jones, *Outcast London: A Study in the Relationship between Classes in Victorian Society* (Oxford: Clarendon Press, 1971), p. 1, *passim*.

8 General Booth, *In Darkest England and the Way Out* (London: International Headquarters of the Salvation Army, 1890), p. 30. Booth's account of the Embankment at night is on pp. 25–31.

9 'This Submerged Tenth – is it, then, beyond the reach of the nine-tenths in the midst of whom they live, and around whose homes they rot and die?', *In Darkest England*, p. 23. Chapter Two is entitled 'The Submerged Tenth' and the phrase 'Sunken Millions' occurs on p. 40.

10 Henry Mayhew, *London Labour and the London Poor*, vol. 4 (New York: Dover, 1968), p. 213. Charles Booth, *Life and Labour of the People in London*, vol. 1, Part 2, 'First Series: Poverty: East, Central and South London' (London: Macmillan, 1902), p. 186.

11 I discuss this idea at greater length in 'Vicious Circles: Hegel, Bosanquet and *The Voyage Out*,' in Diane F. Gillespie and Leslie K. Hankins, eds., *Virginia Woolf and the Arts: Selected Papers from the Sixth Annual Conference on Virginia Woolf* (New York: Pace University Press, 1997), pp. 183–91. There are further allusions to Piccadilly and its prostitutes in *JR*, *Mrs D* and *W*.

12 Richard Trench and Ellis Hillman, *London Under London: A Subterranean Guide* (London: John Murray, 1984), pp. 105, 113, 115. The Thames Tunnel was built by Marc Isambard Brunel and since 1869 it has had either railway or underground trains running through it.

13 Virginia Woolf, *JR*, ed. Sue Roe (Harmondsworth: Penguin, 1992), p. 96. All further page references are given in the text.

14 See, for example, Rick Allen, *The Moving Pageant: A Literary Sourcebook on London Street-life, 1700–1914* (London and New York: Routledge, 1998), pp. 106–7.

15 Mansfield's comments are quoted by Julia Briggs in her essay on *Night and Day* in Julia Briggs, ed., *Virginia Woolf: Introductions to the Major Works* (London: Virago, 1994), pp. 33–60. Quote on p. 34.

16 Virginia Woolf, *ROO [and] TG*, ed. Michèle Barrett (Harmondsworth: Penguin, 1993), p. 187.

17 Virginia Woolf, *TL*, ed. Stella McNichol (Harmondsworth: Penguin, 1992), p. 93. All further page references are given in the text.

18 Clive Bell, *Civilization: An Essay* (London: Chatto and Windus, 1928), pp. 204–5.

19 For an interpretation of the socio-political vision of *Mrs D*, see the Introduction to my Oxford World's Classics edition of the novel.

20 Virginia Woolf, *MB*, ed. Jeanne Schulkind (London: Chatto and Windus for Sussex University Press, 1976), pp. 64–137. Quote from p. 72.

21 Virginia Woolf, *Y*, ed. Hermione Lee (Oxford: World's Classics, 1992), pp. 266, 285, 297. All further page references are embodied in the text.

22 This point is addressed at greater length in my 'Hyams Place: *The Years*, The Jews and the British Union of Fascists,' in *Women Writers of the 1930s: Gender, Politics and History*, ed. Maroula Joannou (Edinburgh University Press, 1999), pp. 179–91.

23 *TG*, p. 271.

24 George Orwell, *The Road to Wigan Pier*, ed. Peter Davison (London: Secker and Warburg, 1998), p. 201.

25 *Ibid.*, p. 199.

26 I discuss this aspect of the novel in '"History in the Raw": Searchlights and Anglo-German Rivalry in *The Years*', *Critical Survey*, Special Issue on Literature of the 1930s, 10, no. 3, September 1998, pp. 13–21.

27 'The Novels of Turgenev,' rep. in Virginia Woolf, *Collected Essays*, vol. 1 (London: Hogarth, 1966), pp. 247–53. Quote from p. 249.

28 'The Novels of George Meredith,' rep. in *E4*, pp. 525–36. Quotes from pp. 531–2.

11

LAURA MARCUS

Woolf's feminism and feminism's Woolf

Feminism, both as a theoretical analysis of gender inequality and oppression and as a political movement, has used literary texts extensively in making and disseminating its meanings. Literary and literary-critical texts were central to 'second-wave' feminist politics and the movement for 'women's liberation' in the late 1960s and 1970s, laying many of the foundations for the developments in feminist and gender criticism and theory that have changed literary studies so radically. The significance of literature for feminism also gives a particular place to those writers whose work spans both feminist polemic and fiction or poetry, including Mary Wollstonecraft, Simone de Beauvoir, Adrienne Rich and, preeminently, Virginia Woolf.

The relationship between Virginia Woolf and feminism, feminism and Virginia Woolf is, as the title of my chapter suggests, a symbiotic one. On the one hand, Woolf's feminism – which includes not just her explicit feminist politics but her concern and fascination with gender identities and with women's lives, histories and fictions – shaped her writing profoundly. On the other, feminist criticism and theory of the second half of this century have fundamentally altered the perception and reception of a writer who, in Anglo-American contexts at least, had largely fallen out of favour by the 1950s and 1960s.[1] The immediate post-war generation tended to perceive Woolf's as an essentially pre-war sensibility. In the decades that followed, women critics and academics creating new feminist approaches found Woolf speaking very directly to their concerns, in the first-person address (albeit one in which the 'I' is diffuse and multiple) of *A Room of One's Own* or in the voice or voices that seemed to speak out from Woolf's newly available essays, letters, diaries and memoirs.

The preoccupations of post-war feminist literary and cultural criticism could, indeed, be traced through accounts of and approaches to Virginia Woolf. Her work has been used as key evidence and example in the most significant and recurrent feminist debates; 'realist' versus 'modernist' writing as the most effective vehicle for a feminist politics; the existence of a specifically female literary tradition and of a woman's language; the place of feminist 'anger' or radicalism; the feminist uses of 'androgyny' as a concept; the significance of gendered perspectives and 'the difference of view' as a counter to difference-blind assumptions of the universal; the relationships between socialism and feminism, feminism and pacifism, patriarchy and fascism.

Woolf's work is also central to recent models and histories of twentieth-century literature and culture; more particularly, definitions of modernism and, most recently, of postmodernism. In previous decades, British modernism was largely defined on the basis of literary themes and forms drawn from the work of T. S. Eliot, James Joyce, Ezra Pound and, though more ambivalently, D. H. Lawrence. When Virginia Woolf was included in this canon, it was most often as an exemplar of 'feminine' modes of writing and of an early twentieth-century (over)subjectivism. In recent years, modernism has come to look more like a 'mouvement des femmes', with Woolf as part of a cluster (or heading a roster) of women writers, including Dorothy Richardson, Katherine Mansfield, May Sinclair, H. D., Djuna Barnes, Mina Loy and Gertrude Stein. Various as these writers are, the question of the 'gender of modernism' has come to provide a powerful centripetal pull. Models of modernism and modernity have become substantially predicated on a set of preoccupations and identities shared by women writers of the first part of the twentieth century and beyond: private and public spheres; urban consciousness; language and the body; gender transformations; lesbian passions; self-presentations.

In biographical terms, feminist criticism has brought about a major shift from accounts of Woolf's relationships with 'Bloomsbury' men (Lytton Strachey, Roger Fry, Clive Bell) and their influences upon her to a concern with Woolf's relationships, personal, sexual and professional, with other women (Vanessa Bell, Violet Dickinson, Vita Sackville-West, Ethel Smyth). A recent collection of essays focuses on the 'lesbian aspects' of Woolf's fictions.[2] Critics have also examined Virginia Woolf in tandem with a female other: 'Vanessa and Virginia', 'Vita and Virginia'.[3]

In a number of feminist biographies, Woolf's history of mental illness and her death by suicide have become the occasion for discussion of those experiences (or their denial and repression) which, in a male-dominated society, make women ill or, more accurately, lead to such a diagnosis. The autobiographical dimensions of her novels, *To the Lighthouse* in particular, contribute to the blurring of boundaries between biography, autobiography and fiction in discussions of her life and work. The narratives created by her biographers seem, almost inevitably, to shape themselves into the life, the scenes, that Woolf, in many different forms, had already composed.

Woolf's feminism

If the feminisms of the second half of the twentieth century have found in Woolf one of their most significant forerunners, it is at least in part because her writing and thinking were so intertwined with the feminisms of the first half of the century. Her responses to the feminist ideas of her time were, however, complex and often contradictory. Alex Zwerdling has written that 'Until we see [Woolf's] work as a response to some of the received ideas of her time about women and "the cause", we will not fully understand it.'[4] Her 'alternating loyalty to and deviation from' the familiar positions of the feminist movement produced contradictions in her thought which late twentieth-century feminisms have often found it difficult to accept, tending to opt for one pole rather than another, instead of recognising and negotiating inconsistencies.

A variety of weights have been attached to the involvement of Woolf (then Virginia Stephen) with the suffragist cause. At the beginning of 1910, she had written to her friend and Greek tutor Janet Case:

> Would it be any use if I spent an afternoon or two weekly in addressing envelopes for the Adult Suffragists?
>
> I don't know anything about the question. Perhaps you could send me a pamphlet, or give me the address of the office. I could neither do sums or argue, or speak, but I could do the humbler work if that is any good. You impressed me so much the other night with the wrongness of the present state of affairs that I feel that action is necessary. Your position seemed to me intolerable. The only way to better it is to do some thing I suppose. How melancholy it is that conversation isn't enough! _(L1, p. 421)_

For Zwerdling, the letter typifies Woolf's 'reluctant' political participation in a cause she nonetheless felt impelled to support. This reluctance was, he suggests, entirely consistent with her subsequent withdrawal from feminist activism, motivated not by an absence of sympathy with broader feminist beliefs and goals, but by her sense that suffrage – the struggle for women's right to vote – was too narrow a cause. It is significant, moreover, that Woolf's short-lived period of suffrage activism affiliated her to the suffragist rather than the more militant suffragette cause.

Naomi Black, who has written extensively about Virginia Woolf and the Women's Movement, uses much of the same 'evidence' to rather different ends. For Black, Woolf's suffrage work, most probably for a body called the People's Suffrage Organization, was significant in both historical and personal terms. The year of Woolf's involvement, 1910, 'was the peak of cooperation among the woman suffrage groups';[5] by implication, the 'shadowy organization' to which Woolf belonged would thus have had extensive contact with the larger and higher-profile women's suffrage groups, including the militant Women's Social and Political Union. Most significantly for Black, Woolf's work for the People's Suffrage Organization, however brief, signalled her entry into a feminist organisational politics which Black defines as 'social feminism'. 'Social feminism' is predicated on assumptions about the *differences* between men and women, and on the belief that women's values and skills, whether innate or culturally constructed, are excluded in male-dominated societies. It calls for a new understanding and valorisation of specifically female values, and is to be contrasted with an 'equal rights' feminism, which campaigns for women's equal access to the civic and social rights and structures enjoyed by men. The contrast is often framed as a distinction between a feminism of *equality* and one of *difference*.

Both Alex Zwerdling and Naomi Black have contributed significantly to an understanding of Woolf's feminism in its historical contexts. Zwerdling's is one of the most thoughtful and comprehensive accounts of the topic, though it may be that he renders Woolf too isolated in her (feminist) perceptions of the limits of suffrage and is thus too eager to withdraw her from a public and political arena. Black, by contrast, insists upon Woolf's continued organisational affiliations, though for the modern British reader the occasional talk Woolf gave to her local Women's Institute smacks more of duty than political commitment. It may be that the place to look for Woolf's feminist activism is in other kinds of institution, such as the Hogarth Press, for which she wrote *Three Guineas* as part of a series on women and feminism: other texts in the series included pamphlets by Willa Muir, Margaret Llewelyn Davies and Ray Strachey.

The equality versus difference arguments (or 'equal rights' versus 'social feminism') also seem too clear-cut and too polarised as a way of understanding Woolf's feminism. Her accounts of the difference of women's values, in literature and in life, are central to her writings but they are also open-ended, and more relativist than absolute. As Mary Jacobus argued in an important feminist essay on Woolf, the 'difference' of 'women's writing', like sexual difference itself, becomes 'a question rather than an answer'.[6]

In her very first writings, primarily reviews and essays for periodicals, Virginia Stephen had addressed the issues of 'masculine' and 'feminine' writing and the nature of their differences, the place of women in the literary tradition and the explanations for their relative absence until the nineteenth and twentieth centuries. In 1905 she reviewed W. L. Courtney's

The Feminine Note in Fiction, asking: 'Is it not too soon after all to criticize the "feminine note" in anything? And will not the adequate critic of women be a woman?'[7] The second question suggests the argument she would later make in her essay 'Women and Fiction' and elaborate in *A Room of One's Own*: 'that both in life and in art the values of a woman are not the values of a man'.[8] The 'too soon' of the first question makes a point to which she would frequently return – that the history of women's freedom of expression, education and experience is a very recent one.

Woolf developed this argument in response to the assertions made by Arnold Bennett in his 1920 collection of essays, *Our Women: Chapters on the Sex-Discord*, and to a favourable review of Bennett's book by her friend Desmond MacCarthy, writing under the pseudonym 'Affable Hawk'. Her diary entry for 26 September 1920 records her 'making up a paper upon Women, as a counterblast to Mr Bennett's adverse views reported in the papers', in particular his claim that 'intellectually and creatively man is the superior of woman' (*D2*, p. 69). In her letters to the *New Statesman*, Woolf anticipates the arguments of *A Room of One's Own*:

> My difference with Affable Hawk is not that he denies the present intellectual equality of men and women. It is that he, with Mr Bennett, asserts that the mind of woman is not sensibly affected by education and liberty; that it is incapable of the highest achievements; and that it must remain for ever in the condition in which it now is. I must repeat that the fact that women have improved (which Affable Hawk now seems to admit), shows that they might still improve; for I cannot see why a limit should be set to their improvement in the nineteenth century rather than in the one hundred and nineteenth. But it is not education only that is needed. It is that women should have liberty of experience; that they should differ from men without fear and express their differences openly (for I do not agree with Affable Hawk that men and women are alike). . .[9]

Woolf's emphases on education and experience as the necessary conditions for women's cultural and intellectual life are a key aspect of her contributions to a 'sociology' of culture, in which the environment and the social sphere become far more significant determinants of literary capacity and production than any concept of creativity as a purely personal property. Such 'materialism' – as in her emphases in *A Room of One's Own* on the importance of financial independence and autonomous space – became central to the socialist-feminist approaches to Woolf of the 1970s, including Michèle Barrett's collection of Woolf's essays, *Women and Writing*, which significantly contributed to the reception of the 'feminist' Woolf.

Woolf's letters to the *New Statesman* also raise the difficult question of male and female 'likeness' and 'difference' and the significance of sexual identity in literature. At times, as in the passage quoted above, Woolf insists upon the difference between male and female perspectives, values and standards. Elsewhere in her writing, she expresses a desire for a freedom from 'the tyranny of sex . . . any emphasis . . . laid consciously upon the sex of a writer is not only irritating but superfluous'.[10] At yet other points – and this emerges in essays written around 1920 – she hints at the illusory nature of our conceptions of sexual identity: 'To cast out and incorporate in a person of the opposite sex all that we miss in ourselves and desire in the universe and detest in humanity is a deep and universal instinct on the part both of men and of women. But though it affords relief, it does not lead to understanding.'[11] The question here is whether the very conception of 'the other' as a fully but single-sexed identity (male/female) is a matter of fantasy and projection, of 'cast[ing] out' and 'incorporation' into an illusory whole. These questions, and the function served by Woolf's seeming absence of a consistent position on questions of sexual difference, are taken up in Woolf's most extended piece of writing on women and literature, *A Room of One's Own*.

Before moving on to this text, however, I want to pause on the slippery ground of women's 'improvement'. On the one hand, Woolf's emphasis on the provisional, incomplete aspects of women's selves could be said to point forward to more recent conceptions of 'women's identity' and 'feminism' as projects without a known goal and end. As Woolf wrote in 'Professions for Women' (first given as a lecture in 1931), the essay in which she introduced the 'Angel in the House', that symbol of Victorian femininity and rectitude whom the woman writer must destroy in order to write freely:

> What is a woman? I assure you, I do not know. I do not believe that you know. I do not believe that anybody can know until she has expressed herself in all the arts and professions open to human skill.[12]

On the other hand, the concept of 'improvement' might suggest the evolutionary, developmental models of femininity and of 'woman' that dominated discussion at the turn of the last century. We should note, however, that by contrast with most representations of the 'New Woman', there is much of culture and little or nothing of biology in Woolf's arguments. I would argue, moreover, that Woolf, to a marked extent, subverted representations and discussions of 'The New Woman', and her later manifestation, 'The Modern Girl', both of which were central personifications for late nineteenth- and early-twentieth-century feminisms. For Woolf, 'The Modern Girl' may well have seemed too slender and shallow a figure through which to explore psychical and temporal complexities, including women's collusions with their unfreedoms.

In *The Voyage Out* Rachel Vinrace's aunt Helen gives her George Meredith's novel *Diana of the Crossways* and Henrik Ibsen's play *The Doll's House*, both extremely influential late-nineteenth-century works of 'New Woman' literature written by men. Rachel's identification with their heroines is total, creating in her 'some sort of change' (*VO*, p. 122), yet Rachel later finds that the experiences of love they delineate have little connection with her own. Here the explicit reference to 'New Woman' writing calls attention to Woolf's own ambivalent relationship to this genre. The nightmare vision of entrapment and monstrosity – 'alone with a little deformed man who squatted on the floor gibbering' (*VO*, p. 74) – that both follows Richard Dalloway's sexual advances to Rachel and accompanies her fatal illness forges the link between sex and death in the novel. Its oneiric obscurity, however, blocks the narratives of female purity and male sexual pollution so central to the 'New Woman' fiction of the 1890s.[13]

Night and Day, like *The Years* and *Three Guineas*, explores changes in women's lives through the contrast between the private house and the life of the city. In *Night and Day* the contrast is made in part through the focus on two women: Katherine Hilbery, whose life is circumscribed by the rituals of upper-class domestic life and burdened by the demands of family, living and dead, and Mary Datchet, who has exchanged her country parsonage childhood for the life of the single woman in the city and for office work in the cause of women's suffrage. The city is central to *Night and Day*: Woolf, like her contemporary Dorothy Richardson, uses its spaces to explore the making of identity and consciousness, and London becomes central to the formation of social being.

Fascinated by the creation of private dreams in public places, Woolf explores the relationship between the 'inner' realms of daydream and reverie (which are often, and paradoxically, enabled by the life of the city streets) and the outer-directed but limited world of feminist and social activism. The novel gives the fullest account of the suffrage campaign to be found in Woolf's writing, but the satire directed against its members has troubled those critics arguing for the strength of Woolf's involvement with feminist *real-politik*, including her rather brief association with the suffragist cause. Although we may wish to nuance Alex Zwerdling's suggestion that 'Woolf's particular contribution to the women's movement was to restore a sense of the complexity of the issues after the radical simplification that had seemed necessary for political action',[14] it is certainly the case that Woolf chose to represent such a 'simplification' in *Night and Day* through the mild absurdities and egoisms of committees and campaigners. The novel also explores the ways in which the apparent singularity and single-mindedness of ambition and activism are always liable to transmutation into fantasies which multiply and dissolve the self and its desires.

At the novel's close, Mary Datchet, excluded from the romance plot, becomes for Katherine and her lover Ralph Denham an image of a bettered future, the 'illuminated blinds' of her London flat 'an expression to them both of something impersonal and serene in the spirit of the woman within, working out her plans far into the night – her plans for the good of a world that none of them were ever to know' (ND, p. 469). The imagined shape of this world to come can only be determined by present knowledges, while the novel's final image is of Katherine standing on the threshold of her family home, poised, like so many fictional 'new women', between past and future.

Three Guineas turns its back on 'The Modern Girl'. Whereas a number of Woolf's feminist contemporaries, in their accounts of the rights and wrongs of women, produced chronological histories leading up to the woman, or girl, of the present day, Woolf makes her closing arguments through the oppressions of Victorian father–daughter relationships. There is undoubtedly an autobiographical element here, and an identification with these nineteenth-century 'daughters of educated men' that Woolf did not have with the déclassée 'contemporary young woman' represented, for example, in Ray Strachey's *Our Freedom and its Results* (published by the Hogarth Press in 1936), who takes her freedoms for granted and is, in the terms we would use today, definitely 'post-feminist'. In electing to represent the workings of patriarchy through Victorian father–daughter relationships in *Three Guineas* – the Barretts, the Brontës and the Jex-Blakes – Woolf was not only caught up imaginatively with her own Victorian upbringing. She also reveals the profound influence of the past on the present, and the ways in which each generation continues to live out and by the values, defences and world-views of the generation, or even generations, preceding its own. In this sense, we can never be fully present in and at our own times.

On the one hand, Woolf was concerned with a form of social and psychic asynchronicity; on the other, a telescoping of time as she explored, for example, the 'ancient and obscure emotions' that fuel, and socially ratify, the desire of fathers to control and possess their daughters. In both cases, there is a psychoanalytically informed understanding of oppression and repression which links Woolf's feminist analyses with her interest in group and collective psychology – for it was at times of social and political, rather than specifically personal crisis, that Woolf turned to psychology and psychoanalysis. Although Elizabeth Abel, in her *Virginia Woolf and the Fictions of Psychoanalysis*, represents Woolf's turn towards Freudian accounts of patriarchal culture as something of a defeat in her imaginings of women's past and future, other feminist critics have seen her analyses of the ways in which patriarchy and fascism interact as her most political, and most prescient, understandings.

A Room of One's Own and *Three Guineas* form the core of Woolf's feminist writings. Renewed critical attention to these texts – and to Woolf's numerous essays on women writers and on women's position in society more generally – has created a Virginia Woolf whose feminism cannot be in doubt, and which is, indeed, at the very heart of her concerns. Nor can a strict line be drawn between her overtly feminist, 'polemical' works and her fiction. Her novels take up the images and imaginings of her pamphlets and essays; her 'non-fiction' uses strategies more often associated with fictional narrative.

A Room of One's Own and *Three Guineas* inevitably invite comparison as Woolf's two most substantial discursive works on women. E. M. Forster, who I discuss later, approved *A Room of One's Own* and deplored the more overtly political and uncompromising *Three Guineas*; more recently, a number of feminist critics have argued that, in contrast to *Three Guineas*, *A Room of One's Own* is overly bound by a need to charm, and by, in Woolf's own phrase, its 'tea-table manner'. I would argue that such a judgement overlooks the biting ironies of *A Room of One's Own* and that it might be more fruitful to think of the differences between the two texts as differences in rhetorical strategy and historical and political contexts rather than as those of feminist conviction or confidence.

A Room of One's Own intervenes in debates about women and creativity, fuelled in part by the obsession with 'genius' of the first decades of the century, and uses fictional strategies to talk about women and about fiction. It is also caught up with the sexual politics of the 1920s, and with the question of love and friendship between women, given new edge by the prosecution for obscenity of Radclyffe Hall's lesbian novel *The Well of Loneliness* in 1928. *Three Guineas*, written in the form of a letter, uses a seemingly more direct first-person address, but its play on and with terms that circulate throughout the text, and its stress on the need for new words and meanings, render it equally rhetorical. *Three Guineas* extends a number of the themes pursued in *A Room of One's Own*, but its contexts – the rise of European fascism and the growing threat of war – shape the concerns of the earlier text in different ways.

Both texts thematise and dramatise women's exclusion – from education, the professions, the public sphere. In *A Room of One's Own*, Woolf represents the structures of inclusion and exclusion as fundamental to patriarchal society and its treatment of women: 'I thought how unpleasant it is to be locked out; and I thought how it is worse perhaps to be locked in' (*ROO*, p. 21). On her visit to 'Oxbridge', Woolf's narrator finds herself repeatedly 'locked out', excluded from chapel, library and the turf of the college quadrangle: 'Only the Fellows and Scholars are allowed here; the gravel is the place for me' (*ROO*, p. 5). Not only is her way physically barred, but these barriers interrupt the free flow of her thoughts, prohibiting her from 'trespassing' on the grounds of intellect and imagination held to be the proper preserve of the male sex.

The effect of such controls, as *A Room of One's Own* represents it, is not to inhibit thought entirely, but to send it down different channels, and along byways other than the straight paths traversed by 'the trained mind' of the college-educated man. *A Room of One's Own* is, indeed, a text about thought and the possibilities of thought. In the scene in the British Museum, 'Woman' becomes a 'thought' in the vast dome of the Reading Room, imaged by Woolf as a 'huge bald forehead'. The amelioration of women's position in society depends, Woolf suggests, largely on their being thought of differently, and on their ceasing to be used as mirrors 'reflecting the figure of man at twice its natural size'. The feminism of *A Room of One's Own* lies, it could be said, less in its concern with what is to be done than with how identities and states of affairs are to be conceptualised. Woolf's claim that 'we think back through our mothers if we are women' (*ROO*, p. 69) has been an immensely powerful support for a feminism seeking to construct a distinct women's history and literary tradition, but, in the contexts of *A Room of One's Own*, the emphasis should be placed as much on the 'thinking' (an activity traditionally associated with a 'rational' masculinity) as on the model of matrilinearity.

A Room of One's Own shares many of the concerns of other early twentieth-century feminist tracts, but transmutes 'issues' and histories into figurations and 'scene-making'. Winifred Holtby's *Women and a Changing Civilization*, for example, begins with a 'factual' account of women in pre-history and ends in the present day.[15] Woolf, by contrast, does not conceal the constructedness of historical imaginings, but turns the histories of the 'Oxbridge' colleges (men's and women's) into 'founding' narratives aligned with fathers and mothers and the births of civilisations:

> Kings and nobles brought treasure in huge sacks and poured it under the earth. This scene was for ever coming alive in my mind and placing itself by another of lean cows and a muddy market and withered greens and the stringy hearts of old men – these two pictures, disjointed and disconnected

and nonsensical as they were, were for ever coming together and combating each other and had me entirely at their mercy.   (*ROO*, p. 17)

Throughout *A Room of One's Own* Woolf plays with the question of origin and generation. Whereas the feminist commentators of her time directly addressed the question of birth control and its impact on women's lives, Woolf encodes it, weaving this issue into *A Room of One's Own* and exploring, indeed, what it means for women to think, and to be able to think, the absence of issue. The fact of childbirth and child-rearing acts as one of the barriers intercepting the narrator's imaginings of a different lot for women.

I have been discussing *A Room of One's Own* as a kind of adventure in thinking differently or as a thought-experiment. Yet the 'conclusion' (or, as Woolf puts it, 'opinion upon one minor point') with which the text (putting the end at the beginning) opens is also a materialist one. Thinking and thought, for Woolf, are not independent of physical and material circumstances but shaped by them: 'a woman must have money and a room of her own if she is to write fiction' (*ROO*, p. 3). The text's admixture of indirectness and directness, of abstraction and situatedness, has helped to make it central to twentieth-century literary and cultural feminism. On the one hand its complexity and obliquity render it virtually inexhaustible by interpretation and limitlessly re-readable. On the other hand, it contains 'detachable' arguments, aphorisms and ideas (those 'nugget[s] of pure truth' which ostensibly elude the narrator's grasp) which have become foundation-stones for feminist theory and criticism: 'we think back through our mothers if we are women'; 'a woman must have money and a room of her own if she is to write fiction'; 'Chloe plus Olivia' (used as the title of a recent anthology of lesbian literature).[16]

'We think back through our mothers if we are women'. This most frequently quoted of Woolf's statements clearly relates to ideas and imaginings of a distinctively female literary tradition and of a language and literature shaped by and for women. The literary and cultural 'turn' in feminist politics has made Woolf's focus on women writers, in *A Room of One's Own* and in numerous essays and reviews, central to her feminism, though it was a less defining feature of a feminist politics in her time. Concepts of a female literary tradition became crucial for feminist literary studies, underlying the creation of presses, in the 1970s and beyond, dedicated to publishing women's writings and, in the academic sphere, of courses devoted to women's writing. These practices have become so naturalised that we now rarely question the assumption of women's 'difference' as writers, or the implications of constructing an independent tradition for women writers. Woolf's fable of Shakespeare's sister, who wanted to be a poet like her brother but committed suicide after finding herself pregnant with the child of the theatre manager who seduced her, also resonated with the feminist model of women's 'silences', the burial and repression of their gifts, and a literary history in which women's absence became constructed as a speaking silence.

In Woolf's time, the question of the woman writer's 'difference' was a particularly vexed one. Woolf reviewed a number of books by male critics – Courtney's *The Feminine Note in Fiction* among them – which sought for some defining essence of the woman writer, and, by extension, the woman, by grouping literary women together as an object of study. One of the contexts for such works was the concern that literature itself was becoming, or had become, 'feminised'. Another was the turn-of-the-century biologism which had pervaded all forms of thought. The obsession with the nature of Woman is satirised by Woolf in *A Room of One's Own* as her narrator, pursuing the topic of 'Women and Fiction' in the British Library, quails before the volume of literature on the topic of Women: 'Have you any notion how many books are written about women in the course of one year? Have you any notion how many are written by men? Are you aware that you are, perhaps, the most discussed animal in the universe?' (*ROO*, p. 24). One of the issues implicitly posed by the text is how to think the question of women as embodied beings outside the reductive terms of much of the biology and anthropology of her day:

> The book has somehow to be adapted to the body, and at a venture one would say that women's books should be shorter, more concentrated, than those of men, and framed so that they do not need long hours of steady and uninterrupted work. For interruptions there will always be. Again, the nerves that feed the brain would seem to differ in men and women, and if you are going to make them work their best and hardest, you must find out what treatment suits them ... what alternations of work and rest they need, interpreting rest not as doing nothing but as doing something but something that is different; and what should that difference be? All this should be discussed and discovered; all this is part of the question of women and fiction. And yet, I continued, approaching the bookcase again, where shall I find that elaborate study of the psychology of women by a woman?   (*ROO*, p. 71)

Male writers taking women as their objects of study, Woolf suggests, have vested interests in distorting the terms of the differences; hence the need for the 'study of the psychology of women by a woman'. The repetition of 'differ', 'different', 'difference' in the passage – three different modalities, used in different contexts – continues the posing of the question of (sexual) difference in the text as a whole. There is 'difference', Woolf seems to be suggesting, but we can as yet make no assumptions about its nature, for which we have no adequate instruments or standards of measurement. Difference, moreover, can only be a relative term – dependent on history, circumstance and perspective.

A Room of One's Own, like *Three Guineas* and many of Woolf's novels, continually explores the different and shifting views created by varying angles of perception. In *A Room of One's Own* Woolf follows her much debated allegory of 'two people [a young man and woman] getting into a cab' as a model of 'unity' within the mind with this passage:

> What does one mean by 'the unity of the mind'? I pondered, for clearly the mind has so great a power of concentrating at any point at any moment that it seems to have no single state of being. It can separate itself off from the people in the street, for example, and think of itself as apart from them, at an upper window looking down on them. Or it can think with other people spontaneously, as, for instance, in a crowd waiting to hear some piece of news read out. It can think back through its fathers or through its mothers, as I have said that a woman writing thinks back through her mothers. Again if one is a woman one is often surprised by a sudden splitting off of consciousness, say in walking down Whitehall, when from being the natural inheritor of that civilisation, she becomes, on the contrary, outside of it, alien and critical. Clearly the mind is always altering its focus, and bringing the world into different perspectives. (*ROO*, pp. 87–8)

The passage names a number of 'stories'; of the founding narratives of generation and of literary heritage (mothers *or* fathers); of urban modernism (the perspectives of 'the man of the crowd' or of the detached observer at the upper window or on the balcony). The discussion is ostensibly about 'states of mind', a prelude to Woolf's discussion of creative 'androgyny'. Yet it marks a political as much as a psychological position, its uneasy pronouns ('it', 'one', 'she') suggesting the uncertain place of women in a culture, a nation, which they cannot fully call their own.

In the passage from *A Room of One's Own* this angle of vision takes the female subject by surprise. In *Three Guineas* it becomes the willed political stance of the woman who assumes her place as outsider. The 'splitting off of consciousness' is closely echoed in a diary entry (15 April 1937) in which Woolf describes dining with Kingsley Martin, Stephen Spender and Julian Bell (who would die in Spain three months later) and discussing politics and war: 'Cant be a pacifist; the irresponsible can. I sat there splitting off my own position from theirs, testing what they said, convincing myself of my own integrity & justice' (*D5*, p. 79). The 'splitting off' also marks the development of the feminist separatism central to the uncompromising radicalism of *Three Guineas*.

While it is possible to isolate themes and images running throughout Woolf's work, from her early essays to her last novel, it is also the case that her writings group themselves into clusters, formed around both personal and public preoccupations. Thus Woolf's fiction and non-fiction of the 1920s, for example, is substantially concerned with the relative fixities or mutabilities of sexual and gender identities. The opening section of *A Room of One's Own* echoes to 'a sort of humming noise' that could be heard before the First World War, which translates into the Victorian love poetry of Tennyson and Christina Rossetti. It is a reverberation from the harmonies of 'two different notes, one high, one low', which was Mrs Ramsay's image of marriage in *To the Lighthouse*, the novel in which Woolf explored most fully the Victorian concept of 'separate spheres' and the chasm separating past and present. *Orlando*, whose writing was intertwined with that of *A Room of One's Own*, takes up, both seriously and satirically, the narratives of gender identity of the culture and period, and exposes the sexual nature of the ostensibly sex-transcendent 'androgyny' that has fuelled so much debate in Woolf criticism. *To the Lighthouse* and *Orlando*, on the surface such different fictions, share a sense of the complex relationships between model and copy, fictional and biographical representations, and a focus on time, memory, historical rupture and sexual identities.

The Pargiters/The Years (which Woolf also thought of as 'first cousin' to *Orlando* (*D*4, pp. 132–3)) and *Three Guineas* were profoundly shaped by the exigencies of the 1930s. Woolf, like so many of her literary contemporaries, was influenced by, and contributed to, the 'documentary' culture, the passion for 'fact', of this period. Woolf's original plan for *The Years* was that it should be an 'Essay-Novel', a 'novel of fact', in which essays would be interspersed with extracts from 'a [non-existent] novel that will run into many volumes': 'Its to be an Essay-Novel, called the Pargiters – & its to take in everything, sex, education, life &; & come, with the most powerful & agile leaps, like a chamois across precipices from 1880 to here & now' (*D*4, 129). 'We must become the people that we were two or three generations ago. Let us be our great grandmothers', she wrote in the first essay of *The Pargiters*, explaining that her use of the fictional extracts was to be an aid to this process for those unused to 'being somebody else'. The past provides 'that perspective which is so important for the understanding of the present' (*The Pargiters*, p. 9).

In early 1933 Woolf decided against the separate 'interchapters' (the essays), instead 'compacting them in the text' (*D*4, p. 146), and later using some of the material in *Three Guineas*. The drafts of *The Pargiters* reveal what a radical and difficult project Woolf had first envisaged. *The Pargiters*, like *The Years*, explores the ways in which girls and women are restricted in the middle-class home, and excluded from the education and public life which their brothers and fathers take for granted. Yet the lives of men, too, are stunted by the inequalities between the sexes. Woolf's analyses are powerful ones, but she encountered immense difficulties in shaping them to the demands of plot, in moving her narrative forward into the 'here and now' and in negotiating the relationship between 'fact' and 'fiction'.

The division of *The Pargiters* into the texts that became *The Years* and *Three Guineas* was at least in part a way of dealing with these difficulties. In the process of turning *The Pargiters* into *The Years*, Woolf also drew back from the 'didactic demonstrative' strain of the novel, her fear of the 'didactic' (*D*4, p. 145) growing as she saw and heard the workings of fascist ideology. Increasingly, Woolf seemed to link political propaganda – both left and right – with the forms of masculine war-mongering or war-enthusiasm to which the feminism of *Three Guineas* is so profoundly opposed. Writing in 'The Leaning Tower' (1940) of and to the group of young male writers we now know as 'The Auden Generation', Woolf argued that the distorting effects of two world wars had resulted in 'the pedagogic, the didactic, the loud speaker strain that dominates their poetry. They must teach; they must preach.'[17]

A Room of One's Own began life as an after-dinner speech, retains a discursive, performative dimension and explores the gendered shape and rhythm of *sentences*. In *Three Guineas* Woolf, by contrast, emphasises the written nature of her text and the politically loaded nature of *words* – 'feminism', 'patriotism', 'influence', 'freedom'. *Three Guineas* is epistolary in form, punctuated by extracts from the writings of 'fact' – biographies, autobiographies, newspaper texts and images ('history in the raw') – and closes with a lengthy and elaborate structure of footnotes and references. The letter form was a device Woolf also used in her response to *Life as We Have Known It* ('Memories of a Working Women's Guild') and which operated there as a form of refusal – to 'introduce', 'preface' or frame the memoirs: 'Books should stand on their own feet.'[18] Interestingly, both *Three Guineas* and 'Memories of a Working Women's Guild' are the Woolf texts which have raised the most questions about the class identifications and limitations of Woolf's feminism. 'Memories of a Working Women's Guild' refuses to imagine cross-class knowledge and empathy: 'One could not be Mrs Giles because one's body had never stood at the wash-tub; one's hands had never wrung and scrubbed and chopped up whatever the meat may be that makes a miner's dinner.'[19] *Three Guineas* makes its specific address to the 'daughters of educated men': Woolf seemed deliberately to have rejected the 'pro-proletarian spectacles' of many of her contemporaries.

Class position and perspective is indeed a complex and troubled dimension of Woolf's feminism, and one of which she was acutely aware – perhaps more aware than many of her recent critics.

The scrapbooks of newspaper and journal cuttings kept by Woolf during the 1930s, on which she drew substantially during the writing of *Three Guineas*, give important insight into Woolf's feminism at this time. In a letter of 1916, Woolf had written (*L2*, p. 76): 'I become steadily more feminist owing to the Times, which I read at breakfast and wonder how this preposterous masculine fiction [the First World War] keeps going a day longer – without some vigorous young woman pulling us together and marching through it.' As fascism spread throughout Europe in the 1930s, Woolf's notebooks place in ironic juxtaposition 'patriarchal' attitudes towards women in England and fascist ideology abroad. Quoting correspondence from the *Daily Telegraph* in which the letter-writers deplore the entry of women into the professions, Woolf comments:

> There, in those quotations, is the egg of the very same worm that we know under other names in other countries.
>
> There we have in embryo the creature, Dictator as we call him when he is Italian or German, who believes that he has the right whether given by God, Nature, sex or race is immaterial, to dictate to other human beings how they shall live; what they shall do.

Woolf reinforces the point with a quotation from Hitler, whose sentiments on women and the home chime directly with those of the newspaper correspondents: 'One is written in English, the other in German. But where is the difference? Are they not both saying the same thing, whether they speak English or German. . .?' (*TG*, p. 175). The Dictator is also one who dictates to women.

Much of the criticism directed against *Three Guineas* expressed the widely held view that feminism should be subordinated to the 'larger' cause of anti-fascism. Woolf pasted into her *Three Guineas* scrapbooks a telling letter from Elizabeth Bibesco, which she also quoted in her diary. In January 1935, Bibesco had asked Woolf to support a proposed anti-fascist exhibition organised by the Cambridge anti-War Council; Woolf had responded by enquiring about the omission of 'the woman question' from the project. Bibesco replied: 'I am afraid that it had not occurred to me that in matters of ultimate importance even feminists could wish to segregate & label the sexes' (*D4*, p. 273). Such attitudes may well have fuelled the insistence in *Three Guineas* that, while the fight against fascism is a common cause, men and women must, for the time being at least, follow their related but separate paths.

In a number of the essays and in the novel written after *Three Guineas*, *Between the Acts*, Woolf explored the question of masculinity as searchingly as that of women and femininity. In *Between the Acts*, Woolf explores masculine sexuality, aggression and fear and their relationship to the coming of war, primarily through the figures of Giles, whose 'anger' dominates much of the novel, and the homosexual William Dodge. Although *Three Guineas* would seem to advocate a feminist separatism, Woolf was throughout her work absorbed by the social and psychological motivations underlying men's need to belittle and exclude women, from the angry professor of *A Room of One's Own* to the regressive and repressive fathers of *Three Guineas*. In 'Thoughts on Peace in an Air Raid', published in 1940, Woolf wrote of the external and internal voices driving 'the young airmen up in the sky' and of 'instincts fostered and cherished by education and tradition'. 'We must help the young Englishmen,' she writes, 'to root out from themselves the love of medals and decorations.'[20]

'Patriarchy' and 'patriotism' share an etymological root. In 'Professions for Women', the lecture, and then essay, which provided the foundation for *The Pargiters*, Woolf wrote of the need to perform a symbolic matricide: 'If I had not killed her,' she writes of the mother-figure, 'The Angel in the House', 'she would have killed me.' In *Three Guineas*, by contrast, it is fathers who threaten to pluck the heart out of their daughters' aspirations and ambitions. Freedom from the law of fathers, *Three Guineas* suggests, is also freedom from the boundaries of nationhood. The basis for 'the anonymous and secret society of Outsiders', imagined as women's alternative to a nation conceived as a male club writ large, is that 'as a woman I have no country. As a woman I want no country. As a woman my country is the whole world.' Woolf's refusal to collude with patriotism – *Three Guineas* is shot through with ironies directed against patriotic and institutional pomp and circumstance – has been variously celebrated and critiqued. Could Woolf's claim to a global identity be too confidently (even imperialistically) inclusive? Does placing women in the position of Outsiders allow Woolf to exempt them from the urgent decisions of the period, and would her position in 1938 have put her very close to a 'politics of appeasement'? 'Thinking is my fighting', Woolf wrote, thus suggesting not a disengagement from the exigencies of her time, but an acute sense of the specific responses she could, and would, make to them.

Feminism's Woolf

The question of Woolf's 'feminism' played a central role in the earliest critical discussions of her work. One of the first book-length studies of

Woolf was written by the novelist and feminist critic and commentator Winifred Holtby. Holtby's book, engaging with the gendered perspectives and politics of Woolf's time, took up the question of 'androgyny', so central to recent feminist Woolf criticism, and, by reading *A Room of One's Own* and *Orlando* in tandem, hinted that Woolf's use of the concept of 'androgyny', far from evading sexual identity, was closely allied to theories of bisexuality and (female) homosexuality. She also explored the provisionality of gender identities in ways which anticipate recent feminist and postmodernist readings of Woolf. Thus Holtby, in her reading of *A Room of One's Own*, understood Woolf to be saying that we cannot 'yet' give an answer to the question 'what is a woman?':

> Looking round upon the world of human beings as we know it, we are hard put to it to say what is the natural shape of men or women, so old, so all-enveloping are the moulds fitted by history and custom over their personalities. We do not know how much of sensitiveness, intuition, docility and tenderness may not be naturally 'male', how much of curiosity, aggression, audacity and combativeness may not be 'female'.[21]

Holtby supported Woolf's model of cultural and historical distortion, whereby the 'natural shape' of men and women is twisted by patriarchy's insistence on the inferiority of women, 'for if they were not inferior, they would cease to enlarge' (*ROO*, p. 32).

In the decades between Holtby's study and Woolf's 'rediscovery' by 'second-wave' feminist criticism, a number of commentators on Woolf had also put 'feminism' at the centre of their analyses – though often in less than sympathetic ways. For Woolf's friend and fellow-novelist E. M. Forster, delivering a lecture on her life and work two months after her death, Woolf's feminism was 'a very peculiar side of her', producing 'one of the most brilliant of her books – the charming and persuasive *A Room of One's Own*', but also 'responsible for the worst of her books – the cantankerous *Three Guineas* – and for the less successful streaks in *Orlando*'.[22] 'There are spots of [feminism] all over her work, and it was constantly in her mind', Forster asserted, representing 'feminism' as a matter of 'streaks' and 'spots', blemishes on the work of art. 'In my judgement', he continued:

> There is something old-fashioned about this extreme Feminism; it dates back to her suffragette youth of the 1910s, when men kissed girls to distract them from wanting the vote, and very properly provoked her wrath. By the 1930s she had much less to complain of, and seems to keep on grumbling from habit ... She was sensible about the past; about the present she was sometimes unreasonable. However, I speak as a man here, and as an elderly one. The

best judges of her Feminism are neither elderly men nor even elderly women, but young women.[23]

Forster's comments typify the inability of many of her contemporaries – women as well as men – to accept Woolf's feminist pacifism of the 1930s or her perception, explored at greatest length in *Three Guineas*, that 'patriarchy', militarism and fascism support and sustain each other.

Forster's identification of feminism with suffrage is also significant. If feminism is defined as the political campaign for women's votes, then its success would indeed render feminism obsolete. Yet many of Woolf's contemporaries continued to work with a broader definition of the feminist project, and to show, as Woolf herself did in *Three Guineas*, that women's rights had in no sense been conclusively 'won' with suffrage. The vote, Woolf's narrator declares in *A Room of One's Own*, had meant far less to her than her aunt's legacy, which had given her the five hundred pounds a year and the room of her own deemed necessary for the woman writer.

For a later critic, J. B. Bachelor, whose 'Feminism in Virginia Woolf', first published in 1968, takes up, and partially refutes, Forster's charges against Woolf's feminism, 'the implications of feminism are antipathetic to [Woolf's] personality'.[24] In an essay singularly unattuned to Woolf's ironies and rhetorical strategies, Bachelor reads the Woolf of *A Room* as arguing that 'women must not emulate men', but give them 'a "renewal of creative power" by the contact of contrasting ways of life, and for this reason women's education should "bring out and fortify the differences rather than the similarities"'. Bachelor writes:

> To return to Forster's original assessment . . . I have suggested firstly that the protests in *Three Guineas* are legitimate in the contest of the 'thirties; secondly, that feminism proper is aesthetically unacceptable to Virginia Woolf and hardly appears in her writings; and thirdly that what is 'constantly in her mind' is not 'feminism' but a passionate concern with the nature of womanhood.[25]

Woolf's 'concern with the nature of womanhood', Bachelor suggests, takes 'two slightly contradictory forms; one with women in their relationships with men and with society, and the special roles that they can play . . . and the other with the full development of women as individuals and as artists'. The focus on women characters in Woolf's fiction was also central to much early feminist criticism, as well as non- or anti-feminist criticism. It would be a revealing exercise to chart the change in critical attitudes towards Mrs Ramsay, Lily Briscoe or Clarissa Dalloway. Whereas, for example, earlier critics tended to celebrate Mrs Ramsay's 'creativity' in human relations and her ability to harmonise the domestic sphere (the 'spinsterish' Lily's passion for her art being seen as a lesser form of creativity), recent critics have seen the portrait of Mrs Ramsay as less positive. Feminist critics have pointed to the ways in which she upholds systems of marriage and a 'separate spheres' ideology of masculinity and femininity which severely disadvantages women; psychoanalytic critics have focused on the ambivalence towards the mother figure which fuels Lily's (and Woolf's) drive to represent her.

A number of mid-century critics, in particular those influenced by 'myth' and 'archetype' criticism, focused less on the *ideologies* of gender identity than on masculinity and femininity as *principles*. Mrs Ramsay becomes perceived as a representation of the mind and sensibility of the female novelist, holding the whole together. J. B. Bachelor was by no means alone in making the critical move from the question of Woolf's *feminism* to that of Woolf's *femininity*, including her 'passionate concern with the nature of womanhood'. Herbert Marder's *Feminism and Art* (1968), by contrast, insists on the centrality of feminism as politics to Woolf's work, although its impulse is also towards the resolution of opposites through the model of 'androgyny'.[26]

Woolf's 'style' was also used as a way of defining by contrast, and shoring up, the 'masculine' writing of her male contemporaries. The famous passage in 'Modern Fiction' in which Woolf offers an account of consciousness and the modern novel – 'Examine for a moment an ordinary mind on an ordinary day. The mind receives a myriad impressions' (an aesthetic from which she in fact takes a critical distance, ascribing it to Joyce and his contemporaries) – was used against Woolf by her detractors, who frequently defined her limitations as those of a purely passive, receptive consciousness. This consciousness is invariably feminised, as in Herbert Muller's 1937 critique of Woolf and other women writers of the early twentieth century, 'the Society of the Daughters of Henry James': 'they render with a nice precision the subtle gradations of perception and sensation – but in this delicious banquet the mere man still yearns for a little red beef and port wine'.[27]

Such a response is anticipated in Woolf's accounts of the difference of value. 'It is probable,' she writes in 'Women and Fiction' 'that both in life and in art the values of a woman are not the values of a man.'[28] She elaborated this claim at length in *A Room of One's Own*, playing, as in *Three Guineas*, with the relationships between money and value:

It is obvious that the values of women differ very often from the values which have been made by the other sex; naturally, this is so. Yet it is the masculine values that prevail. Speaking crudely, football and sport are 'important'; the worship of fashion, the buying of clothes 'trivial'. And these values are inevitably transferred from life to fiction. This is an important book, the critic assumes, because it deals with war. This is an insignificant book because it deals with the feelings of women in a drawing-room. A scene in a battle-field is more important than a scene in a shop – everywhere and much more subtly the difference of value persists. (*ROO*, p. 67)

In her imagined fiction of the future in *A Room of One's Own*, the scene is indeed set in a shop, an 'ever-changing and turning world of gloves and shoes and stuffs swaying up and down among the faint scents that come through chemists' bottles down arcades of dress material over a floor of pseudo-marble' (*ROO*, p. 89). Through this 'ever-changing and turning world' Woolf not only points up but feminises the fleeting, mutable nature of modernity and modern life.

Feminist criticism has, above all, demanded a transvaluation of values (to borrow Nietzsche's phrase), and insisted that the supposedly 'universal' values underlying literary judgements and canon-formation were in fact highly partial, ideological and, for the most part, unsympathetic to the 'difference' of women writers and readers. It has, in this sense, called for a revaluation of the 'perception and sensation' so readily dismissed by Muller. On the other hand, there has also been a significant drive to reveal how unladylike a writer Woolf in fact was, and to show that her writing was fuelled by a proper feminist anger.

'Anger' and 'androgyny' are the two terms most central to feminist debates on Woolf. Their centrality serves to further increase the importance of *A Room of One's Own* as the key text of Woolf's feminism and feminism's Woolf, for it is here that 'anger' and 'androgyny' are most fully discussed. Yet *A Room of One's Own* is seen by many critics to subdue and repress women's anger in favour of a more serene gender-transcendent or androgynous creativity, whereas righteous anger is felt to be the motivating force underlying *Three Guineas*, a text in which 'androgyny' is replaced by an emphasis on women as 'outsiders', both different from and separate from men. More easily assimilable to recent radical feminisms, *Three Guineas* has taken on further significance with the new or renewed interest in women's writing on war and fascism, and with a renewed engagement in literary and feminist studies with cultural and historical contexts and concerns. Whereas a feminist criticism centred on feminine writing, identity and sexuality turned primarily to the poetics of *A Room of One's Own*, *Mrs Dalloway*, *To the Lighthouse* and *The Waves*, those critics concerned with a more overtly feminist Woolf – one whose feminism is an aspect of political and social engagement with the events of her time – have tended to focus on *The Years*, *Three Guineas* and, though to a lesser extent, *Night and Day* and *Between the Acts*.

To an extent, such a divide maps on to the 'modernism' versus 'realism' debates central to literary and cultural studies of the 1970s. This way of dividing up the territory informed Toril Moi's response to Elaine Showalter's chapter on Virginia Woolf in *A Literature of their Own*. Showalter, taking her cues from recently published biographical works on Woolf and arguing against Carolyn Heilbrun's celebration of 'Bloomsbury androgyny', read the message of *A Room of One's Own* as a defensive 'flight into androgyny': 'Androgyny was the myth that helped her evade confrontation with her own painful femaleness and enabled her to choke and repress her anger and ambition.'[29] In Showalter's account, anger founds its articulation in 'madness', while madness, or at least breakdown, is associated with 'crises in female identity': the onset of menstruation at the time of her mother's premature death; Leonard's decision that they would not have children; menopause. 'If one can see *A Room of One's Own* as a document in the literary history of female aestheticism,' Showalter writes, 'and remain detached from its narrative strategies, the concepts of androgyny and the private room are neither as liberating nor as obvious as they first appear. They have a darker side that is the sphere of the exile and the eunuch.'[30] The myth of androgyny and women's 'madness' become linked as different ways of articulating 'resentment and rage'.

Showalter's focus on constructions of and treatment for female insanity makes her chapter on Woolf a dry run for *The Female Malady*, the book in which she explores the history of the concept of women's madness, while the double binds in which she ties Woolf owe something to Ronald Laing's existential psychoanalysis and its accounts of psychic and familial 'knots'. In her response to Showalter's discussion of Woolf, however, Toril Moi takes up the reading of *A Room of One's Own* rather than the psychological and biographical dimensions of the chapter. Starting with Showalter's view of *A Room of One's Own* as an 'extremely impersonal and defensive text', from whose distracting rhetorical devices the feminist critic should take a critical distance, Moi argues that 'remaining detached from the narrative strategies of *Room* is equivalent to not reading it at all'.[31] Picking up on a passing reference to Georg Lukács at the close of Showalter's chapter ('In Georg Lukács' formulation, the ethic of a novelist becomes an aesthetic problem in his writing'), Moi turned her response to Showalter into a replay of the debates between Brecht and Lukács in the 1930s, which had been newly translated and re-presented for the 1970s, with Moi on the side of Woolf's modernism and avant-gardism and Showalter standing for a realist aesthetic opposed to textual innovation and inseparable from that shibboleth of the new cultural theory, bourgeois or liberal humanism. The multiple 'I's' of *A Room of One's Own*, which in Showalter's account are a marker of Woolf's refusal or inability to speak in her own voice, are for

Moi a central aspect of Woolf's challenge to 'the male-humanist concept of an essential human identity', a challenge in turn linked to psychoanalysis' subversions of the old stable ego. Woolf, Moi argues, 'radically under-mine[s] the notion of the unitary self, the central concept of Western male humanism and one crucial to Showalter's feminism'.[32] This feminism is then shown up as a crude 'images of women' aesthetic, which seeks positive role models in its women writers and their characters rather than 'locating the politics of Woolf's writing precisely in her textual practice'. Turning to Julia Kristeva's theories, and in particular her essay 'Women's Time', Moi pitted an aesthetics and politics both avant-gardist and feminist against the 'traditional aesthetic categories' of 'current Anglo-American feminist criticism'. Woolf's 'androgyny', Moi argues, is the deconstruction of sexual identity and of the duality masculinity–femininity, not its attempted resolution or sublation into a unified, sex-transcendent holism.

As significant as the increasingly impassable divide Moi refused to straddle (French versus Anglo-American feminism) is the role played by Virginia Woolf in the construction of feminist theories. Elaine Showalter, in *A Literature of their Own*, presents herself as setting out to save feminist literary criticism, and women's writing more generally, from Woolf's fatal legacy of repression, passivity, sickness and suicide. Using Woolf's own 'murderous imagery' against herself, Showalter argued that Woolf represents the 'Angel in the House' for the twentieth-century woman writer and that she must be demystified, if not killed. Moi, by contrast, sets out to 'rescue' Woolf from her unreconstructed, undeconstructive readers or, rather, non-readers: 'A feminist criticism that would do both justice and homage to its great mother and sister: this, surely, should be our goal.'[33] Woolf is the starting-point and occasion for Moi's history and critique of feminist literary theories: the 'mother' of the feminist critics of the late twentieth century, her right reading will be the result of the right forms of sexual/textual politics. Woolf thus becomes the alpha and omega of feminist criticism, its origin and its 'goal'.

Toril Moi's suggestions for a Kristevan reading of Woolf, in some part anticipated in Mary Jacobus's essay 'The Difference of View' (1979), were pursued by a number of critics. The ramifications of such work have been far-reaching, linking up with new agendas in psychoanalytic literary criticism and theory, and with explorations of the place of women writers, and gender more generally, within modernist and avant-garde culture. In *Revolution in Poetic Language* (1974), Kristeva, drawing upon Freud's distinction between pre-Oedipal and Oedipal sexual drives and Lacan's concepts of the 'imaginary' and 'symbolic', defined the place of the pre-symbolic or 'semiotic' (where the symbolic is understood as the condition of ordered, 'rational' signification) as the space of the maternal chora (enclosed space, womb, receptacle), which in turn corresponds to the 'poetic' function of language. Represented as the transgressive, 'feminine' materiality of signification, the 'semiotic' becomes evident in 'madness, holiness and poetry', and surfaces in literary texts, particularly those of the avant-garde, as musicality and linguistic play.

Kristevan theory, as well as the accounts of 'feminine écriture' in the work of Hélène Cixous and others, opened up for occupancy the 'depths' of Woolf's writing: the female 'room' (perceived by Showalter as a prison-house) or the 'deep lake' of the imagination and of 'unconscious being' in Woolf's essay 'Professions for Women', and its poetics, its 'writ[ing] to a rhythm not a plot'. Some of the most subtle and nuanced recent feminist work on Woolf, including studies by Margaret Homans, Makiko Minow-Pinkney, Patricia Waugh, Sue Roe, Patricia Lawrence and Clare Hanson, has focused on questions of gender, modernism and language, taking as its starting-points Woolf's troubled but imaginatively crucial concepts of a language 'fitted' to women, as in her review of Dorothy Richardson's novel *Revolving Lights*, her models of writing and sexuality, and the intertwining of feminist and modernist subversions of traditional narrative forms and structures in her work.[34]

In 'The Difference of View', Mary Jacobus was both committed to a deconstructionist and psychoanalytic reading of Woolf and concerned with the terms of 'androgyny' and 'anger'. 'Androgyny' is redefined as a way of representing or negotiating 'difference': the model of 'sexual difference' is one in which the difference between the sexes is turned from a question of sexed/gendered entities, identities, and essences to a focus on the process of differentiation itself. 'Androgyny,' Jacobus suggests, is

> a simultaneous enactment of desire and repression by which the split is closed with an essentially Utopian vision of undivided consciousness. The repressive male/female opposition which 'interferes with the unity of the mind' gives way to a mind paradoxically conceived of not as one, but as heterogeneous, open to the play of difference.[35]

On the other hand, women's 'anger' becomes the quantity that is transmitted between generations of women writers. In Jacobus' account, women under patriarchy 'experience desire without Law, wielding language without power', a language of feeling which:

> can only ally itself with insanity – an insanity which, displaced into writing, produces a moment of imaginative and linguistic excess over-brimming the

container of fiction, and swamping the distinction between author and character.[36]

The metonymic chain Jacobus constructs here is then used to link moments of desire, transgression and excess in Mary Wollstonecraft, Charlotte Brontë, George Eliot and Virginia Woolf: 'The overflow in *Jane Eyre* washes into *A Room of One's Own.*' Jacobus takes up the critical moment in *A Room of One's Own* in which Woolf ostensibly condemns Charlotte Brontë's intrusive 'rage' against the nineteenth-century woman's lot. 'Editing into her writing the outburst edited out of Charlotte Brontë's,' Jacobus writes, 'Virginia Woolf creates a point of instability which unsettles her own urbane and polished decorum.' 'Thinking back through our mothers' creates rupture as well as continuity; the legacy of one woman writer to another becomes a 'rift . . . revealing other possible fictions, other kinds of writing'.

For Jane Marcus, Brenda Silver and a number of North American Woolf critics, 'anger' runs throughout Woolf's texts, even where it is most displaced or denied. The focus on women's anger extends the highly influential work of Sandra Gilbert and Susan Gubar, *The Madwoman in the Attic*, which explored the creation of negative, transgressive doubles in nineteenth-century women's writing as ways of both owning and disowning rebellion and rage. Thus Judith Kegan Gardiner, in an essay on psycho-analytic feminist criticism, notes that although Woolf chastised Charlotte Brontë's intrusive anger in *A Room of One's Own*, she 'imagined an angry tale of her own, that of Shakespeare's talented sister who was seduced, abandoned and driven to suicide: "who shall measure the heat and violence of the poet's heart when caught and tangled in a woman's body?"'[37] For Jane Marcus, 'anger' in Woolf's work is the quality transmitted from writer to writer ('We know from *A Writer's Diary* how often anger was the primary impulse of Woolf's art, but here is proof that she was among that sisterhood of great women writers whose pens were driven by anger – Mary Wollstonecraft, George Sand, Olive Schreiner'),[38] and from author to critic. As Marcus writes in her introduction to *Art and Anger*: 'My concern with Woolf's anger clearly grew out of my own anger and the anger of my generation of feminist critics, who were trying to change the subject without yet having developed a sophisticated methodology.'[39]

'Changing the subject', in the case of Woolf studies, entailed, Marcus writes, the attempt to move 'from the study of madness and suicide to a concentration on her pacifism, feminism, and socialism'. Throughout the essays on Woolf in *Art and Anger*, Marcus insists on 'the triple ply' of Woolf as 'artist, feminist, socialist', against what she saw as the depoliticised, aestheticised, and enfeebled Virginia Woolf constructed by her recent biographers and the keepers of her literary estate. 'It is an open secret,' Marcus wrote

> that Virginia Woolf's literary estate is hostile to feminist critics. There are two taboo subjects: on the one hand her lesbian identity, woman-centered life, and feminist work, and on the other her socialist politics. If you wish to discover the truth regarding these issues, you will have a long, hard struggle. In that struggle you will find the sisterhood of feminist Woolf scholarship.[40]

The language of 'sisterhood', like that of mothers and daughters, takes on very specific resonances in a context in which Woolf's editors, biographers and literary trustees were male family members and associates: Leonard Woolf, Quentin Bell (Virginia Woolf's nephew and author of the first official Woolf biography) and Nigel Nicolson, Vita Sackville-West's son and the editor of Woolf's letters. (Anne Olivier Bell, the editor of Woolf's diaries and Quentin Bell's wife, takes on masculine privilege by association.) The increasing friction between a number of feminist critics – the 'lupines', as Quentin Bell termed them, an appellation then taken on as a badge of honour – and the Bells and the estate has been vividly documented by Regina Marler in *Bloomsbury Pie*.[41] It is perhaps enough to note here that controversies arose in part because the release and publication of Woolf's 'personal' writings – diaries, memoirs, letters – coincided with the burgeoning of feminist criticism and, more specifically, of forms of feminist criticism substantially committed to the values of experience, authenticity, voice and presence. Marcus's objections to Olivier Bell's meticulous editorial annotations of the first volume of the diaries, for example, arise from a fantasy of the woman writer speaking out across the decades to her literary daughters. The corollary of this ideal of unmediated communication is the critic's 'anger' at an editorial writing which can only appear to her as a defacement, or as an interruption or silencing of Woolf's voice and message.

Biography becomes the controversial genre at this moment in Woolf and Bloomsbury studies, as it was for Woolf and her contemporaries in the 1920s and 1930s.[42] Quentin Bell elected to separate the 'life' from the 'work', and chose not to discuss Woolf's writings. Jane Marcus commented: 'The Bell view of Virginia Woolf . . . shows her only from the neck down and in the bosom of her family. This is often the trouble with biographies of great women; one never knows what kind of heads graced their feminine shoulders, and sometimes one can hardly see them at all in the family album. Much of Woolf's best writing attacked private property and the family, and she considered herself an outsider to it all.'[43] Interestingly, however, Marcus's writing on Woolf has been substantially concerned precisely with the 'family album'; she reiterates, for example, that Woolf's pacifism is the legacy of her ancestors in the Clapham Sect, and of her Quaker aunt, Caroline Stephen, whose mystical writings Marcus sees as a crucial influence on Woolf, a mysticism rendered feminist in part through its transmission from aunt to niece, bypassing the father and, to some extent, the mother.

Marcus's broader critical–biographical endeavour has been to shift the focus away from Woolf's 'Bloomsbury' relationships, including those with Leonard Woolf, Lytton Strachey and the Bells. Vanessa Bell, for example, receives very little attention from Marcus, whereas for critics like Jane Dunn and Diane Gillespie Vanessa's and Virginia's is the crucial relationship. For Marcus, music, opera and drama – the 'collective' arts – replace painting as the sister medium for Woolf's writing. Marcus also explored Woolf's political, 'feminist', friendships with Margaret Llewelyn-Davies, for whom Woolf wrote her introduction to *Life as We Have Known It*; Ethel Smyth, suffrage activist, writer and composer, to whom Woolf became close later in her life; and Jane Ellen Harrison, the classical scholar whom Marcus describes as the heroine of *A Room of One's Own*.[44] The relationship with the non-biological mother/mentor (the 'mother' for Lily Briscoe rather than for Cam, as it were) is the significant connection for Marcus, for whom Julia Stephen, in her proper Victorian femininity, cannot be an altogether good mother-image and role model for feminist daughters.

Alongside the publication of Woolf's 'personal' writings and the growing number of biographies of Woolf, including Phyllis Rose's important biography *Woman of Letters* (1978), came the manuscript editions of her novels and polemical writings. Jane Marcus defines her own practice as a 'socialist feminist' critic in part through her 'materialist' work with draft and manuscript versions of Woolf's text, arguing that 'the drafts and unpublished versions seemed "truer" texts – spectacularly truer in the case of *The Years* . . . The censorship of editors, publishers, husbands, as well as the enormous pressure of self-censorship on a woman writer, makes the reader mistrust the published text and makes the critic mistrust any methodology that accepts without question the privilege of the printed text.'[45] The late 1970s and early 1980s saw the publication of the 'two enormous chunks' Woolf had omitted from *The Pargiters/The Years* and an edition of *The Pargiters* itself, including the original version of 'Professions for Women'. In *Downhill All the Way*, a volume of his autobiography, Leonard Woolf describes Woolf's extensive revisions of *The Years*: 'I have compared the galley proofs with the published version and the work which she did on the galleys is astonishing. She cut out bodily two enormous chunks, and there is hardly a single page on which there are not considerable rewritings or verbal alterations.'[46] Louise DeSalvo published an edition of *Melymbrosia*, the early version of *The Voyage Out*, and *Virginia Woolf's First Voyage: a Novel in the Making*, a study of the ways in which 'Woolf's changing conception of her first novel was related to her changing life experiences'.[47]

If for Marcus the early, discarded drafts of texts are often seen as the 'truer', more overtly feminist versions which are then suppressed, DeSalvo's work on buried and repressed narratives may well have influenced her contentious biography of Woolf, *Virginia Woolf: The Impact of Childhood Sexual Abuse on Her Life and Work* (1989). For DeSalvo, Woolf's 'life's work – her memoirs and her autobiography, her novels, her essays and biographies – is an invaluable missing link in the history of incest, abuse, and the effects of family violence'. In her work, DeSalvo writes, Woolf 'carved out a way to tell her story . . . and that of other childhood victims of abuse and neglect'.[48]

DeSalvo's book is extreme in its claims, and in its implication that Woolf's writing should be seen as a form of testimonial literature, whose disturbing messages it is the critic and reader's ethical duty to heed. She is by no means alone among recent critics, however, in focusing on representations of violence and trauma in Woolf's work, and on the recurrence in Woolf's work of two 'moments' in particular. The first is the death of the mother; the second an event of violation or rape, which a number of critics have linked to the intrusive sexual explorations the young Virginia Stephen underwent at the hands of her half-brother, Gerald Duckworth, and which she described in 'A Sketch of the Past', published for the first time in 1985. In this memoir, too, she describes vividly Julia Stephen's death and its effects on the family.

'Scene-making' was, Woolf wrote, central to her art, her 'natural way of marking the past' (*MB*, p. 142). Feminist and psychoanalytic critics have sought to understand the ways in which recurrent 'scenes' in Woolf's novels offer a crucial link between 'the life' and 'the work' and open up the complex dynamics of memory and representation in her writing. In their psychoanalytically informed analyses, Françoise Defromont, Elizabeth Abel, Mary Jacobus and others have explored the workings in Woolf's fiction of 'remembering, repeating, and working through', to borrow the title of one of Freud's essays. Defromont makes the question of maternal presence and absence central to an understanding of Woolf's work, and to its recurrent imagery of mirrors and mirroring. Exploring the significance of broken mirrors in *To the Lighthouse* and *Between the Acts*, Defromont writes: 'The mirror is shattered at the moment when there is a double breakage. Biographical echoes resonate through the writing; the two traumatic scenes inscribed in *Moments of Being*, rape and death, are rips which echo everywhere'.[49] While Defromont's focus on traumatic events in Woolf's childhood is not wholly dissimilar from DeSalvo's, it differs radically in its complex understandings of the relationship between event and representation and in its focus on the ways in which 'the two most dramatic moments of Virginia Woolf's life, namely her mother's death and the sexual aggressions she suffered, are symbolised, reduced, displaced and played out in the space of literature'.[50] For Defromont, 'trauma' is displayed and displaced in the text itself; hence the echoic, reiterative nature of Woolf's writing, and its fragmentary syntax and insistent, even excessive, punctuation, so different from, for example, James Joyce's representations of continuous 'feminine' speech in *Ulysses*.

Elizabeth Abel's work on Woolf, in particular her *Virginia Woolf and the Fictions of Psychoanalyis*, is also concerned with the role of repetition and interruption in Woolf's writings. Her focus, however, is less on the fragmenting effects of a violence played out against the self, and both repeated and guarded against in the fiction, than in the narratives of gendered and psychic development represented in Woolf's writing and in psychoanalytic stories of identity and its making. Using the work of Melanie Klein as well as Freud, Abel looks at the 'narrative project' which conjoins Woolf's writing and psychoanalysis in the 1920s and 1930s, while exploring Woolf's fictions as a critique of Freudian versions of the 'family romance'. As Abel writes: 'By questioning the paternal genealogies pre-scribed by nineteenth-century fictional conventions and reinscribed by Freud, Woolf's novels of the 1920s parallel the narratives Melanie Klein was formulating simultaneously and anticipate the more radical revisions that emerged in psychoanalysis over the next half century.'[51]

For Abel, the narratives of female development outlined in *Mrs Dalloway* closely match those simultaneously plotted by Freud in his essays of femininity, while at the same time 'expressly challeng[ing] his normative categories of women's sexuality'. As the narrative is pulled backwards into a remembered past, so Woolf opens up the space of women's affective and erotic relations with other women, Clarissa's with Sally Seton, exploring a realm of identifications Abel links to that of the buried or lost 'pre-Oedipal' space–time gestured towards by Freud, which has become so central to the mother–daughter plots of contemporary feminism and to the focus on maternal identifications.[52] *To the Lighthouse* plays out a Freudian Oedipal narrative which dominates the Ramsay children's past and present while producing a Kleinian challenge to Freudian fictions in Lily Briscoe's 'sustained and recuperative matricentric story'. Following *To the Lighthouse*, *A Room of One's Own* is 'Woolf's most complete and complex interpretation of matrilineage; it is also her last'.[53] *Three Guineas* turns away from mothers to explore the role of fathers, and Woolf becomes more, not less, allied to Freud in the late 1930s. Situating *Between the Acts* in the political and historical contexts of growing European fascism, and reading it alongside Freud's histories of patriarchal culture and its origins, *Totem and Taboo* and *Moses and Monotheism*, Abel finds Woolf's last novel haunted by a void, 'a new inability to think or write the mother, who is already absent or subsumed (like Sohrab) to patriarchy'.[54] In the literary and historical narrative Abel herself constructs, the mother is gradually evacuated from Woolf's fictions; the turning-point is *A Room of One's Own* which, while ostensibly committed to a model of matrilineage and to the mother–daughter plot, in fact conceals an ambivalence towards the mother at its heart.

Psychoanalytic feminist criticism, of which Abel's and Defromont's is some of the most subtle and powerful, has extended the implications of Freud's account of the pre-Oedipal realm of the mother–daughter dyad and of maternal plenitude, finding in Woolf's work, and in *To the Lighthouse* in particular, some of its most compelling explorations and representations. There is a difference, however, between critics for whom there is something like a lost female homeland and those, like Mary Jacobus, for whom the pre-Oedipal relationship with the mother is a myth rather than a place to which women could or should seek to return. As Jacobus writes in *First Things*:

> Mothers and myths of origins have the same function, which may in the end be to remind us that something is always lost in stories of the constitution of the subject, whether we call it the body or an undivided self. Feminism has tried to supply this lack by making the mother the unremembered heroine of the psychoanalytic text – she who would make it whole if we could only tell the entire unexpurgated story.[55]

Throughout her recent work, Jacobus has critically opened up such versions of feminist utopianism and nostalgia to the fragmentations, gaps and divisions they screen and deny.

Rachel Bowlby, while sharing Elizabeth Abel's interest in the relationship between Freud's and Woolf's fictions of femininity and female development, has, perhaps more emphatically than any feminist critic of Woolf, resisted the pull of the past and the elegiac dimensions of Woolf's writing. Bowlby, in her highly original criticism, has represented Woolf as a writer of 'modernity' as well as 'modernism', opening up the place in her work of the city (a topic also explored by Susan Squier[56]), new forms of travel and transport and their relationship to modern subjectivities, consumerism and the fashioning of sexual identities, and exploring 'Woolf's ceaseless fascination with the surprising connections and clashes amid the discontinuous movements of modern life'.[57] This is the Woolf of 'Modern Fiction', who wrote:

> We do not come to write better; all that we can be said to do is to keep moving, now a little in this direction, now in that, but with a circular tendency should the whole course of the track be viewed from a sufficiently lofty pinnacle. It need scarcely be said that we make no claim to stand, even momentarily, upon that vantage ground.[58]

In such passages we find the complexities of Woolf's concept of history as movement rather than linear progress, and her destabilising models of knowledge, in which a perspective is located, only to be undermined in the very next phrase.

Bowlby's work has emphasised the absence of fixities in Woolf's writing. She has also pointed up the ways in which such multivalency has made Woolf the exemplar for any number of different forms of feminism, although the fixing of Woolf to one position rather than another is wholly counter to her strategies and perspectives. Bowlby opens *Feminist Destinations* with a reading of 'Mr Bennett and Mrs Brown' which focuses less on the debate between Edwardian and modernist writing, which has structured so many readings of this essay, than on the train journey itself, and its gendering of passenger and journey:

> It is precisely in her insistence on the sexual inflection of all questions of historical understanding and literary representation that Woolf is a feminist writer. She constantly associates certainty and conventionality with a complacent masculinity which she sees as setting the norms for models of individual and historical development. It makes sense, then, that it will be from the woman in the corner of the railway compartment – or the woman not synchronised with the time of the train – that the most fruitful and troubling questions will be posed, and that new lines may emerge.[59]

Bowlby's readings of Woolf could be situated in the broader contexts of recent work on the 'gender of modernity' and on the feminisation of culture in the late nineteenth and early twentieth centuries.

It is not surprising that Bowlby makes the route taken by the daughter in *Mrs Dalloway* as significant as that of the mother, nor that *Feminist Destinations* focuses on *Jacob's Room* and *Orlando*, the first of which has tended to receive less attention from feminist critics than Woolf's other novels, and the second of which has only recently become a central, and even exemplary, text for feminism and postmodernism. *Jacob's Room* is in one way Woolf's most experimental novel, in its radical deconstruction of 'character'. *Orlando* is similarly 'postmodern' in its production of 'performative' identities, and its radical undermining of fixed gender identities. For Bowlby, these are crucial dimensions of Woolf's work, although she is also concerned with Woolf's 'recurrent and persistent explorations of conceptions of history-writing',[60] including the play with biographical forms of *Jacob's Room* and the historical fictions and fantasies of *Orlando*.

Pamela Caughie's *Virginia Woolf and Postmodernism: Literature in Quest and Question of Itself* (1991) sets out, as its title indicates, 'to read Woolf again from the place of postmodernism'.[61] Caughie, in opening with an account of feminist Woolf criticism to date, suggests that it has been largely inadequate to the play and performance of Woolf's fictions, and that Woolf has been inaccurately represented both by 'modernist' and 'feminist' critics. She returns, as so many critics have done, to Toril Moi's responses to Elaine Showalter as a defining moment not only in Woolf but in feminist studies generally: Mary Eagleton uses their 'debate' as the first section of her reader in *Feminist Literary Criticism*. Caughie argues that the opposition Moi constructed between Anglo-American and French feminisms was in fact part of the 'broader transformation in literature and theory that we have come to call *postmodernism*':

> What has been described as a debate between opposing schools of feminism can now be seen as a change in the very way we conceive the relations between things. Thus, what is needed in Woolf criticism is a perspective that can free Woolf's writings from the cage of modernism and the camps of feminism without denying these relations in her texts . . . By considering Woolf's works in the context of postmodern narrative and cultural theories, I want to change the way we conceive prose discourse so that we do not feel compelled to claim Woolf as a spokesperson for any one group of writers. Virginia Woolf can enter into a variety of literary relations, for she has no essential nature.[62]

For Caughie, Woolf's feminism is '*an effect of* her formal experiments', rather than their cause. As she rethought traditional assumptions and practices in literature, so 'Woolf raised many of the feminist and poststructuralist critical issues that have subsequently emerged as such. Her formal experiments resulted in what many have come to call a postmodern narrative practice, as well as in a feminist textual politics'. Caughie's declared intention is 'to change the way we read Woolf' in order to explode the view that there is a 'right reading' of her work. Changing the way we read Woolf, and literary texts in general, involves a move from an interpretative paradigm of literary analysis (the uncovering of meaning from within the text) to a concern with the rhetoricity and 'pragmatics' of literature: in Caughie's terms, 'how it functions and how it finds an audience'. Woolf's critical essays, in particular, reveal that 'Woolf is more interested in how a reader responds to and shapes a text than in elucidating an author's thematic statements or characterizing forms'.[63]

Caughie notes that she may contravene her own principle of non-dualistic thinking in seeming to oppose two types of writing, modernism and postmodernism, and replacing 'a modernist or feminist referential with a postmodernist one'. The way out of this impasse is, she argues, not to *define* a practice (as much feminist criticism has done) but to *enact* a way of proceeding. Yet, I would suggest, her argument creates further dualisms, with the first term the negative one: properties/production, defining/enacting and, as in the account given in my preceding paragraph, interpretative/pragmatic. We can either call this faulty reasoning or resign ourselves to the inevitability of binary logics and to our messy critical practices, in which attending to 'meanings' *and* to 'strategies' might not be mutually exclusive activities.

One of Woolf's 'strategies', as Caughie suggests, was the construction of the 'feminist reader'. *A Room of One's Own*, Catharine Stimpson has argued, 'is an agitating series of gestures that forbids complacency, security and premature intellectual closure'.[64] In its staging of multiple selves and positions, often internally contradictory, *A Room of One's Own* puts into play – perhaps even constructs – the diversity of feminist views and theories which would subsequently find themselves within it. In this sense, Woolf's *Room* is feminism's project. The question of its continued centrality as a feminist work – as feminism itself is alternately disowned and reclaimed – must remain as open as Woolf's own textual work and play.

NOTES

1 I have focused in this chapter on Woolf's Anglo-American reception. Analysis of her reception, feminist and otherwise, in other national and cultural contexts would reveal rather different histories of reception and response. Work on the European Reception of Virginia Woolf is currently being undertaken at the School of Advanced Study, University of London, under the auspices of a British Academy funded research project led by Dr Elinor Shaffer.

2 *Virginia Woolf: Lesbian Readings*, eds. Eileen Barrett and Patricia Cramer (New York University Press, 1997).

3 See Jane Dunn, *A Very Close Conspiracy: Vanessa Bell and Virginia Woolf* (London: Cape, 1991); Diane Gillespie, *The Sisters' Arts: The Writing and Painting of Virginia Woolf* (Syracuse University Press, 1988); Suzanne Raitt, *Vita and Virginia: The Work and Friendship of Vita Sackville-West and Virginia Woolf* (Oxford University Press, 1993).

4 Alex Zwerdling, *Virginia Woolf and the Real World* (Berkeley and Los Angeles: University of California Press, 1986), p. 211.
5 Naomi Black, 'Virginia Woolf and the Women's Movement', in Jane Marcus, ed., *Virginia Woolf: A Feminist Slant* (Lincoln: University of Nebraska Press, 1985), p. 185.
6 Mary Jacobus, 'The Difference of View', in *Reading Woman: Essays in Feminist Criticism* (London: Methuen, 1986), p. 40.
7 Rachel Bowlby (ed.), *A Woman's Essays* (Harmondsworth: Penguin, 1992), p. 3.
8 Michèle Barrett (ed.), *Virginia Woolf: Women and Writing* (London: The Women's Press, 1979), p. 49.
9 Bowlby (ed.), *A Woman's Essays*, p. 38.
10 'Women Novelists', in Bowlby (ed.), *A Woman's Essays*, p. 12.
11 'Men and Women', in Bowlby (ed.), *A Woman's Essays*, p. 19.
12 Rachel Bowlby (ed.), *The Crowded Dance of Modern Life* (Harmondsworth: Penguin, 1992), pp. 103–5.
13 See, for example, Sarah Grand, *The Heavenly Twins* 3 vols. (London: William Heinemann, 1893).
14 Zwerdling, *Virginia Woolf and the Real World*, p. 217.
15 Winifred Holtby, *Women and a Changing Civilization* (1935) (Chicago: Academy Press, 1978).
16 *Chloe plus Olivia: an Anthology of Lesbian Literature from the Seventeenth Century to the Present Day*, ed. Lilian Faderman (Harmondsworth: Penguin, 1995).
17 Bowlby (ed.), *A Woman's Essays*, p. 172.
18 *Ibid.*, p. 133.
19 *Ibid.*, p. 136.
20 Bowlby (ed.), *The Crowded Dance of Modern Life*, p. 171.
21 Winifred Holtby, *Virginia Woolf: a Critical Memoir* (London: Wishart, 1932; Chicago: Academy Press, 1978), p. 183.
22 E. M. Forster, *Virginia Woolf* (Cambridge University Press, 1942), p. 23.
23 *Ibid.*, pp. 22–3.
24 J. B. Bachelor, 'Feminism in Virginia Woolf', in *Virginia Woolf: a Collection of Critical Essays*, ed. Clare Sprague (Englewood Cliffs, NJ: Prentice-Hall, 1971), p. 171.
25 *Ibid.*, p. 170. This passage, which reveals a strong and symptomatic critical unease with the question of feminism in Woolf's writing, recalls one of Freud's favourite jokes – that of the man who borrows his neighbour's kettle and, when rebuked for returning it with a hole in it, defends himself on the following grounds: 'First, I never borrowed a kettle from B. at all; secondly, the kettle had a hole in it already when I got it from him; and thirdly, I gave him back the kettle undamaged.' *The Standard Edition of the Complete Psychological Works of Sigmund Freud* (London: the Hogarth Press and the Institute of Psycho-analysis, 1953), vol. 8, p. 62.
26 Herbert Marder, *Feminism and Art: A Study of Virginia Woolf* (University of Chicago Press, 1968).
27 Herbert J. Muller, 'Virginia Woolf, and Feminine Fiction', in *Critical Essays on Virginia Woolf*, ed. Morris Beja (Boston, MA.: G. K. Hall & Co., 1985). p. 35.

28 Barrett (ed.), *Women and Writing*, p. 49.
29 Elaine Showalter, *A Literature of their Own* (London: Virago, 1978), p. 264.
30 *Ibid.*, p. 285.
31 Toril Moi, *Sexual/Textual Politics: Feminist Literary Theory* (London: Methuen, 1985), p. 3.
32 *Ibid.*, p. 7.
33 *Ibid.*, p. 18.
34 See Margaret Homans, *Bearing the Word: Language and Female Experience in Nineteenth-Century Women's Writing* (University of Chicago Press, 1986); Makiko Minow-Pinkney, *Virginia Woolf and the Problem of the Subject* (Brighton: Harvester, 1987); Patricia Waugh, *Feminine Fictions: Revisiting the Postmodern* (London: Routledge, 1989); Sue Roe, *Writing and Gender: Virginia Woolf's Writing Practice* (Hemel Hempstead: Harvester Wheatsheaf, 1990); Patricia Ondek Lawrence, *The Reading of Silence: Virginia Woolf in the English Tradition* (Stanford University Press, 1991); Clare Hanson, *Virginia Woolf* (Basingstoke: Macmillan, 1994).
35 Jacobus, 'The Difference of View', p. 39.
36 *Ibid.*, p. 33.
37 Judith Kegan Gardiner, 'Mind mother: psychoanalysis and feminism', in *Making a Difference: Feminist Literary Criticism*, eds. Gayle Greene and Coppelia Kahn (London: Methuen, 1985), p. 121.
38 Jane Marcus, *Art and Anger: Reading Like a Woman* (Ohio State University Press, 1988), p. 138.
39 *Ibid.*, xxi.
40 *Ibid.*, p. 189.
41 Regina Marler, *Bloomsbury Pie* (London: Virago, 1997).
42 For further discussion of 'the new biography' in writings by Lytton Strachey, Harold Nicolson and Virginia Woolf see my *Auto/biographical Discourses: Theory, Criticism, Practice* (Manchester University Press, 1994) and 'Looking Glasses at Odd Corners: the "New Biography" of the 1920s and 30s', in *New Comparisons* (forthcoming, 2000).
43 Marcus, *Art and Anger*, p. 162.
44 Jane Marcus, *Virginia Woolf and the Languages of Patriarchy* (Bloomington, Indiana: Indiana University Press, 1987), p. 181.
45 *Ibid.*, p. xii.
46 Leonard Woolf, *An Autobiography*, vol. 2, *1911–1969* (Oxford University Press 1980).
47 Virginia Woolf, *Melymbrosia*, ed. Louise A. DeSalvo (New York Public Library, 1982), p. ix.
48 Louise A. DeSalvo, *Virginia Woolf: The Impact of Childhood Sexual Abuse on her Life and Work* (London: The Women's Press, 1989), p. 302.
49 Françoise Defromont, 'Mirrors and Fragments', in *Virginia Woolf: Longman Critical Readers*, ed. Rachel Bowlby (Harlow: Longman, 1992), p. 67.
50 *Ibid.*, p. 71.
51 Elizabeth Abel, *Virginia Woolf and the Fictions of Psychoanalysis* (Chicago University Press, 1989), p. 3.
52 See, in particular, Freud's discussions of the female Oedipus complex in his essay 'Female Sexuality' (1931), in which he refers to the female pre-Oedipal

phase, and to the female child's first, 'exclusive attachment', to the mother in the following terms: 'Our insight into this early, pre-Oedipus, phase in girls comes to us as a surprise, like the discovery, in another field, of the Minoan–Mycenaean civilisation behind the civilisation of Greece.' Penguin Freud Library 7, *On Sexuality* (Harmondsworth: Penguin, 1977), p. 372.

53 Abel, *Virginia Woolf and the Fictions of Psychoanalysis*, p. 85.
54 *Ibid.*, p. 118.
55 Mary Jacobus, *First Things: The Maternal Imaginary in Literature, Art and Psychoanalysis* (London: Routledge, 1995), p. 16.
56 Susan Merrill Squier, *Virginia Woolf and London: the Sexual Politics of the City* (Chapel Hill: University of North Carolina Press, 1985).
57 Rachel Bowlby, *Feminist Destinations and Further Essays on Virginia Woolf* (Edinburgh University Press, 1997), p. 261.
58 Virginia Woolf, *The Crowded Dance of Modern Life*, p. 5.
59 Bowlby, *Feminist Destinations*, p. 15.
60 *Ibid.*, p. 125.
61 Pamela Caughie, *Virginia Woolf and Postmodernism* (University of Illinois Press, 1991), p. 207.
62 *Ibid.*, p. 2.
63 *Ibid.*, p. 12.
64 Catharine Stimpson, 'Woolf's Room, Our Project: The Building of Feminist Criticism', in Bowlby (ed.) *Virginia Woolf: Longman Critical Readers*, p. 164.

12

NICOLE WARD JOUVE

Virginia Woolf and psychoanalysis

Psychoanalysis is the science and clinical practice that was born from Freud's discovery of the unconscious and that began to spread with the publication of his *Interpretation of Dreams* in 1900. Freud's invention of the 'talking cure' placed language firmly at the centre of its theory and practice. Throughout the twentieth century, in the West, psychoanalysis has had a huge impact on how human beings think of their own mental and psychic life. It has led to new ways of looking at art, new ways of reading texts, literature in particular.

Woolf's relation to psychoanalysis was manifold. Critics have interpreted it essentially in three ways: in terms of her own mental illness; of her involvement in, knowledge of and attitude to Freud and his followers; of the impact of psychoanalytic concepts upon her own writing and of the occurrence, in her writing and relation to language, of concepts and practices similar or alternative to psychoanalytic ones. In addition, psychoanalytic interpretations of her life and work have been offered. This triple – or quadruple – relation is fraught with paradoxes and questions which this essay will attempt to place before the reader.

Woolf's life is contemporary with the birth and development of psychoanalysis as a therapeutic science and practice. In the 1920s Freud's works and ideas spread to England largely through the so-called Bloomsbury circles in which Woolf moved. Indeed, 40 per cent of the world's psychoanalysts were then in England. Woolf herself suffered from bouts of insanity. Yet psychoanalysis does not seem to have been considered as a possible cure, least of all by herself: might it have helped? Also, moving as she did in a milieu steeped in Freud's ideas, Woolf's recorded reactions suggest strong hostility to those ideas, and her own writing seems to bear no trace of what might be called an influence. Searching the letters and journals for signs of admiration or informed knowledge, one encounters instead ironic or dismissive asides. Yet manifold recent readings of Woolf's novels show her to be consciously re-writing and countering Freudian notions about the unconscious, the Oedipus Complex, female sexuality. Did Woolf gather enough about psychoanalytic concepts through a process of second-hand immersion and osmosis to be able to re-handle or refute them? Or is it the case that such understandings were in the air anyway, that a novelist like Woolf and a scientist like Freud were at the same time and with different means exploring the same psychic realities? Should a fluid notion of intertextuality replace that of influence?

It is worth noting at the outset that interest in Woolf's in-depth relation to psychoanalysis has come almost exclusively from feminist critics. That is not to invalidate or relativise their work: I would be loath to do that, counting myself among them. But I do feel the need to stress that it is so, that such interest bears the mark of its epoch. Woolf criticism as it relates to psychoanalytic issues is gender-marked. And period-marked, as she herself inevitably and fruitfully was. Whatever the degree of her ignorance of or hostility to Freud himself, her own writing about female desire and the relation to the Mother was part and parcel of the question of female sexuality that was being debated in the 1920s through overt or covert dialogue with Freud. It is certainly relevant that from the 1970s onwards, many women writers should have felt that for female identity to be adequately explored, Freudian or Freudian-orientated concepts needed to be eschewed or redefined. This led to new perceptions of Woolf's own redefinitions of such concepts as well as to a desire to make Woolf into a champion: the great woman writer was seen as one who stood for an affirmation of sexual difference and for anti-patriarchal versions of what it is to be a woman. That she did these things deliberately, masterfully as it were, was somehow of the essence of what was being asked of her. This has made Woolf's relation to psychoanalysis as we at present describe it inseparable from the question of gender.

Psychoanalysis and Woolf's 'madness'

Sigmund Freud was almost twenty-six and about to become engaged when Virginia Woolf was born, in 1882. She was two when he went to Paris to study hysteria under Charcot, thirteen when her mother died and Freud co-published the *Studies in Hysteria* (1895). She was close to Dora's age when in 1900 a young hysterical woman called 'Dora' was taken to Freud by her father to be analysed, and when *The Interpretation of Dreams* came out. By 1912, when she married Leonard Woolf, Freud had published much, founded the Psychoanalytic Society, and his ideas were becoming internationally known.

This may be no more than a coincidence of dates: one could establish such parallels with any of Woolf's contemporaries. But it is relevant to how Freud's initiation of psychoanalysis and Woolf's own madness have been perceived and interpreted by recent Western feminisms[1]. They have repeatedly stressed that psychoanalysis was born from work on hysteria – that the hysteric's symptoms spoke of repressed trauma. The hysterics that Freud saw being treated by Charcot were all female. Dora, the young woman whom he attempted to treat by means of the talking cure in 1900, had been traumatised by a complex family situation – sexually pursued by a family friend of her father's age whilst her father was having an affair with the friend's wife. Alice Miller, in *Thou Shalt Not Be Aware*, points out that in 1896 Freud had posited that at the bottom of all cases of hysteria he had studied there were occurrences of premature sexual experiences, generally incest, often seduction by the father.[2] Later on, however, being unwilling to believe so many perverted acts had been committed by respectable family men, Freud abandoned the seduction theory and replaced it with the drive theory, the idea that it was the child's own unconscious desire for the parent that led to the delusion of seduction. In Woolf's time the latter view had been accepted; her own sister-in-law Karin Stephen held it.[3]

Throughout the 1980s in the west awareness has grown of the extent to which children were sexually abused, often by a close member of the family, in incestuous situations. What Florence Rush had called 'the best-kept secret'[4] ceased to be a secret, and one scandal after another erupted, especially in the USA, and in Great Britain as the scale of the problem became clear. Some forms of psychotherapy even came to rest on the idea that sexual abuse was at the core of any psychic disturbance evinced by young women, and that recalling the abuse could constitute the cure. Freud was seen as the man who had first of all come to perceive this (the seduction theory) but who, with the drive theory, had betrayed the 'truth' and his female patients with it.[5] In this perspective, Freudian-based psychoanalysis came to be seen as a new form of repression, resisted by former analysts like Alice Miller, who denounced a parental conspiracy to prevent children from being 'aware'.

There are diverging versions of the severity, frequency and nature of Woolf's mental illness, and even of what the diagnosis should be: manic depression? Cyclothymia (i.e., periodic breakdowns interspersed by long periods of sanity)? Hysteria? Schizophrenia? Should words like 'madness' or 'insanity' be used or are they crude and inappropriate? In her vigorous biography, in what is clearly a rebuff to hard terminology or the search for single causes, Hermione Lee states: 'Virginia Woolf was a sane woman who had an illness . . . Her illness is attributable to genetic, environmental and biological factors. It was periodic, and recurrent.'[6] The rest of her

'Madness' chapter is devoted to a rich description of the intricacies of the case. That it was a major element of Woolf's life, and a component of her talent is difficult to dispute. Virginia Woolf had her first bout of insanity after her mother's death when she was thirteen in 1895. She broke down again after her father's death in 1904, then in 1910 after years filled with family trouble (including her brother Thoby's death), after she had been working on her first novel, *The Voyage Out*. And then again after a year of marriage to Leonard Woolf. Further breakdowns followed, which have often been linked with the strain of working on, or completing, a work of fiction, but not always and not only. In almost all of these attacks, she tried to kill herself. They are dramatically signalled by periodic interruptions in the *Diaries*. There is no clear evidence to connect them with any one cause. Hermione Lee states that the illness: 'was precipitated, but not indubitably caused, by the things which happened to her'.[7] This statement (which is *not* open to more subtle psychoanalytic interpretations) together with the accounts of history of mental disturbance in the Stephen family and the manifold pressures and miseries the Stephen children had to survive, are offered by Hermione Lee as correctives to a psychoanalysis-inspired version of Woolf that has been influential: Louise DeSalvo's.

Louise DeSalvo made a powerful effort to trace the attacks back to abuse which Virginia would have been subjected to as early as when she was six. The whole context of post-1980s discovery of the societal extent of childhood sexual abuse, and its damaging consequences, as well as new feminist research initiated in the United States under Jane Marcus's impact are relevant to her thesis. Hers is the major study, using psychoanalytic concepts and resisting them at the same time, to place Woolf's madness centre-stage and to interpret it in terms of the incestuous advances she suffered at the hands of her two step-brothers, Gerald and George Duckworth. DeSalvo very much counters earlier rosy accounts of the Stephen family, stressing instead the patterns of repression, neglect and even cruelty that made it up. Witness, she argues, the family's pitilessness to Leslie Stephen's daughter from his first marriage, Laura, punished for her 'perverse' behaviour, locked away in the home and eventually sent to an asylum. Or Leslie's exploitation of Stella Duckworth, Julia Stephen's daughter by her first marriage: he used her as a replacement mother to his children after his wife Julia's death. She died early, and then Vanessa, Virginia's other sister, was exploited in her turn. DeSalvo also adduces the violent intrusive visits of a mad cousin, J. K. Stephen, in pursuit of Stella and allowed to roam the house, and the general neediness and predatoriness of the men in the Stephen circle.[8] She points out that Woolf herself had stressed the importance of the abuse she had suffered, and had been prompted to do so by her initial encounter with psychoanalytic notions. In November 1920 she read a paper to the Freudian-inspired Memoir Club: she called it '22 Hyde Park Gate', which was the address at which the Stephen family had been living when she was a child and evoked George Duckworth's 'malefactions', his visits to her bed which lasted through the many years of her adolescence and young womanhood, which she felt 'had spoilt her life for her before it had fairly begun'.[9] But in 1939, when Woolf began to write her autobiography, 'A Sketch of the Past', she went deeper and further back. She embarked upon what she called her 'autoanalysis'[10] – a kind of catharsis through writing – and attempted to recall her feelings as well as tell what had happened. In 'A Sketch of the Past' she came to connect her appalling moments of depression, the sense which she had earlier described as being 'exposed on a high ledge in full light'[11] with a childhood experience: she was six or seven and recovering from a bad bout of 'flu when her step-brother Gerald Duckworth lifted her up 'on a ledge' usually used for stacking dishes and explored her body, down to her 'private parts'.[12] Louise DeSalvo connects Woolf's writing of 'A Sketch of the Past' which induced, or was unable to lighten, a growingly unbearable burden of feelings, with her recent encounter with Freud. She reads Woolf's diary remark that Freud reduced her 'to a whirlpool'[13] as the feeling that she was being yet further repressed: since Freud had ended up denying the seduction theory, he would have been invalidating the memories she was recapturing. This denial, combined with terror of a (bodily) invasion of England by the Nazis, contributed to her suicide. Whilst I would agree with DeSalvo that Woolf's treatment at the hands of her step-brothers and the feelings of rage and outrage that must as a result have been simmering deep inside may well have been one of the determining factors in her psychic illness, I feel one must refrain from laying Woolf's suicide at Freud's door, as DeSalvo almost does. It was *Moses and Monotheism* that Woolf is known to have been reading around 1939, not the *Dora Case* or the *Studies in Hysteria*.

DeSalvo's case may be excessive, and has been questioned, especially in the USA, in a variety of ways but especially on the grounds of simplistic psychoanalytic interpretations.[14] Her readings are one-sided, unsympathetic to the various men in Woolf's life (for what damage had the Duckworth brothers themselves suffered as children, what models of adult behaviour had they been given for them to be so abusive of their half-siblings? Could one not lay Leslie Stephen's neurotic and selfish behaviour at the door of his own 'mad' father?). Damage in families travels in many directions. The French child analyst Françoise Dolto claims that it takes three generations of neurotics to produce one psychotic child: it would be fascinating to apply what she describes in the conclusion to *Le Cas Dominique* about parents and grandparents to Virginia's parents and grandparents.[15] One must baulk at seeing women, especially young girls, as the necessary victims of exploitative or predatory men. Family dynamics are infinitely complex, and human resourcefulness paradoxical and immense. This is not to deny the awfulness of what was done to her: but if one looks at the lives they were able to construct for themselves, Virginia Woolf was much more powerful than her step-brothers.

Yet DeSalvo's case has unquestionable merits: it produces some insightful readings, it corrects other biographical versions that ignore or downplay a crucial element in Woolf's life. It also illuminates a number of metaphors and anchors some of Woolf's characters in her own experience, and our own readings may well be changed as a result. Rose in *The Years* has been traumatised by a childhood experience; in *The Voyage Out* Rachel's father is suspected by Helen Ambrose of 'nameless atrocities with regard to his daughter'. Depressive Rhoda in *The Waves* can also be read as bearing the marks of acute past trauma. Are the Pargiter siblings evoking their creator's childhood when Martin says: ' "What awful lives children live! . . . Don't they, Rose?" "Yes", Rose replies: "And they can't tell anybody".' At this point 'There was another gust and the sound of glass crashing.'[16]

But by the 1920s there was the means to 'tell', the 'talking cure': means that would have brought glass crashing in a liberating way, enabled the then mature woman to escape from her bell-jar. '22 Hyde Park Gate' had been a first step: why did the Woolfs not consult an analyst? The main reason may well have been Virginia Woolf's own suspicion of psychoanalysis, and her downright hostility to its practitioners, of which more later. According to Alix Strachey, it was feared that psychoanalysis might endanger Woolf's creativity: this reasoning is attributed to Leonard Woolf.[17] Frances Partridge told Hermione Lee that it was then regarded as 'dangerous and counterproductive for anyone who had had a major breakdown or attempted suicide'.[18] Jane Marcus provides an additional useful set of answers. Out of the twelve or so doctors who were consulted at one time or at another by the various relatives, especially Leonard Woolf, she picks out the major influence, Dr Savage. She contrasts Virginia Woolf's sister-in-law Karin Stephen's humane *Psychoanalysis and Medicine* (1935) with Dr Savage's *Insanity and the Allied Neuroses* (1884), thereby contrasting the humaneness of psychoanalysis and the lack of it in the psychiatrists and doctors consulted by Virginia's immediate circle. Dr Savage it was who had been called upon by the Stephen family after Virginia had tried to kill herself after long nursing of her father on his deathbed.[19] Savage saw heredity as a primary cause: James Stephen, Virginia's paternal grandfather, had suffered from bouts of madness similar to hers; there was Laura; there was J. K. Stephen, the cousin, also suicidal. Savage had recommended force-feeding, rest, forbade reading: Virginia was to replace her book with a spade. Like the American Dr Weir whose 'rest-and-be-treated-as-a-child' treatment was denounced by Charlotte Perkins Gilman in her autobiographical story *The Yellow Wallpaper*, Savage thought that education and exercise of the intellect was bad for women (and for working men). Woolf's attacks on psychiatrists (Holmes and Bradshaw in *Mrs Dalloway*) has been connected with her experiences at the hands of Dr Savage and his colleague Sir William Gull by Jane Marcus[20] as well as by Elaine Showalter in *The Female Malady*. Marcus's answer to why the Woolf family did not consult a Freudian analyst is persuasive, expecially when added to those already outlined: by the time psychoanalytic help might have been available there had been built at the hand of doctors like Savage such a pattern of belief in hereditary insanity and the connection between insanity and genius, as well as belief in a physical treatment of 'food, rest and no mental work'[21] that other forms of help were not even envisaged. In the debate, as so often in the twentieth century when breakdown occurs, psychiatry goes to war with psycho-analysis. Without wanting to deny the help that psychiatry can give nor exclude genetic elements nor the insights that can be gained through an investigation of childhood abuse, I own that I prefer the more complex version of events that psychoanalysis produces: through seeing the psyche as made through dynamic interaction with others, as acting as well as acted upon, and the seat of unknown submerged and at times strangely emerging forces. It leaves more room for freedom. What has been made psychically, through relationships, can be repaired psychically, through relationship to the analyst or a source of therapeutic help, in ways that call for all the resources of the self rather than put it at the mercy of specialists or blame it on others. Or it can be turned to fruitful uses, aesthetic, moral, spiritual. I admire the manifold ways in which Woolf created out of the tremendous tensions and pressures that were in her, and that at times flooded her, as well as the courage with which she undertook her own autoanalysis towards the end of her life. She wrote in *Moments of Being*, with reference to her writing *To The Lighthouse* where she felt she had exorcised her parents at last, especially her mother's shade: 'I suppose I did for myself what psycho-analysts do for their patients. I expressed some very long felt and deeply felt emotion. And in expressing it I explained it and then laid it to rest.'[22]

Whether Woolf's madness could have been cured or made tolerable at the hands of anyone is of course a matter for speculation. One can dream that her meeting with Melanie Klein, whom she liked, in early 1939 might have encouraged her to seek for treatment.[23] Could relief have come at the hands of Marion Milner, a Woolf admirer who successfully treated a young schizophrenic woman over a period of twenty years, as she recounts in *The Hands of the Living God*?[24] For the presence of a loving and supportive 'mother' figure at times of stress (Violet Dickinson in 1910, Ethel Smyth in the late years) seems to have made a difference. But no talking cure was attempted, probably none ever thought of. What matters, it seems to me, is not to talk away the importance of Woolf's illness, whatever name it be given and whatever cause may be given for it. There are links that are too evident between the childhood traumas and the insanity, between the insanity and the sensibility, the particular vibration of Woolf's genius for the madness to be ignored as some kind of regrettable element in her make-up. In 1924, writing critically about the Stephens, their 'cold fingers, so fastidious, so critical, such taste', she adds: 'My madness has saved me.'[25] In 1930 she wrote in her *Diary* 'I believe these illnesses are in my case – how shall I express it? – partly mystical.'[26] 'On Being Ill' described the 'astonishing' spiritual changes she experienced. 'Undiscovered countries' are revealed 'when the lights of health go down'. Only a 'lion tamer' would have the strength 'to look these things squarely in the face'. 'There is a virgin forest in each.'[27] One must, I think, equally beware of romanticising the illness, of not seeing how much alchemical hard work and determination enabled her to transform the material of madness into the material of art. Left to itself, the madness would only have produced scribbles, as Septimus Warren Smith's does: 'If dreams become too widely divorced from truth they develop into an insanity which in literature is generally an evasion on the part of the artist.'[28] Woolf was not one for evasion.

It must be pointed out, however, that no full-scale analytic study of Woolf has been attempted. There certainly is room for one. Given the amount of documentation that exists about the Stephen family, it would be fascinating to see.

Woolf, Bloomsbury and Freud

Freud's ideas and writings had begun to spread to England before the First World War. Thanks to Frieda, his wife, D. H. Lawrence had become aware of the Oedipus Complex at the time he was revising *Sons and Lovers* in 1912, and several of his correspondents bring Freud's ideas up before and during the war. Leonard Woolf had read *The Interpretation of Dreams* and reviewed *The Psychopathology of Everyday Life* in 1914. Edward Carpenter, Montague Summers and Laurence Housman were among the members of the British Society for the Study of Sex Psychology which was founded in July 1914. It was however, through one of her favourite friends' 'agreeable' talk that Woolf first seems to have become interested:

> [Lytton Strachey] gave us an amazing account of the British Sex Society which meets at Hampstead. The sound would suggest a third variety of human being, & it seems that the audience had that appearance. Notwithstanding, they were surprisingly frank; & 50 people of both sexes & various ages discussed without shame such questions as the deformity of Dean Swift's penis: whether cats use the w.c.; self abuse; incest – Incest between parent and child when they are both unconscious of it, was their main theme, derived from Freud. I think of becoming a member.

Further ironic jibes at the expense of Hampstead follow (*D*1, p. 110).

England after the First World War and Bloomsbury in particular, with its intense cultural openness, provided an ideal setting for the dissemination of Freud's ideas. Stressing how psychoanalysis in England 'most nearly realised Freud's desire for an autonomous movement divorced from psychiatry', Elizabeth Abel, the author of the most sustained study into Woolf's relation to psychoanalysis, quotes anthropologist Malinowski's grumbles about its being 'the popular craze of the day' and the poet Bryher's assertion that 'to me Freud is literary England . . . after the first war'.[29]

The first meeting of the Memoir Club in March 1920 marked the reunion of the Bloomsbury group that had been scattered for the duration of the war. It included Clive Bell, Vanessa and Virginia, their brother Adrian Stephen, Duncan Grant, Maynard Keynes, Lytton Strachey, Roger Fry . . . Some were attracted to psychoanalysis, some hostile: Virginia Woolf lined up with the hostile ones, the art critics, Roger Fry and Clive Bell. Yet it was to the Memoir Club that she shared her memories of her sexual abuse at the hands of her step-brothers: '22 Hyde Park Gate' as mentioned above.

Of the club members only Adrian Stephen trained as a psychoanalyst. But other Bloomsbury members also did: Adrian's wife Karin as well as James Strachey (Lytton's brother) and his wife Alix. The Stracheys are key figures in the history of British psychoanalysis. As early as 1923 they were among the members of the London Psychoanalytic Society, founded by Ernest Jones in 1913. With Alix's help James Strachey was to undertake the huge work of translating Freud's collected papers, which became, through the Hogarth Press that was founded by the Woolfs, the Standard Edition. Woolf's diary entry of 26 May 1924 records expecting Dr James Glover 'to discuss the P.S.S.', that is, the distribution and publication of the papers of the International Psychoanalytic Library, which then led to the publication of Freud's complete works in English (D2, p. 302). Alix Strachey became friends with Melanie Klein, established in Berlin when they were both in analysis with Karl Abraham in 1924–5. Melanie Klein moved to London, where her work was to have profound implications for the future of psychoanalysis. Klein delivered her 1925 lectures at 50 Gordon Square, the home of Adrian and Karin Stephen who were themselves approaching the end of their training. The lectures were translated by the Stracheys. There was intimacy between James Strachey and Adrian Stephen, who boarded with James during the rift in his marriage, between 1923 and 1926. Virginia lived very near, 'next door' by her own account, in Tavistock Square. From the 1920s onward the Woolfs, Bells, Stracheys and Stephens seem to have been ever in and out of each other's homes: 'such is the rabbit warren nature of the place', Virginia records (D2, p. 23).

The wonder is not only are there few traces of interest in, or genuine knowledge of, psychoanalysis in her letters and diaries: there are sibylline entries or none. When there are entries, the tone is distant: 'Lord knows what I didn't read into their reading', she notes about the first Memoir Club meeting where dreams were discussed (D2, p. 23). She often is hostile, sarcastic. The Bloomsbury members involved in psychoanalysis are in for demolition jobs. Woolf's cattiness is in full sway: 'Poor James Strachey was soft as moss, lethargic as an earthworm. James, billed at the 17 Club to lecture on "Onanism", proposes to earn his living as an exponent of Freud in Harley Street. 'For one thing, you can dispense with a degree' is her Thursday 21 November 1918 record of James's decision to train as an analyst (D1, p. 221). She hovers between kindness and cruelty by 2 September 1921, when James and Alix, now training in Vienna, are in England for a visit. She has said goodbye to them 'therefore the whole day is contaminated'. Alix 'certainly provides' 'shade' for James, who is 'low, muted, gentle, modest' – grey. 'Freud has certainly brought out the lines in Alix. Even physically, her bones are more prominent' (D2, p. 135). By 2 September 1921 the disparity between the spouses has grown worse – it almost seems as if Alix is thriving at James's expense – and guess who's to be blamed for it? 'The last people I saw were James and Alix, fresh from Freud – Alix grown gaunt and vigorous – James puny and languid – such is the effect of 10 months psycho-analysis' (L2, p. 482). The Adrian–Karin couple's 'going into practice together as psycho-analysts' draws even more barbed arrows than the James–Alix couple: 'I suppose one'll whisper one's symptoms to Adrian, and he'll bellow them to Karin; and then they'll lay their heads together. Isn't it a surprising prospect? . . . [Karin's] hat is now of the shape of a Welshwoman's hat, only scarlet, then her dress is sage green; and her decorations many-coloured beads; and the whole effect like that of some debauched parrot who has been maltreated by the street boys, but doesn't know it, or only half suspects it, poor fowl' (L2, p. 369). This is to Vanessa. And again: 'I hear you're having Adrian – not Karin? Don't dissuade him from being a doctor. Leonard played bridge there last night and saw something of such girth and grossness on a chair he cried out in horror: it was Karin's leg' (L2, p. 378).

The source of all this nonsensical activity drew the most animus. Woolf's quizzical accounts of Hogarth Press activity that related to the publication of translations from Freud show her reluctant to read him – which she will only do, it seems, quite late into her life: when she met the man himself in January 1939 in Maresfield Gardens, Hampstead, where with the help and patronage of Princess Bonaparte he had fled from Vienna. Freud the refugee who was suffering from the cancer that was to kill him eight months later entertained Leonard and Virginia to tea. He offered Virginia a narcissus: one may well wonder at the choice of a gift . . . She seems to have been moved by the meeting, and it was subsequent to it that, as she records in a letter to John Lehmann of 15 July 1939, she read *Moses and Monotheism*.

In his autobiography Leonard Woolf is celebratory about the Hogarth Press's connection with Freud: 'The greatest pleasure that I got from publishing the psycho-Analytical Library was the relationship which it established between us and Freud . . . He was not only a genius, but also, unlike many geniuses, an extraordinarily nice man'.[30] Virginia does not share the enthusiasm. She seems to feel besieged by a ruinous structure: '[A]ll the psycho-analytic books have been dumped in a fortress the size of Windsor castle in ruins upon the floor'.[31] When she works with James Strachey on the first volume of the *Collected Papers*, she 'in two jackets, for it is freezing, and hair down; he in shirtsleeves', in her account of the day she adds, strangely: 'Thus one gets to know people; sucks the marrow out.' The image, Elizabeth Abel suggests, 'anticipates her hostile portrait of her analyst brother brooding "like a vulture" over a woman in despair'.[32] There was, of course, a great deal of debate about, and suspicion of, Freud's ideas: doubt as to the degree to which they could be regarded as science. Woolf once exclaimed in rage at their preposterousness.

[We] are publishing all Dr Freud, and I glance at the proof and read how Mr A. B. threw a bottle of red ink on to the sheets of his marriage bed to excuse his impotence to the housemaid, but threw it in the wrong place, which unhinged his wife's mind, – and to this day she pours claret on the dinner table. We could all go on like that for hours; and yet these Germans think it proves something – besides their own gull-like imbecility.   (L3, pp. 134–5)

Abel points out what a misreading of Freud this is. What is important, I think, is that it was precisely the scientific status Freud claimed for his ideas that must have infuriated Woolf and made her feel threatened. She must have associated him with those doctors and psychiatrists who had been plaguing her for years and whose stupidity drives Septimus Warren Smith to suicide in *Mrs Dalloway*. She disliked the fictions of psychoanalysis (though in the 1930s she came to use some of the concepts in her own way and to her own purposes, words like 'repression, complex, suppression, ambivalence')[33] but she detested it as a science, a double threat to her own life and art. One of her reviews, 'Freudian Fiction' (1920) sharply attacks J. D. Beresford's *An Imperfect Mother*, in which mother and son are victims of an 'unacknowledged passion' for each other 'in the inarticulate manner of those who lived before Freud'. 'This is strictly in accordance with the new psychology, which in the sphere of medicine claims to have achieved positive results of great beneficence . . . The triumphs of science are beautifully positive. But for novelists the matter is much more complex . . . Yes, says the scientific side of the brain, that . . . explains a great deal. No, says the artistic side of the brain, that is dull and has no human significance.'[34]

Given the strength of Woolf's prejudice against, and hostility to, Freud and psychoanalysis, how is it that so many connections have been traced between her work and that of psychoanalysis?

Psychoanalysis and Woolf's writing

The answer is both simple and infinitely complex: Woolf's work invites endless psychoanalytic interpretation because of the ways it skirts 'madness' – because, like Clarissa Dalloway struggling to make her party hold together, like Lily Briscoe in *To the Lighthouse* straining to make her painting cohere, it seems, with all its grace and surface clarity, to be forever fending off the threat of disintegration, blurred boundaries, insecure identities.

Take, for instance, the final section of *The Waves*:

'Now to sum up', said Bernard. 'Now to explain to you the meaning of my life. Since we do not know each other (though I met you once, I think, on board a ship going to Africa), we can talk freely. The illusion is upon me that something adheres for a moment, has roundness, weight, depth, is completed. This, for the moment, seems to be my life. If it were possible, I would hand it you entire . . .

'But unfortunately, what I see (this globe, full of figures) you do not see. You see me, sitting at a table opposite you, a rather heavy, elderly man, grey at the temples. You see me take my napkin and unfold it . . . But in order to make you understand, to give you my life, I must tell you a story – and there are so many, and so many – stories of childhood, stories of school, love, marriage, death, and so on; and none of them are true . . . How tired I am of stories . . .[35]

If in real life I found myself sitting at a table across from a perfect stranger who began to address me in these terms, I would think he was crazy (why would he want to give me, a perfect stranger, his life 'entire'? How can he imagine it as a globe?), and make my way out as discreetly as I could. As a reader, I first have to accept the fiction I am not a reader but a living party to an encounter with Bernard, one of the characters/voices in the novel, now sadly aged. I have to accept his self-description, make the usual pact one makes as a reader with a fictitious character; but he is a particularly unreliable, unsteady character. I have to accept his lie or enter his fiction about our meeting on a ship bound for Africa (and what does that mean?): but then, he 'thinks' we met, he is not sure. I also have to accept the supposed logic that we can talk freely because we do not know each other (though of course only he will talk). As a reader, that is, I am asked to lose my centre (my own 'globe'), be lost as to who I am supposed to be. And then I am open to the speaker's stark logic: he has a momentary feeling (though only an 'illusion') that he sees his life whole (from the inside; the globe is his image), but since all I see of him is his outside (a rather heavy, elderly man), I cannot see what he sees. He could only 'give' me his life through his talk, by means of a story, and there are so many, and none of them are true, and he is tired of stories. Communication nil; grand designs down in the dust; narrative extinct. 'Now the sun had sunk. Sky and sea were indistinguishable', was the opening of the short, poetic interlude that preceded Bernard's voice. What is left? Bernard begins to long for 'some little language such as lovers use, broken words, inarticulate words, like the shuffling of feet on the pavement.' 'Shuffling of feet on the pavement': is that the language lovers use? We are more in the world of Beckett's Molloy than in the world of lovers. Indeed, Molloy finds himself in a ditch, which is where Bernard ends up: 'Lying in a ditch on a stormy day, when it has been raining, then enormous clouds come marching over the sky, tattered clouds, wisps of clouds. What delights me then is the confusion, the height, the indifference and the fury. Great clouds always changing, and movement; something sulphurous and sinister, bowled up, helter-skelter; towering, trailing, broken off, lost, and I forgotten, minute in a ditch. Of story, of design, I do not see trace then.'[36] A powerful destructive impulse, surged from the unconscious, has swamped and dwarfed consciousness: momentarily.

In the process, boundaries have been blurred, identities have been smudged and dispersed. The possibility of 'story' has disappeared. The reader is down in the ditch, forgotten as a reader, watching clouds with Bernard, who is also 'lost, forgotten', has ceased to be Bernard, a character. Lovers' words equal feet shuffling on the pavement. As for the voice of the author – where might it be found? We can expect no reassurance from such quarters. '*Sky and sea were indistinguishable.*' At the same time, what Bernard's voice is doing with the sense of identity echoes what the 'waves of darkness' are doing in the poetic interlude, '*covering houses, hills, trees, as waves of water wash round the sides of some sunken ship. Darkness washed down streets, eddying round single figures, engulfing them.*'[37] Marvellously subtle, poetic, correspondences give pattern to what seems to have lost all 'design'. That, coupled with the overall patterning, the 'waves' of voices of which the narrative is made, interspersed with the poetic interludes, the sharpness and musicality of the sentences, is what assures us that if this writing skirts the edge of madness, it is not mad.

What is here happening around the name of Bernard (which at times is all that is left of the character) is a characteristic feature in Woolf's fiction. Clarissa Dalloway 'would not say of any one in the world' 'that they were this or were that'.[38] As he falls asleep amid the eddies of his cigar smoke, Peter Walsh's 'thinking' dissolves and fuses: 'I shall try and get a word alone with Elizabeth to-night, he thought – then began to wobble into hour-glass shapes and taper away; odd shapes they take, he thought.'[39] Being 'oneself', to Mrs Ramsay, is being 'a wedge-shaped core of darkness'.[40] There is some shape at least to this image from *To the Lighthouse*, but in *The Waves* instability and dissolution are potent. 'Yet these roaring waters,' said Neville, 'upon which we build our crazy platforms are more stable than the wild, the weak and inconsequent cries that we utter when, trying to speak, we rise; when we reason and jerk out these false sayings, "I am this; I am that!" Speech is false.'[41] 'Even I who have no face, who make no difference when I come in . . . flutter unattached, without anchorage anywhere, unconsolidated, incapable of composing any blankness or continuity or wall against which these bodies move.'[42] This is Rhoda, also from *The Waves*. An inspired essay by Lee R. Edwards juxtaposes a passage spoken by Rhoda with quotations recorded from schizophrenic patients as well as extracts from the French surrealist poet Artaud in his period of breakdown, challenging the reader to guess which is by whom, and pointing out that the 'imagined utterances' of Woolf's and Artaud's characters 'render them, in this context in particular, indistinguishable literally from lunatics'.[43] Now it is, of course, of crucial importance that Rhoda, like Neville, like Bernard, should be a character created by Woolf as part of the pattern of a highly intricate and beautifully controlled novel.

This is art that records near madness, that skirts the edge of madness: not madness. Yet the depth with which Woolf plumbs such states is something specific (as Artaud's letters and poems are to him), not something that could for instance be accounted for by the states of disintegration of the self and of classical narrative and poetic form so often, and justly, associated with modernism and the impact of the First World War. Lee R. Edwards argues that Woolf does not have to be defended against the charge of madness, as a number of critics have done. Madness here is taken to mean a 'particular ontological position', one that she knew and used as a source of insight:

> For her, the feeling or perceiving self is inherently – categorically – an unfixed entity, porous and inconstant, uncontained by any continuous limit or consistent definition, evading every social label, warring against its own embodiment. Insecurely bounded and ungrounded, Woolf's characters are obsessively preoccupied with the maintenance and collapse of systems that alternately support and threaten their own emotional – or even physical – integrity: sequences of time, spatial distinctions, categories of knowledge.[44]

Daniel Ferrer similarly argues that 'there is a certain relationship between madness and writing, for Virginia Woolf as a writer as well as for us as readers'. Because of the continuum that exists between her self and her work (so much of it is made up of diaries, letters, etc.), psychoanalytic interpretations have to come in, even though they may not be verified. For Woolf's writing shows a 'dynamic' subject 'in process'. One feels that the subject of the author is at stake in the writing that is taking place, as are the identities of the characters. As I tried to show through the above quotation about Bernard from *The Waves* (Ferrer uses other examples) there are no stable or grounded points in Woolf, there is no 'representation', and neither guaranteeing authorial voice nor secure bounds:

> Very far from being the enclosure *containing* the inner excesses, the narration combines with them to multiply their virulence. The interpenetration of the different levels does not stop . . . This absence in the place of the ultimate subject guaranteeing the enunciation reactivates all the gashes which the text opened up but immediately pretended to mend, in order to carry on, in order to exist.[45]

Ferrer celebrates this in Woolf: 'through their relation to madness, these texts systematically challenge the frontiers that constitute novelistic fiction'.[46] She thus becomes an avant-garde writer. And well might she be: I have suggested earlier that bits of her are already plumbing Beckett territory.

Interestingly, however, the bulk of psychoanalytic interpretations of Woolf's work have in the past twenty years or so come from feminist quarters that whilst (like Edwards and Ferrer) placing 'madness' at the core of the work, have read it very differently: as the assertion of a certain kind of femininity; as a protest against a dominant male economy. I have outlined above, when discussing treatments for Woolf's madness, how feminists read it alongside female hysteria, misinterpreted, it was argued, by psychoanalysis with its anti-feminine bias. Some saw madness, as Phyllis Chesler put it, as the 'acting out of the devalued female role or the total or partial rejection of one's sex-role stereotype'. Others, like Luce Irigaray,[47] saw it as central to womanhood: the feminine element is rejected by traditional philosophy with its totalitarian principle of so-called 'logo-centrism', that is, the privileged status of the logos, the authority of a *presence-to-being*, of a rational centre, of concepts like Origin, God, Truth, Being, Reason. Irigaray pointed out a latent design in western metaphysics to exclude the woman from the production of speech, to subjugate her to the masculine, logical principle of identity. This would leave woman either in a state of silence, or speaking in ways that shake up the normal workings of language and identity. The passage I quoted above would be a good example of this: were Bernard able to speak his life, give it 'entire', like a globe, he might accomplish the logocentric act. But he cannot. Identities dissolve as he goes on speaking, and something that is not representation but something in process becomes expressed. Though Bernard is a male character, one might say that through his voice Woolf inscribes a novel, 'feminine', de-centred relation to speech.

For Woolf's feminist critics then the stress is not on the madness, but on the subversiveness and novelty of the enterprise, on the inscription of something specific that had not been allowed before. Essays like *A Room of One's Own* (in which a protest is being voiced in the name of repressed femininity against the patriarchal 'law' that silences women and puts writing outside their reach) and *Three Guineas* are adduced to show that throughout her fiction Woolf sets out to destabilise systems of perception and of value that are essentially male: like Mr Ramsay's famous attempt to work his way through knowledge from A to Z in *To the Lighthouse*. Mr Ramsay is read as the archetypal logocentrist, with all the blindness and limitations that such a world-view entails. He has stopped at Q, before the letter R which begins his name and which, had he reached it, might have indicated that he had arrived at some degree of self-knowledge. The systematic linear rationality of his attempt is seen to contrast with Mrs Ramsay's more inclusive poetic and empathetic awareness and female artist Lily's own fluid and shifting perception of the world. This rationality itself is seen as bound up with the primacy of male sexuality, of the 'phallus' as the French analyst Lacan called it.

Mr Ramsay has been much read as the Freudian patriarch: as a dominant figure, he is the father who says 'no' to his son James who is hoping to go to the lighthouse, the house of light, the mother's house. He separates James from his mother. It seems that in the portrayal of this relationship, Woolf was deliberately setting out to show the Oedipus complex at work.

The Oedipus Complex

It was a question that Freud returned to repeatedly in the 1920s and early 1930s. One of his earliest major discoveries, and the one which made him most famous, was that of the Oedipus complex, inspired by the Greek myth and Sophocles' plays: 'King Oedipus, who slew his father Laius and married his mother Jocasta, merely shows us the fulfilment of our child-hood wishes', *The Interpretation of Dreams* states.[48] We repress these wishes so strongly we end up not even knowing we ever had them. Oedipus solved the Sphinx's riddle, and just so Freud solved the riddle of dreams. There was much identification with Oedipus in Freud, and on the whole it was the man-child's drives that he focused on until the 1920s. The little boy learned to direct his desire away from his mother towards other females by going through the castration complex: the father enforced a separation from the mother by symbolically threatening to 'cut it off' unless the little boy renounced his desire to seduce his mother.

In *To the Lighthouse* Mr Ramsay's destruction of his young son James's hope to go the next day to the lighthouse ('it won't be fine'), and James's own reaction of anger are so strong as to be almost caricature, yet of a piece with the violent images that throughout the text contradict the apparent smoothness and politeness of the overt exchanges:

> Had there been an axe handy, a poker, or any weapon that would have gashed a hole in his father's breast and killed him, there and then, James would have seized it. Such were the extremes of emotion that Mr Ramsay excited in his children's breasts by his mere presence; standing, as now, lean as a knife, narrow as the blade of one, grinning sarcastically.[49]

Well may Woolf have intended Mr Ramsay to stand as a phallic shadow, the powerful phallus that both shows the child how impotent he is and symbolically threatens to cut off the child's own weaker organ. Rachel Bowlby points out that James's hatred for his father who keeps staking 'prior claims to his mother parallels Freud's Oedipal scenario, where the boy wants nothing less than to put out of the way the father who asserts his right to the mother',[50] and it is difficult to escape the thought that the parallel is intended. There are odd features to this, though, which I have pointed out in one of my essays[51] and which Rachel Bowlby implicitly acknowledges when she underlies how repeated and endless Mr Ramsay's demands for reassurance are: indeed as I argue Mr Ramsay behaves as a rival for his children, he demands of his daughter or female companions that they mother him, instead of behaving (except in that opening scene) like a law-giving, castration-threatening Freudian father. One might even say that his very relish at the pain he is causing his son is not just sadistic, it is puerile. Whether Woolf was quietly exploding a patriarchal myth – that fathers are powerful, the corner-stones of society – or simply recording the truth about the kind of father she herself had is an open question. Probably both. It is certainly interesting that towards the end, when James, through a series of equally violent images, comes to accept that there is something impersonal about the way his father keeps crushing him, something is being suggested about how not just Victorian patriarchy, but power and oppression in general work. One sane way out of the Oedipus Complex, of hatred against the father, appears at the same time:

> He sought an image to cool and detach and round off his feelings in a concrete shape. Suppose then as a child sitting helplessly in a perambulator, or on someone's knee, he had seen a waggon crush ignorantly and innocently, someone's foot? Suppose he had seen the foot first, in the grass, smooth and whole; then the wheel; and the same foot, purple, crushed. But the wheel was innocent. So now, when his father came striding down the passage knocking them up early in the morning to go to the Lighthouse down it came over his foot, over Cam's foot, over anybody's foot. One sat and watched it.[52]

How terrible: yet it is not long after this that James gets a 'Well done!' from his father, which gets him what he was after . . .

Elizabeth Abel records the ongoing debate generated in the 1920s by Freud's *Totem and Taboo*. Freud boasted of having made sense of anthropologists' findings by revealing the same structure at work in the tribal murder of the father by the brothers, which leads to the incest taboo, so that the situation be not repeated, and in the Oedipus Complex, which also leads to the acceptance of the incest taboo for the little boy: the desire to kill the rival father gets transformed into an acceptance of a taboo forbidding access to the mother (sisters etc.). Abel points out that Freud is relying on some of the anthropologists only, and not necessarily the best-informed ones. He ignores other work that would have contradicted his findings, in particular the work of Jane Harrison, a woman anthropologist publishing her findings in the same period, and which drew attention to the importance of the Mother figure, which Freud largely leaves out. Woolf had read Jane Harrison.[53] It may not be unrelated that in *To the Lighthouse* Mrs Ramsay, the mother, is by far the most powerful and central figure.

The Pre-Oedipal and the mother–daughter relationship
The question of female sexuality was a central and disputed one in the
1920s. This is one of the reasons why Woolf, who in her search for a
distinctive form of writing and in her thinking endlessly articulated the
question of female quiddity, has appealed so much to 1970s and later
feminists engaged in the same questioning. Freud himself repeatedly
returned to the question in the 1920s and early 1930s after a gap of more
than twenty years since the Dora case. 'Some Psychical Consequences of
the Anatomical Distinction Between the Sexes' (1925) maps out female
sexuality in relation to the male and elaborates the celebrated conception
of 'penis envy'. The little girl is described as falling 'a victim to envy for the
penis' upon having made the 'momentous discovery' of a brother or
playmate's 'superior counterpart of their own small and inconspicuous
organ'.[54] She turns in anger and reproach against her mother, who has sent
her into the world so 'insufficiently equipped'. Later she will turn to her
father who alone could give her a symbolic penis by giving her a baby.
Later yet, if she successfully negotiates all these twists and turns, she will
redirect her desire towards a man. My essay on Woolf in *Female Genesis*
dares ask whether there might not be a case of penis-envy in *A Room of
One's Own* – whether, as analyst Maria Torok has argued, penis-envy in
women does not conceal a repressed womb?[55] I say, 'dares', for what is
normally done is to see Woolf as refuting Freud rather than – as I see her –
both producing alternatives to Freud *but also* open to psychoanalytic
readings.

In 'Female Sexuality' (1931) however, Freud acknowledged that the little
girl's desire, like the boy's, is initially directed towards her mother. The
'pre-Oedipal', the period of polymorphic desires that precedes language
and a sense of self, lasts longer and is deeper in little girls than in little boys.
It is archaic, mysterious, a layer under the subconscious layers, like 'the
Minoan–Mycenaean civilisation behind the civilisation of Greece'. It is
uncharted: the 'dark continent' of femininity.[56]

As I have suggested at the outset, psychoanalytical approaches to Woolf
are contemporary with the development of feminisms from the early 1970s
onwards. French feminisms, which from the start had relied upon psychoanalytic concepts, had dialogued with, or denounced, Freud and Lacan
around the question of female sexuality and language, have been the source
of inspiration for much Woolf criticism. In her essays of the mid-1970s
Hélène Cixous attacked traditional philosophical binaries such as man/
woman which placed one term – man – above the other – woman (Freud
and Lacan were seen as having reinforced these binaries by asserting the

primacy of male sexuality, of the 'phallus'). Cixous championed instead a play of pluralities, a new form of bisexuality. In a similar vein though with different emphasis and concepts, Julia Kristeva drew attention to the very period in the infant's development which Freud had called the 'pre-Oedipal'. There is no sense of a centre then, of 'I'; but manifold 'drives', and a 'babble' instead of language. Kristeva showed how this babble, these primary sounds, which she called the semiotic in opposition to fully structured language which she called the symbolic, are connected with desire for the mother's body, and what a large incidence of babble, or pure sounds as it were, remains in poetic language. Following Cixous, Mary Jacobus in 1979 advocated what she saw as a kind of bisexuality or 'neither/nor' in Woolf, something that goes beyond binaries: 'The repressive male/female opposition which "interferes with the unity of the mind" gives way to a mind paradoxically conceived of not as one, but as heterogeneous, open to the play of difference'.[57] Kristeva's interest in the pre-Oedipal was linked by Mary Jacobus to Woolf's writerly practice: a plurality, a dissolution of boundaries is found in Woolf's watery metaphors, such as the 'thought-fish' that 'darts' and sinks and flashes inside the narrator as a 'dominating phallic shadow' falls across her.[58] The vision was shared by Gillian Beer, arguing that against a male-driven fixed form of plot and realism Woolf works 'through a dislimning of the edges of identity'. In *The Waves* 'the self is in undetermined relations with objects, surfaces, heat and cold'. In that novel 'we can observe some of the qualities shared by feminist and *avant-garde* writing, such as Kristeva commented on in her remark about the dissolution of identities, even sexual identities'.[59] In such readings, and in many that followed, the stress is no longer on psychotic disintegration, on the threat of madness. The indeterminacies, the lack of a stable subject, are read as the positive inscription of a form of feminine identity that has never before been allowed to exist. Woolf's struggles against exclusive male precincts and the 'male sentence', so inappropriate for women as she sees it, thus are read as an early protest against Freud. It is implied that in the 1920s Woolf had been engaged in the very same struggle about female sexuality and feminine forms of writing as 1970s French feminists and those women writers and critics who like them were committed to a sexually different form of identity.[60]

From the 1930s onwards Melanie Klein, working intensively with infants and young children, had begun to map out the crucial importance of the mother in the child's development. Her work, along with that of other analysts like, later on, Winnicott, placed great stress on the maternal element, on the mother–child dyad. It came to be seen that it is not only the successful negotiation of the Oedipus complex (so much more difficult for girls than for boys according to Freud) but the mother's or the parents' capacity to 'hold' the child, both protect it and withstand its aggressive impulses, that enables the child to develop a strong sense of self. Klein's work in particular came to challenge and even displace the stress placed by Freud on the figure of the father. In a similar way, often with reference to Melanie Klein, Woolf from the 1970s and 1980s onwards came to be seen almost as an anti-Freud, a writer who offers an alternative vision to Freud's, sometimes one that downright corrects or contradicts him: a spokesperson for the Mother as against Freud the apostle of the Father. Thus, for instance, for both Abel and Hanson Woolf is close to Melanie Klein.[61]

Those 'undiscovered countries', then, that became perceptible to Woolf through her madness are seen by her feminist critics as bound up with the pre-Oedipal, connected with the mother, with whom the bond for the little girl is deeper (if we are to believe Freud himself). Klein concentrated on the mother–infant dyad, seen as primary and active, and as already containing all the psychic potentialities that will later develop in the Oedipal triad of mother–father–child. The mother is seen not only as the object of both girls and boys' desire, but as 'the self-contained source of life and creativity'.[62] In Woolf, the mother is also the spurting fountain of happiness, the object of the heart's desire. The father, or the would-be man–lover, is the one who intrudes into the dyad: Peter Walsh in *Mrs Dalloway* turns up at the point when Sally is kissing Clarissa, Mr Ramsay in *To the Lighthouse* interrupts James's tête-a-tête with his mother. For Woolf the mother seems to be the warrant of life, the one who guarantees order and continuity – the order-giving role is played in Freud by the father. As against Freud's *Moses and Monotheism*, which laid fascism at the door of a collapse of paternal power, Woolf writes *Between the Acts*, where there is no motherly presence to contain the collapse of the social and familial fabric, and *Three Guineas*, where the evils of patriarchal power are denounced. Abel sees them as diametrically opposed: 'The world that for Woolf had newly consecrated patriarchy was for Freud reviving the sensuous chaos of archaic matriarchy.'[63] For Woolf on the contrary the archaic matriarchy that prevails at the beginning of *To the Lighthouse* is one in which harmony, potency and fertility are ensured by the motherly presence – at least this is how James sees it:

[Mrs Ramsay] half turning, seemed to raise herself with an effort, and at once to pour erect into the air a rain of energy, a column of spray, looking at the same time animated and alive as if all her energies were being fused into force, burning and illuminating (quietly though she sat, taking up her stocking again), and into this delicious fecundity, this fountain and spray of life, the fatal sterility of the male plunged itself, like a beak of brass, barren and bare.[64]

The fascistic danger, here, made strident by the alliterated 'bs' ('beak of brass, barren and bare'), is all on the father's side.

Homoerotic desire and the ambivalence to the mother

Against Freud's complicated route to heterosexuality for the female, Woolf is seen as articulating lesbian desire: through Clarissa Dalloway's relationship with Sally Seton, the celebration of Mary Carmichael's 'Chloe liked Olivia' in *A Room of One's Own*; above all through Lily's desire for Mrs Ramsay. In what is a dream of the adoptive artist daughter's incest with the mother, the desire for an all-female fusion is strongly contrasted with logocentrism, with male knowledge. Lily wants to penetrate into the 'chambers of the mind and heart of the woman who was, physically, touching her':

> What art was there, known to love or cunning, by which one pressed through into those secret chambers? What device for becoming, like waters poured into one jar, inextricably the same . . .? Could loving, as people called it, make her and Mrs Ramsay one? For it was not knowledge but unity that she desired, not inscriptions on tablets, nothing that could be written in any language known to men, but intimacy itself, which is knowledge.[65]

Elizabeth Abel interprets Lily's painting, in the third section, as a return to origins and as the entry into that very shadowy world of female prehistory, the 'dark continent' which Freud had described as unconquerable and which Klein was exploring in her work with infants. The desired fusion somehow, however briefly, takes place.[66] I read Lily's desire for Mrs Ramsay as more ambivalent, more mixed with death. There is a lot of darkness and void in Woolf's images of the womb, which Sue Roe describes as an 'empty' space.[67] Mrs Ramsay's 'chambers of the mind and heart' into which Lily wishes to press in the passage I have just quoted are related to Egyptian burial chambers, 'treasures in the tombs of kings'. Is Mrs Ramsay also the Terrible Mother, a figure of Death, does she hold death at the heart of her? There is a powerful account of the disturbing imagery connected with her figure in Daniel Ferrer. He shows that like the sea, with which she is much associated, she is both 'the waters of annihilation' and the source of infinite riches. He points out, for instance, a very short section in the third part of the novel, in which Lily the artist is trying to complete her picture whilst Mr Ramsay takes his children to the lighthouse. Between brackets, it is recorded that:

> [Macalister's boy took one of the fish and cut a square out of its side to bait his hook with. The mutilated body (alive still) was thrown back into the sea.]

This is preceded and followed by, Lily's anguished calls to Mrs Ramsay: '"Mrs Ramsay!" Lily cried, "Mrs Ramsay!" But nothing happened. The pain increased . . . No one had seen her step off her strip of board into the waters of annihilation'. The bracketed passage with its air of being quite about something else 'marks the intensity of the vital lack (a square cut out of living flesh) for which [Mrs Ramsay, the mother's] absence is responsible'. And so, the sea with all it signifies, the maternal fluid 'cradles and overwhelms, nourishes and poisons'. Lily's ambivalent feelings towards Mrs Ramsay, Ferrer argues, thus again offering a psycho-analytic reading of the fictional text, are close to Woolf's about her mother. And like Lily, for whom artistic practice 'attempts to operate an ordering and reintegration of the destructive drives', for Woolf 'art is not only a discharge of aggressivity, but simultaneously an attempt at repara-tion, a will to fill in an empty space, to close the wounds opened in the maternal body'.[68]

And so, whether it turns to the figure of the father or that of the mother, psychoanalysis, according to how it is used, leads to powerfully ambiva-lent readings of Woolf. Some see destructive impulses and a subject dangerously in process where others see the fruitful subversion of mascu-line discourse. Nowhere is that subversion more in evidence, perhaps more praised, but to my mind also more paradoxical, than in Woolf's manifold use of androgyny. She does claim in A Room of One's Own that the creative mind is androgynous. This is seen by Minow-Pinkney as exemplified by Bernard in The Waves, who absorbs the consciousness of the other characters and becomes a kind of androgyne. He is caught in an alternation of identity and its loss, and this makes feminine writing possible, with a 'regression to the pre-Oedipal stage, to the jouissance of an as yet undissociated mother and child'. The pre-Oedipal makes itself felt through the rhythms of Woolf's prose, its refusal of linear narrative, its attempts at capturing the evanescent present, its 'surface equality', its 'absence of rupture'. The character Orlando, the hero of the fiction by that name, in a way exemplifies the complex of qualities that androgyny stands for, in which resistance is shown to the Freudian model where certain paths to masculinity and femininity need to be followed. Orlando's name contains both 'and' and 'or', as Defromont points out. He defies the laws of time, since he is first found in the days of Elizabeth I, and ends in the 1920s, Woolf's present. He begins as a man, changes sex in the latter part of the seventeenth century, and continues as a woman. He loves people from both sexes, and cross-dresses too. For Minow-Pinkney again the character's sex change is not so much change (a metaphor) as metonymy, a sliding through fantastical boundaries.[69] There is a play of difference rather than sexual difference, which returns us, yet again, to the pre-Oedipal, multiple desire.

Indeed, Orlando's desire for the extraordinarily seductive princess brings out of him a fertile world of images that seem easily and amusingly to mutate into each other:

> Images, metaphors of the most extreme and extravagant twined and twisted in his mind. He called her a melon, a pineapple, an olive tree, an emerald, and a fox in the snow all in the space of three seconds.[70]

In Orlando that 'vacillation from one sex to the other'[71] which, we are told, takes place in every human being, is allowed full sway. So is multiple desire: 'For the probity of breeches she exchanged the seductiveness of petticoats and enjoyed the love of both sexes equally'.[72] Ambiguities and multiplicity delightfully infect the text itself, astride many genres as it is astride gender: we read it largely as fiction, but it calls itself 'a biography', is a brief suggestive potted history of three centuries of English upper-class life, a compound of skilful parodies and pastiches of styles of writing through the ages, a lesbian romance, and was described by Woolf as a 'love letter' to Vita Sackville-West, her lover at the time of the writing. And yet – and this is where I see the paradox – whilst it undoes the Freudian models of masculinity and femininity, carnivalises logocentric discourse, shakes notions of sexual identity (since Orlando goes on perfectly unperturbed from being a man to being a woman), it is also the text from the mature Woolf that most relies on character, centre and linear narration. It might require again psychoanalytic interpretation to work out why this is so, and I like to leave the reader with this as a puzzle. Is it because Woolf was particularly happy, on a high as it were, on account of her affair with Vita, that she could give herself over to the gleeful creation of a character? Because Orlando had Vita for a model, and the steadiness of the model allowed for endless play with language? Because writing about multiple desire removed a repression for Woolf and stabilised her? Because the text was written for somebody? It is at any rate striking that where Clarissa Dalloway, Lily Briscoe, Mrs Ramsay, Bernard, are left so much at sea, reach moments of identity so precariously, cannot find the unity, the 'globe' they are longing for, Orlando is treated to a full paragraph of selfhood – of being. It is towards the end, close to the present, and Orlando is a she. She has ceased to call 'Orlando', and 'the Orlando whom she had called [comes] of its own accord':

> The whole of her darkened and settled, as when some foil whose addition makes the round and solidity of a surface is added to it, and the shallow

becomes deep and the near distant; and all is contained as water is contained by the sides of a well. So she was now darkened, stilled, and become, with the addition of this Orlando, what is called, rightly or wrongly, a single self, a real self. And she fell silent. For it is probable that when people talk aloud, the selves (of which there may be more than two thousand) are conscious of disseverment, and are trying to communicate, but when communication is established they fall silent.[73]

NOTES

1 For a bibliography see Elizabeth Abel, *Virginia Woolf and the Fictions of Psychoanalysis* (The University of Chicago Press, 1989), p. 132, note 6; on hysteria also see Elaine Showalter, *The Female Malady: Women, Madness and English Culture 1830–1980* (London: Virago, 1987).

2 Alice Miller, *Thou Shalt Not Be Aware: Society's Betrayal of the Child* (London: Pluto Press, 1986), see discussion pp. 109–20. For a bibliography on abuse see Louise DeSalvo, *Virginia Woolf: the Impact of Childhood Sexual Abuse on her Life and Works* (London: The Women's Press, 1991), p. 311, note 9. On Dora see C. Bernheimer and C. Kahane (eds.), *In Dora's Case* (London: Virago, 1985).

3 DeSalvo, *Virginia Woolf: the Impact of Childhood Sexual Abuse*, p. 308, note 12.

4 Florence Rush, *The Best Kept Secret: Sexual Abuse of Children* (New York: McGraw-Hill, 1980).

5 DeSalvo, *Virginia Woolf: the Impact of Childhood Sexual Abuse*, p. 7.

6 Hermione Lee, *Virginia Woolf* (London: Chatto and Windus, 1996), p. 175; also p. 789, note 6.

7 *Ibid.*, p. 175.

8 DeSalvo, *Virginia Woolf: the Impact of Childhood Sexual Abuse*, see Chapter 2.

9 DeSalvo, *ibid.*, pp. 3, 5, 100, 121; Lee, p. 155.

10 DeSalvo, *Virginia Woolf: the Impact of Childhood Sexual Abuse*, p. 99.

11 *Ibid.*, p. 110.

12 *Ibid.*, p. 104.

13 *Ibid.*, p. 129.

14 Lee, *Virginia Woolf*, note 68, pp. 786–7.

15 Françoise Dolto, *Le Cas Dominique* (Paris: Editions du Seuil, 1985), p. 246.

16 *The Years* (London: Hogarth, 1958), p. 171.

17 Abel, *Virginia Woolf and the Fictions of Psychoanalysis*, p. 14, and p. 138, note 58.

18 Lee, *Virginia Woolf*, p. 197.

19 Jane Marcus, *Virginia Woolf and the Languages of Patriarchy* (Bloomington and Indianapolis, 1987), p. 101.

20 Showalter, *Female Malady*.

21 *Ibid.*, p. 100.

22 *Moments of Being: Unpublished Autobiographical Writings* (1976) ed. with an introduction by Jeanne Schulkind (London: Triad/Granada, 1982), p. 94.

23 Abel, *Virginia Woolf and the Fictions of Psychoanalysis*, p. 19.

24 Marion Milner, *The Hands of the Living God: An Account of a Psychoanalytic Treatment* (London: Hogarth, 1969).

25 To Jacques Raverat, 8 March 1924, *L*3, p. 92.
26 Lee, *Virginia Woolf*, p. 192.
27 'On Being Ill' in *The Moments and Other Essays* (New York: Harcourt Brace, 1948), p. 10.
28 Lee, *Virginia Woolf*, p. 195.
29 Abel, *Virginia Woolf and the Fictions of Psychoanalysis*, pp. 16–17.
30 Leonard Woolf, *Downhill All The Way* (London: Hogarth, 1967), p. 64.
31 Quoted Abel, *Virginia Woolf and the Fictions of Psychoanalysis*, p. 14.
32 *Ibid.*, p. 15.
33 Lee, *Virginia Woolf*, p. 191.
34 *E*3, pp. 196–7.
35 *The Waves*, from *Collected Novels of Virginia Woolf*, ed. by Stella McNichol (London: Macmillan, 1992), p. 475.
36 *Ibid.*
37 *Ibid.*, p. 474.
38 *Mrs Dalloway*, from *Collected Novels*, p. 38.
39 *Ibid.*, p. 74.
40 *To the Lighthouse*, in *Collected Novels*, p. 225.
41 *The Waves*, p. 414.
42 *Ibid.*, p. 404.
43 Lee R. Edwards, 'Schizophrenic Narrative', *Journal of Narrative Technique*, 19 (Winter 1989), p. 27.
44 From a paper delivered at a Woolf colloquium, University of Massachusetts, October 1989, p. 4 (privately lent; with thanks).
45 Daniel Ferrer, *Virginia Woolf and the Madness of Language*, trans. by Geoffrey Bennington and Rachel Bowlby (London: Routledge, 1990), p. 140.
46 *Ibid.*, p. 141.
47 Phyllis Chesler as quoted in Shoshona Felman, 'Women and Madness: The Critical Phallacy' in C. Belsey and Jane Moore (eds.), *The New Feminist Criticism* (London: Macmillan, 1989), p. 134; what follows is a brief summary of Irigaray, *This Sex Which Is Not One* (Ithaca and London: Cornell University Press, 1985), pp. 135–6.
48 Standard Edition (London: Hogarth, 1953–74), 4, pp. 262–3.
49 *To the Lighthouse*, p. 182.
50 Rachel Bowlby, *Feminist Destinations and Further Essays on Virginia Woolf* (Oxford: Basil Blackwell, 1988) second rev. edition (Edinburgh University Press, 1997), p. 59.
51 Nicole Ward Jouve, 'Virginia Woolf: Penis Envy and the Male Sentence,' in *Female Genesis: Creativity, Self and Gender* (Oxford: Polity Press, 1998), pp. 123–4.
52 *To the Lighthouse*, p. 316.
53 Abel, *Virginia Woolf and the Fictions of Psychoanalysis*, pp. 21–9.
54 Standard Edition, 19, p. 252.
55 Ward Jouve cit. Torok, in 'Virginia Woolf', *Female Genesis*, pp. 132–3.
56 Standard Edition, 21, p. 226.
57 Mary Jacobus (ed.), *Women Writing and Writing about Women* (London: Croom Helm, 1979), p. 20.
58 *Ibid.*, pp. 12, 19.

59 Gillian Beer, 'Beyond Determinism: George Eliot and Virginia Woolf', in Jacobus ed., *Women Writing*, p. 97.

60 Both Mary Jacobus and Gillian Beer have continued to reflect on Woolf with distinctiveness and flair. In the United States, Jane Marcus had separately built up readings of Woolf's work as a wholesale protest against patriarchal power and values. She uses psychoanalytic concepts at various points to make her case in *Virginia Woolf and the Languages of Patriarchy*. Her highly perceptive and original book however is turned more towards radical political argument than a study of Woolf's relation to psychoanalysis. Other studies, on the other hand, interestingly pick up on the points made early on by Jacobus and Beer. Woolf's androgyny had already been explored in relation to the figures of the father and the mother in terms of 'manic-depressive psychology' by Nancy Topping Bazin's *Virginia Woolf and the Androgynous Vision* (New Brunswick, NJ: Rutgers University Press, 1973). The mother–daughter relationship is explored in Ellen Bayuk Rosenman's sensitive *The Invisible Presence* (Baton Rouge: Louisiana State University Press, 1986). Makiko Minow-Pinkney's skilful *Virginia Woolf and the Problem of the Subject* makes much use of French feminist perspectives. Minow-Pinkney dialogues with Lacan, with Cixous, Irigaray but above all with Kristeva, regarding *The Waves* as 'the high point of [Woolf's] achievement in terms of the dialectic of symbolic and semiotic' and as a 'challenge' to 'the dominant, phallocentric mode of discourse and the masculine social order that underpins it' (Brighton: The Harvester Press, 1987). In France, Françoise Defromont has made a most perceptive contribution to an understanding of Woolf's metaphors and verbal play and their relation to unconscious processes, especially in relation to the Mother and to bisexuality, in *Vers la maison de lumière* (Paris: Editions des femmes, 1985). In her subtle study of Woolf's writing practice, Sue Roe deals with the theme of Woolf and creation (*Writing and Gender: Virginia Woolf's Writing Practice* (Hemel Hempstead: Harvester Wheatsheaf, 1990)), also explored in Shirley Panken's psychoanalytic *Virginia Woolf and the 'Lust of Creation'* (Albany: State University of New York Press, 1987). Rachel Bowlby is concerned with issues of sexual difference in her *Feminist Destinations*, arguing that Woolf shows the 'untenability of the prevailing constructions of masculine and feminine identities'. The two 'are neither complementary, making a whole, nor ever reached in their imaginary completion by individuals of either sex'. Clare Hanson's compact *Virginia Woolf* suggestively draws on links between Woolf and psychoanalysis, and makes a particularly apposite use of Melanie Klein (London: Macmillan, 1994). However, the main study to tackle the topic head-on and in a systematic way has already been quoted from. It is Elizabeth Abel's *Virginia Woolf and the Fictions of Psychoanalysis*.

61 Abel, *Virginia Woolf and the Fictions of Psychoanalysis*, p. 70.

62 Clare Hanson, *Virginia Woolf*, p. 75.

63 Abel, *Virginia Woolf and the Fictions of Psychoanalysis*, p. 114.

64 *To the Lighthouse*, p. 206.

65 *Ibid.*, p. 216.

66 See Abel, *Virginia Woolf and the Fictions of Psychoanalysis*, chapter 4.

67 Roe, *Writing and Gender*, p. 174.

68 Ferrer, in Maud Ellmann (ed.), *Psychoanalytic Literary Criticism* (London: Longman, 1994), pp. 152–3 and 156–7.
69 Minow-Pinkney, p. 122. See also Hanson, pp. 101–11.
70 *Orlando: A Biography* (London: Grafton Books, 1977), p. 24.
71 *Ibid.*, p. 118.
72 *Ibid.*, p. 138.
73 *Ibid.*, p. 196.

GUIDE TO FURTHER READING

Abel, Elizabeth, *Virginia Woolf and the Fictions of Psychoanalysis* (Chicago University Press, 1989)

Anderson, Linda, 'Virginia Woolf: "In the Shadow of the Letter 'I'"', in *Women and Autobiography in the Twentieth Century: Remembered Futures* (Hemel Hempstead: Prentice Hall/Harvester Wheatsheaf, 1997)

Annan, Noel, *Leslie Stephen. The Godless Victorian* (London: Weidenfeld and Nicolson, 1984)

Auerbach, Erich, 'The Brown Stocking', in *Mimesis: The Representation of Reality in Western Literature*, trans. Willard Trask (Princeton: Yale University Press, 1953)

Ayer, A. J., *Russell and Moore: The Analytic Heritage* (London and Basingstoke: Macmillan, 1973)

Barrett, Eileen, and Patricia Cramer (eds.), *Virginia Woolf: Lesbian Readings* (New York University Press, 1997)

Barrett, Michèle (ed.), *Virginia Woolf: Women and Writing* (London: The Women's Press, 1979)

Barthes, Roland, 'The Grain of the Voice', in *Image Music Text*, trans. and ed. Stephen Heath (London: Fontana, 1977)

Beer, Gillian, 'The Body of the People in Virginia Woolf', in *Women Reading Women's Writing*, ed. Sue Roe (Brighton: The Harvester Press, 1987)
  'The Island and the Aeroplane: The Case of Virginia Woolf', in *Nation and Narration*, ed. Homi K. Bhabha (London: Routledge, 1990)
  Virginia Woolf: The Common Ground (Edinburgh University Press, 1996)

Beja, Morris (ed.), *Critical Essays on Virginia Woolf* (Boston, Mass.: G. K. Hall and Co., 1985)

Bell, Clive, *Art* (London: Chatto and Windus, 1914)
  Since Cézanne (London: Chatto and Windus, 1922, repr. 1929)
  Civilization: An Essay (London: Chatto and Windus, 1928)
  'Bloomsbury' in *Old Friends* (London: Chatto and Windus, 1956)

Bell, Quentin, *Bloomsbury* (London: Weidenfeld and Nicolson, 1968)
  'Reflections on Maynard Keynes' in *Keynes and the Bloomsbury Group*, eds. Derek Crabtree and A. P. Thirlwall (London and Basingstoke: Macmillan, 1980)
  Virginia Woolf: A Biography, 1972 (repr. London: Hogarth, 1982)

Bishop, Edward, *A Virginia Woolf Chronology* (London: Macmillan, 1989)
  Virginia Woolf (London: Macmillan, 1991)

Blodgett, Harriet, 'Food for Thought in Virginia Woolf's Novels', *Woolf Studies Annual* 3 (New York: Pace University Press, 1997)

Boswell, Samuel, *Boswell's Life of Johnson*, 1787 (Oxford University Press, 1946)

Bowlby, Rachel (ed.), *The Crowded Dance of Modern Life* (Harmondsworth: Penguin, 1992)

    A Woman's Essays (Harmondsworth: Penguin, 1992)

    Virginia Woolf: Longman Critical Readers (Harlow: Longman, 1992)

    Feminist Destinations and Further Essays on Virginia Woolf (Edinburgh University Press, 1997)

Bradbury, Malcolm, and James McFarlane (eds.), *Modernism: 1890–1930*, 2nd edn (Harmondsworth: Penguin, 1991)

Breuer, Josef, and Sigmund Freud, 'On the Psychical Mechanism of Hysterical Phenomena: Preliminary Commentary', in *Studies on Hysteria*, 1893–5, trans. James and Alix Strachey, ed. Angela Richards, *Penguin Freud Library*, 3 (Harmondsworth: Penguin, 1974)

Briggs, Julia (ed.), *Virginia Woolf: Introductions to the Major Works* (London: Virago Press, 1994)

Brosnan, Leila, 'Virginia Woolf's Essays and Journalism' (unpublished thesis, University of Edinburgh, 1994)

Butler, Christopher, *Early Modernism: Literature, Music and Painting* (Oxford University Press, 1994)

Calinescu, Matei, *Five Faces of Modernity* (Durham, NC: Duke University Press, 1987)

Carey, John, *The Intellectuals and the Masses: Pride and Prejudice among the Literary Intelligentsia, 1880–1939* (London: Faber and Faber, 1992)

Caughie, Pamela, *Virginia Woolf and Postmodernism* (University of Illinois Press, 1991)

Cixous, Hélène, 'Sorties', in *The Newly Born Woman*, trans. by Betsy Wing (Manchester University Press, 1986; Minneapolis, University of Minnesota Press, 1993)

Clark, Kenneth, *Landscape into Art* (London: J. Murray, 1979)

Clements, Patricia, and Isobel Grundy (eds.), *Virginia Woolf: New Critical Essays* (London: Vision, 1983)

Daiches, David, and John Flower, 'Virginia Woolf's London', in *Literary Landscapes of the British Isles: A Narrative Atlas* (New York and London: Paddington Press, 1979)

Denvir, Bernard, *Post-Impressionism* (London: Thames and Hudson, 1992)

DeSalvo, Louise A., *Virginia Woolf's First Voyage: A Novel in the Making* (Totowa, NJ: Rowman and Littlefield, 1980)

    Virginia Woolf: The Impact of Childhood Sexual Abuse on Her Life and Work (London: The Women's Press, 1989)

    ed. *Melymbrosia: An Early Version of 'The Voyage Out'* (New York Public Library, 1982)

DiBattista, Maria, *Virginia Woolf's Major Novels: The Fables of Anon* (London: Yale University Press, 1980)

Dick, Susan, *Virginia Woolf* (London: Edward Arnold, 1989)

    (ed.), *The Complete Shorter Fiction of Virginia Woolf* (London: Hogarth, 1985)

Dunn, Jane, *A Very Close Conspiracy: Vanessa Bell and Virginia Woolf* (London: Cape, 1991)

DuPlessis, Rachel Blau, *Writing Beyond the Ending: Narrative Strategies of Twentieth-Century Women Writers* (Bloomington: Indiana University Press, 1985)

Dusinberre, Juliet, *Virginia Woolf's Renaissance* (Basingstoke and London: Macmillan, 1997)

Eagleton, Terry, 'Capitalism, Modernism, and Postmodernism', repr. in *Modern Criticism and Theory: A Reader*, ed. David Lodge (Harlow: Longman, 1988)

Eliot, T. S., 'Ben Jonson', *The Sacred Wood* (1920; London: Methuen, 1928)

The Complete Poems and Plays of T. S. Eliot (London: Faber and Faber, 1969)

Selected Prose of T. S. Eliot, ed. Frank Kermode (London: Faber and Faber, 1975)

Faderman, Lilian (ed.), *Chloe plus Olivia: An Anthology of Lesbian Literature from the Seventeenth Century to the Present Day* (Harmondsworth: Penguin, 1995)

Faulkner, Peter, *Modernism* (London: Methuen, 1977)

Ferrer, Daniel, *Virginia Woolf and the Madness of Language*, trans. Geoffrey Bennington and Rachel Bowlby (London: Routledge, 1990)

Flint, Kate, 'Virginia Woolf and the General Strike', *Essays in Criticism* 36 (1986)

Forster, E. M., 'The Early Novels of Virginia Woolf', in *Abinger Harvest* (London: Edward Arnold, 1936)

Virginia Woolf (Cambridge University Press, 1942)

A Room with a View, 1908 (Harmondsworth: Penguin, 1978)

Frank, Joseph, 'Spatial Form in Modern Literature' (1945), repr. in *The Widening Gyre* (New Brunswick: Rutgers University Press, 1963)

Freud, Sigmund, 'On Narcissism: An Introduction', 1914, in *General Psychological Theory*, ed. Philip Rieff (New York: Collier, 1963)

'Slips of the Tongue', in *The Psychopathology of Everyday Life*, 1901, trans. Alan Tyson, ed. Angela Richards, Penguin Freud Library, 5 (Harmondsworth: Penguin, 1975)

Friedman, Susan Stanford, 'Spatialisation, Narrative Theory, and Virginia Woolf's *The Voyage Out*', in Kathy Mezei, ed. *Ambiguous Discourse: Feminist Narratology and British Women Writers* (Chapel Hill: University of North Carolina Press, 1996)

Froula, Christine, 'Out of the Chrysalis: Female Initiation and Female Authority in Virginia Woolf's *The Voyage Out*', *Tulsa Studies in Women's Literature*, 5, No. 1 (Spring 1986)

Fry, Roger, *Vision and Design* (Harmondsworth: Penguin, 1961, 1920)

Fussell, Paul, *The Great War and Modern Memory* (Oxford University Press, 1975)

Garnett, Angelica, *Deceived With Kindness* (London: Chatto and Windus, 1984)

The Eternal Moment (Maine: Puckerbrush Press, 1998)

Gillespie, Diane F., *The Sisters' Arts: The Writing and Painting of Virginia Woolf* (Syracuse University Press, 1988)

(ed.), *The Multiple Muses of Virginia Woolf* (Columbia and London: University of Missouri, 1993)

Goldman, Jane, *The Feminist Aesthetics of Virginia Woolf: Modernism, Post-Impressionism and the Politics of the Visual* (Cambridge University Press, 1998)

Gordon, Lyndall, *Virginia Woolf: A Writer's Life* (Oxford University Press, 1984)

Gillespie, Diana F. and Leslie K. Hankins (eds.), *Virginia Woolf and the Arts: Selected Papers from the Sixth Annual Conference on Virginia Woolf* (New York: Pace University Press, 1997)

Grand, Sarah, *The Heavenly Twins*, 3 vols. (London: Heinemann, 1893)

Green, Gayle and Coppelia Kahn (eds.), *Making a Difference: Feminist Literary Criticism* (London: Methuen, 1985)

Hanson, Clare, *Virginia Woolf* (London: Macmillan, 1994)

Holtby, Winifred, *Virginia Woolf: a Critical Memoir* (London: Wishart, 1932; Chicago: Academy Press, 1978)

Women and a Changing Situation (Chicago: Academy Press, 1978)

Homans, Margaret, *Bearing the Word: Language and Female Experience in Nineteenth-Century Women's Writing* (University of Chicago Press, 1986)

Howarth, Tony, *Twentieth Century History: The World Since 1900*, 2nd ed. Josh Brooman (London: Longman, 1979; 1993)

Hulme, T. E., *The Collected Writings of T. E. Hulme*, ed. Karen Csengeri (Oxford University Press, 1994)

Hussey, Mark, *The Singing of the Real World: The Philosophy of Virginia Woolf's Fiction* (Ohio State University Press, 1986)

ed., *Virginia Woolf and War: Fiction, Reality, and Myth* (Syracuse University Press, 1991)

Jacobus, Mary, 'The Difference of View', in *Reading Women: Essays in Feminist Criticism* (London: Methuen, 1986)

First Things: The Maternal Imaginary in Literature, Art and Psychoanalysis (London: Routledge, 1995)

Jameson, Fredric, '"Ulysses" in History', *James Joyce and Modern Literature*, ed. W. J. McCormack and Alistair Stead (London: Routledge and Kegan Paul, 1982)

Joannou, Mary (ed.), *Women Writers of the 1930s: Gender, Politics and History* (Edinburgh University Press, 1998)

Johnstone, J. K., *The Bloomsbury Group* (London: Secker and Warburg, 1954)

Jones, Gareth Stedman, *Outcast London: A Study in the Relationship between Classes in Victorian Society* (Oxford: Clarendon Press, 1971)

Keynes, J. M., *Two Memoirs* (London: Rupert Hart-Davis, 1949)

Kirkpatrick, B. J., and Stuart N. Clarke, *A Bibliography of Virginia Woolf*, 4th edn (Oxford University Press, 1997)

Kolakowski, Leszek, *Bergson* (Oxford University Press, 1985)

Kolocotroni, Vassiliki, Jane Goldman, and Olga Taxidou (eds.), *Modernism: An Anthology of Sources and Documents* (Edinburgh University Press, 1998)

Lacan, Jacques, 'The Mirror Stage as Formative of the Function of the I as Revealed in Psychoanalytic Experience', in *Ecrits: A Selection*, trans. and ed. Alan Sheridan (New York: Norton, 1977)

Lawrence, Patricia Ondek, *The Reading of Silence: Virginia Woolf in the English Tradition* (Stanford University Press, 1991)

Lee, Hermione, *Virginia Woolf* (London: Chatto and Windus, 1996)

Levenson, Michael H., *A Genealogy of Modernism: A Study of English Literary Doctrine, 1908–1922* (Cambridge University Press, 1984)

ed. *The Cambridge Companion to Modernism* (Cambridge University Press, 1999)

Lyons, Brenda, 'Textual Voyages. Platonic Allusions in Virginia Woolf's Fiction' (Oxford University, D.Phil, 1995)

McLaurin, Allen, 'Virginia Woolf and Unanimism', *Journal of Modern Literature* 9 (1981–2)

Marcus, Jane, '*The Years* as Greek Drama, Domestic Novel and Gotterdammerung', *Bulletin of the New York Public Library*, Virginia Woolf Issue, vol. 80 (Winter 1977) no. 2

Virginia Woolf and the Languages of Patriarchy (Bloomington: Indiana University Press, 1987)

Art and Anger: Reading Like a Woman (Ohio State University Press, 1988)

'Britannia Rules *The Waves*', in *Decolonizing Tradition: The Cultural Politics of Modern Literary Canons*, ed. Karen Lawrence (Urbana: University of Illinois Press, 1991)

ed. *New Feminist Essays on Virginia Woolf* (London: Macmillan, 1981)

Marcus, Laura, *Auto/biographical Discourses: Theory, Criticism, Practice* (Manchester University Press, 1994)

Virginia Woolf (*Writers and their Works* series, London: Northcote House, 1997)

Marder, Herbert, *Feminism and Art: A Study of Virginia Woolf* (University of Chicago Press, 1968)

Marler, Regina, *Bloomsbury Pie* (London: Virago, 1997)

Meisel, Perry, *The Absent Father: Virginia Woolf and Walter Pater* (New Haven: Yale University Press, 1980)

Mepham, John, *Virginia Woolf: A Literary Life* (Basingstoke and London: Macmillan, 1991)

Minow-Pinkney, Makiko, *Virginia Woolf and the Problem of the Subject* (Brighton: Harvester, 1987)

Moi, Toril, *Sexual/Textual Politics: Feminist Literary Theory* (London: Methuen, 1985)

Naremore, James, *The World Without a Self: Virginia Woolf and the Novel* (New Haven: Yale University Press, 1973)

Naylor, Gillian (ed.), *Bloomsbury: The Artists, Authors and Designers By Themselves* (London: Octopus, 1990)

Nicholson, Nigel, *Portrait of a Marriage* (London: Phoenix, 1995)

Pater, Walter, *The Renaissance*, ed. Donald L. Hill (Berkeley: University of California Press, 1980)

Marius the Epicurean (1885), ed. Michael Levey (Harmondsworth: Penguin, 1985)

Paul, Janis M., *The Victorian Heritage of Virginia Woolf: The External World in her Novels* (Norman, Oklahoma: Pilgrim, 1987)

Phillips, Kathy J., *Virginia Woolf Against Empire* (University of Tennessee Press, 1994)

Prins, Yopie, *Victorian Sappho: Declining a Name* (Princeton University Press, 1999)

Raitt, Suzanne, *Vita and Virginia: The Work and Friendship of Vita Sackville-West and Virginia Woolf* (Oxford: Clarendon Press, 1993)

Roe, Sue, *Writing and Gender: Virginia Woolf's Writing Practice* (New York: St Martin's Press, and Hemel Hempstead: Harvester Wheatsheaf, 1990)

Romains, Jules, *Death of a Nobody*, trans. Sydney Waterlow and Desmond MacCarthy (London: Howard Latimer, 1914)

Rosenbaum, S. P. (ed.), *The Bloomsbury Group* (London: Croom Helm and University of Toronto Press, 1975)

Victorian Bloomsbury (Basingstoke and London: Macmillan, 1987, 1994)

'The Philosophical Realism of Virginia Woolf', in *Aspects of Bloomsbury: Studies in English Literary and Intellectual History* (London: Macmillan, and New York: St Martin's Press, 1998)

Rosenberg, Beth Carole, and Jeanne Dubino (eds.), *Virginia Woolf and the Essay* (New York: St Martin's Press, 1997)

Russell, Bertrand, 'My Mental Development', in *The Philosophy of Bertrand Russell*, vol. 1, ed. P. A. Schilpp (New York: Harper and Row, 1963)

Scott, Bonnie Kime, *Refiguring Modernism*, 2 vols. (Bloomington: Indiana University Press, 1995)

Sellers, Susan, *Language and Sexual Difference: Feminist Writing in France* (Basingstoke: Macmillan, 1991)

Hélène Cixous: Authorship, Autobiography and Love (Cambridge: Polity Press, 1996)

Showalter, Elaine, *A Literature of their Own* (London: Virago, 1978)

Spalding, Frances, *Vanessa Bell* (London: Weidenfeld and Nicolson, 1983)

Duncan Grant (London: Chatto and Windus, 1997)

Sprague, Clare (ed.), *Virginia Woolf: a Collection of Critical Essays* (Engelwood Cliffs, NJ, Prentice-Hall, 1971)

Squier, Susan M., *Virginia Woolf and London: The Sexual Politics of the City* (Chapel Hill: University Press of North Carolina, 1985)

Stape, J. H., *Virginia Woolf: Interviews and Recollections* (London: Macmillan, 1995)

Stephen, Leslie, *Hours in a Library* vol. 1 (London: Smith, 1874)

Stevenson, Randall, *Modernist Fiction: An Introduction* (Hemel Hempstead: Harvester Wheatsheaf, 1992)

Stimpson, Catharine R. 'The Female Sociograph: The Theater of Virginia Woolf's Letters', in *The Female Autograph*, ed. Domna C. Stanton (The University of Chicago Press, 1984)

Sutherland, John, 'Clarissa's invisible taxi', in *Can Jane Eyre Be Happy? More Puzzles in Classic Fiction* (Oxford University Press, 1997)

Watney, Simon, *English Post-Impressionism* (London: Cassell, 1980)

Waugh, Patricia, *Feminine Fictions: Revisting the Postmodern* (London: Routledge, 1989)

Wheare, Jane, *Virginia Woolf: Dramatic Novelist* (London: Macmillan, 1989)

Williams, Raymond, *Problems in Materialism and Culture* (London: Verso, 1980)

Willison, Ian, Warwick Gould and Warren Chernaik (eds.), *Modernist Writers and the Marketplace* (London: Macmillan, 1996)

Woolf, Leonard, *Quack, Quack!* (London: Hogarth, 1935)

Sowing: An Autobiography of the Years 1880–1904 (London: Hogarth, 1960)

Wussow, Helen (ed.), *New Essays on Virginia Woolf* (Dallas: Contemporary Research Press, 1995)

Zuckerman, Joanne P., 'Anne Thackeray Ritchie as the Model for Mrs. Hilbery in Virginia Woolf's *Night and Day*', *Virginia Woolf Quarterly*, 1 (1973)

Zwerdling, Alex, *Virginia Woolf and the Real World* (Berkeley and Los Angeles: University of California Press, 1986)

INDEX

Novels by Virginia Woolf are entered directly under their titles. Her shorter works are grouped as: essays, articles and reviews; lectures and broadcasts; memoirs; stories. VW is used to stand for Virginia Woolf. Abbreviations for the titles of her books are as listed on page xix.

Index

Index